Theology of the Prophetic Books

Also by Donald E. Gowan from
Westminster John Knox Press

Theology in Exodus:
Biblical Theology in the Form of a Commentary

Theology of the Prophetic Books

THE DEATH AND RESURRECTION OF ISRAEL

Donald E. Gowan

Westminster John Knox Press
Louisville, Kentucky

Book design by Douglas & Gayle Ltd.
Cover design by Pam Poll
Cover illustration: Giorgio Vasari (1511–1574). The Prophet Elijah. Uffizi, Florence, Italy. Courtesy of Alinari/Art Resource, New York.

First edition
Published by Westminster John Knox Press
Louisville, Kentucky

This book is printed on acid-free paper that meets the American National Standards Institute Z39.48 standard. ∞

PRINTED IN THE UNITED STATES OF AMERICA
98 99 00 01 02 03 04 05 06 07 — 10 9 8 7 6 5 4 3 2 1

Library of Congress Cataloging-in-Publication Data

Gowan, Donald E.
Theology of the prophetic books : the death and resurrection of Israel / Donald E. Gowan. — 1st ed.
p. cm.
Includes bibliographical references and indexes.
ISBN 0-664-25689-9 (alk. paper)
1. Bible. O.T. Prophets—Criticism, interpretation, etc.
2. Bible. O.T.—History of Biblical events. I. Title.
224'.06—dc21   98-6184

*In memory of Joseph L. Mihelic,
my first teacher of Hebrew and Old Testament*

CONTENTS

Abbreviations   viii

1. The Prophets as Theologians   1
   1.1 Approaches to the Prophets   1
   1.2 Ways of Reading the Prophetic Books   4
   1.3 The Uniqueness of the Prophetic Books   6
   1.4 The Three Key Moments, and a Theology of the
       Prophetic Books   9
   1.5 The Reality of Exile   10
   1.6 Land and Covenant Outside the Prophetic Books   16

Part One
Death: 722 and 587 B.C.E.

2. The Eighth Century: The Assyrian Threat and the Death of Israel   24
   2.1 Amos   25
   2.2 Hosea   37
   2.3 Micah   50
   2.4 Isaiah 1—39   59

3. The Late Seventh and Early Sixth Centuries:
   The Neo-Babylonian Threat and the Death of Judah   78
   3.1 Zephaniah   79
   3.2 Nahum   84
   3.3 Habakkuk   90
   3.4 Jeremiah   98
   3.5 Obadiah   117
   3.6 Ezekiel   121
   3.7 Jonah   137

Part Two
Resurrection: 538 B.C.E. and the Postexilic Period

4. The Mid-Sixth Century and Later:
   Restoration to the Promised Land   144

   4.1 Isaiah 40—55   146
   4.2 Haggai and Zechariah   162
   4.3 Isaiah 56—66   170
   4.4 Malachi   177
   4.5 Joel   181

5. The Continuing Influence of Old Testament Prophecy   188
   5.1 The "End of Prophecy"   188
   5.2 Did the Prophetic Mission Succeed or Fail?   190
   5.3 New Manifestations of the Prophetic Message   193

Notes   201

Index of Scripture and Other Ancient Writings   235

Index of Names and Subjects   245

TABLES

1. Historical Setting of the Prophetic Books   xii
2. The Old Testament Prophets and the
   Three Key Moments in Israel's History   8

ABBREVIATIONS

AB	Anchor Bible
AnBib	Analecta biblica
ANET	J. B. Pritchard (ed.), *Ancient Near Eastern Texts Relating to the Old Testament*
ANESTP	J. B. Pritchard (ed.), *Ancient Near East Supplementary Texts and Pictures*
ATANT	Abhandlungen zur Theologie des Alten und Neuen Testaments
ATD	Das Alte Testament Deutsch
BARev	*Biblical Archaeology Review*
BASOR	*Bulletin of the American Schools of Oriental Research*
BBET	Beiträge zur biblischen Exegese und Theologie
BETL	Bibliotheca ephemeridum theologicarum lovaniensium
BJRL	*Bulletin of the John Rylands University Library of Manchester*
BN	*Biblische Notizen*
BWANT	Beiträge zur Wissenschaft vom Alten und Neuen Testament
BZAW	Beihefte zur ZAW
CBOTS	Coniectanea biblica, Old Testament Series
CBQ	*Catholic Biblical Quarterly*
Ebib	Etudes bibliques
EvTh	*Evangelische Theologie*
FRLANT	Forschungen zur Religion und Literatur des Alten und Neuen Testaments
HAR	Hebrew Annual Review
HBT	*Horizons in Biblical Theology*
HSM	Harvard Semitic Monographs
HTR	*Harvard Theological Review*
IB	*Interpreter's Bible*
ICC	International Critical Commentary
IEJ	*Israel Exploration Journal*
Int	*Interpretation*
ITC	International Theological Commentary
JAOS	*Journal of the American Oriental Society*

JBL	*Journal of Biblical Literature*
JJS Mono	Journal of Jewish Studies, Monographs
JNES	*Journal of Near Eastern Studies*
JPSV	Jewish Publication Society Version
JQR	*Jewish Quarterly Review*
JR	*Journal of Religion*
JSOT	*Journal for the Study of the Old Testament*
JSOTSup	Supplements to *JSOT*
JTS	*Journal of Theological Studies*
KPG	Knox Preaching Guides
LXX	Septuagint
MT	Masoretic Text
NCB	New Century Bible
NCBC	New Century Bible Commentary
NEB	New English Bible
NIB	*New Interpreter's Bible*
NICOT	New International Commentary on the Old Testament
NIV	New International Version
NRSV	New Revised Standard Version
OTE	*Old Testament Essays*
OTG	Old Testament Guides
OTL	Old Testament Library
OTS	*Oudtestamentische Studiën*
PEQ	*Palestine Exploration Quarterly*
PTMS	Pittsburgh Theological Monograph Series
REB	Revised English Bible
RHPR	*Revue d'histoire et de philosophie religieuses*
RSR	*Recherches de science religieuse*
RSV	Revised Standard Version
RTP	*Revue de théologie et de philosophie*
SBLDS	*Society of Biblical Literature Dissertation Series*
SBLMS	Society of Biblical Literature Monograph Series
SBS	Stuttgarter Bibelstudien
SBT	Studies in Biblical Theology
SJT	*Scottish Journal of Theology*
SOTSMS	Society for Old Testament Study Monograph Series
ST	*Studia theologica*
TBü	Theologische Bücherei
TD	*Theology Digest*
ThZ	*Theologische Zeitschrift*
TLZ	*Theologische Literaturzeitung*
VT	*Vetus Testamentum*
VTSup	Supplements to VT

WBC	Word Biblical Commentary
WMANT	Wissenschaftliche Monographien zum Alten und Neuen Testament
ZAW	*Zeitschrift für die alttestamentliche Wissenschaft*
ZTK	*Zeitschrift für Theologie und Kirche*

Table 1

Historical Setting of the Prophetic Books:
Assyrian Period

Kings of Israel	Prophet	Kings of Judah	Kings of Assyria
Jeroboam II (785–745)		Uzziah	Shalmaneser IV (782–773) Ashur Dan (772–755) Ashur-nirari IV (754–745)
	Amos (760)		
		Jotham	
	Hosea (750–724)		
Zechariah, Shallum (745) Menahem (745–736)			Tiglath-pileser III (745–727)
		Jehoahaz (742–727)	
Pekahiah (736–735) Pekah (735–732) Hoshea (732–723)	Isaiah (738–701) Micah (730–700)		
		Hezekiah (727–698)	Shalmaneser V (726–722) Sargon II (722–705) Sennacherib (704–681)
		Manasseh (697–642)	
			Esarhaddon (680–669) Ashurbanipal (668–627)
		Amon (642–640)	

Table 1 (Continued)

Historical Setting of the Prophetic Books:
    Babylonian and Persian Periods

Prophets	Kings of Judah	Kings of Babylon
	Josiah (639–609)	
Zephaniah (630–620)		
Jeremiah (627–583)		Nabopolassar (626–605)
Nahum (612)		
Habakkuk (609–597)	Jehoahaz II (609) Jehoiakim (608–598)	
		Nebuchadnezzar (605–562)
	Jehoiachin (598–597) Zedekiah (597–587)	
Ezekiel (593–571)		Evil-merodach (562–560) Neriglissar (560–556) Nabonidus (556–539)

Prophets	Kings of Judah	Kings of Persia
Isaiah 40–55 (550–538)		Cyrus (559–530) Cambyses (530–522)
Haggai (520) Zechariah (520–518) Isaiah 56–66		Darius I (522–486)

All dates are B.C.E.
Malachi is probably to be dated in the middle of the 5th century B.C.E.
The dates of Joel, Obadiah, and Jonah are uncertain.

1

THE PROPHETS AS THEOLOGIANS

This is a study of a unique group of books that came into existence because of the destruction of the kingdoms of Israel and Judah and the beginning of the restoration of Judeans to their homeland. They are works of theology, in that they claim to be able to explain what Yahweh, God of Israel and Judah, was doing in the midst of those events, and this book focuses exclusively on that theological explanation. It thus differs from most books on the Old Testament prophets. It does not deal with the general phenomenon of "prophecy," so will devote little attention to the psychology of prophetism or to the roles played by the prophets in their society, subjects that have been extensively discussed in recent literature.[1] This study confines itself to the messages of the canonical prophets (formerly called writing prophets): Isaiah, Jeremiah, Ezekiel, and the Book of the Twelve.[2] Their messages have, of course, been expounded many times over, and yet there is a way of looking at this corpus of literature which has not been overworked, and indeed has not been recognized as the unifying factor that explains why this collection of books was made. A brief survey of the ways the prophets have been understood should be useful to the reader as a way of locating what this book attempts to do, in comparison with the long history of interpretation.

1.1 Approaches to the Prophets

In postexilic Judaism the term "prophet" came to be used eventually of any inspired person. The origins of this usage may be found already in the Old Testament, where Abraham (Gen. 20:7) and Moses (Deut. 34:10) are so designated. In the New Testament, John the Baptist (Matt. 21:26) and Jesus (Matt. 21:11) are called prophets, so it is clear that by the New Testament period the term had come to be used in ways not necessarily defined by those books we now call the canonical prophets. John Barton has provided an extensive study of the various uses of the concept of prophet in this period.[3] The canonical prophets themselves had been cast in the roles of martyrs, in keeping with the need for examples of faithfulness in the midst of suffering brought about by the persecutions of both Jews and Christians (cf. Matt. 5:12; 13:57; 23:30–31, 37; Acts 7:52; Rom. 11:3; 1 Thess. 2:15; James 5:10; Rev. 16:6). The noncanonical work *Lives of the Prophets* (first century

C.E.) would more accurately have been called "deaths of the prophets," for it considered them all to have been martyrs, and the legendary material which it adds to what is known from the Bible deals mostly with their deaths.

Through much of Christian history, the prophetic books have been read primarily as sources of predictions of the coming of Christ, and of the eschaton. In contrast, Judaism has understood the prophets to be teachers of the Torah.[4] The historical and biographical interests that came to dominate nineteenth-century biblical scholarship led to a greater interest in the prophets as individuals, and efforts began to reconstruct the backgrounds, religious experiences, and distinctive theologies of each of them. The traditional understanding of prophets as people inspired by God tended to be transmuted into a picture of them as great, creative religious thinkers. The opinions of influential German scholars such as Ewald, Wellhausen, and Duhm have tended to be echoed in scholarship as a whole throughout the nineteenth and much of the twentieth century, and their definition of "prophet" has widely influenced the way prophets are viewed in the church, as well. To "prophesy" is still regularly used to mean "predict the future," but to be "prophetic" now means to take a lonely stance for truth and justice, against popular opinion. This corresponds with the scholarly understanding of the canonical prophets as the virtual creators of ethical monotheism, lonely individualists who stood for spiritual religion and against organized religion's ritualistic observances, which were devoid of concern for justice. Thinking of the prophets as individualists led to the effort to learn as much about their lives as possible. The Old Testament shows little interest in that subject, so the efforts to reconstruct their biographies inevitably led to a considerable exercise of the imagination. For example, the location of Amos's home, Tekoa, on the edge of the Judean wilderness, and his reference to himself as a herdsman, could produce a rather romantic picture of one whose religious experience had been shaped by the severity of life in the desert. The fact is, we do not know whether Amos spent any time in the Judean wilderness, let alone whether he had any religious experiences there.

This biographical interest took a new turn early in the twentieth century, when Gustav Hölscher and others began to emphasize the psychological aspects of prophetic experience, as they are recorded in the accounts of visions and other paranormal phenomena, and eventually a full account of the "ecstatic personality" was produced by Johannes Lindblom.[5] Some have tried to confine these phenomena to the kind of prophet mentioned in the books of Samuel and Kings, claiming they were not important aspects of canonical prophecy, but Amos, Isaiah, Ezekiel, and others do claim to have seen visions, and it seems most likely that Israelites identified people as nebi'im, "prophets," because they were known to have had ecstatic experiences of this kind.

By the middle of the twentieth century, a reaction to the claim that the prophets rejected ritual in favor of a spiritual religion had set in. Numerous studies showed that the prophets all used cultic materials extensively, mostly in positive ways, and some even concluded that many, if not all, the canonical prophets were in fact employed at the Israelite sanctuaries.[6] That theory has gained few adherents, but the study of the use of cultic forms showed at least that the prophets were well acquainted with the language of worship of their people, and by no means were starting afresh with a new vocabulary and new concepts.[7]

This move away from seeing them as individuals largely isolated from their community took another form in the writings of those who stressed the centrality of the covenant in the life of Israel. Even though the word "covenant" seldom appears in the prophetic books earlier than Jeremiah and Ezekiel, other forms associated with the covenant were identified, and the picture of prophets filling a formal office in Israel, carrying out God's covenant lawsuit against his people, was created. Thus their oracles of judgment were claimed not to be original creations, after all, but part of Israel's worship.[8] Recent studies of the history of the covenant have questioned whether the covenant concept in Israel was even as early as the period of the prophets, and although that seems to be hyperskeptical, the evidence to support the idea that they were "covenant-officials" is largely lacking.[9]

Another possible source for the prophets' teaching was located in the wisdom literature. Attention was drawn to the presence of certain genres, vocabulary, and ideas typical of the wisdom books, especially in Amos, Isaiah, and Habakkuk.[10] For example, Hans Walter Wolff's commentary on Amos takes the position that his thought was profoundly influenced by his "intellectual home," which was tribal wisdom. Further studies showed that wisdom influence is widespread throughout the Old Testament, so it seems better to think of the prophets as using both wisdom and cultic materials known to everyone, without assuming that gave them a special relationship to either aspect of Israel's institutional life.

Late in the twentieth century, efforts were made to shed additional light on the roles Israelite prophets may have played in their society by comparing them with figures in other, better-known cultures who are thought to have been similar to the Old Testament characters.[11] Comparisons with the texts produced by oracle givers at the ancient Syrian city of Mari have been of interest, although they are dated long before the prophetic period in Israel. The efforts to interpret the roles of Israelite prophets by studying the activities of shamans in contemporary cultures runs the danger of circular reasoning, however, for the criteria for choosing individuals from other cultures must be drawn from one's preconceptions of what the Old Testament prophets were really like.[12]

Contemporary studies have thus moved significantly away from the earlier picture of the prophets as highly creative individuals, who produced something truly new.[13] These trends may lead to the extreme represented by these sentences from Lester Grabbe's book: "The contents of the prophetic books are certainly not unique in the Bible." "The differences between the pre-classical seer, the classical prophet, the post-exilic prophet, and the apocalyptic visionary dwindle at most to matters of degree rather than kind."[14] At another extreme, a study of the Old Testament uses of the word *nabi'*, traditionally translated "prophet," has suggested that Amos and the others associated with the "prophetic books" were probably never called by that title in the postexilic period, and it was given to them only much later.[15] What then remains of those noble figures, martyrs, mystics, reformers, heroes of the faith, that earlier readers thought they had found in their books?

The fact is that there is not enough evidence about the biographies of the prophets or about the social setting of the words in these books to make any of the reconstructions just cited demonstrable. A great deal of extrapolation has been used in every case, and that explains why such a wide variety of pictures of who the prophets really were is possible. These efforts were probably inevitable, for the nineteenth and early twentieth centuries had a strong historical and biographical interest. The search for the historical Jesus was accompanied by these searches for the historical prophets. Late-twentieth-century scholarship has been strongly influenced by materialist approaches to history, with religion itself to be accounted for by social and political factors, and so the study of the prophets has now been made to conform with those interests. But the variety of results is not due solely to presuppositions; it is also, and primarily, due to the scarcity of evidence of the kind being sought. Israel clearly had little or no interest in the kinds of questions being asked by modern readers, for they preserved very little evidence of the sort needed to answer these questions. We know nothing about Obadiah and Habakkuk except their names, and only the name and place of residence of Nahum. We know Amos's hometown, occupation, and one incident from his life, and that is more than we know about the other minor prophets. There is more information about Isaiah, Jeremiah, and Ezekiel, but not enough to write the life story of any of them. Jeremiah's book does contain a lengthy series of stories about his later years, but the chapter on Jeremiah in this book will claim that was not an early effort at biography. The incidents from the lives of the prophets which are contained in the canonical books quite clearly have been preserved because they have within them a message from God to Israel, and not because the prophets lived such interesting lives.[16] This book will follow Israel's lead, and will claim that our inability to reconstruct biography or social location is not a serious defect. These efforts to get at the "historical Amos (or Isaiah, etc.)" certainly involve questions of great interest to us, and we cannot avoid asking them, but since the lives, religious experiences, and social status of those responsible for these books seem to have been of little or no interest to the Israelites who collected and produced the final editions of the material, this book will not attempt to get beyond what we have, written in the prophetic books, and will take them as Israel's testimony to what the prophets meant to them, a subject of sufficient interest in its own right.

1.2 Ways of Reading the Prophetic Books

The prophets have been compared with shamans, with Nostradamus, with one's favorite reformer, or one's favorite evangelist, et al., but the books ascribed to them have no truly close parallels anywhere else in literature. The uniqueness of this collection will provide a starting point for our work in the theology of the books, but before moving in that direction some reflection on scholarly approaches to the books themselves will be helpful. For centuries the prophets were thought of as authors, so they were designated writing prophets to distinguish them from Nathan, Elijah, and the others in the books of Samuel and Kings. With the application of form criticism to these books, the homiletical nature of their words was noticed, and they were recognized to have been preachers whose work was originally oral in form, set in writing later (cf. Jeremiah 36). Whether the written forms were composed by themselves or by disciples, or even later by scribes dependent on oral tradition remains an unanswerable question. Once the interval between production of the words orally and their setting down in writing had been acknowledged, with the possibility that the prophet did not do any of the writing, then another possibility emerged: Perhaps the prophet himself did not say everything in the book ascribed to him. Given the nineteenth century's strong interest in the prophet as an individual, with the assumption that he was a great, creative, religious genius, it then became important to know which words came from the genius and which were the work of lesser minds. Source criticism, which had succeeded in answering many of the questions about the composition of the Pentateuch, was applied to the prophetic books in the effort to determine what was "authentic."[17] Serious efforts were made to find objective criteria for making such decisions, but the enterprise inevitably had a strong subjective element. How does one decide where to begin? Which are the authentic words with which to compare all the rest? Consequently, the results have varied widely from commentator to commentator.

More recently, redaction criticism has worked with the prophetic books, using similar analytical methods, but with interest not just in recovering the authentic words of the prophet himself, but with an almost equal interest in the assumed levels of redaction of the book. There is evidence that the books took shape in several stages, with material being added to an original collection of oracles, and the redaction critic not only attempts to dissect the book into its various levels, but then tries to locate the historical setting for each of them.[18] This method depends just as much on subjective elements as source criticism, however, with the result that no two redaction critics have produced results that agree. This book will take the position that there certainly is evidence for redaction, but that we do not have adequate evidence to enable us to identify the original words of the prophet with any hope of certainty, and neither is it possible to determine in detail the process by which it has taken its present form.[19]

Recently it has been claimed that nothing in these books came from the eighth and seventh centuries and that the prophets are fictional characters created by postexilic authors who produced an imaginative history for the Jewish community of their time.[20] It is said that scribes produced the prophetic books in order to create messages that would correspond to the picture of the prophets found in the Deuteronomistic Historical Work (Joshua through 2 Kings). They appeal to the great interest the Historian shows in prophecy (e.g., 2 Kings 17:13; chs. 18—19; 21:10–15), but in fact the History has a very different understanding of prophecy from that found in the prophetic books. For the Historian the prophets were preachers of repentance, but exhortations to change accompanied by promises of reward for it are extremely rare in the prophetic books.[21] The difference between the messages of the canonical prophets and the picture of prophet in the History is the likely explanation for the fact that the History mentions only one canonical prophet by name (Isaiah; although there is also a Jonah in 2 Kings 14:25), and does not quote anything from the prophetic books.[22] Those books in no way reflect the postexilic view of prophecy as it is found in the Deuteronomistic literature and Chronicles, but contain a quite different message from that assumed to be "prophetic" in later times. Only the obviously Deuteronomistic materials in Jeremiah (e.g., Jer. 7:5–7; 22:1–5) correspond to the outlook of the Historian, and this may be what has led to the notion that the other books also reflect the Deuteronomistic point of view. Even the claims that the prophetic corpus has undergone extensive Deuteronomistic editing are now being shown to be unlikely on the basis of careful reevaluation. The judgmental parts of the books traditionally dated in the preexilic period are so shockingly thoroughgoing that it is hard to imagine why any postexilic author would have thought to create them, for they do not correspond to anything we find in the later parts of the Old Testament or the intertestamental literature.

Another approach is the "canonical" reading of a prophetic book, as advocated by Brevard Childs. It does not deny that the book contains early material and has been formed by a process of redaction, but considers its history of composition to be of no great interest to the interpreter. It is the final, "canonical" form that has influenced the history and faith of synagogue and church, and his approach focuses on the message of that form, no matter how many authors or periods may be represented in it.[23] My approach will also find it important to consider the final form of each book as postexilic Judaism's mature reflection on the exile/restoration experience, but it will also attempt to identify material contemporary with the disasters that befell the two kingdoms. I give the benefit of the doubt to passages that show no obvious indications of being addressed to a later audience, and find that large portions of the books attributed to preexilic prophets betray no evidence of awareness of the exilic or postexilic situation. The sections on many of the books to be discussed, then, will deal with two levels of theology: words that appear to be contemporary with the events surrounding the demise of Israel and Judah, interpreting what is happening and is about to happen; and the book in its final form, reflecting exilic or postexilic interpretations of what did happen and what that means for the community which now accepts these books as definitive for their faith and life.

1.3 The Uniqueness of the Prophetic Books

Grabbe's sociohistorical study of prophecy led him to the conclusion (noted above) that the differences between the canonical prophets and preclassical prophets, postexilic prophets and apocalyptic visionaries are matters of degree rather than kind, and that the contents of these books are not unique in the Bible. His approach may have led him to consider unimportant two facts that raise questions about each of those conclusions; facts that will be of great importance for a theological reading of the prophetic books. As a challenge to his first conclusion: Only these prophets are credited with an extensive written collection of their words. There are no true parallels to the corpus composed of Isaiah, Jeremiah, Ezekiel, and the Book of the Twelve. This is more than a difference of degree. As to the second conclusion: These books contain a message that is not ascribed to prophets elsewhere, one that appears elsewhere in the Old Testament only as a result of the influence of these books, and in mitigated forms. The message is, as

Amos put it: "The end has come upon my people Israel" (Amos 8:2). The characteristic message of the preexilic, canonical prophets contains no calls for repentance, no specifications of what the people must do to avoid disaster, no program for reform; it is an announcement that disaster is at hand, with an explanation of why it must come. This has been recognized for some time, but there is still resistance to accepting it in some quarters. It will be of such importance for what follows that it may be worth quoting the various ways recent scholars have stated it:

> the new discovery of the pre-exilic prophets . . . was that Israel had fallen away from Yahweh, her God, had been rejected as a nation and would be punished.[24]

> the new feature in their preaching, and the one which shocked their hearers, was the message that Yahweh was summoning Israel before his judgment seat, and that he had in fact already pronounced sentence upon her: "The end has come upon my people Israel" (Am. VII.2).[25]

> The new feature that came into prophecy with Amos was the foretelling of the end of Yahweh's covenant relationship to Israel, and it was especially on this account that his oracles were preserved and ultimately given canonical status.[26]

> So that is the new, hard message of the classical prophets. God's great history of salvation with Israel, which began with the Exodus from Egypt and received a final seal in the election of Jerusalem, will be pushed inexorably to its end.[27]

This is the one element that clearly distinguishes the work of the canonical prophets from their predecessors, and it most likely accounts for the fact that in the mid-eighth century the words of certain prophets began to be collected in books. This kind of prophecy has a beginning and an end, marked by the books now called Latter Prophets in the Hebrew Bible.[28] The beginning is sharply delineated; it is the book of Amos. The end cannot be dated with any definiteness, and the reason for that is clear. The last of these prophets dealt with restoration, and restoration began shortly after 538, but was a continuing matter. Eventually the Jewish community ceased to acknowledge persons who may have claimed to be speaking under divine inspiration as having the same stature and authority as those who had preceded them, whose words were already collected in books and were being used as a continuing source of guidance. So, they spoke of prophecy coming to an end—meaning that *kind* of prophecy—even though they also used the word "prophet" in other ways (Zech. 1:4; 7:7, 12; 13:2–5; Prayer of Azariah 15; 1 Macc. 4:46; 9:27; 14:41).

Since we no longer think of the preexilic prophets as authors in the modern sense, no one accounts for the existence of Amos and Hosea in the Bible by thinking those men decided to write a book. We understand the books to be anthologies, collections of oracles that were mostly oral in their original form. The question concerning the existence of these books is thus, Why did someone begin to collect the words of just these prophets, and preserve them long enough that they eventually became a part of the collection of books considered to be definitive for the

Table 2

The Old Testament Prophets and the Three Key Moments in Israel's History

	800 B.C.E.		
	-		
		Amos	
	-		
		Hosea	
		Micah	Isaiah 1—39
	-		
722 B.C.E. - Fall of Samaria			
	700 B.C.E.		
	-		
		Zephaniah	
	-		Jeremiah
		Nahum	
		Habakkuk	
	600 B.C.E.		
			Ezekiel
587 B.C.E. - Fall of Jerusalem			
	-		
		Isaiah 40—55	
538 B.C.E. - Cyrus' Decree			
	-		
		Haggai and Zechariah	
		Isaiah 56—66	
	500 B.C.E.		
	-		
		Malachi	
	-		
	400 B.C.E.		

Jewish faith? Why?—when the words of Amos and Hosea were so unacceptable; the announcement that one's national existence was soon to come to an end. The chronology of these books affords an answer. Table 2 makes the answer visible. There is a clustering of books, according to the way they are normally dated, and the clustering corresponds to the major emphasis of the message of each of them, and to a key date in history.[29] Four books, Amos, Hosea, Micah, and Isaiah 1—39, are dated from the middle to the end of the eighth century. Samaria, capital of the Northern Kingdom, fell to the Assyrians in 722 B.C.E., bringing the history of that kingdom to an end. Judah survived as a vassal to the Assyrians until shortly before the fall of Nineveh in 612 B.C.E. There were prophets in Judah during that period (2 Kings 21:10–15), but no collections of prophetic messages were made (or at least preserved) until near the end of the Southern Kingdom. Another cluster surrounds the fall of Jerusalem in 587 B.C.E.: Zephaniah, Nahum, Habakkuk (perhaps

Obadiah), Jeremiah, and Ezekiel. After a generation, with the decree of Cyrus in 538, restoration to Judah became possible, and collections of prophetic words of promise began to be produced, beginning with Isaiah 40—55 and continuing with Isaiah 56—66, Haggai, Zechariah, and (probably in the next century) Malachi. There is little evidence to enable us to date Jonah and Joel, but there are reasons for thinking they belong with this group. The simple matter of dating suggests that these three turning points in Israel's history account for the existence of just this collection of prophetic words. Whether the clustering means any more than that will depend on the success of the approach taken here, which is to show that these books are unified by the prophets' intention to explain what God was doing in the midst of these events, and that the unifying theme can be identified, with Ezek. 37:1–14, as the death and resurrection of Israel.

1.4 The Three Key Moments, and a Theology of the Prophetic Books

If one insists, it could be claimed that judgment prophecy in the Old Testament was produced after Samaria and Jerusalem fell, and was a simple application of retribution theology in the effort to account for these disasters; namely, God must have been punishing us for something.[30] As a writer of theology, however, I am willing to allow for the possibility of divine inspiration, and to take these works as more than just human ingenuity at explaining the unacceptable. At the purely human level, an approach found in many books on the prophets, one may see them as keen observers of what was developing in international affairs, recognizing the danger to the continuing freedom of their nation before many others did, or in the cases of Isaiah and Jeremiah, showing more political skill than their rulers possessed. As is typical, they may also be credited with a heightened ethical sensibility which enabled them to diagnose their people as a sick society, without the moral strength to enable them to withstand a severe time of tribulation. Without denying the elements of truth in these approaches, this is a work of theology, and the theologian will dare to claim that God has been involved in all of this, both at the level of communication with certain chosen individuals, and at the level of actual participation in the events of world history.[31]

A theological explanation of the existence of the prophetic books may put it this way: God had called a people into a special relationship with himself, giving them a land of their own, addressing them in their cultic ceremonies with the assurance that he had made a covenant with them, and defining their character as his people in terms of a law. He had given them priests to instruct them, kings to maintain justice, sages to guide them, and prophets to warn and exhort them when they forgot who they were. It had not worked. Neither Israel's worship nor daily life was truly distinct from their neighbors. They were no true witness to the nations concerning the character of their God, and the fate of widow, orphan, immigrant, and the poor in their midst was no better than in other countries. With the rise of the great empire builders in the Middle East—Assyria, followed by Babylon and Persia—God determined to do a new thing, in effect to start over. The little kingdoms of Israel and Judah would lose their political existence forever, but out of the death of Judah, God would raise up a new people, who would understand about God what most of their preexilic ancestors had never been able to comprehend, and who would commit themselves to obeying his will to an extent their ancestors had never done. The first step in making that happen was to raise up a series of prophets, messengers of God, whose responsibility was straightforward. They were no reformers; it was too late for that. They were to announce what was about to happen, to insist that it would not happen because God could not protect them from their enemies, but that God intended to use the disaster for his own purposes. They were also preachers of the law; the standards of behavior which, if obeyed, would produce a community of peace and harmony in which all would benefit. The standards had failed, so far, but when the disaster came, and all was lost, the words of the prophets were remembered. Other prophets began to explain that God had a future in mind for a renewed people, and the combined message of judgment and promise was finally taken with the utmost seriousness by the exiles in Babylonia. If there was to be a future for them as the people of Yahweh, they had better pay attention, and they did, for out of the exile experience did come a new people. Once the new community, Judaism, had begun to be formed there was no more need for divine messengers of that kind, and eventually the Jews recognized they were no longer being addressed in that way. The more normal attributes of religion—organized worship and instruction in faith and ethics—were working with this transformed people as they had not worked with Israel prior to the exile. The kind of prophet represented in the canonical books is thus the one who appears when God determines that a radical change in human history must come about.

The preceding paragraph is in effect a synopsis of the book that follows. It remains now to show how each of the prophetic books contributes to the drama of the death and resurrection of the people of God.

1.5 The Reality of Exile

. . . for there is nothing dearer to a man than his own country and his parents, and however splendid a home he may have in a foreign country, if it be far from father or mother, he does not care about it.
(Homer, Odyssey, Book IX, Butler's translation, lines 34–36)

Exile and restoration became theological topics for the prophets, the basis for reflection on human nature and the character and purpose of God. Because of that, exile is likely to become an abstraction for us, if we have not experienced anything like it. This section will thus be devoted to the attempt to re-create what it was like for individuals in Israel and Judah to be forceably deported from their homeland. Unfortunately, the Neo-Babylonian records from the early sixth century provide little information of this kind, but Nebuchadnezzar was continuing (with variations) a policy developed by the Assyrians, and from Assyrian records we can learn a good deal about what it was like to become an exile during the eighth to sixth centuries.

The twentieth century has been called the century of the refugee. The term "displaced person" came into common use to describe one of the major effects of World War II. But exile is a common and ancient human experience. Often it involves terrible physical distress, sometimes not, but in every case a special kind of suffering is involved, for what each experience has in common with the next is the peculiar anguish of being separated from one's homeland. "This is the worst violation of historic truths and of the rights of man: when the right to their homeland is denied to certain human beings so that they are forced to leave their homesteads."[32]

The causes have been various (and here we are concerned with the deportation of large groups of people rather than with individual exiles).[33] Groups have fled or been driven out of their homeland because they were out of favor politically, or have left more voluntarily in order to seek better lives elsewhere. Others have been forced to leave because of their religion.[34] The Nazis uprooted millions from their homes in order to murder them. Refugees have fled in large numbers before invading armies, or to escape internal conflict. The Soviet Union under Stalin moved tremendous numbers of their own citizens from their homes into forced labor camps. The experiences of those who became the victims of the Assyrians and Babylonians were not quite the same as any of the groups just mentioned, however, so it will be important not to project what is known about later displaced persons back onto the data from the eighth to sixth centuries.

The Old Testament authors wrote of the fate of the exiles in the briefest of terms, so most of what is available may be quoted here, as the first step in our reconstruction. The details of the history of Israel and Judah, as they are relevant to the understanding of exile in the prophetic books, will be provided later, where appropriate.

> In the days of Pekah king of Israel Tiglath-pileser king of Assyria came and captured Ijon, Abelbethmaacah, Janoah, Kedesh, Hazor, Gilead, and Galilee, all the land of Naphtali; and he carried the people captive to Assyria. (2 Kings 15:29, RSV)

> The people of Israel walked in all the sins which Jeroboam did; they did not depart from them, until the LORD removed Israel out of his sight, as he had spoken by all his servants the prophets. So Israel was exiled from their own land to Assyria until this day. (2 Kings 17:22–23, RSV)

> He carried away all Jerusalem, and all the princes, and all the mighty men of valor, ten thousand captives, and all the craftsmen and the smiths; none remained, except the poorest people of the land. . . . So Judah was taken into exile out of its land. (2 Kings 24:14, 25:21b, RSV)

From the annals of the Neo-Assyrian kings, from letters, and from the reliefs in their palaces depicting their campaigns we can learn more about why and how they deported thousands of conquered people from their homelands.[35] Exile could be used by a powerful king as a punishment for an unruly vassal. Treaties included threats of this kind: "May Melqart and Eshmun deliver your land to destruction, your people to be deported."[36] The Assyrian kings usually treated those responsible for rebellion with the utmost brutality, however, and they probably did not live long: "On their return (march) they (lit., their hands) seized Shuzubu, king of Babylon, alive in open battle. They threw him fettered into a cage and brought him before me. I tied him up in the middle city gate of Nineveh, like a pig."[37]

The deportation of large numbers of conquered people was ordinarily not for punishment but for various practical purposes as the emperors sought to add to the security and prosperity of the empire. There had been occasional forced movements of populations earlier than the eighth century, but it became a regular part of Assyrian policy from the reign of Tiglath-pileser III on (745–727 B.C.E.).[38] It was a major enterprise, moving hundreds or thousands of people for many miles, sometimes from one side of the empire to the other, keeping them fed and as healthy as possible, since they were intended to be useful to the empire in their new location. The reliefs show lines of captives leaving their city after defeat, their status made evident by guards with upraised clubs or spears.[39] The male captives might have their hands bound, but the women walked freely, and sometimes rode with children in carts.[40] The women are typically shown carrying sacks over one shoulder, with a small container in the other hand. An Assyrian scribe, with clay tablet and stylus, and an Aramaic scribe, with scroll and brush, are shown making records of what has been captured. Letters indicate the responsibility laid upon those in charge of the deportation:

> The people and the large cattle which they bring to me from the city of Gozan, I went forth to the city of Shabirishu to meet. I was prospered. I met them. I caused them to take shelter for inspection on the spot. Kina the *kelek* boatman (lacked) three persons; Sandapi the gardener, three persons; Huli the irrigator, five persons; Kuza the officer, the sinew of his hands, four persons—a total of fifteen persons are lacking according to my invoice. I sent back after them, from the city of Shabirishu to the city of Gozan, a member of the body-guard, saying, "Go bring the rest of the people with you.[41]

In order to keep the people alive, provisions had to be made available at regular intervals along the route, and the letters also show how difficult that was at times:

> In the midst of the month Adar, this is my course: I will certainly go up, that the face of the king my lord I may see; and the prisoners, that are a thousand in number, whom I have captured, I shall bring up with me; and many fugitives have taken refuge with me, and the king my lord knows that there are no provisions in the land. Grain and dates for money, from the Pukudi I might purchase and distribute to them. Behold now I am bringing them up with me. Let the lord of kings my lord send a body-guard official and let him furnish provisions for the prisoners on the journey.[42]

These records help bring to life the brief description of the treatment of Judeans by Nebuchadnezzar after the fall of Jerusalem in 587 B.C.E., for the Neo-Babylonians seem to have borrowed the practice of deportation from the Assyrians:

> The king of Babylon slaughtered the sons of Zedekiah at Riblah before his eyes; also the king of Babylon slaughtered all the nobles of Judah. He put out the eyes of Zedekiah, and bound him in fetters to take him to Babylon. The Chaldeans burned the king's house and the houses of the people, and

broke down the walls of Jerusalem. Then Nebuzaradan the captain of the guard exiled to Babylon the rest of the people who were left in the city, those who had deserted to him, and the people who remained. Nebuzaradan the captain of the guard left in the land of Judah some of the poor people who owned nothing, and gave them vineyards and fields at the same time. (Jer. 39:6–10)

The Old Testament mentions several places where the exiles from the Northern Kingdom were settled: Halah, on the [river] Habor, the river of Gozan, and in the cities of the Medes (2 Kings 17:6; 18:11). The first three places can be located in northern Mesopotamia, along the upper Euphrates, and the cities of the Medes were probably Harhar and neighboring townships west of the Hamadan-Kirmanshah line (in what is now Iran).[43] Several new cities were built by the Assyrian kings during the height of their power (eighth to seventh centuries), and sometimes exiled people were brought in to form part of the new population. After defeating Abdi-Milki of Sidon, Esarhaddon (680–669 B.C.E.) reported:

> His people, from far and near (lit., widespreading), which were countless, (with their) cattle, flocks and asses, I deported to Assyria. I gathered together the kings of the Hittite-land (i.e., Syria) and of the seacoast, all of them; I built a city in another place and called its name Kar-Assur-ah-iddina (Esarhaddonburg). Conquered people (lit., peoples, the conquest of my bow) from the mountains and sea of the east (rising sun) I settled therein. My official I set over them as governor.[44]

Old cities were rebuilt, as well, in the effort to enrich Assyria by bringing in booty and people. The annals of Tiglath-pileser III and of other kings contain records such as: "Nikur, together with the cities of its environs, I rebuilt. People of the lands my hands had conquered I settled therein."[45]

Other exiles were settled in border areas, such as the "cities of the Medes" mentioned in 2 Kings 17:6. It is thought that because these displaced persons would realize their safety and well-being in these potentially troubled areas depended on the Assyrians, their loyalty could be expected.[46] The soldiers of conquered armies were actually conscripted into the Assyrian army, on numerous occasions. The Old Testament alludes to it, in 2 Kings 24:16 (RSV): "And the king of Babylon brought captive to Babylon all the men of valor, seven thousand, and the craftsmen and the smiths, one thousand, all of them strong and fit for war." Earlier, Sargon II had enlarged his army with conscripts from the Northern Kingdom:

> I fought with them (the Samarians) and I counted as spoil 27,280 people who lived therein, with their chariots and the Gods of their trust. 200 chariots for my royal bodyguard I mustered from among them, and the rest of them I settled in the midst of Assyria.[47]

After conquering Hamath, "300 chariots, 600 cavalry, bearers of shield and lance, I selected from among them and added them to my royal host."[48]

Sometimes the exiles would be put to forced labor in construction projects,[49] but the deportations recorded during this period seem not ordinarily to have led to the permanent enslavement of the captives. Most of them were settled in new areas and put to work at their old trades, it would seem. Skilled labor was especially desired. 2 Kings 24:16 mentions craftsmen and smiths, and Sennacherib specifically lists musicians as one of the prizes he took from Judah after his invasion of 701 B.C.E.[50] Most seem to have been settled as farmers, in order to add to the productivity of the land. Jeremiah's advice to the Babylonian exiles, to "build houses and live in them; plant gardens and eat what they produce" (Jer. 29:5), is not unrealistic in the light of earlier Assyrian records that exiles were given plots of land, and were identified as farmers, gardeners, or shepherds.[51] Ezekiel seems to have lived in a relatively self-contained Jewish community with its own elders, on the canal Chebar, near Nippur (Ezek. 1:1–3; 3:15; 14:1; 20:1). Records from Nippur, later in the Persian period, show that people with Jewish names owned or rented fields and canals, and held minor administrative positions.[52] It would thus appear that once resettled, it was possible for most of the exiles to lead their own lives, with one restriction— they could not return home. The Assyrian kings regularly said of the deportees, "With the people of Assyria I counted them. Dues and service, as of the Assyrians, I laid upon them."[53] By the time of Ezra, in the fifth century, there were communities of the descendants of the Judean exiles in Telmelah, Telharsha, Cherub, Addan, Immer (Ezra 2:59), Casiphia, and near the river Ahava (Ezra 8:17, 21, 31), and some of them, at least, seem to have been fairly well-to-do. Most of them did not return to Judea, when the Persians made it possible to do so, for they evidently had made good lives for themselves, and this was the land in which they had been born. By the Roman period, there is evidence for Jewish communities throughout the Tigris-Euphrates river valleys, and eastward into Persia.[54] This remarkable increase and dispersion of the Jewish population has yet to be explained, for there are no early records of these communities, but it is evident enough that those few thousands of displaced persons from earlier centuries had prospered, maintaining their ethnic and religious identity. It may be that some of those living in the heart of what had once been Assyria were the descendants of the exiles from the Northern Kingdom. That was thought to be the case by Jews in Palestine in the Roman period (Tobit 1:1–2; As. Mos. 3:5–14; 2 Esd. 13:39–50; Mishnah, *Sanh.* 10:3), but it cannot be demonstrated from the evidence presently available.

"When two elephants fight, it is the grass that gets hurt" (African proverb). Few of the exiles may have been enslaved, and many of them may eventually have been able to build houses and plant gardens, as Jeremiah advised, making reasonably comfortable lives for themselves, but they could not have predicted that during those terrible days after they lost the war. They had survived fighting, hunger, burning, rape, and brutal slaughter. Neighbors and loved ones were dead or lost. Those who left Jerusalem to go into exile in 597 and 587 had walked about seven hundred miles by the time they reached Babylon. The records of warfare, in the Old Testament and in the official documents of the ancient Near East, tell us nothing of how all this affected the people who were its victims, but other parts of the Old Testament do so. There was cynical bitterness: What have *we* done to deserve this? "The parents have eaten sour grapes, and the children's teeth are set on edge" (Ezek. 18:2). There was hatred:

By the rivers of Babylon—
  there we sat down and there we wept
  when we remembered Zion.
On the willows there
  we hung up our harps.
For there our captors
  asked us for songs,
and our tormentors asked for mirth, saying,
  "Sing us one of the songs of Zion!"
How could we sing the LORD's song
  in a foreign land?
If I forget you, O Jerusalem,
  let my right hand wither!
Let my tongue cling to the roof of my mouth,
  if I do not remember you,
if I do not set Jerusalem
  above my highest joy.
Remember, O LORD, against the Edomites
  the day of Jerusalem's fall,
how they said, "Tear it down! Tear it down!
  Down to its foundations!"
O daughter of Babylon, you devastator!
  Happy shall they be who pay you back
  what you have done to us!
Happy shall they be who take your little ones
  and dash them against the rock!
                                    (Psalm 137)

There was grief:

Judah has gone into exile with suffering
  and hard servitude;
she lives now among the nations,
  and finds no resting place;
her pursuers have all overtaken her
  in the midst of her distress. . . .
Is it nothing to you, all you who pass by?
  Look and see
if there is any sorrow like my sorrow,
  which was brought upon me,
which the LORD inflicted
  on the day of his fierce anger.
                                    (Lam. 1:3, 12)

And there was despair: "Our bones are dried up, and our hope is lost; we are cut off completely" (Ezek. 37:11). Israel is dead, Ezekiel heard his fellow exiles saying, and that was in fact what the prophets beginning with Amos had said would happen. The forceable loss of one's homeland, in the midst of the terror and suffering inflicted by those enemy armies, must have been a profoundly shattering experience for all those displaced persons of the eighth to sixth centuries, but for Israel and Judah it struck at the very heart of their religion. They believed in a God who had promised them that land, and now they had lost it. Before beginning to consider what the prophets said about the death of Israel, it will be helpful to look at those divine promises, and to attempt to determine whether the thought of losing the promised land may ever have been taken seriously by Israelites before it actually happened.

1.6 Land and Covenant Outside the Prophetic Books

People need land—a place with the resources to enable life to continue, and ideally to live safely and comfortably. The land is the source of almost every resource we use, and so real property has been coveted and fought over for millennia of human existence. Animals also sense the same need, for they mark and defend their territories. From the family with its home, to the tribe with its territory, to the nation with its strictly regulated boundaries, the stability, security, and prosperity of groups of humans are normally inseparable from the possession of land.[55] So Israel associated becoming a people (as over against being strangers in another's land—Egypt) with the promise of a land to be their own possession (e.g., Exod. 3:7–8; 6:8). When they were forced to consider the possibility that they might lose that land, the thought was at first inevitably the same as thinking of their death, as a people. In fact, however, the Jews who survived the loss of their land have become one of the most remarkable people on earth. They did cease to exist as a nation, but unlike others who have suffered the same fate, they did not lose their identity. They have continued to exist—and to thrive—as a congregation and as an *ethnos*, within the territories of other nations. That anticipates the end of the prophets' story, however. The story must begin with the theology of the land in the Old Testament, for the death of Israel which the prophets find they must announce is directly associated with the loss of the land.

Most of the peoples of the ancient Near East, with the exception of the Israelites, seem to have taken for granted their association with their land, for it is only in the Old Testament, among the ancient literatures available to us, that possession of, conditions for living in, and the possibility of losing one's homeland play a prominent role.[56] The theology of the land in the Old Testament had not attracted much attention among scholars until fairly recently, but its importance is now widely recognized.[57] It would be most helpful for the purposes of this study if we could determine with some certainty which of the various ideas concerning possession of the land were present in the minds of Israelites prior to the work of the canonical prophets, and which must be dated later, showing the influence of the experiences of exile and restoration. Unfortunately, many of the generally accepted bases for dating Old Testament material are now being challenged, so it seems best at this time to present various points of view without claiming certainty about their chronological relationship, unless the evidence is very explicit.

An Unconditional Covenant

Some Old Testament authors speak of Canaan as an eternal and irrevocable gift from Yahweh to Israel. This point of view appears primarily in the promise to the ancestors, beginning with Gen. 12:7, continuing throughout Genesis, reappearing occasionally in Exodus–Numbers, and prominently in Deuteronomy, but seldom occurring in the rest of the Old Testament.[58] Abraham and Sarah, and their descendants, are remembered as moving about in a country not their own, living mostly at peace with the owners of the land, and dying without owning more than a burial plot in Canaan (Genesis 23). But Yahweh had taken an oath to give that land to Abraham and his descendants (Gen. 13:15; 17:8), or more often, just to his descendants (e.g., Gen. 12:7; 15:18). Three times in Genesis, once each in Exodus and Deuteronomy, and eight times elsewhere possession of the land is said to be "forever" (*'ad-'olam, le'olam*, once *kol-hayyamim*). Associated with this is the divine promise not to forget the covenant with the ancestors (Lev. 26:40–45; Deut. 4:30–31), for land and the covenant with Abraham are inseparable (Gen. 17:7–8; Exod. 6:4; 7:12–13; Judg. 2:1–2; Neh. 9:8). The Priestly source in Genesis also speaks of that covenant as an eternal one (Gen. 17:7, 13, 19; cf. Ps. 105:8–11).

The references to the land in the passages that speak of the covenant with Abraham do not suggest that possession of it can be jeopardized in any way. The covenant itself was unconditional, and the promise of the land thus would appear to be as certain as Yahweh is faithful.[59] The Sinai covenant, as described in Exodus, has conditions attached to it ("if you obey my voice and keep my covenant," Exod. 19:5), but nothing is said about any circumstance that would lead God to abrogate it.[60] Certainly the possibility is broached in Exodus 32, as a result of the sin with the golden calf, but the covenant remained in effect in spite of Israel's faithlessness, solely because Yahweh is "merciful and gracious, slow to anger, and abounding in steadfast love and faithfulness" (Exod. 34:6; cf. Exod. 32:13). The book of Exodus contains no threat of loss of the land, but only two warnings of potential insecurity, if Israel adopts the ways of the Canaanites.

Warnings

A group of six closely related passages shows an awareness of a tension created by God's gift to Israel of a land already occupied by other people. They combine references to the expulsion of those people with warnings not to associate with the remnant of those who continue to live in the land.[61] The threat in these passages is expressed in a curiously cryptic way. The central term in all but one (Num. 33:55) is *moqesh*, "snare."

> You shall make no covenant with them and their gods. They shall not live in your land, or they will make you sin against me; for if you worship their gods, it will surely be a snare to you. (Exod. 23:32-33)

> Take care not to make a covenant with the inhabitants of the land to which you are going, or it will become a snare among you. (Exod. 34:12)

The Sinai covenant thus forbade the making of any other covenant, which might involve recognizing other gods. The consequences of doing so are remarkably vague, in Exodus and the parallel passages (Deut. 7:16; Judg. 2:3; Josh. 23:13), as compared with what we shall see in Leviticus and Deuteronomy. The word translated "snare" may be either a trap, that is, the trouble itself that will result from going wrong, or the bait, the enticement to go wrong (as in Exod. 10:7; Judg. 8:27; 1 Sam. 18:21). In Josh. 23:12–13, however, the warning is expanded to make it clear that the "snare" is a punishment for wrongdoing:

> For if you turn back, and join the survivors of these nations left here among you, and intermarry with them, so that you marry their women and they yours, know assuredly that the LORD your God will not continue to drive out these nations before you; but they shall be a snare (*pah*) and a trap (*moqesh*) for you, a scourge (*shotet*) on your sides, and thorns (*tsininim*) in your eyes, until you perish (*'abad*) from this good land that the LORD your God has given you.[62]

The Joshua text has added an element not found in the other warnings, which seems to suggest that involvement with the Canaanites and their religion may lead to very serious jeopardy. Joshua 23 adds "until you perish from this good land," an expression that is the result of the combining of two traditions—the Sinai tradition of the book of Exodus (warning of the "snare") and the plains of Moab tradition of Deuteronomy.[63] For the book of Deuteronomy and a few other texts clearly dependent on it do confront the reader with the possibility of losing the land and of dying in it or somewhere in exile. These are the only texts outside the prophetic books that consider this unacceptable idea, but in contrast with the prophets, the Deuteronomic material contains some remarkable ambiguities that need to be taken seriously. These passages have for a long time been assigned to the period after the fall of Jerusalem in 587 B.C.E., but here it will be suggested that some of them may have originated after the fall of Samaria in 722 B.C.E.

The Reaction to 722 B.C.E. in Deuteronomy and Related Texts

The framework to Deuteronomy (chs. 4—11 and 28—30) makes the covenant relationship conditional to an extent not found anywhere in Exodus. Threats of destruction and/or exile appear with remarkable frequency, but there is a strange ambiguity about those that are the most developed. For example:

> When you have had children and children's children, and become complacent in the land, if you act corruptly by making an idol in the form of anything, thus doing what is evil in the sight of the LORD your God, and provoking him to anger, I call heaven and earth to witness against you today that you will soon utterly perish (*'abad*) from the land that you are crossing the Jordan to occupy; you will not live long on it, but will be utterly destroyed (*shamad*). (Deut. 4:25–26)

That would seem to be the end of it, but it is not. There will be survivors, who will be exiled:

> The LORD will scatter you among the peoples; only a few of you will be left among the nations where the LORD will lead you. There you will serve other gods made by human hands, objects of wood and stone that neither see, nor hear, nor eat, nor smell. (Deut. 4:27–28)

What had been their sin—idolatry—will next be part of their punishment, it would seem. But Deuteronomy understands this to be a corrective punishment:

> From there you will seek the LORD your God, and you will find him if you search after him with all your heart and soul. In your distress, when all these things have happened to you in time to come, you will return to the LORD your God and heed him. Because the LORD your God is a merciful God, he will neither abandon you nor destroy you; he will not forget the covenant with your ancestors that he swore to them. (Deut. 4:29–31)

For some reason, the author wants to speak both of being "utterly destroyed" and of some going into exile.[64] Unlike the prophets, this author's promissory material will not speak explicitly of return to the land. A similar prediction appears in Deut. 29:18–28, threatening exile but without any reference to promise. Other texts take the form of warnings, which would seem to make the best sense in a reforming document that seeks to avoid this terrible fate (thus perhaps to be dated earlier than 587):

> If you do forget the LORD your God, and follow other gods to serve and worship them, I solemnly warn you today that you shall surely perish (*'abad*). Like the nations that the LORD is destroying before you, so shall you perish, because you would not obey the voice of the LORD your God. (Deut. 8:19–20; cf. 6:15; 7:4; 11:17; 30:18)

The curses in Deuteronomy 28 are like 4:25–31 in that they threaten both complete destruction and exile, but they elaborate on what exile will be like:

> The LORD will bring you, and the king whom you set over you, to a nation that neither you nor your ancestors have known, where you shall serve other gods, of wood and stone. You shall become an object of horror, a proverb, and a byword among all the peoples where the LORD will lead you. (Deut. 28:36–37)

> Because you did not serve the LORD your God joyfully and with gladness of heart for the abundance of everything, therefore you shall serve your enemies whom the LORD will send against you, in hunger and thirst, in nakedness and lack of everything. He will put an iron yoke on your neck until he has destroyed (*hishmid*) you. (Deut. 28:47–48)

> The LORD will scatter you among all peoples, from one end of the earth to the other; and there you shall serve other gods, of wood and stone, which neither you nor your fathers have known. And among these nations you shall find no ease, and there shall be no rest for the sole of your foot; but the LORD will give you there a trembling heart, and failing eyes, and a languishing soul; your life shall hang in doubt before you; night and day you shall be in dread, and have no assurance of your life. In the morning you

shall say, "Would it were evening!" and at evening you shall say, "Would it were morning!" because of the dread which your heart shall fear, and the sights which your eyes shall see. And the LORD will bring you back in ships to Egypt, a journey which I promised that you should never make again; and there you shall offer yourselves for sale to your enemies as male and female slaves, but no man will buy you. (Deut. 28:64–68)

Some of these details leave the impression that the author is imagining what exile will be like, without any firsthand knowledge. All these passages have been dated in the Babylonian exile, but they show little awareness of the actual experiences of those exiles, as we learn of them from the books of Jeremiah and Ezekiel, and show little evidence of being influenced by the language and theology of the prophets. Deuteronomy's favorite verbs, 'abad "perish," and shamad, "destroy," are seldom used in the prophetic books to refer to the fate of Israel, and the author never uses the root galah of exile, as the Deuteronomistic Historian does, fifteen times in 2 Kings.[65] The book shows no awareness of the prophets' promises of eventual restoration to the promised land, except for ch. 30, which contains an outlook on the future like that in the prophetic books and significantly different from the rest of Deuteronomy.

There is strong evidence for locating the formation of the original book of Deuteronomy in the Northern Kingdom, late in the eighth century B.C.E.[66] Although the texts just discussed have regularly been dated in the Babylonian exile, it may well be that, with the exception of ch. 30, these rather ambiguous threats of complete destruction, mixed with descriptions of exile, are the result of the exiling of northern Israelites in the eighth century. Deuteronomy contains a program for reform, combining dire threats for faithlessness to Yahweh with a course of behavior which if followed will lead to abundant blessings for Israel. If its earliest form was produced in the Northern Kingdom, then it was apparently taken to Judah and reworked there (perhaps less than is usually proposed) as a message intended to save Judeans from the fate of their neighbors.

A few echoes of the language of Deuteronomy appear in Joshua–Kings. In Josh. 23:13–16, both 'abad and shamad are used. Joshua 24:20 contains the same idea, but uses the root kalah (piel) "consume." Elsewhere in the Deuteronomistic Historical Work, the root 'abad is used once in this way, to speak of the destruction of Judah (2 Kings 24:2). The Historian has also inserted at appropriate places three predictions of exile, using vocabulary different from that found in Deuteronomy: 1 Kings 9:6–7; 14:15–16; and 2 Kings 21:14. The content of these texts rather clearly indicates that they are to be dated in the exilic period.

One more text outside the prophetic books speaks of the destruction and exiling of Israel, with significant parallels to Deuteronomy 4 and 28, but with its own unique interest in the land. Leviticus 26 contains a series of blessings and curses reminiscent of Deuteronomy 28, and concluding with the threat of exile, as the former text does. If Israel insists on continuing in rebellion against Yahweh, the land will be devastated (Lev. 26:32–33) and the people scattered among the nations (cf. Deut. 4:27, although the vocabulary is different). Whereas Deut. 4:26 has the people utterly perish ('abad) from off the land, Lev. 26:38 uses the same verb for what will happen to the exiles among the nations. But, as in Deuteronomy 4, the author of Leviticus does not really mean total annihilation by this verb, since the wretched fate of those who survive is described in v. 39. There is a greatly increased interest in the land itself in Leviticus. The law of the sabbatical year had been elaborated in Lev. 25:1–6, and now exile (thought to be the complete depopulating of the country, contrary to what actually happened) is explained as God's way of giving the land its right to rest every seven years (26:34–35, 43). This is an idea that occurs nowhere else in scripture.

Like Deut. 4:29–30, Lev. 26:40–41 introduces the possibility of repentance on the part of future exiles, leading to God's mercy, based on the covenant with Abraham. Deuteronomy says, "he will neither abandon you nor destroy you; he will not forget the covenant with your ancestors that he swore to them" (4:31). Leviticus elaborates the same promise: "Then will I remember my covenant with Jacob; I will remember also my covenant with Isaac and also my covenant with Abraham, and I will remember the land" (26:42). Note the emphasis on the land, again. The passage ends with the promise reaffirmed:

> Yet for all that, when they are in the land of their enemies, I will not spurn them, or abhor them so as to destroy them utterly and break my covenant with them, for I am the LORD their God; but I will remember in their favor the covenant with their ancestors whom I brought out of the land of Egypt in the sight of the nations, to be their God: I am the LORD. (Lev. 26:44–45)

The land has been emphasized here more than in any other text of this type, and everyone knew the covenant with Abraham included the promise of the land to his descendants, so perhaps restoration from exile is implicit here, but it is striking that it is not made explicit, either here or in any of the texts in Deuteronomy, except for the unique passage, ch. 30. Leviticus 26 in its present form may well come from the exilic period, as is usually claimed, with these final verses intended as a message of hope for exiles, based on the promises of the covenant with Abraham, but like Deuteronomy it shows little evidence of being influenced by the restoration promises of the prophets, and seems to belong to a different line of tradition. It may be that Deuteronomy and Leviticus 26 represent a trajectory of thought in Israel that attempted to hold to the belief in the unconditional covenant with Abraham as best it could, while at the same time being influenced by the shock of the end of the Northern Kingdom, which had led to the exiling of parts of its population. Although they use the strong verbs of destruction, 'abad and shamad, they find various ways to mitigate those threats, and never speak in the radical way that Amos and his successors do, announcing the impending death of Israel.

PART ONE

DEATH: 722 AND 587 B.C.E.

2

THE EIGHTH CENTURY: THE ASSYRIAN THREAT AND THE   DEATH OF ISRAEL

The superscription to the book of Amos dates it during the reign of Jeroboam II, who ruled the Northern Kingdom from c.785 to 745 B.C.E. This appears to have been a time of relative peace and prosperity for Israel (and also Judah, under Uzziah), but about twenty years after Jeroboam's death the kingdom had come to an end, never again to be restored. The book of Hosea reflects the internal chaos that followed the death of Jeroboam, but Amos does not, and so most scholars have accepted the traditional dating, c. 760. For the political, social, and religious background of the first of the canonical prophets we must thus look to the scanty records of this period that are presently available.

The Deuteronomistic Historian gives Jeroboam the same failing grade as all the other kings of Israel (2 Kings 14:24), accusing him in general terms of the same sins committed by Jeroboam I; that is, schism from the house of David and the maintenance of sanctuaries rivaling Jerusalem, at Dan and Bethel. He does get credit, however, for saving Israel from bitter distress (14:26–27), probably a reference to the end of the period when Damascus dominated the Northern Kingdom and occupied significant amounts of its territory (2 Kings 10:32–33; 13:3–7, 22–25). He apparently recovered the Transjordan, from the Golan heights to the northern border of Moab (2 Kings 14:25).[1] Amos refers to the reoccupation of the Transjordan as something that has happened recently, in Amos 6:13–14. The additional reference to Jeroboam's recovery of Damascus and Hamath (2 Kings 14:28) is hard to interpret, since there are no records indicating that these city-states were actually subjugated by Israel. There is no other direct evidence about Jeroboam's long rule, but secondary evidence of various kinds may be used to help understand Israel's last period of prosperity before the end.

Egypt had been going through a long period of relative weakness, ruled by kings of Libyan descent (the Twenty-second and Twenty-third Dynasties, c. 950–730 B.C.E.). Near the end of this period several of the city-states in the delta had become independent from the central government, so Israel and Judah were subject to little interference from their southern neighbor.[2] To the northeast, Assyria, which had been a serious threat to the Syrian city-states earlier in the eighth century,[3] now had its attention drawn by serious threats from Urartu (now Armenia) and by problems in Babylonia.[4] According to 2 Kings 13:24–25 Jeroboam's father, Jehoash (or

Joash), took advantage of the defeat of Damascus to recover Israelite towns that had been annexed by the Arameans. The reign of Jeroboam II was thus a time when Israel (and also Judah) could control their own political fortunes, for a brief period.

2.1 Amos

There is very little evidence for internal affairs in the Northern Kingdom during this period except for a few suggestive details that can be gleaned from the book of Amos itself. The sense of security, even complacency, that a time of relative peace might produce is referred to in Amos 6:1–3, 13. The economy apparently was flourishing, for Amos speaks of those who have both summer and winter houses, decorated with ivory (3:15), and of building with hewn stone (requiring skilled masons) rather than with fieldstone as Israelite houses were typically constructed (5:11). He had evidently witnessed, or at least heard of, elaborate and extended feasting on the part of the wealthy (6:4–6). If the figures in 2 Kings 15:20 are correct, Menahem, who ruled for ten years after Jeroboam II, was able to find 60,000 landowners from whom he could exact a tax of fifty shekels of silver (about 1.6 pounds) in order to pay tribute to Tiglath-pileser III. We cannot estimate the extent of poverty in the country, but what Amos saw he found to be very offensive, blaming it on a breakdown of the court system (Amos 5:10–12) and on a class that put luxury above justice (2:6–8; 6:4–7; 8:4–6).

The principal references to religion in Amos are claims that worship in the sanctuaries at Bethel and Gilgal will not assure Israel's security (4:4; 5:5; cf. 5:21–24). Beersheba, a Judean sanctuary, is also included. It is known that the religion of Israel (and Judah) was highly syncretistic at that time,[5] but Amos does not take up that as a major issue, mentioning other gods only in 5:26 and 8:14 (if 8:14 is translated correctly by NRSV, REB).

What we know about the international situation between 785 and 745 correlates well with the little that is said about Jeroboam's reign in 2 Kings and with the circumstances described in Amos. It is especially important to note that although Amos speaks of a future attack by an enemy army (e.g., 3:11; 6:14), he never mentions Assyria.[6] Once Tiglath-pileser III (745–727) began his systematic acquisition of territory in Syria/Palestine, Assyria would dominate the thought of the prophets, so the major part of the book of Amos was almost certainly produced during this "prelude to disaster," when something other than an ability to evaluate trends in international affairs led one prophet to announce to a prosperous nation that it did not have long to live.[7]

Israel Must Die

In a time and place where things seemed to be going relatively well, Amos dared to take the familiar language used to express deep grief, mourning the death of a young person, and to make of it a lament over the death of Israel. The theme of this study of prophetic theology (the death and resurrection of Israel) is introduced by the book of Amos, for it has a great deal to say about death. The most poignant passage in the book is a funeral song, the lament over the virgin Israel:

> Hear this word that I take up over you in lamentation, O house of Israel:
>> Fallen, no more to rise,
>>> is maiden Israel;
>> forsaken on her land,
>>> with no one to raise her up.
>>>> (Amos 5:1–2)

The death of a young, unmarried person, who had no children to carry on his or her name, was the occasion for the most intense feelings of grief in ancient Israel. In the second line of the song, Amos alludes to another misfortune which would exacerbate the usual sense of mourning for the death of a loved one: for some reason the body has not been properly buried, but is left lying in the field.[8] Amos exercises great freedom and creativity in his uses of genres and ideas familiar to the Israelites, and this is the first such example. He identifies the genre in advance: *qin'ah,* "lamentation," or more exactly "funeral song," so his hearers think they know what to expect. Instead of mourning the death of an individual, however, he laments the death of a nation, and in advance. It must have been a highly offensive message, but is one of the various ways Amos tried to get the attention of a people who, from what we know, would have had no reason to think he could be speaking the truth.

The theme reappears later in the same chapter, now referring to a time of great community lamentation in the future:

> Therefore thus says the LORD, the God of hosts, the Lord:
>> In all the squares there shall be wailing;
>>> and in all the streets they shall say, "Alas! alas!"
>> They shall call the farmers to mourning,
>>> and those skilled in lamentation, to wailing;
>> in all the vineyards there shall be wailing,
>>> for I will pass through the midst of you, says the LORD.
>>>> (Amos 5:16–17)

The last line of this oracle seems to be one of Amos's many reversals of what had been positive traditions in Israel, for in Exod. 12:12, 23 God is said to have "passed through" Egypt in order to destroy all the firstborn except those of Israel, but this time Israel will not be spared. Reversal appears in another reference to community lament; feasts turned into funerals, with the allusion to the death of an only son perhaps recalling both the death of the Egyptians' firstborn in Exodus and the cutting off of one's name in Amos 5:2:

> On that day, says the Lord GOD,
>> I will make the sun go down at noon,
>>> and darken the earth in broad daylight.
>> I will turn your feasts into mourning,
>>> and all your songs into lamentation;
>> I will bring sackcloth on all loins,

and baldness on every head;
I will make it like the mourning for an only son,
and the end of it like a bitter day.
(Amos 8:9–10)

The same reversal appears in the explanation of Amos's fourth vision (8:1–3), accompanied by the most blunt statement in the book of the essence of his message: "The end has come upon my people Israel" (v. 2). There is a remarkable and disturbing growth of intensity among his five visions. The first (7:1–3) depicts a fairly common natural phenomonon: a locust plague. Amos intercedes for Jacob (Israel's other name, Gen. 32:28), as Moses had done before him (Exod. 32:11–14): "O Lord GOD, forgive, I beg you! How can Jacob stand? He is so small!" And the Lord changed his mind.[9] The second vision (7:4–6) portrays no natural event, for Amos saw a supernatural fire that devoured the very depths of the ocean (the *těhom* of Gen. 1:2). This time Amos just asked the Lord to cease, not to forgive, and once again the Lord changed his mind.

The third vision is not as clear to us as the others. Translations all speak of a plumb line, but the Hebrew word used four times in Amos 7:7–9 has now been shown to mean "tin."[10] "Plumb line" first appeared as a guess in the medieval commentaries by Ibn Ezra, Rashi, and Qimhi, and has no support in etymology or in any of the ancient versions. It seems likely that Amos introduced the word *'anak* not because of its meaning (tin) but in order to create a play on words (as he did with *qayits* and *qets* in 8:1–2). The word would sound much like two similar roots, *'anah* and *'anaq*, both of which mean "sigh." The mourning that appears in 5:16–17 and 8:3, 10 would thus reappear here, if Amos said, "See, I am setting *'anak* in the midst of my people Israel," intending them to think *'anah* or *'anaq*—sighing.[11] The sighing would correspond with the explanation that follows:

The high places of Isaac shall be made desolate,
and the sanctuaries of Israel shall be laid waste,
and I will rise against the house of Jeroboam with the sword.
(Amos 7:9)

This is the one reference to Jeroboam (or to kingship in Israel, in contrast with Hosea) in the speeches of Amos, and that led to the insertion within the sequence of visions of the account of an incident in Amos's career (7:10–17), which will be dealt with shortly.

The sequence is resumed with the fourth vision-account in 8:1–3. The first two depicted phenomena in nature, and according to my reading the third and fourth correspond to one another in making use of wordplay. What Amos sees is in itself of no importance—tin and summer fruit—but their names call to mind words that are meaningful. In 8:1–2 that is made explicit. God asks Amos what he sees: *qayits*, "summer fruit." But the Lord says, "*qets*—End—has come upon my people Israel." As in the third vision, Amos makes no attempt to intercede. After "End" there is not much more to be said. But the sequence of increasing terror reaches its climax in a final passage that is identified as a vision, since it begins "I saw the LORD," although its content is a speech, with nothing more said about what Amos sees (9:1–4). It emphasizes, probably more strongly than any other passage in the book, the thoroughness of the destruction that is to come:

> Those who are left I will kill with the sword;
>> not one of them shall flee away,
>> not one of them shall escape.
> Though they dig into Sheol,
>> from there shall my hand take them;
> though they climb up to heaven,
>> from there I will bring them down.
> Though they hide themselves on the top of Carmel,
>> from there I will search out and take them;
> and though they hide from my sight at the bottom of the sea,
>> there I will command the sea-serpent, and it shall bite them.
> And though they go into captivity in front of their enemies,
>> there I will command the sword, and it shall kill them;
> and I will fix my eyes on them
>> for harm and not for good.
>
> (Amos 9:1–4)

Even exile will be no escape from the divine judgment. This is the last threat of exile in the book, and for some reason it uses a root (*shabah*) that is common elsewhere in the Old Testament, but is otherwise not Amos's choice when he speaks of exile, as he does in nine other passages.

If the end of the kingdom of Israel was a radically new and unprecedented message, Amos's use of the root *galah* to designate exile was also unprecedented in the Old Testament.[12] It does not occur in any text earlier than Amos, is missing from Hosea, appears once in Micah (1:16), and only twice in Isaiah 1–39 (5:13; 20:4), but appears thirteen times in the nine passages in Amos. It is frequently used in Jeremiah (32 times), Ezekiel (16 times), and in the Deuteronomistic History (18 times), and the noun forms, *golah* and *galuth*, became the standard words used in Judaism to denote exile, from that time until the present. One might then suspect that an exilic editor introduced them into the book of Amos, but they are used in such original and various ways (and were not introduced in the editing of Hosea, Micah, or Isaiah) that it seems more likely to have been vocabulary distinctive to this book, until it influenced the work of Judean authors in the Babylonian exile.[13] Amos condemns Gaza and Tyre for exiling whole peoples (1:6, 9), and threatens the Arameans with exile (1:5). He uses assonance between Gilgal and *galah* to create a fairly elaborate wordplay, for by emphasizing "exile" (which calls for using the root twice, in the imperfect and the infinitive absolute) he created *hagilgal galoh yigleh* (Amos 5:5). Never mind that the sanctuary Gilgal could scarcely go into exile; the play on words made his point, and was too good to overlook. Another of his effective uses of words appears in 6:1–7. He introduces the wealthy partyers as "notables of the first (*re'shith*) of the nations (*goyim*)," and declares that in the future they will still be first (*ro'sh*), but first of the exiles (*golim*) to go into exile.

Exile was thus associated with the time-honored sanctuaries (Gilgal, 5:5) and with those who live in luxury at the expense of the poor (6:7). In a difficult passage it also appears to be connected with idolatry. The words *sikkut* and *kiyyun* in 5:26 have been taken by several scholars (and NRSV) as distorted forms of the names of Assyrian deities: Sakkuth and Kaiwan. If so, the question is raised how and when the people of the Northern Kingdom became aquainted with these deities. Others (e.g., REB, NIV) take the words to be derivatives of common Hebrew words, meaning "shrine" and "pedestal," but in both cases the picture presented is that of people marching away into exile beyond Damascus carrying their false gods with them. The reference to Damascus has led some to think Amos must have Assyria in mind as the enemy, but that does not seem necessary. All the danger had come from the north for the past century or more, and he would naturally think of exile taking place in that direction.

The most sweeping, and ultimately most influential use of the term *galah* appears in the confrontation between Amos and the priest of Bethel, Amaziah, in Amos 7:10–17. Amaziah advised (or ordered) Amos to leave Bethel, the king's sanctuary, and return to Judah, for his words threatening king and nation had been reported to Jeroboam himself. The message was summarized by Amaziah as follows: "Jeroboam shall die by the sword, and Israel must go into exile away from his land" (7:11). Amos refused to accept the priest's assumption that as guardian of the sanctuary Amaziah could forbid him to speak. We shall return to what this book says about the prophet's commission later. Amos's condemnation of the priest's assumption of authority is important at this point; Amaziah and family will be punished for it, he will die in an unclean land, and then Amos repeats the second part of the message he had been quoted as giving earlier: "and Israel shall surely go into exile away from its land." In Hebrew the wording is identical in 7:11 and 7:17 (unlike NRSV), and as in 5:5 the root is used twice for emphasis, in the imperfect and the infinitive absolute. The Deuteronomistic Historian must have known this oracle, even though he shows no other awareness of the book of Amos, for he summarizes the fall of Samaria and the fall of Jerusalem using the same formulation, and these are the only other places in the Old Testament where it occurs: "and Israel went into exile away from its land" (2 Kings 17:23); "and Judah went into exile away from its land" (2 Kings 25:21; my translations).

The book of Amos thus makes exile a prominent part of its picture of the disastrous future in store for the kingdom of Israel, and if the earliest words in the book are to be dated around 760 B.C.E., with the majority of scholars, that threat came true about forty years later. Amos does not contain anything that could be called a theology of exile, however. Evidently the idea was too new for an Israelite or Judean to be able to correlate it in any way with the accepted traditions. The exiling of populations had been practiced from time to time in earlier history, and it was taken up by Amos in order to emphasize the thoroughness of the end of the political entity, Israel. Death would be widespread, and those who did not die would be removed from their homeland.

Why Death?

Was it that bad? Why should God have decided that this part of the people he had chosen for a covenant relationship should be judged so severely, so thoroughly? The simplest answer leaves God out of it and either bypasses the prophets' message or declares them to be wrong: The Assyrians were coming, and nothing could stop them. Ethics had nothing to do with it.[14] But the prophets claimed that God was at work in the midst of the disaster and that there was a reason for it. Amos does not know that there is also a purpose beyond it, but Hosea and others who follow will begin to get intimations of that.

Did Amos think that God was passing the death sentence on Israel because of a series of misdemeanors, crimes for which nothing more than probation might be expected today? Was he really stretching things to find a moral justification for the disaster he expected? The question can be answered correctly only if one starts in the right place, and that is with Amos 3:1–2. The poor probably fared no worse in Israel than in the surrounding nations, but Amos claimed Israel was a special case, and there is little doubt that the Israelites would have agreed with that point: "You only have I known of all the families of the earth." But here also, Amos makes a new and disturbing use of familiar tradition:

> Hear this word that the LORD has spoken against you, O people of Israel,
>   against the whole family that I brought up out of the land of Egypt:
>> You only have I known
>>   of all the families of the earth;
>> therefore I will punish you
>>   for all your iniquities.
>
> (Amos 3:1–2)

This is an appeal to the Exodus and Sinai traditions. "Thus says the LORD: Israel is my firstborn son" (Exod. 4:22). "You shall be my treasured possession out of all the peoples. Indeed, the whole earth is mine, but you shall be for me a priestly kingdom and a holy nation" (Exod. 19:5–6). These traditions clearly played a central role in the theology of the Northern Kingdom (cf. 1 Kings 12:29 and see the discussion of Hosea), so Amos here reaffirms what the people believed: They had been chosen by Yahweh for a special relationship. Amos does not use the word "covenant," but "you only have I known" is covenant language. This was election for privilege, yes; they had been saved from slavery and they had been given a land that once belonged to others. But privilege involves responsibility as well. They were to become a priestly kingdom, a holy nation, and their special character as a nation among others was defined by the law given on Mount Sinai.[15] Amos asserts that they have enthusiastically claimed the privilege, but have forgotten responsibility. The basis for his words of judgment is summed up most effectively in a saying of Jesus: "From everyone to whom much has been given, much will be required; and from the one to whom much has been entrusted, even more will be demanded" (Luke 12:48). The word translated "punish" in NRSV is *paqad*, which can be used of either a favorable or an unfavorable response, depending on the situation. Thus it would be more appropriately translated here "hold you accountable for" (with JPSV). The issue is a relationship that has been violated. Israel had been put where they are in order to become a truly healthy community, in which everyone could live in harmony, a witness to the nations ("a priestly kingdom"). God's intention for Israel has failed. Later prophets will announce that God will find a way to start over, but Amos does not know that. He knows only of failure, and can say only that the relationship is ended. Since Amos is usually so vague about the danger that lies ahead, speaking more often of God than of an enemy army as the agent of judgment, the basis for his dire view of the future would seem to be not political analysis but awareness that a relationship has been broken. So, many interpreters have appropriately taken 3:2 to be a theme verse for the entire book.

Examples of the way Israel has failed its part of the relationship are given in the first oracle against Israel (2:6–15), and they are combined with reminders of their special status: "I brought you up out of the land of Egypt, and led you forty years in the wilderness, to possess the land of the Amorite" (v. 10). The text of this passage is difficult in several places, and we cannot be sure exactly what some of the offenses were,[16] but the beginning and end are clear. He begins with debt slavery (2:6), and when he speaks of selling the *righteous* for silver he means those who were in the right, who evidently did not owe what they were being charged with. He ends with another reference to debts, to feasting in sanctuaries, drinking wine bought with fines, and lying on garments taken in pledge for a debt from people so poor they had nothing else to offer (cf. 6:4). Since that outer garment was ordinarily the only thing the poor person would have for warmth at night, it was supposed to be returned each evening (Exod. 22:26–27 [MT vv. 25–26]). The passage is thus bracketed with references not only to unconcern for the poor but also to taking advantage of them intentionally.

The same attitudes are condemned in other passages. The wealthy women of Samaria not only order about their husbands—"Bring something to drink!"—but in general terms are accused of oppressing the poor and crushing the needy (4:1–3).[17] This accounts for Amos's insistence that those of the upper classes who revel in luxury will lead the rest into exile, in 6:1–7. It was not that he found something wrong with luxury in itself. The Old Testament never advocates asceticism as a superior way of life, but insists that God wants his people to have plenty (e.g., Lev. 26:3–10; Ps. 72:3, 16; Jer. 31:12–14). How they get it and what they do with it is what matters to God.

Two specific examples of how they got it are provided in the book. In 8:4–6 Amos claims that commercial practices are trampling the needy, bringing ruin to the poor of the land. The merchants are using small measures for the grain they sell and extra heavy weights to measure out what they charge (v. 5b), and they adulterate the product as well (v. 6b). They do so well at it that even though custom requires them not to trade on new moon or sabbath, they chafe at having to give up a day of business.

Most serious of all was the corruption of the legal system, according to Amos. The word "justice" (*mishpaṭ*) for which he has become famous occurs only in 5:7, 15, 24; and 6:12, and it is in ch. 5 that the question of justice in the gate becomes prominent. The gate was the entrance to the city, where the elders who were responsible for deciding matters of law could be found during the day. The "one who reproves," who speaks the truth (5:10), was probably the person who attempted to uphold the cause of a poor person who had no influence with those elders when he tried to bring a case against a rich and prominent community member. Worse yet, Amos knows that bribery was leading the "righteous" (*tsaddiq*), those who were in the right, to lose their cases (v. 12). Apparently, then, there was little recourse for those who were being cheated in commerce, who were being forced even into slavery for debts they did not owe, since justice could not be found in the courts.

We might ask, What is so unusual about that? Cannot similar conditions be found in every society, to this day—even forms of servitude that amount to slavery? Amos's answer would be, It was not unusual, but Israel was supposed to be different. The Exodus/Sinai traditions spoke of a God whose special concern is for the helpless on earth, and that conviction must lie behind the accusations Amos makes, even though the book contains no exact quotations of the law. The first oracle against Israel in the book cites offenses against the poor in the immediate context of a reminder of the exodus (2:6–8, followed by 9–11). There is a connection between Amos and the book of Exodus that seems to account for the severity of the judgment Amos pronounced against Israel, and also to explain the basis for his oracles against the nations (to be discussed in the next section). The law codes in the Pentateuch are filled with motive clauses, explanations of law intended to persuade the Israelites to obey. They may appeal to memory of what God has done, hoping for a response of gratitude (e.g., Deut. 15:12–15). They may be reminders of generally accepted truths or common sense (e.g., Deut. 12:23; 20:19), or may offer promises (Deut. 12:25). It seems odd, given the human tendency to threaten in order to get people to obey, to find only one motive clause associated with a law that is a dire threat of direct, divine punishment. The nature of the offense must be the reason for it:

> You shall not wrong or oppress a resident alien, for you were aliens in the land of Egypt. You shall not abuse any widow or orphan. If you do abuse them, when they cry out to me, I will surely heed their cry; my wrath will burn, and I will kill you with the sword, and your wives shall become widows and your children orphans. (Exod. 22:21–24 [MT vv. 20–23])

Mistreatment of the widow, the orphan, or the alien (best translated in our day, "immigrant"), the Old Testament's classic examples of those without enough "clout" to be able to maintain their own rights, is the basis for the single motive clause that speaks of the wrath of God.[18] Yahweh had taken the role of an *advocate* for the slaves in Egypt and had made war on Egypt in order to set them free. The Exodus/Sinai traditions continued to remind Israel, "for you were aliens [elsewhere, slaves] in the land of Egypt," and you have a God who continues to take the role of advocate for all who are too weak to maintain their own cause, intervening in human affairs as the enemy of oppressors. In Amos's time, Israel appears to have neglected to apply that principle to themselves, but Amos does so. This was thus not a new idea, making Yahweh the upholder of social justice, but the drawing of conclusions about where Israel stood in Yahweh's sight based on what they had long been taught about the character of the God of the exodus.

If Israel believed that the God of the exodus was an advocate for the helpless, although without necessarily applying that to their own behavior, then the much-debated basis for Amos's oracles against the foreign nations may be readily accounted for. Amos claimed that Yahweh, God of Israel, stood in judgment of Damascus, the Philistines, Tyre, Edom, Ammon, and Moab (1:3–2:3) without saying they necessarily knew anything about demands that God had placed upon them. Frequently this has been explained by saying Amos assumed all the nations were subject to Yahweh's judgment whether or not they knew his laws, but this raises questions of fairness—punishment for something they did not know was wrong. A stronger explanation notes the nature of the crimes cited—atrocities against humanity—and says these were ideas generally accepted in the international community as to what was acceptable behavior in warfare, so there was nothing specifically Yahwistic in Amos's thought. Others have suggested that these six nations were part of an idealized Davidic empire, and Amos condemns them for treaty violations.[19] The notion of advocacy, drawn from the way Yahweh is depicted in Exodus, offers another way of reading the oracles. Egypt knew nothing of Yahweh. The Pharaoh responded to Moses's demand with, "Who is Yahweh, that I should heed him and let Israel go? I do not know Yahweh, and I will not let Israel go" (Exod. 5:2). An advocate may have to act with force, precisely because his principles are not accepted by the power from whom he is trying to rescue an oppressed people, and Israel remembered Yahweh acting with devastating force in the plagues that came on Egypt.

In Amos's oracles against the nations the prophet speaks of war crimes, violations of the integrity of individual human beings. Some of them were crimes against Israelites (1:3, 11, 13), others may have been (1:4, 9), one clearly has nothing to do with Israel (2:1). Amos is not expressing a nationalistic, but a humanistic point of view, making one of his universal claims for the sovereignty of Yahweh. Wherever human beings are mistreated, Yahweh is offended, Amos says. The individual oracles in chs. 1—2 make a new use of an old tradition. They follow the pattern of "holy war oracles" once delivered by prophets to declare that Yahweh would assure victory for his people (cf. 1 Kings 20:28). But now, Amos uses the old form to announce widespread judgment, including not only all the surrounding nations, but also Israel itself, thus reversing the original intent of holy war. The reason for it, in each case, is Yahweh's intervention because of mistreatment of the helpless. That reversal appears also in his depiction of the Day of Yahweh as darkness, not light (5:18–20), for the term "Day of Yahweh" probably originally referred to the day of God's victory over Israel's enemies.[20]

One of the most remarkable statements in Amos is that an exodus itself, under the guidance of Yahweh, is not something only Israel has experienced. The final reference to the exodus is in 9:7: "Are you not like the Ethiopians to me, O people of Israel? says the LORD. Did I not bring Israel up from the land of Egypt, and the Philistines from Caphtor and the Arameans from Kir?" Caphtor was probably

Crete, and Amos knew what archaeology can now confirm for our benefit, that the Philistines had in fact migrated from the islands of Greece to settle eventually on the coast of Palestine. We also have some evidence for migration of the Arameans into north Mesopotamia and Syria, although Kir cannot be located with certainty. For Amos, Yahweh was not only the judge of the nations when their wars led to the cruel treatment of human beings, he was also the one who led other nations, as well as Israel, into their present homelands.[21]

Amos makes no explicitly monotheistic statement about Yahweh. Only Second Isaiah ("There is no other god besides me," Isa. 45:21) and Deuteronomy ("Yahweh is God; there is no other besides him," 4:35) use that language. But Amos seems implicitly to be a practical (rather than theoretical) monotheist, for in addition to claiming Yahweh's sovereignty over the nations his book also contains nature hymns extolling God's power as creator. Brief stanzas have been inserted at three places in the book. In 4:13 and 9:5–6 the hymn forms an impressive conclusion to a section (4:6–13 and 9:1–6), leading up to the declaration "Yahweh [the God of hosts] is his name!" The reason for the location of 5:8–9 is not so obvious, and the announcement of Yahweh's name comes in the middle of the stanza rather than at the end.[22] These may once have been stanzas of a single hymn, as some think, but there is no way to demonstrate that. They use language reminiscent of the theophanies elsewhere in the Old Testament (e.g., Psalm 18; Nahum 1:2–8; Habakkuk 3), and the thought moves from creation to destruction. Yahweh made the mountains and the wind (4:13), the constellations Pleiades and Orion, day and night (5:8a), but also pours the waters of the sea out upon the earth (surely a recollection of the Flood 5:8b; 9:6b), and touches the earth so that it melts (9:5). Amos's claims for the universal power of Yahweh thus extend far beyond the affairs of Israel, and beyond the affairs of the nations who are also responsible to him. It is the creator of heaven and earth who is offended by cruelty to one human being; who surely can bring human oppressors to judgment since he has the power to destroy the world itself.

Israel knew this already. Amos uses traditional language drawn from various parts of the daily life of the people, although often in shockingly unorthodox ways. In the passages just mentioned it is the language of worship, and he appears to make no change in the way it had always been used. Worship did not escape his critical evaluation, however, and he declared that what was going on in Israel was a hypocritical, hence useless exercise. Later prophets would call for confession in the cult as the appropriate response to times of trouble (e.g., Joel 2:12–17 and the use of confession and lament in Isa. 59:9–20; 64:1–12). Amos claims to find no such sensitivity in the Israelite worship of his time. When trouble comes, whether it is good theology or not, people normally ask what they may have done to bring it upon themselves. But Israel is so dense, according to 4:6–12, that a whole series of disasters in the past had no effect on them whatever. Worship has evidently become routine. The best-known text in the book (5:21–24) is not a rejection of sacrifice as a form of worship, as it has sometimes been read. Note that singing is also called useless! The problem Amos identified was carrying out acts of worship without showing any regard for what God expects of his people in daily life. Without evidence that justice and righteousness prevail in the community, praise of any sort is hypocrisy. Elsewhere, Amos creates a mock call to worship, another of his reversals of the normal meaning of words:

> Come to Bethel—and transgress;
>   to Gilgal—and multiply transgression;
> bring your sacrifices every morning,
>   your tithes every three days;
> bring a thank-offering of leavened bread,
>   and proclaim freewill offerings, publish them; for so
> you love to do, O people of Israel!
>
> (Amos 4:4–5)

Complacency, reinforced not only by the relative security and prosperity of the time but also by the comforting routines of worship, was the major barrier to understanding which Amos's brutally creative use of language attempted to breach.

Was there no hope? Readers of scripture naturally want to find messages of hope wherever they look, and the Deuteronomistic picture of the prophets as preachers of repentance has supported the effort to find an option to judgment, even in Amos. There is in the book one appeal with a promise attached, expressed in two slightly different ways: "Seek me and live" (5:4; "Seek Yahweh and live," 5:6) and "Seek good and not evil, that you may live; and so Yahweh, the God of hosts, will be with you, just as you have said" (5:14). The first of these appeals is attached to Amos's insistence that the sanctuaries cannot save them; the second defines exactly what he means by seeking good: "Establish justice in the gate" (5:15). The expression "Seek the LORD and live" is another of Amos's ironic uses of cultic language (cf. Pss. 24:6; 27:8; 34:10 [MT v. 11]). Note that these offers of "life" occur in a chapter the main theme of which is death (5:1–3, 9, 16–20). As to the promise in 5:15, there is not much that Amos can offer. It begins, "It may be." Amos has never spoken of repenting; perhaps because he knows there is no guarantee of automatic forgiveness. He knows also that there is no future for Israel as it now is, for the highly uncertain promise is offered only to the *remnant* of Joseph.[23] But he will use, here only, one of the most potent theological words of the Old Testament: "It may be that the LORD, the God of hosts, will be *gracious* (*hanan*) to the remnant of Joseph." That has led a good many scholars to question whether even this highly uncertain promise could come from the same source as the words of certain judgment that dominate the book. It is good Israelite theology, however, to make allowances for the freedom of God to be gracious, even though it did not logically fit with the equal insistence on his justice (Exod. 33:19; 34:6–7; Joel 2:12–14; Jonah 4:2). It need not, then, be thought to contradict the message of the rest of the book, but neither does it define the whole message of Amos as an appeal to repent so that the disaster may be averted. The best this book can hope for is that some individuals will be spared.

Some interpreters will say that such a message was only to be expected from a Judean. They read the book as an expression of nationalism. The Northern Kingdom, which had rejected the line of David and Jerusalem as Yahweh's chosen city, could do nothing right. But a few have questioned whether Amos was in fact from Judah. There was a Tekoa in Galilee also, and some have claimed he was a northerner, thus a subversive, a traitor to his own country.[24] Amos's own explanation of why he said what he did was different. He claimed to have no choice in the matter, but to be under divine compulsion. When Amaziah told him to "flee away to the land of Judah, earn your bread there, and prophesy there" (7:12), Amos's answer was cryptic in part, but made it clear why he had brought his messages to Bethel: "The LORD took me from following the flock, and the LORD said to me, 'Go, prophesy to my people Israel'" (7:15).[25] There is another reflection on the reason for prophecy in 3:3–8. It is a series of rhetorical questions, the point of which is inevitability: "Does a lion roar in the forest, when it has no prey? . . . Is a trumpet blown in a city, and the people are not afraid? . . . The lion has roared; who will not fear? The Lord Yahweh has spoken; who can but prophesy?"

There is little that we can say about any personal experiences the man Amos may have had in the eighth century B.C.E., but these passages and similar ones in other books are important for the information they provide as to what Israel and early Judaism understood as the basis for the prophets' claim to authority. At the time, who could know whether they were right or wrong (cf. 1 Kings 22 and Jeremiah 27—28)? It was finally the test of history that proved these prophets knew something that had been hidden from others.

Amos as Part of the Whole Prophetic Message

Amos found that he must speak of death; there is no evidence in the book of any intimation that a resurrection might follow. Indeed, since his concern was the Northern Kingdom and there never was a restoration of those exiled from the north, such a message would have been inappropriate. His words, shocking and unacceptable though they must have been when uttered, were preserved somehow, and made their way to Judah. We can only speculate about the process, and that is not profitable. There is evidence that this collection of oracles was thought by those who preserved them to be relevant to Judah, and not just to be an explanation of what had happened to Israel. We cannot be certain about the origin of the oracle against Judah in 2:4–5, but its contents are remarkably vague and general, in comparison with the other seven oracles in ch. 1—2. They sound like the summaries that later prophets produced, after they had detailed specific charges. A later insertion of this oracle may thus be one of the ways Amos was made to speak directly to his homeland. Other passages would have supported the application of his words to Judah. The "theme verse" in 3:2 is introduced: "Hear this word that the LORD has spoken against you, O people of Israel, against the whole family that I brought up out of the land of Egypt" (3:1). Here, Amos used "Israel" in its ideal sense, as other prophets will do, to include both the Northern and Southern Kingdoms. Amos the Judean may have spoken this way, and may also have mentioned Zion/Jerusalem a few times (1:2; 6:1), but it seems unlikely that the two promises that conclude the book (9:11–12, 13–15) would have originated from any eighth-century source. There are no relationships of vocabulary or themes with the rest of the book, and each oracle presupposes that disaster has already come. The first refers to the fallen booth of David, the second to ruined cities, with a promise that the people will never again be plucked up out of the land. These would be meaningless promises for people who had not already lost everything, but their place in the final, canonical form of the book of Amos makes good sense. The original book accounted for the cataclysm that befell first Israel, then Judah, as something that was no accident and not due to the will of some foreign emperor or another god. It insisted that Yahweh was still in charge. Those who eventually took Amos's words seriously heard an imperative addressed to them in Amos's analysis of what he had found in Israel that was incompatible with the way the people of Yahweh ought to live. It called them back to the law of Sinai, but they could have taken that as a basis for a new life only because of what later prophets said, those who spoke of Yahweh's intention to bring a new people out of the ruins of the past. The earliest form of the book of Amos knew only part of the story, but the first act without the second left them with no future. So it should not be thought a weakening of his message of judgment when later prophets added these promises to the book. They make the book a full part of the whole prophetic canon.

2.2 Hosea

The book of Hosea presents a very difficult challenge to the writer of a commentary. The text is poorly preserved, there is very little structure, and the thought is not always consistent. It is not as difficult to write a study of the theology of the book, however, for it contains many variations on a limited number of themes. The superscription of the book dates it in the time of Uzziah and Jeroboam II, suggesting that Hosea may have been contemporary with Amos, but adds the names of three more kings of Judah—Jotham, Ahaz, and Hezekiah—certain evidence that Hos. 1:1 is part of a Judean edition of the book. Unlike Amos, Hosea makes frequent references to Assyria, and the condemnations of kings and princes that appear in the book show that much of it is appropriately dated during the chaotic years after Jeroboam's death (745 B.C.E.). The book shows no awareness of the fall of the capital city Samaria (722/21). The commentaries on Hosea suggest that the material in the book may be arranged roughly in chronological order, and attempt to associate certain oracles with events known from 2 Kings and the Assyrian records, perhaps with a fair degree of success, but Hosea's language is vague and highly poetic, so this study of his theology will make little use of those efforts.[26] It will be enough to be aware that the turmoil in the book is a reflection of the troubles afflicting Israel during this twenty- to thirty-year period.

When Jeroboam died he was succeeded by his son Zechariah, but after only six months on the throne he was assassinated by Shallum, bringing to an end the dynasty established by Jehu four generations earlier (2 Kings 15:8–12; Hos. 1:4–5). Shallum survived only a month, and was in turn assassinated by Menahem, who was able to hold the throne for ten years (745–736; 2 Kings 15:13–22). In the meantime Tiglath-pileser III had come to power in Assyria, and by 743 was campaigning in Syria. An inscription of his dated in 738 lists Menahem among a series of kings of nations ranging from north Mesopotamia to Arabia who paid tribute to him (*ANET*, 283). This may be the same tribute recorded in 2 Kings 15:19–20, which is said to have dissuaded the Assyrian king (there called by his Babylonian name Pul) from occupying the land. Menahem was succeeded by his son, Pekahiah, but after a two-year reign he was assassinated by another usurper, Pekah, aided by a band of Gileadites (2 Kings 15:23–26; note the references to Gilead in Hos. 6:8; 12:11). Pekah is said to have reigned twenty years, in 2 Kings 15:27, but that seems to be a textual error, and his probable dates are 735–732. He became involved in an effort by the kings of the region to break free from tribute paying to Assyria. Only Ahaz, king of Judah, seems to have remained pro-Assyrian, leading to an invasion of Judah by the armies of Israel and Damascus, and an appeal to the Assyrians for help by Ahaz (2 Kings 16:5–9; Isa. 7:1–17). Tiglath-pileser soon dealt severely with the rebellion, invading Gilead and Galilee, and adding them to his empire as provinces (733/32). Of the Northern Kingdom, only the central hill country around Samaria was left as a semi-independent, tribute-paying state (2 Kings 15:29; 16:9). Pekah was then assassinated by Hoshea (1 Kings 15:30) and the latter was confirmed as vassal king by Tiglath-pileser (*ANET*, 284). The details of the last years of the kingdom of Israel are unclear, and the debate among historians continues, but they need not concern us in this context.[27] Tiglath-pileser died in 727, and was succeeded by Shalmaneser V, who ruled until 722, when Sargon II came to power. According to 2 Kings 17:4, Hoshea attempted to with-hold tribute from Shalmaneser, hoping for help from Egypt, but was imprisoned by the Assyrians, who then laid siege to Samaria, taking it after three years (see also 2 Kings 18:9–12). The Assyrian records credit both Shalmaneser V and Sargon II with the victory over Samaria, leading to suggested dates ranging from 722 to 720.[28] I have chosen 722 as "close enough" for our purposes.

The Bible records the exiling of Israelites from Gilead and Galilee by Tiglath-pileser III (2 Kings 15:29), and another exile after the fall of Samaria (2 Kings 17:6; 18:11). Sargon II claimed, "I besieged and conquered Samaria (*Sa-me-ri-na*), led away as booty 27,290 inhabitants of it. I formed from among them a contingent of 50 chariots and made remaining (inhabitants) assume their (social) positions. I installed over them an officer of mine and imposed upon them the tribute of the former king."[29] So ended the political history of the Northern Kingdom, and these were the events which appear to have brought forth the prophecy of Hosea.

The Death of Israel

Hosea is well-known for the reversals of words of judgment that appear in the book; for example, "In the place where it was said to them, 'You are not my people,' it shall be said to them, 'Children of the living God'" (Hos. 1:10; MT 2:1), and, "I will not execute my fierce anger" (Hos. 11:9). Is it inappropriate, then, to approach it as we did Amos, beginning with the message that Israel must die? It would seem to be, if one read only the first three chapters, for although they speak of punishment to come, apparently it will be of short duration, and for disciplinary purposes. These chapters introduce a tension that does not appear in any significant way in Amos, but they must not be allowed to dominate the reading of the whole book. Others have pointed out that Hosea's words of judgment are no less severe than those of Amos.[30] His language has a poetic extravagance about it that forbids us to take it all literally. For example, the adulterous wife is said to be killed with thirst in 2:3 [MT 2:5], but she is very much alive a few verses later. In chs. 9—13, however, the death of Israel is spoken of in a variety of ways that cannot be explained away:

> For even if they escape destruction,
>   Egypt shall gather them,
>   Memphis shall bury them.
>   (Hos. 9:6)

The latter part of ch. 9 contains a terrible description of the time to come when Ephraim will have no children, ending with the threat of exile, as in Amos (vv. 11–17). But Hosea ascribes a ferocity to Yahweh surpassing anything in Amos:

> So I will become like a lion to them,
>   like a leopard I will lurk beside the way.
> I will fall upon them like a bear robbed of her cubs,
>   and will tear open the covering of their heart;
> there I will devour them like a lion,
>   as a wild animal would mangle them.
> I will destroy you, O Israel;
>   who can help you?
>   (Hos. 13:7–9)

The last words of the book before the exhortation and promise in ch. 14 are the most terrible of all:

> Samaria shall bear her guilt,
>   because she has rebelled against her God;
>   they shall fall by the sword,
>   their little ones shall be dashed in pieces,
>   and their pregnant women ripped open.
>   (Hos. 13:16; MT 14:1)

Like Amos and their contemporaries in Israel, Hosea knew about the horrors of warfare, and he announced that they were to fall upon his people in the near future.

Hosea is noted for his teaching about the love of God, but he also speaks of hate: "Every evil of theirs began at Gilgal; there I came to hate them. Because of the wickedness of their deeds I will drive them out of my house. I will love them no more; all their officials are rebels" (9:15). Unike Amos, he will speak of the wrath of God: "I gave you a king in my anger, and I took him away in my wrath" (13:11; cf. 5:10). Although Hosea can identify the international threat—Assyria— he is like Amos in saying more about God than the nations, as the one who will carry out the judgment. In 5:14, as in 13:7–9, he compares God to a wild beast who will attack his people: "I myself will tear and go away; I will carry off, and no one shall rescue." Just prior to that he makes the most shocking comparison of all: "Therefore I am like maggots [some commentators translate the word "pus"] to Ephraim, and like rottenness to the house of Judah" (5:12).

The book begins with the message of judgment; indeed, of the rejection of Israel by Yahweh, but already in ch. 1 that message seems to be nullified by promises. At this point we must leave the promises to one side, to return to the tension this creates in the book at a later point. We need not enter into the lengthy and inconclusive debate over Hosea's marriage in order to understand the first chapter of the book, for the point of that chapter is to be found in the symbolic names he gave to his three children.[31] Hosea's ministry is introduced with the order to "take a promiscuous wife and promiscuous children, for the land has been promiscuous away from Yahweh."[32] We shall consider the meaning of this term in the next section, for Hosea makes nothing of it in ch. 1. Some of the efforts to produce an imaginative biography of the marriage of Hosea and Gomer have made a great deal of it, but we shall say no more than the author of the chapter does (note that Hosea is referred to in the third person). His first child was to be named Jezreel, with an explicit explanation added. It was in the valley of Jezreel that Jehu, the usurper, had killed the reigning king, Joram, and his mother, Jezebel (2 Kings 9; note that Jezreel is mentioned ten times in the chapter). Jehu receives mild praise from the author of 2 Kings, since he led a reaction against Baal worship (2 Kings 10:28–36), but it involved bloody massacres, and the message Hosea was told to associate with the name of his child was, "I will punish the house of Jehu for the blood of Jezreel." The message probably came during the reign of Jeroboam II, who was Jehu's grandson, for Jeroboam's son, Zechariah, ruled only six months and the dynasty came to an end. But there is more to the message: "and I will put an end to the kingdom of the house of Israel." The first words attributed to Hosea speak not only of the end of a dynasty but of the end of the kingdom.

The second child was to be named Lo-ruhamah, meaning "Not pitied." The root *raham* is one of the potent theological terms in the Old Testament, occurring in a special form, used only of God, in Yahweh's self-definition in Exod. 34:6–7. The sense of it is probably best represented in English by the word "compassion." For God to say "no compassion" would be devastating under any circumstances, but if a direct allusion to Exod. 34:6–7 was intended, that was already a threat to the very covenant relationship itself.[33]

The third child was to bear the worst name of all: Lo-ammi, "Not my people." If we made an assumption that the second child's name implied an end to the covenant relationship, no assumption is called for here, for the Lord explains the name by negating the covenant formulary, "I will be your God and you shall be my people" (cf. Exod. 6:7). The Hebrew of the last part of v. 8 reads literally, "And I am not I AM to you," which could mean simply, "I am not yours," but may be another reference to Exodus, namely, to God's revelation of his name to Moses, beginning with "I AM" (Exod. 3:14).

Even though 1:11 [MT 2:2] has always been taken as part of the promise in Hos. 1:10–2:1 [MT 2:1–3], there are reasons for thinking it should be read as a final threat, concluding the first section of the book: "The people of Judah and the people of Israel shall be gathered together, and they shall appoint for themselves one head; and they shall go up from the land, for great shall be the day of Jezreel" (1:11, RSV). Since 1:10 and 2:1 are clearly promises, commentators have struggled to understand "go up from the land" in such a context, since its literal meaning would clearly be to leave the land.[34] "Gather" (*qabats*) is often used of the restoration from exile, and would thus seem to fit a promissory passage, but it has not been noticed that the other two occurrences in Hosea have quite a different sense. There is an evident reference to death in exile in 9:6: "For even if they escape destruction, Egypt shall gather them, Memphis shall bury them." The last line of the other verse (8:10) has a very difficult text, but the general sense is almost certainly negative. The first part reads, "Though they bargain with the nations, I will now gather them up." The NRSV, with only a little emendation reads the last line, "They shall soon writhe under the burden of kings and princes." If correct, the gathering here would also refer to exile. There are two other parts to Hos. 1:11. Jezreel has been introduced as a judgmental term in 1:4–5. Eventually its meaning will be reversed, in 2:22 [MT 2:24], but it seems premature to do that here. "Day of Jezreel" ought to echo the meaning of "on that day" in 1:5. "They shall appoint, for themselves, one head" is an odd sort of promise for Hosea, since elsewhere he says, "They made kings, but not through me" (8:4). Each of the four clauses of this verse are thus most naturally taken as negative in meaning, and both the "gathering" and the "going up" may be references to exile. [35]

This may thus be the first, though previously unrecognized, reference in a series of references to exile. In the time of Jeroboam II, Amos's threats of exile would have been understood primarily as an attack on the Israelite understanding of the land as a divine promise, with perhaps some awareness of what it meant because of reports of deportations of whole populations elsewhere. With the conquest of Gilead and Galilee by Tiglath-pileser III, exile became a reality for Israel, so it would be surprising if Hosea did not speak of it. He has his own, distinctive way. He never uses Amos's favorite root *galah*, and chooses terminology that is not used by any other prophet. Amos had not found a way to associate such a radical idea with traditional theology, but Hosea did so. One of his favorite roots is *shub* "turn, return," and he found a remarkable variety of uses for it, one of them being to predict a reversal of the exodus:

Now he will remember their iniquity,
  and punish their sins;
  they shall return to Egypt.
           (Hos. 8:13)

They shall not remain in the land of the LORD;
  but Ephraim shall return to Egypt,
  and in Assyria they shall eat unclean food.
           (Hos. 9:3)

> They shall return to the land of Egypt,
>   and Assyria shall be their king,
>   because they have refused to return to me.
>   (Hos. 11:5)[36]

Although every interpreter of Hosea comments on his extensive use of the historical traditions of Israel,[37] the references to a return to Egypt are usually taken literally, with the discussion focusing on whether he meant appealing to Egypt for help or refugees fleeing in that direction. Both things did happen, but given the great importance of the exodus tradition to Hosea, we should not overlook the possibility that he spoke of the reversal of the exodus as a way to work the threat of exile into his theology.

The many echoes of the book of Exodus in Hosea support reading his references to exile as the undoing of the history of salvation. His favorite theme, harlotry, introduced in 1:2, appears in Exod. 34:14–16. The name of his second child, Lo-ruhamah ("Not pitied," Hos. 1:6), uses one of the roots that appears in God's own self-description in Exod. 34:6 (*raham*, translated there as "merciful" by NRSV). That root reappears along with another from Exod. 34:6, *'aman* "faithfulness," in Hos. 2:20 [MT 2:22]. The interpretation of the third child's name, "you are not my people and I am not yours" (Hos. 1:9) reverses the covenant formulary that appears first in Exod. 6:7, and may also contain an allusion to the I AM of Exod. 3:14, as noted above. The expression "other gods" in Hos. 3:1 echoes the First Commandment, "You shall have no other gods before me" (Exod. 20:3), and the commandments appear more prominently a few verses later, in Hos. 4:2. Less obvious, but probable, given the number of reflections of the Sinai material in these chapters, is the reference to the Lord's goodness in 3:5, which recalls Exod. 33:19: "I will make all my goodness pass before you." The exodus itself is referred to in Hos. 2:15 [MT 2:17]; 11:1; 12:9, 13 [MT 12:10, 14], and Egypt is mentioned in various ways thirteen times. Since it is only in Exod. 15:26 that the title "Healer" is used of Yahweh, the appearance of the root *rapha'* "heal" in Hos. 5:13; 6:1; 7:1; 11:3, and 14:4 [MT 14:5] may also be due to the influence of the exodus traditions.

"Return to Egypt" in Hosea is thus more than a reference to current and future events; it is a reversal of the classic account of how Israel came to be, and thus a challenge to the continuing validity of their beliefs in Yahweh as their savior. Once this is recognized, other, less obvious ways of speaking of exile begin to appear.

Once Hosea uses a verb that was used of refugees from war in other prophets: "Because they have not listened to him, my God will reject them; they shall become wanderers among the nations" (9:17).[38] Other references become evident once we are aware that he is working with the reality of exile to say something about what it means in terms of his people's traditions. "Therefore, I will now allure her, and bring her into the wilderness, and speak tenderly to her" (2:14 [MT 2:16]) is probably too tender a translation, for "allure" (*pathah*) usually means "deceive, fool, seduce," and "speak tenderly" is literally "speak upon her heart." This is the beginning of a restoration passage, truly, but "wilderness" is not a place the adulterous wife goes willingly, and the restoration begins with some plain talk. A similar use of wilderness as a reversal of salvation history appears in Hos. 12:9 [MT

12:10]: "I am the LORD your God from the land of Egypt; I will make you live in tents again, as in the days of the appointed feast." He used yet another original verb for exile in 8:8: "Israel is swallowed up; now they are among the nations as a useless vessel." The following verse, "For they have gone up to Assyria, a wild ass wandering alone; Ephraim has bargained for lovers," may refer to the efforts of some of the last kings to negotiate with Assyria, as most commentators take it, but may also allude to the exiling of Israelites by Tiglath-pileser III.[39] Finally, there is one promise of return, using the verb *shub* for movement in the opposite direction:

> They shall go after the LORD,
>   he will roar like a lion;
> yea, he will roar,
>   and his sons shall come trembling from the west;
> they shall come trembling like birds from Egypt,
>   and like doves from the land of Assyria;
> and I will return (*shub*, hiphil) them to their homes, says the LORD.
> (Hos. 11:10–11, RSV)

Once again Egypt and Assyria are paired. He may have been thinking of actual exiles coming from both places, but the claim has been made here that Egypt is for Hosea a key word, intended to recall the exodus, and thus to provide a theological explanation for what the exile to Assyria will really mean; that is, salvation history is coming undone.

The book of Hosea moves from these terrible threats of judgment to affirmations about a divine purpose lying beyond, but before turning to those passages it is appropriate to consider why this prophet was certain that judgment was inevitable. There are differences in this between Amos and Hosea. Amos seems to have spoken because of what was *about* to happen *to* Israel, but Hosea gives the impression of being motivated more by what had *already* happened *in* Israel. If Amos's words were driven by the conviction that disaster was about to befall Israel, Hosea's words are driven more by the conviction that it had already befallen Israel, since he dwells at length on what has gone wrong within the nation that will lead to its inevitable collapse.

What Has Gone Wrong?

Amos does not focus on the relationship between Yahweh and Israel. He alludes to it in an important text, 3:1–2, but for the most part assumes it rather than discussing it. He also assumes another relationship between Yahweh and the nations, as Amos 9:7 and chs. 1—2 reveal. Hosea has no interest in the latter, but shows an intense interest in the former. It is almost the sole subject of chs. 1—3, and it leads him to use the risky metaphors of husband and parent for Yahweh. He might have chosen to emphasize "safe" relational language. He does use the word "covenant" (*bĕrith*) more often than the other eighth-century prophets (2:18 [MT 2:20]; 6:7; 8:1; 10:4; 12:1 [MT 12:2]), and might have elaborated further on covenant breaking. He develops the parenthood imagery in an impressive way in ch. 11, but in chs. 1—7 prefers instead to describe Israel's failings in terms of sexual irregularity: prostitution or adultery. When the metaphor for Israel is an adulterous wife, then God becomes the husband, and the language becomes risky because it speaks of Yahweh the way the Canaanite religion spoke of Baal, as we know from the Ugaritic texts.[40] For the most part, rather than providing specific details as to what has gone wrong with the relationship between Yahweh and Israel, Hosea prefers to use the metaphors of prostitution (harlotry, RSV; whoredom, NRSV) or adultery.

He seems to have been the first to speak of unfaithfulness to Yahweh as adultery (root *na'ap*), for that root is used metaphorically only in Hosea, Jeremiah, and Ezekiel. Prostitution (root *zanah*) is widely used in a metaphorical sense in the Old Testament, however; about 71 times (38 in Ezekiel) as against about 31 times with a literal reference. In many sources the worship of other gods was called prostitution (e.g., Exod. 34:15–16; Lev. 17:7; Deut. 31:16; Ps. 106:39; Isa. 1:21). It may be that there were sexual rites associated with Canaanite worship, which led to the choice of this metaphor, but there is very little explicit evidence for what they may have been.[41] Whatever its origin may have been, the sense of the imagery is clear in all sources: The worship of another god besides Yahweh is compared with the promiscuity of a prostitute. Hosea offers explicit definitions of what he means by this promiscuity. The people have forsaken Yahweh (1:2; 4:10, using two different terms); they do not know him, and their deeds do not permit them to return to their God (5:4; introducing two of the key terms of the book: *yada'*, "know," and *shub*, "turn, return").

Hosea speaks of adultery in a literal sense four times (3:1; 4:2, 13, 14) and metaphorically twice. In 7:4 (RSV) he says of Ephraim, "They are all adulterers; they are like a heated oven, whose baker ceases to stir the fire, from the kneading of the dough until it is leavened," thus mixing metaphors in a not very helpful way. In 2:2 ([MT 2:4] he uses harlotry and adultery in parallel, with reference to Yahweh's wife. While the metaphor of prostitution implies that there should be a unique relationship between Yahweh and Israel, adultery makes it explicit, and in ch. 2, Hosea spins out the metaphor into an extended allegory. The children of the broken marriage are addressed, rather than the adulterous wife (and note that Hosea makes no distinction between adultery and prostitution in 2:2 [MT 2:4]). Most interpreters assume that Hosea is thinking of a marriage between God and Israel, but Klaus Koch may be right in identifying the wife as the land, and the children as the Israelites.[42] Everything Hosea says, through v. 13, applies very directly to the land, and if that is in truth the way the allegory begins, we may think that in vv. 14–15 the prophet's thought begins to shift to the people. In 1:2 it was in fact the land that was said to prostitute itself, forsaking Yahweh. But why imagine a marriage between Yahweh and the land of Canaan? This may well be one of Hosea's bold polemics against the Baal worship that he refers to in 2:8 and 13. Baal, the storm god, was known in Canaan to be the source of the fertility of the land, and also of animal fertility. The sexual imagery that is so prominent in the first half of Hosea thus played a very natural role in Canaanite theology, as we know it from the Ugaritic texts.[43] In order to insist on the claim that it was Yahweh, not Baal, who was the storm God, source of the life-giving rain (cf. Elijah in 1

Kings 18), Hosea thus dared to create an allegory in which it was Yahweh who was the legitimate husband of the land, not Baal. This limited ascription of sexuality to Yahweh (limited because allegorical) was a very risky move, for it would seem to be giving up too much to the enemy, but Jeremiah and Ezekiel took it up as well and developed it further, evidently finding that in that environment it was the most easily understood way to speak of God as the source of the blessings of nature.[44]

Baal worship was thus one of the major issues that concerned Hosea, and its sexual overtones must have contributed to the prophet's choice of prostitution and adultery as metaphors for Israel's acceptance of another god alongside Yahweh. There is still inadequate evidence to indicate to what extent sexual activity was a part of Canaanite religion, so we cannot be sure to what extent the terms were more than metaphors. The clearest reference of that sort in Hosea is 4:13–14.[45] He does have a good deal to say about other forms of worship of which he disapproves, although it is often hard to tell whether they involve the cult of Yahweh or of Baal. Perhaps they were rather thoroughly confused, as practiced in Israel at that time.[46] Hosea considered the sanctuaries to be as useless as Amos did: "Do not enter into Gilgal, or go up to Beth-aven, and do not swear, 'As the LORD lives'" (Hos. 4:15; cf. 12:11). He was highly offended by the presence of images of calves in the sanctuaries, which may have been intended to represent the presence of Yahweh or Baal, or both (8:4b–6; 10:5–6; 13:2). Given the thoroughness of the corruption of worship, so that the true nature of Yahweh (as Hosea understood God) could no longer be distinguished, sacrifice and the appointed feasts were also now worthless (4:13; 8:11–13; 9:4–5; 10:1).

The true nature of Yahweh could no longer be distinguished—a major theme in this book, expressed by the term "knowledge of Yahweh."[47] The wife in the allegory was unfaithful because she did not know that Yahweh was the source of grain, wine, oil, silver, and gold (2:8 [MT 2:10]), and Israel's lack of knowledge is lamented repeatedly (4:1, 6; 5:4; 7:9; 11:3). If there is to be any future for Israel, knowledge of Yahweh will be an essential gift (2:20 [MT 2:22]). Given the polemical treatment of nature religion in the book, knowledge of Yahweh clearly involves recognition that he alone is the source of all the blessings in nature. But it also must involve acceptance of the standards of behavior laid upon Israel in the covenant relationship: "For I desire steadfast love (*ḥesed*) and not sacrifice, the knowlege of God rather than burnt offerings" (6:6). The lack of knowledge meant "there is no faithfulness or loyalty . . . in the land. Swearing, lying, and murder, and stealing and adultery break out; bloodshed follows bloodshed" (4:1b–2). This is a clear allusion to some form of the Ten Commandments. Elsewhere Hosea also upholds the same ethical standards taken to be essential for Israel's health and continuing life by the other prophets: righteousness and justice, steadfast love and mercy (2:19 [MT 2:21]; 10:12; 12:6 [MT 12:7]). Instead, however, he has seen bloodshed, banditry, and dishonesty in the land (1:4; 4:2; 6:8–9; 7:1; 12:1, 7, 14 [MT 12:2, 8, 15]).

Hosea's analysis of the sickness in his society was thus not very different from that of Amos, although he expressed it in highly original ways. He did lay the blame on the leadership of the nation in very explicit terms not to be found in

Amos. His initial indictment of the inhabitants of the land (4:1) moves quickly to focus on priest and prophet (4:4–9).[48] In addition to maintaining the holiness of the sanctuaries, it was the priests' responsibility to be teachers of the Torah, and Hosea, like later prophets, found they had sadly neglected it (4:6). His references to prophets have been taken, as a result of the work of Hans Walter Wolff, to be positive (with the exception of 4:5), and this has even influenced modern translations of the difficult verses, 9:7–8 and 12:11 [MT 12:12]. Margaret Odell has reconsidered those texts (and 6:5), however, and suggests that all are consistent with 4:5 in linking prophet with priest as having led Israel astray.[49]

The leaders most frequently condemned are Israel's kings and princes, and once we know the political misfortunes the nation suffered during the last twenty years of its existence, it is easy to understand why Hosea treated them so severely. He never states in any detail his basis for wholesale disapproval, however, except to claim they are all acting contrary to the will of Yahweh (5:1, 10; 7:3). Several possibilities can be imagined: (a) Four kings were assassinated during this period, and that in itself may have been enough to lead Hosea to judge the whole system to be hopeless (7:7). (b) He makes several brief references to the government's dealings with Egypt and Assyria, and we know from 2 Kings that the desperate efforts of these last kings were of no avail (5:13; 7:11). Their ineptness is another likely basis for his charges. (c) Following Albrecht Alt's claim that Israel held a concept of charismatic kingship, in contrast to the dynastic understanding in Judah, it might be that Hosea believed the only legitimate kings were those chosen and anointed by prophets,[50] or it might be that he was completely opposed to kingship, on principle (8:4; 13:10–11). (d) In contrast to that theory, those who accept the reference to David in Hos. 3:5 as coming from Hosea suggest that although a northerner he believed the heirs of David were in fact the kings chosen by Yahweh to rule over all Israel. Since there is no evidence for these latter two theories, it seems best to be satisfied with a and b as reasons enough for focusing in such a thoroughly negative way on kingship.

Judgment as Discipline?

Hosea's message of judgment was not so clear and straightforward as that of Amos, but we have seen that what he says is as severe, if not more so. It seems to be not so straightforward only partly because of his style and the confusing structure of the book. There is more to it than that. Amos simply announced what God impressed on him. "The Lord Yahweh has spoken; who can but prophesy?" (Amos 3:8). We do not know what he thought about it. But there is evidence in the book of Hosea of struggle with the message of judgment. There are outcries placed in the mouth of God himself:

What shall I do with you, O Ephraim?
                    (Hos. 6:4)

How can I give you up, Ephraim?
    How can I hand you over, O Israel?

How can I make you like Admah?
  How can I treat you like Zeboiim?
My heart recoils within me;
  my compassion grows warm and tender.
(Hos. 11:8)

And there is the effort, especially prominent in chs. 1—3, to interpret the disaster that is sure to come as being for corrective purposes; not the end after all. Hosea is extremely vague about how that might work, and so his promises do not have the detail found in those produced by exilic prophets, but like those prophets he was convinced that God did not intend to give up completely on his people.[51]

Hosea's second symbolic act is recorded in a very cryptic fashion in ch. 3. That it was intended to be symbolic, that is, representing in the prophet's life what was happening in the relationship between God and Israel, is made evident by the comparison: "Go, love a woman who has a lover and is an adulteress, just as the LORD loves the people of Israel, though they turn to other gods and love raisin cakes" (3:1). Israel has been promiscuous, so the prophet must deal with some promiscuous woman the same way God deals with Israel. But, the command says nothing about acting judgmentally; the key verb for both parties is "love"!

We are not told who the woman is, and will not take the time to evaluate all the hypotheses concerning the relationship between chs. 1 and 3. If it had been important to know who she was, probably the author would have told us. What matters is her character—like Israel's—and what Hosea is to do. First, God and Israel are no equals, and in the society of that time it was possible for Hosea to play the role of God in a way that we cannot, to deal with another human being to some extent the way God deals with people—as their sovereign. Hosea could buy a person and become her master, telling her what she could and could not do, and he does that as the first necessary step in carrying out the symbolic act. As the initiative was all God's in choosing Israel, so now the initiative in this relationship is all Hosea's. Perhaps that is why the price is mentioned.

He is to love the woman as God loves Israel, and that means, we are told, that she will belong to him and to no other man for many days and give up her promiscuous life—so Hosea will act out God's exclusive claim. The Hebrew reads literally: "Many days you shall dwell with [to?] me; you shall not play the harlot [be promiscuous]) and you shall not be to [i.e., belong to] a man, and also I (am [or will be]) to you." The prepositions are not the same in the last two clauses, but the first clause clearly indicates possession, and it would seem likely the same thing is meant in the second. They will belong to each another. Does this indicate a period of confinement, during which the woman will have no intercourse with others or with the prophet (cf. RSV, NRSV), symbolic of the period of judgment that soon will befall Israel? Does the promise in v. 5 (which corresponds to nothing in the symbolic act) mean that eventually a loving, marital relationship will eventually be established with the woman? Nothing in the text enables us to answer those questions, so perhaps they are the wrong ones to ask, even though they have been widely debated. The literal translation above suggests another reading. As God made Israel his own, so Hosea will make this woman his own. She has been promiscuous, as Israel has been. But Hosea's symbolic act (called "love") focuses entirely on establishing an exclusive relationship with this woman, and that is what God intends to do with Israel. This scarcely fits our notion of a love story, but "love" as used in the Old Testament makes good sense in terms of the reading just offered. Love and hate are terms of choice, and Hosea must choose this woman to live with him in spite of her qualifications, just as God has chosen Israel.[52] Note that this way of understanding the symbolic act makes it another echo of Exodus.

The literal interpretation of Israel's promiscuity is provided in 3:4: kings and princes, sacrifices and pillars, ephods and teraphim—pairs representing in turn the corrupt government, the useless cult, and the futile efforts to learn the future by manipulative methods. What will replace those worthless things is then stated in v. 5: return to Yahweh and to Davidic kingship. Nothing in the symbolic act corresponds to this, and the advocacy of the Davidic dynasty is puzzling, if from the mouth of Hosea, so this may be a later elaboration of the text.

We are thankful that this symbolic act—buying a person—could not be carried out today. But there is something inherently shocking about many of the symbolic acts of the prophets, as we shall see. Isaiah walked around naked and barefoot for three years (Isaiah 20). Knowing the power of names, then and now, imagine what the lives of Hosea's children must have been like, carrying about those threatening names. The terror of what was soon to happen to their people had to be borne in the life of the prophet himself (and his family), it seems. What that means will be taken up in the section on Ezekiel, when it will be possible to reflect on this series of disturbing events in the prophets' lives.

If there is nothing explicit about discipline in Hosea 3, the same cannot be said for Hos. 2:2–23. Punishment appears at first (vv. 3–4), then an effort of the husband to restrict the wife's freedom until she repents (vv. 6–7, cf. ch. 3). More punishment follows, however (vv. 9–13), until a return to the wilderness is introduced, a place of testing, hence of purging, in Israelite tradition (vv. 14–15; cf. Ezek. 20:34–38). The prophet declares that time of testing will at last lead to the recognition they belong to Yahweh, not Baal (vv. 16–17), and they will enter into a perfect covenant relationship that will even include all of nature. Then the inauspicious names, Not Pitied and Not My People can be changed (vv. 18–23).[53]

Another passage from which the mitigation of punishment cannot be edited out is ch. 11. Unfortunately the text of this chapter is extremely difficult, and every effort at translation involves emendation and a considerable amount of guesswork.[54] It begins as an allegory, with God appearing as a parent—perhaps a mother, although the text is not clear enough for us to be certain.[55] "When Israel was a child, I loved him, and out of Egypt I called my son" (11:1). "Love" is a verb of choosing again; God adopted Israel in Egypt and called him his son (cf. Exod. 4:22). God's care, which the allegory in ch. 2 described in terms of the bounty of nature, is now described as the care of a mother or father for a little child. He is an ungrateful and rebellious child, however, and this leads to the typical prophetic message of judgment (vv. 5–7)—momentarily. This time God himself interrupts the oracle of judgment with a reversal of his own intentions:

How can I give you up, Ephraim?
  How can I hand you over, O Israel?
How can I make you like Admah?
  How can I treat you like Zeboiim?
My heart recoils within me;
  my compassion grows warm and tender.
I will not execute my fierce anger;
  I will not again destroy Ephraim;
for I am God and no mortal,
  the Holy One in your midst,
  and I will not come in wrath.

(Hos. 11:8–9)

If this were the end of the story, then the mercy of God would have triumphed, and somehow Israel could have escaped disaster even though they had done nothing to change things. But it did not happen this way. Assyria came, and Israel died. Is this just false prophecy, then? It was the judgment messages of Hosea that came true, and Ephraim was destroyed. Understand it this way: Hosea is one of the few Old Testament authors who dares to claim he knows something about what goes on within the godhead, specifically what it is costing God to allow his people to suffer under the Assyrians as they will do. The tensions in the book, ch. 11 tells us, reflect tensions within God himself, who is something like the loving parent who must severely discipline a rebellious child.

Both chs. 2 and 11 provide excellent examples of the way Hosea rings the changes on a single verb that appears throughout the book: *shub,* "turn, return." His message can actually be summed up by noting the uses of this verb. Israel has turned to Baal, thus turned away from Yahweh (7:16). They refuse to return to Yahweh (7:10; 11:5b); even though they claim to do so (2:7 [MT 2:9]; 6:1), their deeds do not permit it (5:4; 6:11–7:1). As a result God will turn away from them (5:15), will requite (a form of *shub*) them for their deeds (4:9; 12:2, 14 [MT 12:3, 15]), will *take back* the grain, wine, wool, and flax (2:9 [MT 2:11]), and they will return to Egypt (8:13; 9:3; 11:5). But in this book not all is lost; not only are there appeals to return to Yahweh, assuming they still can (12:6 [MT 12:7]), but God also turns back to them of his own initiative. In "I will not again destroy Ephraim" (11:9), it is *shub* that is translated "again." Near the end of the book comes the promise that God's anger will turn away (14:4 [MT 14:5]). So Israel will finally be able to return to Yahweh (3:5) and be returned to their homes (11:11), where they will flourish like a garden (14:7 [MT 14:8]).

The promises that appear at the beginning and end of the book thus leave the impression that the severe treatment the Northern Kingdom will soon undergo will be a temporary thing and will have salutary results, leading the people to give up their practice of Baal worship and to acquire the "knowledge of Yahweh" that is their true destiny. Hosea thus moved beyond Amos's conviction that judgment was inevitable to offer an explanation of judgment as part of a divine plan to create a new people. Hosea's hopes did not come true, however. The upper classes were taken into exile, as he said, but never returned. Yahwism did not die out in the north, but did continue to be practiced among those who were left, who became the ancestors of the Samaritans. It might be said that in them Hosea's promises of correction and healing did come true, for the Samaritan religion is a very conservative form of Yahwism, completely free of the kinds of syncretism with nature religion Hosea condemned.[56] But ironically, that does not seem to be due to the influence of Hosea, for his book is not part of the Samaritan canon, which includes only the Pentateuch. Hosea, the northerner, became instead God's spokesman to Judah, and his understanding of God's intention for Israel became reality for Judah instead.

Hosea as Part of the Whole Prophetic Message

We have assumed throughout that Hosea was a citizen of the Northern Kingdom, but that is in fact an assumption, for the book never says so. There would be nothing accomplished by questioning it, even though we cannot prove it. Perhaps he was an Ephraimite, since Ephraim is his favorite term for the Northern Kingdom, but the book in its present form does show a continuing interest in Judah.[57] With the growing Assyrian presence in Palestine during the ministry of Hosea, it would not be at all surprising that when he considered the dire fate that seemed in store for Israel he might also have expected Judah to be included. Most of the references do add Judah to the words of condemnation and predictions of disaster for Israel (e.g., Hos. 5:5, 12–14; 6:4). They may be Hosea's work, or may be the work of a Judean redactor who believed the northern prophet's words were equally valid for his own country. At any rate, the book did make its way to Judah somehow, and eventually was accepted as the word of Yahweh to them, even though Judah did not fall in the eighth or seventh centuries. There do seem to be at least two overly optimistic references to the Southern Kingdom. "Judah is still known by God, and is faithful to the Holy One" (11:12, RSV) is certainly no typical prophetic word, and may have been added rather early, before Judah's fate became unmistakable. The promise of deliverance of Judah in 1:7 interrupts the context, and is also not meaningful as part of Hosea's message at that point.

Eventually this book was placed at the beginning of the scroll containing the twelve minor prophets. They are arranged roughly by date, as best that could be determined, and the reason Hosea precedes Amos may be partly just because it is the longest of the twelve, but also perhaps because unlike Amos, Hosea already contains in a preliminary way that "second act," which will bring a new people out of the deaths of the two nations.

2.3 Micah

As Amos and Hosea faced the end of the Northern Kingdom, so Micah and Isaiah faced the end of the Southern Kingdom, but there was a difference. The end did not come, after all. Judah suffered terribly under the Assyrians, but Jerusalem did not fall and the Davidic dynasty continued for more than a century longer. The willingness of Micah and Isaiah to confront the expected end of their nation and the need to account for unexpected continuity probably explain the tensions in these books between announcements of irrevocable judgment and promises concerning Zion and Davidic kingship.

Jerusalem was severely threatened in 735/34 by the Syro-Ephraimite coalition (2 Kings 16:5–9; Isaiah 7) and in 701 by the Assyrian army under Sennacherib (2 Kings 18:13–19:36; Isaiah 36–37), and Samaria fell in 722/21. As indicated in chapter 1 of this book, I take 722, the end of the Northern Kingdom, to be the decisive moment that explains not only the existence of Amos and Hosea but also that of Micah and Isaiah. Is it forcing things, associating these two Judean prophets so closely with the fall of Samaria? Their references to the Northern Kingdom have tended to be neglected by many interpreters, since Zion is so obviously a major concern for both prophets. In addition to those explicit references, which will be noted, the implicit effects of 722 on the contents of these books become evident once the reader keeps in mind what that event would have meant to Judeans. With the fall of Samaria, Assyrian control extended to within ten miles of Jerusalem. Would not many have expected Jerusalem to be next? It is evident that Micah did. Archaeological surveys of Jerusalem show that its population increased greatly during the latter part of the eighth century B.C.E., and it has been suggested that was in part the result of an influx of refugees from the north.[58] That may have produced some of the problems cited in Micah and Isaiah. Both prophets use the names Jacob/Israel with reference to Judah, evidently claiming that Judah is the authentic successor to the Northern Kingdom. Both take the theme of death, applied by Amos and Hosea to Israel and now come true for that kingdom, and declare that it will be the fate of Judah as well. They found the inner life of Judah to be not significantly different from that of Israel, but differed in what they said about the success of the Assyrians. Micah predicted the complete destruction of Jerusalem (3:12), a message found nowhere in Isaiah.

The book of Micah does not show the originality of Amos or Hosea. In it we find an extensive use of traditional forms, especially of cultic origin, but without the creative alterations, reversing their meaning, that appear in Amos (an exception: the entrance liturgy in 6:6–8). The most often used typical prophetic form is the reason/announcement oracle (1:5–7; 2:1–5; 3:1–4, 5–8, 9–12; 6:9–16). The influence of the two earlier prophets is evident in several places. We do not know whether their words were available in written form to Micah, but one may think their messages were so striking that they had become known in Judah, especially after Samaria fell.

There has been a long scholarly debate about the relationship of the promises that dominate chs. 4—7 to the threats in the first three chapters of the book. That story need not be retold here, although a decision will have to be made as to whether anything can be made of those promises with reference to a late–eighth-century setting.[59] In brief, there is a significant group of scholars who claim Micah was responsible for nothing but threats, and attribute only chs. 1—3 to him, while another group find reasons to account for most, if not all, of the book as his work.[60] To put it perhaps too bluntly, if Micah himself was responsible for only what is ascribed to him by Mays or Wolff, then he must be judged a minor and not very creative figure, and one may wonder why his words were preserved. His most memorable statement, "Zion shall be plowed as a field . . ." (3:12), was in fact a prophecy that did not come true. It might rather have been his words about Samaria (1:5–7) that made him memorable. The most creative parts of the book are to be found in chs. 4—7, so if they do not in fact come from Micah, this is a case where materials that source critics used to call "inauthentic" or "spurious" are of greater lasting value than the words of the original prophet.

The approach that will be taken here will be to claim that the book in its present form (like Isaiah) reflects the ambiguity of the situation of late-eighth-century prophets in Judah. They took up the messages of Amos and Hosea and reaffirmed them concerning the Northern Kingdom. They saw Judah equally threatened by Assyria, and saw internal injustice and political ineptness in Jerusalem comparable to what Amos and Hosea had condemned in the north. So they formulated similar messages against Judah. Judah was indeed severely injured during the latter years of the eighth century, and some of its citizens went into exile, but Jerusalem was spared. Zion theology, it will be claimed, was already a part of the Jerusalem cult, as the Psalms reveal, and it must have been strongly reinforced by the retreat of Sennacherib in 701.[61] Chapters 4—7 represent a prophetic use of those cultic materials, by Micah or a later prophet, to account for what really happened, projecting Zion theology into the future, as the starting point of Old Testament eschatology.

Facing the End

The lament plays an even more prominent role in Micah than it did in Amos. He calls for more extravagant behavior than was probably normal for mourners, because of the incurable wound of Samaria, which has now reached the gate of Jerusalem:

> For this I will lament and wail;
> I will go barefoot and naked;
> I will make lamentation like the jackals,
> and mourning like the ostriches.
> (Micah 1:8)

The text of the lament itself, in 1:10–16, is very difficult, partly because the prophet tends to choose words that sound like the place names, rather than being explicit about the details of the expected disaster. It concludes with another reference to extravagant behavior:

> Make yourselves bald and cut off your hair,
> for your pampered children;
> make yourselves as bald as the eagle,
> for they have gone from you into exile.
> (Micah 1:16)

This is the only use in the book of Amos's term for exile, *galah*. The reference to lamentation in vv. 8–9 thus links Micah's prediction of the complete destruction of Samaria, with an expectation of disaster for a series of Judean towns in the Shephelah region. According to the inscriptions of Sargon II, he had the city rebuilt after he conquered it in 720 B.C.E., so Micah's words are probably to be dated before that. He foresaw:

> Therefore I will make Samaria a heap in the open country,
>> a place for planting vineyards;
> I will pour down her stones into the valley,
>> and uncover her foundations.
>>
>> (Micah 1:6)

His message was thus that both Samaria and Jerusalem (3:12) would be wiped out. The poem concerning the Judean cities has been dated in connection with Sargon's campaign against Ashdod in 713/12 and with Sennacherib's invasion of Judah in 701, but the difficulties of the text make certainty impossible.

Lamentation continues in the next passage (Micah 2:1–5) with the outcry *hoy* ("woe," RSV; "alas," NRSV) used as Amos did in Amos 5:18 and 6:1 to express his grief at the ways people have gone wrong. Widespread lamentation appears later in the oracle (Micah 2:4). The death of "my people" is described in one of the most gruesome passages in the prophets, in Micah 3:2–3. His comparison of Israel with sheep just before (2:12) may have led to the imagery. Later, Ezekiel spoke of worthless shepherds (i.e., kings) treating their sheep in a similar, though less severe way. The guilty parties in Micah 3 are called "heads" (*ra'shim*) and "rulers" (*qĕtsinim*) in v. 1 and again in v. 9, leading to the announcement of the results of their mistreatment of the people:

> Therefore because of you
>> Zion shall be plowed as a field;
> Jerusalem shall become a heap of ruins,
>> and the mountain of the house a wooded height.
>>
>> (Micah 3:12)

Chapters 1 and 3 thus end with dire threats, of exile and of the destruction of Jerusalem. For most readers, ch. 2, in contrast, ends with a promise, leading some commentators to reject its originality, and others to find reasons to explain it. It may, however, be a threat of exile, and thus be a perfect fit where it is. Although verbs for "gathering" (*'asaph* and *qabats*) are often used in promises of restoration from exile, that is not always the meaning, as I suggested for Hos. 1:11 (cf. Hos. 8:10; 9:6). Being gathered like sheep in a fold is more suggestive of rounding up prisoners to be taken into exile than of bringing people back to their homeland. Parts of 2:12–13 are not very clear, but the opening of the breach is reminiscent of Amos 4:3, which also speaks of going out through breaches in the wall, on the way to exile. This may be another use of *'alah*, "go up," with reference to exile, as I suggested for Hos. 1:11 (cf. Hos. 8:9), and the picture of being led by the king recalls Amos's claim that the notables of the first of the nations will be the first to go into exile (Amos 6:1, 7). Amos's word "first" is formed from the same root that is translated "head" in Micah 2:13 and 3:1. The case has been argued before, by W.E.

Barnes and by Gershon Brin, and although it has not been been adopted by any commentator, it seems worth considering again.[62]

Two indictments with threats of judgment appear in the latter, disputed part of the book, and some commentators will ascribe them to Micah. Chapter 5:10–15 [MT 5:9–14] speaks largely of a purification of the land, but includes destruction of their cities (v. 14). Micah 6:9–16 is a reason/announcement oracle leading to the conclusion, "Therefore I will make you a desolation, and your inhabitants an object of hissing; so you shall bear the scorn of my people." There is no debate among scholars as to the inevitablity of judgment as it is spoken of in any part of the book. The book contains no exhortations associated with promise. Those who claim Micah as the source of the promissory texts recognize that, and insist that as he saw the future, judgment was irrevocable, and restoration would come, by the free choice of Yahweh, only afterward.[63] He shows no evidence of influence of Hosea's concept of disciplinary punishment, and does not consider any possibility of averting the judgment. To this extent, the book sees the immediate future of Samaria as Amos did, and now speaks of Jerusalem in the same way.

What Has Gone Wrong?

Micah's analysis of the sickness that has befallen both Israel and Judah (1:9) contains nothing strikingly new, for echoes of Amos and Hosea appear in every chapter except 4 and 7. Here is evidence for the existence of a prophetic tradition, which can be traced no earlier than Amos, but which is maintained throughout the latter part of the eighth century, then is revived late in the seventh. He uses Hosea's term, *zonah,* "prostitute," with reference to Samaria in 1:7, associating it with images and idols. Elsewhere in that chapter he is not explicit, speaking generally of transgression (*pesha'*) and sin (*hatta'th*) in 1:5, 13. The indictment parts of the reason/announcement oracles in chs. 2, 3, and 6 become more explicit, and these have led to the theories that Micah, from the small town of Moresheth, was an upholder of traditional values over against the corruptions he found in the city.[64] Those who covet and sieze fields, oppress a man, his house and inheritance, and drive out women and children from their homes are condemned in 2:2, 9. He seems to refer to the same conditions of which Isaiah spoke in Isa. 5:8. Cheating in commerce of the kind Amos found in the Northern Kingdom (Amos 8:4–6) is the focus of the indictment in Micah 6:10–12. Like Hosea, his principal targets are the leaders of the nation. Whereas Hosea spoke of kings and princes, Micah's terms are heads and rulers (Micah 3:1, 9), and it is justice (*mishpat*, a key word for Amos) which he says they abhor. He is also like Hosea in condemning priests and prophets for failing to fulfill the vocations entrusted to them (Micah 3:11; Hos. 4:4–5). The announcement of judgment in 5:12–14 [MT 5:11–13] includes bringing cultic irregularities to an end. The lament in 7:2–6 speaks of a thorough breakdown of stability in society, to the extent that crime is widespread, and no one, even one's neighbors and family members, can be trusted. Whether it was ever that bad in eighth-century Judah, or later, we cannot know. Commentators have pointed out that such language is traditional in laments from elsewhere in the ancient Near East as a way of expressing despair at the loss of traditional values.[65] Although some have tried to develop a profile of Micah and of the society he challenged from these scanty data, it should be noted that the passages just cited say very little that is distinctive. Micah, as much as any prophet, is a traditionalist, as will become evident when the prominence of liturgical language in the book is traced.

Micah as Part of the Whole Prophetic Message

The book of Micah may be thought of as a kind of sampler, containing examples of materials that reappear frequently in other prophetic books, so it may be used as an introduction to the books that follow. Whether Micah himself could have been responsible for all of it continues to be debated, but since the interest here is not biographical, the approach taken will be to consider what relevance it may have to the crises of the late eighth century. At first, all the traditional material in the book will be surveyed, with reference to its uses in other prophetic books, and elsewhere. Then a conclusion will be tried out: attempting to read the largely promissory parts, chs. 4—7, as having been formulated originally in order to deal with the fact that although Judah was severely punished by the Assyrians, Jerusalem was saved, not destroyed, and the Davidic dynasty continued. It might have been Micah himself who dealt with that need, as several scholars have recently claimed, or may have been another prophet, but for our purposes the effort to see whether these materials can reasonably be associated with the eighth century will be of importance first as an introduction to the same phenomenon in Isaiah (the mixture of threats and promises), and as a "preview of coming attractions," an introduction to many of the other prophetic books.

The book begins with a theophany, a cultic form, introduced as Yahweh's witness against the people, and indeed the whole earth. Yahweh speaks from his "holy temple," a term drawn from Zion theology which appears in Hab. 2:20, just before another theophany.[66] Theophanic language uses the most awe-inspiring of natural phenomena to speak of the way awareness of the immediate presence of God affects one.[67] The classic theophany was the appearance of God on Mount Sinai (Exodus 19—20), but it must have played a role of some kind in the Jerusalem cult, for poetic descriptions appear in Psalms 18; 68; 77; and 97. This cultic language was used where appropriate by the prophets, to announce the imminent coming of Yahweh, either to save or to punish, as in Isa. 29:5–6; 30:27–33; Nahum 1:2–11; and Habakkuk 3.[68]

The next kind of traditional language to appear in the book is the funeral lament, already a part of the prophetic repertoire since Amos (Micah 1:8–16; 2:1–5). The theme of lamentation is prominent throughout the prophetic books, but plays an especially important role in Jeremiah (e.g., Jer. 6:26; 7:29; 9:10–11, 17–22; 25:34–38). During the last years of the kingdom of Judah the prophets witnessed the deaths of many individuals, but like Amos they were speaking of the death of the people of God, as well.

The poem depicting the glorification of Zion in the latter days, in Micah 4:1–4, was the part of the book that first raised questions about authorship, for almost the identical passage also appears in Isa. 2:2–4, and its location in Micah seems to make it a contradiction of the prediction of Jerusalem's complete destruction in

3:12. Arguments may be found claiming either Micah or Isaiah as the original author, claiming the passage must be very late, exilic or postexilic, and claiming it may even be earlier than either eighth-century prophet. In contrast to the arguments for a late date, it should be noted that this text differs from the eschatological pictures of Zion that are typical in the prophets. It makes no reference to a destruction and rebuilding of Jerusalem or to exile and return. The closest parallels to the ideas in Micah 4:1–4 are not in Jeremiah, Ezekiel, or Second Isaiah, but in the psalms of Zion, which speak of the glories of the city and temple Yahweh has chosen (Psalms 46, 48, 84, 87, 122). These psalms are likely to be earlier than Micah and Isaiah,[69] and the most significant difference between them and the poems in Micah 4 and Isaiah 2 is that what the psalms spoke of in the present tense has now been projected into the future. This is probably one of the earliest stages in the development of Old Testament eschatology, which, as will be seen later, took as its center hopes focused on Zion. Its appearance in two prophetic books suggests to me that it was produced by neither Micah nor Isaiah, and its character suggests that it may well have originated earlier than either book. Its location in Micah, with its completely untroubled picture of peace among nations, remains a problem, however, and we shall return to that.

Chapters 4 and 5 contain a series of short oracles, all eschatological in content, and these chapters have been identified as a distinct unit by many commentators. The rescue of exiles and their restoration to Zion, promised in 4:6–8 and 4:9–10, is the kind of theme that appears frequently in the books of the sixth-century prophets, and the reference to Babylon in 4:10 suggests that these texts may well be the latest additions to the book. Some scholars claim, however, that having predicted exile for Judeans, with the destruction of Jerusalem, Micah already looked forward to a time of restoration.[70] Chapter 4 contains another piece of traditional, cultic material (4:11–13), the depiction of an attack on Jerusalem by a coalition of nations who are defeated by the intervention of Yahweh. This is another part of Zion theology and as such cannot be dated, but it is likely to be as early as the Yahwistic cult in Jerusalem. It appears in Psalms 2; 48; 76; and takes on a prominent role in Isa. 29:1–10, Ezekiel 38–39, and Zechariah 12; 14.

The Psalms show that Zion theology included affirmations of Yahweh's choice of both Jerusalem as the place for his temple, and David as the one to rule over his people (most explicitly in Psalm 132). The mysterious description of "one who is to rule in Israel" in 5:2–4 [MT 5:1–3] thus follows naturally on the collection of Zion oracles in ch. 4. This ruler is called neither king nor messiah, but since his origin is Bethlehem, David's hometown, it is taken by all interpreters to be an expression of hope for a future king in the dynasty who will bring peace (v. 5a). This is thus another use of theology already present in the Jerusalem cult, as the royal psalms reveal (cf. Psalms 2; 20; 21; 45; 72; 110). The hope for the coming of a righteous king plays a role of some prominence in Micah's contemporary, Isaiah, and will reappear occasionally in later prophetic books. It represents, of course, the roots of the later messianic hope, to be discussed in connection with the Isaiah texts.

Chapters 6 and 7 say nothing of Zion, and have even been called the work of a prophet from the Northern Kingdom by some scholars.[71] The section begins with what is now called a "covenant lawsuit."[72] Whether this was in fact a traditional form with a cultic setting in which a prophetic figure played a specified role can be debated. Formulas reminiscent of the way court procedures may have been carried out have been projected into heaven, so to speak, by the prophets, as they make Yahweh both plaintiff and judge (cf. Hosea 4 and Isa. 1:2–3). In Micah 6, God begins by asking whether Israel in fact has a complaint against him (v. 3), reminding them of his continued gracious acts on their behalf in the past. Amos offered a similar reminder as part of his indictment of Israel in Amos 2:9–11, and Jeremiah will also ask what Judah has against the one who brought them up from Egypt, in Jer. 2:4–13. In Micah 6 the lawsuit language does not lead immediately to an accusation or a sentence, however, but to an imitation of another cultic form, the priestly torah or entrance liturgy (6:6–8). Although the chapter clearly divides into three parts, concluding with a reason/announcement oracle in vv. 9–16, it probably was intended to be understood as a unit. The entrance liturgy then functions as the defendant's inquiry as to what God expected, and the reason/announcement oracle as the indictment and sentence.

Psalms 15 and 24 show that there was a form to be followed by a worshiper when entering a sanctuary. Set questions were to be asked of the priest responsible for guarding the holiness of the place, and the answers given, in the records we have, concerned the righteousness of the worshiper's life, rather than matters of ritual cleanness, although we may suspect they were also included. Micah 6:6–8 is thus traditional in its conclusion, but it takes an original route in the formulation of the questions, for they are highly exaggerated, and are not to be taken as literal expressions of what any worshiper might think Yahweh required. The text, with its emphasis on justice (*mishpaṭ*) and kindness (*ḥesed*), thus lies in two lines of tradition; the cultic, represented by Psalms 15 and 24, and the prophetic, in which righteousness is exalted above sacrifice (Amos 5:21–24; Hos. 6:5; Isa. 1:12–17; Jer. 7:21–23; but see also Ps. 50:7–15).

Chapter 7 is regularly divided into two parts, vv. 1–7 and vv. 8–20, but Bo Reicke has shown that it can be read as a liturgical unit, for there are parallels throughout with the psalms of lament.[73] Psalms 69 and 79, for example, contain similar complaints and expressions of confidence. There are no certain historical references in the chapter, and its liturgical character really makes it undatable.[74] The appearance of a psalm in a prophetic book is no more unusual than the other cultic forms we have found in Micah. Fragments have already been found in Amos 4:13; 5:8–9; and 9:5–6, a hymn appears in Isaiah 12, and the psalms of lament are put to effective use in Habakkuk 1 and in the so-called confessions of Jeremiah (Jer. 11:18–23; 12:1–6; 15:10–21; 17:9–10, 14–18; 18:18–23; 20:7–18). The book of Micah is thus not unusual in its extensive use of traditional forms of speech, most of which had their original location in the cult. Although he and the other prophets were highly critical of worship as they saw it practiced, finding it necessary to condemn the priesthood for failure to uphold the ethical standards of Yahwism, as the prophets understood it, their intent was not "liturgical reform." The language of worship was their own language. The problem, as identified by Amos, Micah, Isaiah, and others, was the failure to understand that the righteous life is both a prerequisite for approaching Yahweh and the necessary result of true worship.

Is the book of Micah an anthology of essentially disconnected materials of prophetic and liturgical origin, does it represent successive reapplications of the words of the eighth-century prophet to new situations of the sixth and fifth centuries (as Wolff and Mays read it), or can most of it be understood as a theological interpretation of the crises involving Samaria and Jerusalem produced by a contemporary of those events? Most of those who take the last of these approaches think of Micah as already foreseeing a divine plan, extending beyond the expected disaster, through a time of exile, to a new age. How meaningful that would have been to Judeans who could still look to the temple in Jerusalem as evidence of the invulnerability of that city and of Yahweh's certain presence among them may be questioned. It is worth considering whether chs. 4 and 5 might have been a response to the fact that Jerusalem did not fall to the Assyrians in 701. The references to exile would make sense, for captives from Lachish and other cities were exiled by Sennacherib. "Babylon" in 4:10 remains a problem, although some have suggested it need not be understood as the enemy here, but as the place where Assyrians took the exiles. The cultic theme of God's defeat of the nations who surround Jerusalem (4:11–13) could have been appealed to and added to the book as a counter to Micah's prediction of total destruction. The oracle concerning the peacemaker from Bethlehem might have referred to Hezekiah, at the beginning of his reign, or even at the beginning of his revolt against Assyrian domination, and the verses that follow (5:5–15) could be a promise of deliverance from Sennacherib, together with purification of Judah from the abuses the prophet found there.

All this is speculative (like the other theories alluded to above), but it does act as a preface to a major issue in the book of Isaiah: Was he responsible for the promises of deliverance for Jerusalem, given the negative character of the rest of his message? It also points toward a major issue that will confront Jeremiah and Ezekiel. By the time they came on the scene, the fact that Jerusalem had been saved from Sennacherib had so reinforced the old Zion theology that those prophets found it impossible to convince their people that Yahweh would ever let the city fall. They mount major attacks on the theology that appears in positive ways in Micah and Isaiah. They are also thoroughly critical of the kings who rule in Jerusalem, although they do not seem to reject the idea of kingship. The promises that appear in their books, however, take up Zion theology again, elaborate it and project it into the future. Jerusalem, the temple, the king, and all the rest were gone, but the ideas associated with them in these earlier prophets became the basis for new hope.

Micah 7 adds something that was hinted at in Hosea, and will reappear in Habakkuk and Jeremiah. It turns to the effects of internal injustice and invasion by a foreign army on an individual Israelite.[75] We need not be concerned whether this is Micah or not; this is traditional language suited to anyone facing the kind of distress that affected both kingdoms from the eighth through the sixth century. This provides an acceptable setting for words about forgiveness, which could not be addressed to the people as a whole, since these prophets were convinced it was too late for the nation to be able to repent, change its ways, and be delivered from certain disaster. But Amos had spoken of a tiny remnant that might yet seek the Lord and live, and this passage, in a prophetic book, shows that there were some in every generation who understood the true character of what it meant to be the people of Yahweh. This has produced one of the most important forgiveness passages in the Old Testament; unfortunately largely overlooked by commentators whose interests are date and authorship. There are actually two, separate references to forgiveness. The first (v. 9) involves a remarkable use of vocabulary:

> I must bear the indignation of the LORD,
>   because I have sinned against him,
> until he takes my side (*yarib ribi*)
>   and executes judgment for me (*wĕ'aśah mishpaṭi*).
> He will bring me out to the light;
>   I shall see his vindication (*tsidqatho*).
>   (Micah 7:9)

Here the roots *rib*, *shapaṭ*, and *tsadaq*, which are normally used of God's just punishment of evildoers, are used by one who admits his sinfulness, makes no claims to deserve to be forgiven, but appeals to the fact that these terms not only have juridical content, but were used in Israel to speak of God's saving action.[76] The righteousness of God as Paul spoke of it was thus already anticipated long ago.

The second reference to forgiveness is the hymn in 7:18–20. Only Psalm 103 is comparable to it in the Old Testament. More will be said in connection with the sixth-century prophets about their hope for eschatological forgiveness, but this passage, with its present-tense language, reminds us that in every age, no matter how hopeless the prospects seemed to be, there were faithful people who maintained a close relationship with their God.

2.4 Isaiah 1—39

Isaiah is the most complex of the prophetic books, and its interpreters have taken a wide variety of approaches.[77] For example, on the question of authorship, opinions range from ascribing all sixty-six chapters to the eighth-century Isaiah[78] to questioning whether any of it comes from him.[79] Within chs. 1—39, which are the subject of this section, some scholars find a prophet who preached only judgment;[80] others one whose message was a call for repentance.[81] If all or most of the materials in chs. 1—39 are thought to come from Isaiah, then one needs to explain his apparently inconsistent message, sometimes threatening disaster (e.g., 6:11–12; 28:22), sometimes promising divine intervention to save Jerusalem (e.g., 31:5; cf. 29:1–4 with 29:5–8). Our approach to each prophetic book is to take seriously its consistent message, without finding it necessary to solve all the problems of authorship and composition that are present, but consistency is a serious problem in this book, so it will be necessary to devote more space to its composition than is true for the others.

The book of Isaiah offers significant commentary on each of the three key moments in Israel's history—the falls of Samaria and Jerusalem, and the restoration of exiles to the promised land—and it adds a fourth: the unsuccessful siege of Jerusalem by the army of Sennacherib in 701 B.C.E. This complicates the relatively straightforward approach to Israel's history followed so far in this book, and it will be shown that 701 has a great deal to do with the complexity of the book of Isaiah itself. But a prior question for the organization of this book arises: Does my use of the death/resurrection theme logically call for a discussion of all 66 chapters at this point? It might be possible to organize the book so as to do that, but I have concluded that clarity will be served by making the now traditional division between chs. 1—39 (as representing for the most part preexilic prophecy) and 40—66 (as exilic and postexilic material). Chapters 40—55 not only take the promise of return from exile in Babylonia as their central message, as all recognize, but show every appearance of having originated in the mid-sixth century. Chapters 56—66 not only deal with the problems faced by returnees from exile to Jerusalem, but appear to have originated in Jerusalem some time after 538 B.C.E. It thus seems better to deal with them as if they were separate books, even though they were long ago combined with chs. 1—39 as the canonical book of Isaiah.[82] There is evidence that the materials in chs. 1—39 come from various dates, some long after the time of Isaiah himself, but for the purpose of understanding the major theological themes of this part of the book, it can be treated as the result of two redactions—one shortly after 701 and another during the exile.[83]

Isaiah 1—39 is rather clearly divided into blocks of material as follows:

ch. 1	An introductory collection of oracles
chs. 2—12	Oracles concerning Israel and Judah
chs. 13—23	Oracles against foreign nations
chs. 24—27	Oracles largely eschatological in content
chs. 28—31	Oracles concerning Judah (except for 28:1–4)
chs. 32—35	Oracles largely eschatological in content
chs. 36—39	Narratives about Isaiah

Three crises account for much of the material in these chapters: the threat to Judah from the coalition of Damascus and Israel in 735–733 (see especially chs. 7—8), the fall of Samaria in 722 (e.g., Isa. 9:8–21), and the siege of Jerusalem in 701 (e.g., Isa. 36–37). Most interpretations of Isaiah pay a great deal of attention to the events of 735–733 and 701, because of the narratives associated with them. They typically deal at length with Isaiah's political advice, found in the narratives and in associated passages elsewhere. The interest in this book is the theology motivating that "advice" (if it can properly be called that), and the theology itself is remarkably consistent, amid the great variety of materials the book contains. This means that much of the typical discussion, involving the dating of passages to one crisis or another, and the details of the history of the period, plus trying to evaluate what Isaiah himself may or may not have said, can be left to the margins.[84]

In general terms, these are the key events that led to the message that runs through most of chs. 1—39: Both kingdoms were threatened with death by Assyria, beginning with the invasion of Galilee by Tiglath-pileser III, and continuing through the invasion of Judah by Sennacherib. Israel died in 722 (2 Kings 17), but Jerusalem was twice saved, from the attack by the Syro-Ephraimite coalition in 735–733 (Isaiah 7–8; 2 Kings 16) and from the siege by Sennacherib in 701 (Isaiah 36–37; 2 Kings 18–19). Isaiah continued the prophetic tradition found in Amos and Micah, with reference to Israel's demise, and he applied the same traditional message to Judah (as Micah also did), but unlike the others, he needed to account for the fact that Jerusalem did not fall. I have said Isaiah did that. Other scholars attribute the passages concerning the deliverance of Jerusalem to later writers, but I will attempt to show that the book in its present form is so dominated by 701 that it must have taken its essential shape shortly after that event. Thus Isaiah himself or someone chronologically close to him may have been responsible for it.

Death and Deliverance in Isaiah

We begin with ch. 6, which most scholars believe to be the account of Isaiah's call, the beginning of his prophetic work, located out of chronological order in the book. Some interpreters believe that it is not in fact a call story and that chs. 1–5 represent his work as a prophet before the death of Uzziah. The vision in ch. 6 is then read as the mark of a change in Isaiah's divine commission.[85] Given our approach to the book, ch. 6 is the appropriate place to begin, no matter when the incident occurred, for the message Isaiah received in that vision was in continuity with the one originally introduced by Amos, namely, "death." Early in this section we shall note a great deal of continuity between Isaiah 1–39 and the prophets already studied, but very soon will observe much that is new, as well. Chapter 6 is rich, theologically, but for our purposes we must focus on only two elements: the nature of the God revealed here, and the devastating message given to Isaiah.[86]

Isaiah, like Amos, claims that he "saw Yahweh" (Isa. 6:1, 5; Amos 9:1), a most remarkable statement from one who emphasizes more than any other prophet the holiness of God. "The Holy One of Israel" is Isaiah's favorite title for Yahweh, and he uses it to designate both the otherness and the righteousness of God.[87] Although scripture normally insists no one can see God and live (Exod. 33:20; cf. John 1:18), a few passages dare to speak of some such experience (Exod. 24:9–11; 1 Kings 22:19–22). It is important to observe that none of these passages, however, undertakes to say what God looks like. A few writers have recorded an experience in which the sense of the immediacy of God's presence was so intense that they dared to use the verb "saw."[88] The imagery in Isaiah 6 and in the even more elaborate vision in Ezekiel 1 serves to emphasize the absolute difference between the divine and the human. That difference is a major theme in Isaiah; it is a difference of power, of wisdom, and of goodness. It is an understanding of God that Isaiah shares with other Old Testament writers, but he has distinctive ways of emphasizing it. One is by the word "holy" (as in 6:3); another is by designating pride as the most serious of human sins, taking pride to mean rejecting the difference between God and humanity (Isa. 2:6–22 and many other texts); and another is the elaboration of the claim that already surfaced in Amos—that Yahweh is sovereign over all of nature and over every human system and endeavor. The seraphim in 6:3 express that claim in a unique way, rendered inexactly by the standard translations as "the whole earth is full of his glory." The Hebrew literally makes this remarkable statement: "The fullness of all the earth is his glory." Koch says, "What Isaiah experiences therefore is not merely a transcendent God, but a God who also dwells completely within the world, even though innerworldliness only represents one of his manifestations—that is to say, his *kabod*." Otto Kaiser elaborates the same idea:

> Thus heaven and earth, and day and night, tell of his glory (Ps. 19.1f.). Even the destiny of the Gentile nations points towards him as the true ruler of history, and so maintains his glory, which excludes every other claim (Isa. 42.8). Yet there can be no greater misunderstanding of this hymn than as the expression of a rationalist natural theology. For man is blind to the glory of God to which all reality bears witness, until he is convinced of his holiness. Both God's glory and God's holiness are always recognized simultaneously. Only someone who knows of his holiness also recognizes his glory.[89]

That insight leads to Isaiah's insistence that all of history is subject to the will of Yahweh, and that human plans are thus completely futile, unless based on faith and trust in his work (Isa. 7:9; 30:15).

The vision indicates that the basis of Isaiah's sense that something has gone fatally wrong in the life of his people is not his observation of social injustice, as we might deduce from Amos or Micah, or his awareness of the ways contemporary worship made knowledge of the true nature of God impossible, as Hosea suggests. It was a more deeply existential matter, based on Isaiah's encounter with the One who is holy—holy in the sense of perfectly righteous, perfectly pure. "Woe is me! I am lost, for I am a man of unclean lips, and I live among a people of unclean lips; yet my eyes have seen the King, the LORD of hosts!" (6:5). That awareness made the prophet one with his sinful people, for as a human being he also was too impure to come near the Holy One. Unlike those whose pride he will condemn elsewhere, he knew there was an absolute distance between himself and Yahweh, but confessing it led to his forgiveness, symbolically represented in the vision by the purifying fire of a coal touching his lips. The forgiveness of sin ("atonement" *těkuppar*) thus appears in this key passage, but it is only the prophet, who has confessed his unworthiness, who is forgiven. Forgiveness makes it possible for him to respond to the divine call, "Whom shall I send, and who will go for us?" (6:8b),[90] but his work is to be as thoroughly negative as that of Amos, if not more so. As with Amos the trial has been held and the sentence, "Guilty," has been passed. It was the prophets' task to announce it and explain it, but Isaiah is apparently told that he must also make sure there will be no escaping it.

> Go and say to this people:
>   "Keep listening, but do not comprehend;
>   keep looking, but do not understand."
> Make the mind of this people dull,
>   and stop their ears,
>   and shut their eyes,

so that they may not look with their eyes,
   and listen with their ears,
and comprehend with their minds,
   and turn and be healed.

                   (Isa. 6:9–10)

This is the most disturbing of the parallels between Isaiah 6 and the vision of Micaiah ben Imlah in 1 Kings 22:19–23, for like the lying spirit in the latter passage, Isaiah's task was to make sure judgment will come to pass.[91] The rest of the prophetic message does not support the apparently obvious conclusion from these words that God did not want his people to repent (cf. Isa. 30:15). This is probably best understood as one of the extravagant uses of language typical of Hebrew poetry, with the intent being to make it completely clear that Isaiah's role was not to be a preacher of repentance. And in fact he was not, even though parts of ch. 1 have been read that way, as will be seen shortly.

It is no wonder that he responded with the lament, "How long, O Lord?" Surely that could not be God's intention for his life's work! God shows no mercy here, however, for what lies ahead is the desolation of the land (6:11, 12b, a very common theme in Isaiah) and exile (12a, relatively rare in this book). Amos's remnant theme, which was used more by Isaiah than any other prophet, is finally made even more threatening. Even if a tenth (cf. Amos 5:3) remains, it will be burned. The text of v. 13 is very difficult, and is perhaps untranslatable, but it seems very unlikely that the many who have thought to find a final note of hope in this verse are correct.[92]

One of Isaiah's masterworks, the song of the vineyard in 5:1–7, expresses in a powerful way the message he received in his commission: Judgment is coming, is deserved, and is unescapable. It is a highly creative use of familiar images in a way that has tantalized scholars who have tried to find a simple description of the genre.[93] Isaiah's supposed love song (v. 1) is used the way Nathan used his parable of the poor man with one ewe lamb in 2 Sam. 12:1–7 and the way the wise woman of Tekoa used her fictitious account of her two sons in 2 Sam. 14:1–20. Jesus also appealed to the lawyer whose question brought forth the parable of the Good Samaritan to make a judgment about it which ought to apply to himself: "Which of these three, do you think, was a neighbor to the man who fell into the hands of the robbers?" (Luke 10:36). He also told his own parable of the vineyard which led the hearers to recognize themselves in it (Mark 12:1–12). The technique is thus to attract the interest of listeners by a story that arouses their sympathy or sense of justice, then to show that it is a story about them.

Isaiah identified the genre as a love song, but then began to tell about a farmer's labors to make a fine vineyard. His most literal-minded listeners may have thought he was talking about a real vineyard, but most would hear the clue, "love song," and would take this to be a metaphor for the love relationship between a man and his wife. Suddenly, it is no longer Isaiah speaking, but the man himself, bringing charges of unfaithfulness, in spite of all that he had done for her.

And now, inhabitants of Jerusalem
   and people of Judah,

judge between me and my vineyard.
What more was there to do for my vineyard
   that I have not done in it?
When I expected it to yield grapes,
   why did it yield wild grapes?
                              (Isa. 5:3–4)

He sees divorce as the only possibility, described metaphorically as the destruction of the vineyard—but with a human impossibility included: "I will also command the clouds that they rain no rain upon it" (v. 6b). With that, Isaiah finally makes clear his real subject, and moves rapidly to the denouement of the song. The subjects are not farmer and vineyard, not husband and wife, but Yahweh and his people (both Israel and Judah, v. 7). The song ends with the reason judgment is coming, expressed in two words Isaiah uses frequently, *mishpat* "justice" and *tsedaqah* "righteousness," here formulated in a powerful play on words that cannot be reflected adequately in an English translation such as the NRSV's "he expected justice, but saw bloodshed; righteousness, but heard a cry!" Isaiah paired justice and righteousness with two words that sounded like *mishpat* and *tsedaqah*, but meant something very different: *wayqaw lᵉmishpat wᵉhinneh miśpaḥ litsdaqah wᵉhinneh tsᵉ'aqah.*[94] It is a brutal conclusion, but the song has a center that must not be overlooked, for it reminds us of Hosea's emphasis on the pathos of God: "What more was there to do for my vineyard that I have not done in it?" (v. 4a).

Isaiah thus participated in the tradition of judgment prophecy begun by Amos and Hosea and continued in Judah by Micah. The entire book is dominated, however, by a new element that would have profound effects on the work of the later prophets—the theology of Zion and David. We shall turn to the first chapter of the book, in which Zion theology is introduced, but first it may be useful to note the variety of elements Isaiah has in common with the other eighth-century prophets. God as parent and Israel as rebellious child, in Isa. 1:2–3, reminds us of Hos. 11:1–4, and Isa. 1:3 also uses Hosea's "know" and "understand." Isaiah frequently begins his oracles with the lamenting cry *hoy,* "alas" (1:4; 5:8–22; etc.) as Amos did in Amos 5:18; 6:1. He insists that worship without justice is futile (Isa. 1:10–17), following the lead of Amos 5:21–24; Hos. 6:6; Micah 6:6–8. He sings dirges over his people (e.g., 1:4–9, 21–23), as Amos did (Amos 5:1–2). He condemns the leaders (3:14; 28:14; reminding us of both Hosea and Micah); the wealthy (Isa. 3:16; cf. Amos 6:4–7); and pays special attention to wealthy women (Isa. 3:18–4:1; Amos 4:1–3). Later we shall note his use of the holy war oracle, different from Amos's use, in Isaiah 7; 10; and 37. Unlike Hosea or Micah, Isaiah's book contains a series of oracles against foreign nations, something that first appeared in Amos. Isaiah also had to deal with rival prophets, who must have challenged each of the canonical prophets because their words were so unacceptable (Isa. 9:15; 28:7; 29:10; cf. Hos. 4:4; Micah 3:5–8). Other examples could be added, but this should be enough to demonstrate the continuity among these books.[95]

This kind of prophecy was called forth, as emphasized earlier, by the crisis introduced by Assyrian empire building, which led to the declaration that the old ways were not working and that God was about to bring them to an end and start again. The predictions of Amos and Hosea that the Northern Kingdom's political existence was near its end soon came true. Micah and Isaiah followed their lead, found conditions in Judah to be similar, saw the Assyrians drawing ever nearer, and Micah predicted the destruction of Jerusalem. That did not happen. Isaiah's commissioning experience (ch. 6) led to a similar message, but the fact that Jerusalem did not fall led to the collection in his book of a much more complex evaluation of the work of God in history than appears in Micah. Jerusalem did not fall in 735–733 or in 701, but according to prophetic insights it should have. Both Micah and Isaiah identified the same problems in Judah that Amos and Hosea found in Israel. The book of Isaiah is thus dominated by the tension between what had already become the traditional prophetic way of evaluating their people's unfaithfulness to the true character of Yahwism (as the prophets understood it), and the fact that Jerusalem was saved, temple worship continued, and the Davidic king still reigned.

Zion Theology in Isaiah

The first chapter of Isaiah suggests a way to deal with those tensions as they appear throughout the book. There are two introductions to the book, Isa. 1:1 and 2:1, and this seems to call for an explanation. Does ch. 2 mark the beginning of an earlier collection of Isaiah's oracles, to which ch. 1 was later added? Georg Fohrer proposed that ch. 1 was in fact added as an introduction to and summary of the book, and this explanation has been accepted by many.[96] It will be taken here as providing the key to the way the book was intended to be read when that chapter was added. The two oracles in ch. 2 will also be understood as passages deliberately placed at the beginning of a collection in order to emphasize two major themes of the book.

Isaiah differs from the other eighth-century prophetic books in that it begins with the description of a disaster that has already occurred. Chapter 1 introduces a collection of oracles made during a time of severe distress. The words, "I reared children and brought them up, but they have rebelled against me" (Isa. 1:2b) are thus as much divine lament as they are accusation. We understand the list that begins the next unit (1:4–9)—sin, iniquity, evil, corruption, forsaking, despising, estrangement—once we notice that it begins with the outcry of grief, *hoy*,[97] and see that it leads to the question of the divine parent, which may be paraphrased, "Why have you chosen a life that has led to such suffering?" (vv. 5–8). Metaphorically, the whole country is sick; they have not turned to be healed (cf. 6:10). Literally, the land has been overrun by foreigners, cities have been burned and the population decimated. Only Zion is left. There is debate over the setting of this oracle, but surely the reference to Zion as the only survivor of the disaster is most naturally to be understood as a reference to the events of 701.[98] I take this to be the key not only to the way this chapter should be read, but also to the reading of much of the rest of Isaiah 1—39, except for those parts that obviously presuppose an exilic setting.

The chapter laments over the sorry state of a country that had suffered under the cruelty of the Assyrian army. Isaiah will have much to say about the Assyrians elsewhere, but at this point, just after they have left Jerusalem still standing, he (like Amos and Micah) blames what has happened on the absence of justice and righteousness among his own people (1:17, 21, 23). The temple still stands and worship continues as usual, without concern for the plight of a suffering people (1:10–17). Jerusalem had been saved, but not because they deserved it. They have the *Torah*, of which Isaiah reminds them (vv. 16–17; cf. Pss. 15:1–5; 24:3–6), they know its threats and promises (vv. 18–20), but reality is that the city that was once full of justice (Isaiah believes) is now filled with murder (vv. 21–23). Surely God will do something about that, but the latter part of this chapter speaks of a different kind of judgment from what we have found elsewhere. Verses 24–31 speak of refining, of purging out evil (vv. 24–25, 27–28), somewhat reminiscent of God's work of correction in Hosea 2, although the imagery is different. If the chapter is a unit to be dated shortly after 701, then it offers a significantly different outlook from that found in Amos, Hosea, and Micah. Judgment *has* fallen, but Jerusalem still stands, and society is still sick. There is a theology being taught in the temple that might account for Jerusalem's survival: namely, God's ideal for Zion. Zion had been delivered; that might be the clue to what God intended to do next. So, the latter verses of this chapter speak of a possibility that still remains—that God will purge Jerusalem of its rebelliousness and make it what it should be. "Afterward you shall be called the city of righteousness, the faithful city" (1:26b; cf. 1:21). The tensions between judgment and promise in much of the rest of the book may be understood as resulting from this ideal of Zion which is held up against present reality.

Psalm 132 celebrates both Yahweh's choice of Zion to be his "resting place forever" (v. 14), and his covenant with David (cf. Ps. 78:67–72). David had captured Jerusalem from the Jebusites and had brought the ark of the covenant there in order to associate that symbol of the presence of Yahweh with his kingship. The Psalter reflects those events in a theology that associates both the temple and kingship with Yahweh's intention to bless his people from Mount Zion. The Judeans who inhabited Jerusalem from David's time on may have inherited some elements of earlier Canaanite theology and worship practices, which are reflected in these psalms. There is, for example, the unexplained association of the Davidic king with Melchizedek, king of Salem in Abraham's time (cf. Psalm 110 with Gen. 14:18–24), and the association of Zion with rivers and the far north (Psalms 46; 48), which does not fit the topography of Jerusalem. At any rate, there is general agreement that the psalms of Zion (Psalms 46; 48; 76; 84; 87; 122; and elements of others), the psalms celebrating the kingship of Yahweh (Psalms 47; 93; 95–99), and those focusing on the Davidic king (Psalms 2; 20; 21; 45; 89; 110; 132) antedate the eighth-century prophets.[99]

J. J. M. Roberts has neatly summarized the Zion theology, and the following modification of his outline, comparing some citations from the Psalter with texts from Isaiah will help to show the importance of the tradition for this prophetic book:[100]

I. Yahweh is the great king—Ps. 48:2; Isa. 6:5

II. He chose Jerusalem for his dwelling place—Pss. 78:67–69; 132:13–14;
Isa. 8:18
    A. Yahweh's choice has implications for Zion's topography:
        It is on a high mountain—Pss. 48:1–2; 68:16, 18; Isa. 2:2; and
        is watered by a river—Ps. 46:4; Isa. 33:21–23a
    B. Yahweh's choice has implications for Zion's security:
        1. Yahweh protects it from his enemies—Pss. 48:4–7; 76:5–9;
           Isa. 17:12–14; 31:4–5
        2. The nations acknowledge Yahweh's suzereignty—Pss. 46:10;
           76:12; Isa. 2:3–4; 18:7
        3. There will be no more war—Ps. 46:9; Isa. 2:4; 11:9
    C. Yahweh's choice has implications for Zion's inhabitants
        1. They share in the blessings of God's presence—Pss . 48:12–
           14; 132:13–18; 133:3; 147:12–20; Isa. 4:2–6; 24:23; 25:6–8;
           30:19–26; 33:17–24
        2. But they must be fit to live in his presence—Pss. 24:3–6;
           84:11; 125:1–5; Isa. 1:16–17; 33:15

To this list should be added the evidence for the close relationship between
Zion theology and the theology of Davidic kingship, for that helps to account for
elements in the book of Isaiah. Yahweh's choice of David and his descendants was
to make them king in Zion (Pss. 2:6; 78:70–71; 122:5), to support them (Pss. 20:2,
6; 84:9), and to give them victory over their enemies (Pss. 2:9; 20:9; 110:2). Isaiah's association of justice and righteousness with both Zion (Isa. 1:26–27; 33:5)
and the king (Isa. 9:7; 11:4–5; 16:5; 32:1) also had its parallels in Israel's traditional language of worship. For Zion, see Pss. 76:9; 84:11; 97:6, 8, 10–12; 99:4;
125:3, and for the king, see Pss. 45:7 and 72:1–2, 4, 7, 12–14.

The movement in Isaiah 1 from lament over the desolation of Judah at a time
when only Jerusalem was left unscathed (vv. 4–9) through an analysis of what has
gone wrong (vv. 10–23) to an oracle in which Yahweh declares he will purify that
corrupt city suggests that the events of 701 led to this line of reasoning: Jerusalem
was saved, but not because they deserved it. It must be, then, because God has a
purpose specifically focused on that city—as Zion theology had long declared—
but not the city as it is now. The Jerusalem cult had celebrated all these glorious
things about Zion and the king as if they were true in the present, but they seldom
if ever were. Jerusalem must be purified, and so the book of Isaiah both holds up
the ideal Zion as the standard against which the city is now being judged and
found wanting, and as the goal which Yahweh will one day achieve.

Chapter 2 begins with a picture of this ideal Zion, drawn from elements that had
long been celebrated in the cult, but now projected into the future with the addition of a universalistic outlook that does not seem to have been traditional.[101] This
is one way of expressing Isaiah's insistence on the universal sovereignty of Yahweh, for it will be to Zion that all the nations will freely come to have their differ-

ences adjudicated. Zion will be the source of instruction—*Torah*—and the word of Yahweh, and once that is recognized and accepted, peace will be possible. If it is true, as claimed here, that Zion theology dominates the book of Isaiah, then it was very appropriate to begin this earlier collection with the ideal against which the present is to be judged and toward which God is working.

The second unit in ch. 2 also has a universalistic sweep, but it stands in stark contrast with vv. 2–4, for it is a terrifying vision of wholesale destruction (Isa. 2:6–22). It has been associated with earthquake or windstorm, but in fact no agent is mentioned except God himself. It is a vision of the leveling of everything high, meaningful not in a literal sense, but in terms of the uses in Hebrew of several roots for "height" to mean also "pride" (like our use of "haughty"). Various forms of the roots *ga'ah*, *gabah*, and *rum* appear twelve times in these verses, used in three ways: to denote physical height which is brought low (the visionary part), human pride, and the only thing deserving to be called "high" in Isaiah's theology —Yahweh. Pride is the moral obverse of Isaiah's insistence on Yahweh's universal sovereignty, so it is one of the major themes of the book, appearing as the basis for explaining the present misfortunes of Israel, and for predicting the eventual downfall of the other nations.[102] It has taken the form, in Ephraim and Judah, of human plans that have no regard for the will of God (e.g., 5:21; ch. 7; 9:8–10; 30:1–17; 31:1–3), and in Assyria, of the claim to be all-powerful, responsible to no one (Isa. 10:5–19; 37:23–29).

"Oh, Rebellious Children, Who Carry Out a Plan, but Not Mine" (Isa. 30:1)

John Barton has reminded us that "in Isaiah, as in hardly any other prophet, we are told about the underlying *attitudes* or states of mind of those who are condemned."[103] The key word that sums up those attitudes is "pride," of the kind that leads to arrogance and insolence. The *hoy* oracles in Isa. 5:8–24; 10:1–4 provide a series of examples of how attitude led to action that had to be condemned. They contain the most detailed description of social ills in the book, reapplying Amos's critique of Israelite society to the leaders of Judah. In their midst appears an echo of the poem against pride in ch. 2: "People are bowed down, everyone is brought low, and the eyes of the haughty are humbled. But the LORD of hosts is exalted by justice, and the Holy God shows himself holy by righteousness" (5:15–16; cf. 2:11, 17). The words seem to interrupt the context here, but they are appropriate reminders of the way pride and injustice are connected in Isaiah's thought. The outcry, *hoy*, that appears throughout the series, is taken by most interpreters to be accusatory, but it seems not inappropriate to hear overtones of the original sense of lamentation, as Isaiah uses it. The word appears here as the introduction to the reason part of a varied sequence of reason/announcement oracles (5:8–10, 11–17; 18–24; 10:1–4). The first, accusing landowners of expanding their estates, probably by unjustly taking over the land of the poor, leads to an announcement of judgment reminiscent of Amos 5:11. The second speaks of drunkenness and feasting, a frequent theme in Isaiah, which reappears already in 5:22. The result will be exile (5:13) as also in Amos 6:4–7. Those who behave this way are the same ones responsible for injustice in the court (5:23; 10:1–4), as in Amos 5:12. Then Isaiah goes his own way, with references to attitude. He cries out *Hoy* over those who say, "Let him make haste, let him speed his work that we may see it; let the plan of the Holy One of Israel hasten to fulfillment, that we may know it" (5:19). "Is there really a 'divine plan'?" they ask. "We would like to see some evidence of it—and in the meantime we make our own plans"—so Isaiah reads the thoughts of the leaders of his people. And they operate by a reverse morality: "You who call evil good and good evil" (5:20). We wish Isaiah had provided some examples of that. But their pride leads them to believe they know best: "You who are wise in your own eyes, and shrewd in your own sight" (5:21).

That last evaluation sums up Isaiah's attitude toward the government's frantic and futile efforts during the years of his ministry. The first crisis Judah faced during this period came in the time of King Ahaz (Isaiah 7; 735–733 B.C.E.). The two northern neighbors, Israel and Damascus, planned to rebel against paying tribute to Assyria, and attempted to force Ahaz to join them. The chapter has been discussed at great length in the commentaries and periodical literature, and much of that need not detain us here.[104] The focus of the chapter is Isaiah's use of a holy war oracle, in its traditional sense (unlike Amos's new use of it in Amos 1—2). As an unnamed prophet had once appeared before Ahab with the promise of deliverance from the Arameans (1 Kings 20:28), Isaiah also offered an oracle saying of the plans of the kings of Israel and Damascus, "It shall not stand, and it shall not come to pass" (Isa. 7:7). The oracle concludes with another of Isaiah's plays on words, using a root that means both "believe" and "be firm": *'im lo' ta'ăminu ki lo' te'amenu*. Translators now use "stand" twice in order to reflect the wordplay: "If you do not stand firm in faith, you shall not stand at all (Isa. 7:9, NRSV)." Ahaz's unwillingness to believe the promise led Isaiah to offer him a sign, and when the king refused to ask for one, a sign was given anyway, in the form of the prediction of the birth of a child, to be named Emmanuel, "God is with us."[105] That name has taken on great importance in Christianity because of Matthew's citation of Isa. 7:14 and his use of the theme "God with us" throughout his Gospel (Matt. 1:18–25; cf. 28:20). For Isaiah's time, however, the meaning of the sign was made explicit in 7:16–17: "For before the child knows how to refuse the evil and choose the good, the land before whose two kings you are in dread will be deserted. The LORD will bring on you and on your people and on your ancestral house such days as have not come since the day that Ephraim departed from Judah—the king of Assyria." Ahaz's plan, which he did carry out, was to ask Assyria for help, with the result that he became a tribute-paying vassal (2 Kings 16). The political wisdom of Isaiah's words was the reminder that Assyria would certainly take care of the rebels to the north without Ahaz having to subject himself to that great power, but the theology behind it, as reflected in other oracles, seems to have been the conviction that God was working out a plan, with reference to Assyria, and that it would come to pass no matter what Ahaz did.

In fact, Jerusalem was saved, and Israel and Damascus suffered the wrath of Tiglath-pileser III. The next crisis to concern Isaiah was the complete demise of the Northern Kingdom in 722 (see Isa. 8:1–4; 9:8–21; 17:4–6; 28:1–4). The earlier defeats they had experienced had taught them nothing, and he spoke of their complacency, which led them to recognize no need for change, as pride:

> The Lord sent a word against Jacob,
>> and it fell on Israel;
> and all the people knew it [a veiled reference to Amos?]—
>> Ephraim and the inhabitants of Samaria—
>> but in pride and arrogance of heart they said:
> "The bricks have fallen,
>> but we will build with dressed stones;
> the sycamores have been cut down,
>> but we will put cedars in their place."
>
> (Isa. 9:8–10)

Although the Northern Kingdom had been an enemy of Judah in the past, and was again in the crisis of 735–733, Isaiah, like the other prophets, thought of the people of God as properly including both kingdoms (note "both houses of Israel" in 8:14 and cf. 5:7), so he took it to be his responsibility to speak of the will of Yahweh for that politically distinct neighbor whose destiny was also part of the divine plan.

In 713 the Philistine city of Ashdod rebelled against Assyria, with the promise of help from Egypt (Isaiah 20; *ANET,* 287–88). Edom, Moab, and Judah (now under king Hezekiah) were also involved, and this led to one of the more bizarre symbolic actions to be found in the prophetic books. God ordered Isaiah to "loose the sackcloth from your loins and take your sandals off your feet" (Isa. 20:2) and he is said to have walked about naked and barefoot for three years, as a sign of the way the Egyptians would be taken away captive by the Assyrians. Scarcely any commentator will allow Isaiah to strip himself completely, in spite of what the text says, and they insist he must have worn something. We can scarcely imagine life without clothes for three years in Jerusalem, but the text confronts us with that shocking statement. Nakednesss was considered extremely shameful in ancient Israel, but depictions of captives of war in Egyptian and Assyrian art show that it was frequently inflicted on them. Why should Isaiah have had to participate in the shame that Egyptians were expected to experience? It was, of course, primarily a message to Judah: Egypt will be no help to you. There was more to it, however, as will become clearer with reference to the symbolic acts of Jeremiah and Ezekiel. Yahweh's prophet, the one who condemned the haughtiness of others, had to accept the lowest and most humiliating role for himself, and that was part of what it meant to be a prophet.

With the death of Sargon II (705 B.C.E.), Sennacherib came to power in Assyria, but he was faced immediately with a major rebellion in Babylonia. It seemed the opportune time for the western vassals to declare their independence, and Hezekiah became the leader of a movement involving Judah, Ekron, and Ashkelon, with the promise of help from Egypt (2 Kings 18:7; *ANET,* 287–88). Isaiah opposed this alliance, as he had earlier opposed Ahaz's willingness to ally himself with Assyria. Parts of chs. 28–31 probably come from this time. There are no words for pride here (he reserved them for Assyria at this time), for at this point he preferred to speak of folly—scoffers who have made a covenant with death (28:14–15), who could do better than to try to ensure their future by their efforts at armed resistance (30:1–5; 31:1–3), but who will not listen to the truth (30:8–11, 15–18). Here, Isaiah's so-called quietism appears most prominently. He was a prophet, not a politician, and his work was to explain what God was doing in history, not to give practical advice about armies and defenses. Evidently (as will become clear when we look at 10:5–6), he believed it was the will of Yahweh to put the immediate future in the hands of the Assyrians, and that meant there was no averting it, no matter what the leaders of Judah might do. Even so, it is not easy to ascribe everything in these chapters to the same person. The oracle concerning the covenant of death (28:14–22) concludes with the announcement, "for I have heard a decree of destruction from the Lord GOD of hosts upon the whole land," reminding us of Isaiah's commission in ch. 6. The "Ariel" speech in 29:1–4 makes God the enemy of Jerusalem, and uses mysterious language in v. 4 that may have been intended to indicate its destruction, but then speaks of the annihilation of the nations that fight against Ariel (vv. 5–8). Chapter 30 threatens the "rebellious children" with defeat until the remnant is left "like a flagstaff on the top of a mountain" (vv. 12–14, 16–17), but offers a better way:

> In returning and rest you shall be saved;
>> in quietness and in trust shall be your strength.
>>> (Isa. 30:15b)

> Therefore the LORD waits to be gracious to you;
>> therefore he will rise up to show mercy to you.
> For the LORD is a God of justice;
>> blessed are all those who wait for him.
>>> (Isa. 30:18)

The ambiguity (see also 31:4–9) can probably be explained by the events of 701. The plans of Judah's leaders did lead to disaster. Sennacherib's army ravaged the land, but the passages that speak of Yahweh's protection of Jerusalem represent a prophetic interpretation of the deliverance of Jerusalem in 701 that may already have been pronounced by Isaiah during the siege, or may have been added shortly after. The account in 2 Kings 18–19 suggests three explanations for the breaking off of the siege. Hezekiah paid a large tribute (2 Kings 18:14–16; also recorded in Sennacherib's inscriptions), there was a miraculous destruction of the Assyrian army (2 Kings 19:35), and he may have hurried home because he received news of a plot against him, which eventually succeeded (2 Kings 19:37).[106] For Isaiah, however, the arrival of Sennacherib had been a part of Yahweh's plan, and the deliverance of Jerusalem must also have been his will. "Trust" thus becomes a significant theme in this part of the book. It speaks of the wrong kind of trust in 30:12 and 31:1, and uses the same word, *batah*, of the "complacent women" in 32:9, 10, 11. A different kind of confidence, in the sovereignty of Yahweh, whose will is ultimately for the good, led to sayings such as 30:15b, 18, quoted above, and 32:17:

"The effect of righteousness will be peace, and the result of righteousness, quietness and trust forever" (cf. 26:2–4).

Shall the Ax Vaunt Itself Over the One Who Wields It?" (Isa. 10:15)

Other prophets had spoken of Yahweh's use of a foreign army as his agent to judge Israel and then Judah for the injustice in their midst, but Isaiah was the first to consider the problem raised by Assyrian cruelty. Those armies did not bring justice, but increased suffering. Isaiah offered a preliminary answer, in line with his theme of pride and with his insistence on the universal sovereignty of Yahweh. Later, Habakkuk found that it was not an adequate answer, but it was a bold, first step, challenging the Assyrian king's pretensions to world domination. The most important texts are Isa. 10:5–19; 14:4b–21, 37:22b–29. The authorship of the last two and parts of the first has been questioned, but they represent the same theology, and each is a poem of great power and originality.

The poem in ch. 10 begins as a *hoy* oracle, but soon changes to a disputation speech. As in 5:26–29; 7:18–20; 8:5–8, it is Yahweh who has sent the Assyrian against his people, but the reason for it is made explicit in v. 6: "against a godless nation I send him." "Godless" may sound a bit too modern; the sense of the Hebrew word is to be alienated from God. Isaiah is fully aware that the Assyrian king has no awareness of being sent by Israel's God to carry out his will. The Assyrian's intention is to rule the world (vv. 7–11), and he is certain of his power to do it (vv. 13–14). The words put into the king's mouth here and also in 37:24–25 are remarkably accurate echoes of what Assyrian kings actually put into their inscriptions, showing that their royal propaganda was well known in Judah.[107] Isaiah does not exaggerate the boasting of which he accuses them, but for him that represents overweening pride, *hybris*, which will surely be brought low. Given Isaiah's theology, it is the Assyrian's pride for which he will be judged, rather than condemnation for the excessive cruelty that was a part of Assyrian policy:

> Shall the ax vaunt itself over the one who wields it,
>   or the saw magnify itself against the one who handles it?
> As if a rod should raise the one who lifts it up,
>   or as if a staff should lift the one who is not wood!
>
> (Isa. 10:15)

> Because you have raged against me
>   and your arrogance has come to my ears,
> I will put my hook in your nose
>   and my bit in your mouth;
> I will turn you back on the way
>   by which you came.
>
> (Isa. 37:29)

The empire builder as oppressive tyrant does appear in Isa. 14:4b–21, however. The poem is introduced as a taunt against the king of Babylon, who was no world conqueror in Isaiah's time, so the passage has often been dated during the Neo-Babylonian period. The theme of *hybris* is so important in Isaiah, however, that it seems likely the poem comes from Isaiah and has been provided with a new introduction (14:1–4a) at a later time.[108] This is a mock funeral song, developing at length the familiar theme of the reversal of fortune, which in the true dirge was a natural way of expressing grief. At the death of a great tyrant, however, reversal of fortune is the occasion for rejoicing: "The whole earth is at rest and quiet; they break forth into singing" (14:7). Even the dead kings in Sheol greet the newly deceased emperor with surprise: "You too have become as weak as we! You have become like us!" (v. 10b). The prophet then introduces a mythological theme that is well known from ancient Near Eastern texts, that of rivalry over who is to be king of the gods.[109] He accuses the king of claiming to be a god himself, speaking of him as *Helel ben Shaḥar* (NRSV "Day Star, son of Dawn"), a reference to the planet Venus, the morning star. This lesser astral deity, as the prophet retells the myth, thought himself able to raise his throne above the stars of God, to make himself like the Most High (vv. 13–14). In the original myths, some of the claims to divine kingship issued by younger gods were successful, some were not, but for a prophet in Israel the king's efforts at world domination were taken to be a claim of divinity, and that was a challenge to Yahweh, the only God. Such human pretensions were no serious challenge at all. For the prophets, *hybris* was nonsense, and since the king was only human, the true God's last word is "Death" (vv. 15–21).[110]

Unlike Amos, Isaiah does not generally condemn the foreign nations for their inhuman treatment of others.[111] The rather lengthy collection of oracles against the nations in chs. 13—23 contains several that were probably formulated in the attempt to discourage Judah from looking for help from their neighbors, but the appearance of the theme of pride in the oracles against Moab and Tyre (scarcely rivals of Assyria for wealth and power) may indicate that another reason for the collection is to emphasize the claim that it is Yahweh alone who determines the future for all the nations.

"For Unto Us a Child Is Born" (Isa. 9:2–7)

Yahweh alone was king, according to Isaiah, and that formed the basis for his prediction of the downfall of the king of Assyria. But there was a king in Jerusalem, a descendant of David, who had been chosen by Yahweh to rule over his people, and that aspect of the theology of Zion clearly influenced Isaiah's work. His book does not contain the kind of wholesale condemnation of kings that appears in Hosea and in Jeremiah 22, even though he clearly disapproved of their foreign policy. One of his oracles, taken for centuries to be a messianic prophecy, shows itself to be, when read without presuppositions, a powerful description of how God intended his people to be ruled. The oracle in Isa. 9:2–7 [MT 9:1–8] does not take the form of prediction at all, but is an announcement of a change from darkness to light in the life of the people because of the birth of a royal child. We cannot be sure whether this was an actual birth announcement, or was an oracle proclaimed at the accession of a new king to the throne, although the latter seems more likely. The "birth" referred to would then be a reference to God's "adoption" of the new king as his son, as in Ps. 2:7: "You are my son; today I have begotten you." The names Wonderful Counselor, Mighty God, Everlasting Father, Prince of Peace are similar to the throne names given kings in other nations at the time of their accession.[112] The passage appears to function in a way similar to the ideal picture of Zion in Isa. 2:2–4, holding up in its perfection what God intends for his people. Note that the most important functions of the king are to establish justice and righteousness, as in Psalm 72 and in the second important passage concerning the king in Isa. 11:1–9.

The oracle in 11:1–9 differs from 9:2–7 in that it does speak of a future king, a shoot from the stump of Jesse, as if the dynastic tree established by David had been cut down. The passage thus seems to presuppose a time much later than Isaiah, after 587 B.C.E., but it is included here because the ideal of kingship is similar. The new king's wisdom is praised at first, with a piling up of synonyms (v. 2). He is no divine figure, but a human being who has been given the spirit of the Lord, and who lives in the fear of the Lord. As in Isa. 9:2–7, his main function is to establish and maintain good government: "Righteousness shall be the belt around his waist, and faithfulness the belt around his loins" (v. 5). The king then disappears from the next stanza of the poem, but the two parts probably belong together, for the prophets believed God's future would involve peace not only among human beings, but also in the natural world. Isaiah 11:6–9 is the most striking example of that belief, as it describes a time when animals are no longer carniverous or in need of deadly weapons for protection, leading to the moving conclusion: "They will not hurt or destroy on all my holy mountain." This passage probably should be dated, with other developments of Zion theology, during the exilic and postexilic period, but it is a faithful outgrowth of the ideas Isaiah proclaimed in the eighth century.[113]

Isaiah as Part of the Whole Prophetic Message

At this point logic would lead to a discussion of the whole 66-chapter collection, but as noted above, for the sake of clarity chs. 40–66 will be reserved for later. Isaiah is certainly the major example of the way the works of earlier prophets were kept relevant to new circumstances. We found limited evidence of that in Amos, Hosea, and Micah, but for some reason the Isaiah scroll attracted more new prophetic work than any other.[114] Without speculating further on the reasons for that, we conclude this section by looking at several themes that seem to be relevant to the time after 587 B.C.E.

There are threats of exile and promises of return from exile in the prophetic books, but the two do not appear in the same passage, as if a prophet were laying out the plan of history far in advance. The promises of return in Isaiah presuppose that people are already in exile. The promise in Isa. 11:11–16 might at first appear to come from the eighth century, because of its references to Assyria, but it speaks of both Israelite and Judean exiles, and of a very extensive dispersion, so it seems likely to come from a later time (cf. also Isa. 27:12–13). It contains hopes that appear in other exilic material: hope for the reunion of the northern and southern tribes (v. 13; cf. Ezek. 37:15–28) and for military victories over the neighboring countries (cf. Zeph. 2:5–11). The latter does not seem to correspond well with the outlook on the nations found elsewhere in First Isaiah.

The passage that now forms an introduction to the mock funeral song over the great tyrant, identifying him as a king of Babylon (probably secondarily) also promises restoration of exiles to their land and contains another hope for Israelite superiority over their former captives, similar to what appears in Second Isaiah (Isa. 45:14–17; 49:22–23). The relationship between ch. 35, which speaks throughout of the return of exiles to Zion, and Second Isaiah is even more striking, and some scholars have considered it to be the work of that prophet, displaced for some reason by the narrative in chs. 36–39.[115] The glorification of Zion does not appear here, as it does in Isa. 4:2–6; 30:19–33; 33:17–24; chs. 40—66, but the emphasis falls on the transformation of the natural world (including the healing of human disabilities in Isa. 35:5–6) to accompany the triumphal procession of exiles across the desert to Zion. This is a theme that appeared briefly in the final chapters of Amos and Hosea, and is one that carries several theological overtones that have not been as thoroughly discussed as other aspects of the prophetic books. At the level of basic human need, the transformation of nature was hoped for so that there might be no more hunger, as Ezek. 34:25–31 explicitly states, and as remains implicit in other promises of abundant crops (e.g., Amos 9:13–14). The remarkable insight that although God allows certain kinds of killing (cf. Gen. 9:3–6 with Gen. 1:29–30), it is not his ultimate intention that there be any killing on earth is put forth in the picture of peace among the animals in Isa. 11:6–9 (cf. Hosea's covenant in 2:18 [MT 2:20]). The ethical implications of that should be explored in another context. Another association of ethics with nature is found in the idea that the subhuman world suffers under a curse brought upon it by human sin (Gen. 3:17–18). Judgment of human sin also includes turning arable land into uninhabitable desert, as in Isa. 13:21–22; 34:9–15, as a the result of the curse. Isaiah 24:3–13 is the Old Testament's most striking expression of that idea:

> The earth lies polluted under its inhabitants;
> for they have transgressed laws,
> > violated the statutes,
> > broken the everlasting covenant.
> Therefore a curse devours the earth,
> > and its inhabitants suffer for their guilt.
>
> (Isa. 24:5–6a)

Paul would eventually allude to that idea in Rom. 8:19–23. For an eschatological picture such as Isaiah 35, then, the transformation of nature was more than an accompaniment, making the glorious return easier; it also implied the removal of the curse, and the bringing of peace to all creation.

The cosmic dimension of the judgment passage in ch. 24, just alluded to, is one of the aspects of the section, chs. 24–27, that has led to its designation as the "Isaiah Apocalypse." This is a misnomer, as most of the typical elements of the Jewish apocalyptic literature produced between c. 200 B.C.E. and c. 100 C.E. are not present in these chapters. That they are later than Isaiah is suggested by their reuse of themes found elsewhere in the book. "The earth shall be utterly laid waste and utterly despoiled" (24:3) is an elaboration of the poem of worldwide judgment in Isa. 2:6–22. A promise is offered that one day the meaning of the song of the vineyard in Isa. 5:1–7 will be reversed (Isa. 27:2–6), and Israel and Yahweh will be at peace. The section is a mixture of liturgical (25:1–5; 26:1–18) and eschatological (24:1–23; 25:6–12; 26:19–21; 27:1–12) material, not always well connected, and some have attempted to explain it as a prophetic liturgy. It has been dated as early as Isaiah and as late as the second century B.C.E.[116] It may contain one of the earliest Jewish references to an expectation of the resurrection of the dead in the last days:

Your dead shall live, their corpses shall rise.
O dwellers in the dust, awake and sing for joy!
For your dew is a radiant dew,
and the earth will give birth to those long dead.
(Isa. 26:19)

A recent study claims, however, that the passage speaks of a historical resurrection of Israel, rather than the resurrection of individuals.[117] If it is the latter, it suggests a relatively late date for these chapters, since there is little evidence for interest in the fate of individuals after death in Judaism earlier than the third century (when Ecclesiastes denied an idea that obviously was in the air, Eccl. 3:19–22).

Concern about the future of the human enemy after Judeans had lost everything in the defeat of 587 took the form of texts that promised, in violent language, divine judgment of Babylon (Isaiah 13) and of Edom (Isaiah 34). It was Babylon that brought the kingdom of Judah to an end, and there would have been no occasion for this kind of language earlier than the sixth century. There had been intermittent hostility between Judah and Edom for many years, but the depth of hatred expressed in ch. 34 must have been the result of the Edomites' treatment of refugees from the Babylonian army and their eventual occupation of areas that had belonged to Judah (cf. Ezek. 25:12–14; 35; Obadiah). These passages reflect the normal human emotions of those who have suffered cruelty, and should be taken as no more than that. We should rather be impressed by the inclusion in the prophetic books of materials accepting the existence of nations that had been their rivals or their enemies, and promising that Yahweh's intention for the future was peace for all.

The most surprising of such "peace pictures" appears in a series of brief oracles in Isa. 19:18–24. There is little evidence to date them, but to be able to speak of Assyria in this way probably means the Assyrian threat was long past. Assyria and Egypt represent Israel's two archetypal enemies, to the north and the south, but this prophet looks forward to a time when there will be a center for the worship of Yahweh in Egypt, and when Egypt and Assyria will worship together (19:19–23). Israel, Egypt, and Assyria will be equals, all of them blessed by Yahweh, who will say, "Blessed be Egypt my people, and Assyria the work of my hands, and Israel my heritage" (v. 24). This is the only place in the Old Testament where any group other than Israel is called by Yahweh "my people" or "the work of my hands," and these designations are expected one day to be applied to the old enemies who had caused them so much suffering![118]

Finally, a bit of speculation, called forth by the reading of Isaiah 1—39: If Jerusalem had fallen in 701, what might have become of the Yahwistic faith? We must not dwell for long on that, for it is historical fiction which we can make to come out any way we like. It may be worth a moment, however. If Jerusalem had fallen in 701, the upper classes would have been exiled to Assyria, as the north Israelites had been. Judah would have been incorporated into the Assyrian empire as a province, so there would be no reason to think of any continuity of the Davidic line. So much would be almost certain. Would there have been any way to preserve the words of the eighth-century prophets? We cannot answer that, for we do not even know what form they had taken in 701. Neither can we project the history of the people who worshiped Yahweh into the Neo-Babylonian and Persian periods, but we can make some guesses and raise some additional questions. Probably there would have been no restoration of Judean exiles from the Assyrian exile, since that did not happen for exiles from the Northern Kingdom. A Yahwistic cult may well have continued in Jerusalem, but would other prophets have arisen, there, or in exile, to help purify the religion, which at that time was highly syncretistic? In real history, Samaritanism, a conservative form of Yahwism, developed in the central part of the country—would that have happened if the history around them had been entirely different? Speculation—but it suggests that the deliverance of Jerusalem in 701 was as important as Isaiah 1—39 makes it out to be.

3

THE LATE SEVENTH AND EARLY SIXTH CENTURIES: THE NEO-BABYLONIAN THREAT AND THE DEATH OF JUDAH

After 701 Judah did not suffer invasion again for almost one hundred years, and the first two-thirds of that period of relative peace was a time of prophetic silence. If any prophetic voices were raised to interpret the meaning of that time, their words were not preserved. When the life of the kingdom of Judah drew near its end, however, prophets once again began to explain what God was doing in the midst of the coming disaster. They were Zephaniah and Jeremiah, with Nahum and Habakkuk adding comment on single aspects of the turmoil that began to sweep over the Near East.

Sennacherib did not campaign again in Syria/Palestine. What had been the kingdom of Israel remained under Assyrian rule as the provinces of Megiddo, Gilead, and Samaria. Judah was a tribute-paying vassal kingdom, as were Ammon, Moab, and Edom to the east and the Philistine cities of Ekron, Ashdod, Ashkelon, and Gaza to the west. Judah had been laid waste in 701. Sennacherib claimed he had destroyed forty-six cities, and he assigned some of the region of Judah to the rule of Ashdod, Ekron, and Gaza (*ANET*, 288). Apparently Hezekiah was left with only the territory immediately around Jerusalem. But, in spite of the fact that Hezekiah had been a leader of the revolt, his city and he himself were spared the terrible fate usually meted out to those who challenged Assyrian power. The temple and its cult remained, and a son of David was still on the throne. The words of the eighth-century prophets must have been preserved in written form by people (not identifiable, unfortunately) for whom their explanation of the fall of Samaria and Judah's bondage to Assyria remained important. There is no evidence that the message of those prophets effected any change in the lives of Judeans as a whole, however, as it would eventually change the entire outlook of Judeans in exile in the next century.

Sennacherib was followed by Esarhaddon (680–669 B.C.E.), who was determined to add the wealth of Egypt to his empire. The Phoenician and Philistine coastal regions thus experienced repeated forays by Assyrian armies during the seventh century, but Samaria and Judah seem to have been bypassed. Esarhaddon dealt with a revolt of Sidon in 677/6, invaded Egypt unsuccessfully in 675, and succeeded in conquering Egypt and Nubia in 670 (*ANET*, 293). The last of the successful Assyrian emperors was Ashurbanipal (668–627 B.C.E.). Egypt was too far from upper Mesopotamia for Assyria to maintain tight control, and Ashurbanipal had to deal with two rebellions, in 667 and 663. Soon he faced serious trouble nearer home, the revolt of his brother Shamash-shum-ukin, vassal king of Babylon (652 B.C.E.). His last campaign in the west was against Acco and Tyre in 645 (*ANET*, 300). By 635, Psammeticus I, who had made himself king of Egypt, had laid siege to Ashdod, finding it possible to move into Philistia without fear of reprisal from Assyria. With Ashurbanipal's death in 627, the empire rapidly began to fall apart, and kings in every part of the Near East were moving toward independence and conquests of their own.

Manasseh succeeded his father Hezekiah as king of Judah, and by paying regular tribute to Assyria was able to hold the throne for fifty-five years (2 Kings 21:1–18; *ANET*, 291, 294, 301). He was judged to be the worst king ever to rule in Judah by the author of 2 Kings, largely because of his advocacy of pagan religious practices (vv. 3–7), although he was also accused of shedding much innocent blood (v. 16). Studies by J. McKay and by Morton Cogan have shown that Assyria did not make a practice of imposing its own religion on conquered countries, so Manasseh's court appears to have been dominated by syncretists intent on assimilating Judean ways to those of the world at large.[1] The author of 2 Kings does claim that prophets were active in Manasseh's time, quoting an oracle which "the LORD said by his servants the prophets" (2 Kings 21:10–15). It has the familiar two-part reason/announcement form that appears throughout the prophetic books, and its use of "line and plummet" recalls Isa. 28:17, so it may be an authentic oracle from the time, although its attribution to "servants the prophets" is vague. It is the only suggestion of prophetic activity during this long period, and was clearly used at this point in the history to strengthen the author's point: that the fall of Judah was the result of the sins of Manasseh (2 Kings 23:26–27).

Manasseh's son Amon reigned only two years, then was assassinated by people of his own court. A counterrebellion led by an otherwise unidentified group called "the people of the land" was successful, and they declared Amon's son Josiah to be king, even though he was only eight years old (639 B.C.E.; 2 Kings 21:19–26). Presumably a regent ruled for him during his early years. In the eighteenth year of his reign he began a renovation of the temple, followed by extensive religious reforms, guided by a law book found during the repairs, a book now generally agreed to have been an early edition of Deuteronomy (2 Kings 22–23). Ashurbanipal was dead, Assyrian power was crumbling, Egypt now moved at will through the coastal region, and for a short time it was possible for a Judean king to chart his own course. This is the time of the ministry of Zephaniah and probably of the early part of the work of Jeremiah.

3.1 Zephaniah

During the years when the prophetic books were admired largely for their originality of language and thought, Zephaniah tended to be noticed only for its powerful description of the Day of Yahweh in 1:14–18, the basis for the great hymn *Dies Irae*. The rest of the book was much like those of the other judgment prophets, lacking the originality of Amos or Isaiah, and conveying essentially the same message. The present interest in the prophetic tradition should draw more attention to Zephaniah, however, for the book appears in an important place in the sequence. He was the first prophet on record to take up anew the message of judgment, applying it now exclusively to Judah, after a long interval from which no prophetic words have been preserved (except perhaps for additions to Micah and Isaiah, as noted earlier).

There is no hint in the book of Zephaniah that any religious reform has taken place in Jerusalem, so his work is usually dated before the events recorded in 2 Kings 22–23, c. 630.[2] The world was in turmoil. The Assyrian empire was crumbling, their posts in Philistia and Judah were deserted, Egypt was moving to take control of the Philistine cities, and reports of the movements of the Chaldeans from southern Mesopotamia, the Medes from Iran, and the northern tribes such as the Cimmerians and Scythians, may have reached Jerusalem. Hopes for independence must have been growing, and recovery of lost territory may have been a fleeting goal during Josiah's time.[3] Josiah's religious reforms were supported by a group influenced by the program contained in the book of Deuteronomy, as it existed at the time. Zephaniah cannot be identified with either of those aims, political or religious. He revived the message of Amos, from more than a century earlier: The end is near. When the first signs of hope had appeared on the international scene, and the cautious optimism of Deuteronomy was also current, he saw things differently, taking his place in the line of the eighth-century prophets.[4] The unusual superscription to his book, tracing his genealogy back four generations to one Hezekiah, has been much discussed. Why four generations, and was the Hezekiah really the eighth-century king of Judah? If he was, then it might be that the intention of the long genealogy was to make the claim that his ancestry connected him with the reforming king, and that he revived the words that had been addressed to his forefather.

The nations stood as much under divine judgment in 630 B.C.E. as they had in the time of Amos. Like Isaiah, Zephaniah includes Assyria, condemning them for their arrogance (Zeph. 2:13–15; cf. Isa. 10:5–19). But he found Judah to be worse than in the time of Isaiah. All the cultic variety promoted during Manasseh's reign still flourished: worship of Baal, of the host of heaven, and of Milcom (god of the Ammonites) or Molech (2 Kings 23:10).[5] Like Micah, he found the ruling class to be corrupt:

The officials within it
    are roaring lions;
its judges are evening wolves
    that leave nothing until the morning.
Its prophets are reckless,
    faithless persons;
its priests have profaned what is sacred,
    they have done violence to the law.
              (Zeph. 3:3–4; cf. 1:8–9)

Jerusalem was a "soiled, defiled, oppressing city" (3:1). The most striking accusation of all concerned a sort of practical atheism he found in his city. He claims there are some who say, "The LORD will not do good, nor will he do harm" (1:12). No need to deny the existence of God, when God does nothing. The idea is strongly reminiscent of that expressed by those Isaiah quoted as saying, "Let him make haste, let him speed his work that we may see it" (Isa. 5:19), but Zephaniah heard the denial that Yahweh is capable of doing anything put more bluntly. His list of the wrongs done in Jerusalem is shorter than those provided by the eighth-century prophets, but they suffice to show that things were no better than when Micah spoke of the death of the nation (Micah 3:9–12).

The turmoil affecting the world around Jerusalem is reflected in the book. Amos had in his own way spoken of universal judgment, with the condemnation of all of Israel's neighbors, and Israel as well (Amos 1—2). Micah had addressed the peoples and the earth before moving to the sentencing of Samaria and Jerusalem (Micah 1:2). Zephaniah is closest to Isa. 2:6–22 in his depiction of worldwide judgment in ch. 1. The international situation may help to account for his picture of cosmic death. It begins:

> I will utterly sweep away everything
> > from the face of the earth,
> > says the LORD,

and it ends:

> for a full, a terrible end
> > he will make of all the inhabitants of the earth.
> > > (Zeph. 1:2, 18b)

But what begins as the undoing of creation itself—humans and animals, birds of the air and fish of the sea (1:3)—moves quickly to Zephaniah's real concern: Judah and Jerusalem (1:4). It appears we are not to take the destruction of the whole earth literally, for later the book does not speak of restoration in terms of re-creation, as would seem to be necessary, and as other prophets did. One of those later prophets may help us to understand Zephaniah's outlook. In Isa. 65:17–25, the promise that God is about to create new heavens and new earth moves immediately to Jerusalem, and it seems all the prophet needs to say about the new creation can be said about Zion. So, in Zephaniah, the judgment of Jerusalem involves the whole world.

Death is as powerful a theme in Zephaniah as in the earlier prophets. The Day of the Lord, which Amos warned would be darkness not light, when feasts would be turned into mourning (Amos 5:18–20; 8:9–10), is described by Zephaniah at length (1:7–18) as a time of outcries and wailing,

> a day of distress and anguish,
> a day of ruin and devastation,
> a day of darkness and gloom,
> a day of clouds and thick darkness,
> > a day of trumpet blast and battle cry.
> > > (Zeph. 1:15–16a)

The Assyrian threat is over, so for Zephaniah, as for Amos, the enemy army is unnamed, and it is the Lord who brings about the judgment. This is no evaluation of the current international situation, but represents a contrary outlook in a time when there might have been hope, an outlook based on the conviction that God had another agenda.

This book reminds us of Amos and Isaiah in another way, because of its inclusion of oracles against a group of foreign nations. The nations chosen for attention do fit the circumstances of the time of Josiah. The Philistine cities had suffered repeatedly under the Assyrians, for a time they would be under Egyptian control, then would face the army of Nebuchadnezzar. Zephaniah's promise, "The seacoast shall become the possession of the remnant of the house of Judah," may allude to the fact that for a long time the Philistines had occupied Judean territory (Zeph. 2:5–7). Moab and Ammon would have been two of the vassal kingdoms looking for independence at this time (2:8–11). They are condemned for making boasts against Judean territory, something for which we do not have additional evidence in this period. In addition, their pride and arrogance are cited, a theme that reappears in the Moab oracles of Isaiah and Jeremiah (Isa. 16:6; Jer. 48:29–30). Pride is a major theme in both Isaiah and Zephaniah, and we shall soon see that it takes on a new form in the latter book. Both prophets also condemn Assyria for its *hybris*: "Is this the exultant city that lived secure, that said to itself, 'I am, and there is no one else'?" (Zeph. 2:15; cf. Isa. 10:15; 37:23–29). The nearest neighbors and the old enemy are thus the nations chosen for attention.[6]

The oracles against the nations are located between two passages that speak of the judgment of Jerusalem (1:4–18 and 3:1–8). One way of looking at the structure of the book is to note that a theme original to Zephaniah is introduced just after these two passages. In 2:1–4 and 3:9–13 the "humble" appear. If we think of those two texts as dividing the major part of the book into two parts, then it is apparent that the sovereignty of Yahweh, who is judge of all the earth, is portrayed in two, related ways. In 1:2–2:4 the judgment of Judah is described with language of cosmic proportions. In the section 2:5–3:13 the pattern used by Amos in chs. 1—2 is echoed: first the nations then God's own people are held responsible for their deeds. Both ways of affiming the universal sovereignty of Yahweh had already become traditional in the work of the earlier prophets, but what role do the humble now play, and who were they?

Zephaniah uses four words drawn from the vocabulary of lowliness, humility, poverty, and even affliction:

> Seek the LORD, all you humble (*'anaw*) of the land,
>   who do his commands;
> seek righteousness, seek humility (*'ănawah*);
>   perhaps you may be hidden on the day of the LORD's wrath.
>
> (Zeph. 2:3)

> For I will leave in the midst of you
>   a people humble (*'ani*) and lowly (*dal*) . . .
>   the remnant of Israel.
>
> (Zeph. 3:12–13a)

Except for Isa. 66:2, a postexilic text, these terms are used elsewhere in the prophetic books to refer only to physical distress, from which people ought to be saved, and never in a spiritual, positive sense.[7] There is a body of literature in the Old Testament that speaks of poverty or lowliness in a metaphorical way, however, using the terms to refer to one's appropriate opinion of oneself in the presence of God:

> For you deliver a humble people,
>> but the haughty eyes you bring down.
>>> (Ps. 18:27)

> He leads the humble in what is right,
>> and teaches the humble his way.
>>> (Ps. 25:9)

> For though the LORD is high, he regards the lowly;
>> but the haughty he perceives from far away.
>>> (Ps. 138:6)

> For the LORD takes pleasure in his people;
>> he adorns the humble with victory.
>>> (Ps. 149:4)

> Toward the scorners he is scornful,
>> but to the humble he shows favor.
>>> (Prov. 3:34)

> When pride comes, then comes disgrace;
>> but wisdom is with the humble.
>>> (Prov. 11:2)

> It is better to be of a lowly spirit among the poor
>> than to divide the spoil with the proud.
>>> (Prov. 16:19)

The literature of wisdom and of prayer used these terms as the opposites of pride, haughtiness, and scornfulness, and Zephaniah has clearly chosen them because the pride that leads humans to choose their own course, scorning the way of life provided by Yahweh, is a major theme of his work (e.g., 1:6, 12–13; 2:10, 15; 3:2, 11). These two passages, each of them following an extended announcement of judgment, are thus a distinctive part of Zephaniah's message, and would appear to deserve more attention than they have been given.

The text of 2:1 is difficult, but A. Vanlier Hunter and Adele Berlin have shown that 2:1–2 continue the words of judgment in ch. 1. The verbs chosen compare the nation with straw—worthless, as Hunter sees it, or highly flammable, according to Berlin.[8] Verses 1–2 are thus taken to be an ironic call, similar to Amos's "Come to Bethel— and transgress" (Amos 4:4), while v. 3 is addressed to another audience, those Zephaniah identifies as "the humble, who do his commands." To them presumably the prophet can address a serious exhortation to "seek righteousness, seek humility," but he maintains the basic outlook on the future held by Amos, offering only a highly conditional promise: "Perhaps you may be hidden on the day of the LORD's wrath" (recall the "perhaps" [NRSV "it may be"] in Amos 5:15). Neither Amos nor the other eighth-century prophets indicate whether they can identify any likely prospects for the exhortations contained in their books (cf. Hos. 10:12; 12:6; 14:1–3; Isa. 1:18–20). Zephaniah has a word for them, but who were "the humble" in his time? Unfortunately he does not identify them further, so it would be only guesswork at this point to ponder whether there existed a group within Judah who not only preserved the words of the prophets but sought to live them, and who may have designated themselves in this way. The terms may simply be used as they are in Psalms and Proverbs, to denote anyone whose life was not marked by pride, hypocrisy, and arrogance.

The use of these words to designate some people within Judah who might truly be called a faithful remnant (contrary to what the preexilic prophets usually say) reappears in the promise for a better future in Zeph. 3:9–10. Recent commentaries are more inclined than those of the past to accept this as the work of the seventh-century prophet, and it certainly does contain the same contrast of pride with humility that appears earlier in the book (3:11–12). Here is a prophetic form of the promise found in the Psalms and Proverbs, that one day God will justify those who know themselves to be spiritually humble and lowly.

Zephaniah as Part of the Whole Prophetic Message

Most of this book fits what we know of the late seventh century very well, but the hymn that concludes it (3:14–20) seems likely to have been another of the additions made to the preexilic prophetic books in order to add to them the insights of later prophecy. The most important clue here is the reference to restoration from exile, in v. 20. Zephaniah's understanding of the coming judgment has been wholesale destruction, and he has never spoken of exile. It seems most appropriate to understand promises of restoration to have been made to people who needed such promises, those who actually were in exile. With this in mind, we then note in this psalm a good many features typical of Isaiah 40—55, the exilic prophet. Although there is much in Zephaniah that seems to be a reapplication of the message of Isaiah 1—39, two things are missing from Zeph. 1:1–3:13: Zion theology and the theology associated with Davidic kingship. But Zion appears in the hymn, as the recipient of promises of a glorious future—with a tone rather different from the promises in 3:11–13. The true king is Yahweh, as in the psalms of the enthronement of the Lord (e.g., Psalms 95; 97; 98). For those in exile who had experienced the fulfilment of Zephaniah's awful message and had learned that the prophets had been right, the words "And I will save the lame and gather the outcast, and I will change their shame into praise and renown in all the earth" were a necessary addition to the earlier work, a reassurance that "the sound of the day of the LORD is bitter" (Zeph. 1:14) represents only the first act.

3.2 Nahum

The fall of the Assyrian capital, Nineveh, in 612 B.C.E. marked the end of the world's first great empire, and it must have been a cause for rejoicing—briefly—

for many people in the Middle East. Unfortunately, other empire builders would follow—Babylonians, Persians, Greeks, and Romans—but the feelings of those from whom oppression was momentarily lifted have been expressed in their classic form in the book of Nahum. This prophet is known among scholars as one of the greatest poets of the Old Testament, but his status as a prophet, among modern interpreters, is not so secure.[9] His is a one-subject book (like Obadiah), the subject is the fall of a foreign nation, and he says nothing of the sins of Israel and Judah. If bad news is the mark of a true prophet, as Jeremiah once claimed (Jer. 28:8–9), then Nahum would not seem to qualify. Israel, however, appears to have judged him according to another standard, that of Deut. 18:21–22, for his prediction of the fall of Nineveh did come true, and his book was added to the collection of prophetic works.

There are two dates of obvious importance for locating the book in history. Nahum 3:8 refers to the conquest of Thebes by Assyria (663/61), so the book is later than that date, and most agree that it was written before the fall of Nineveh in 612. Some scholars argue that it is best understood as having been written not long after the fall of Thebes, when the memory of that event would still be fresh. It would thus speak of Nineveh's demise when Assyria was still strong, and would be a message of hope to a subject people at a time when there seemed to be little basis for hope. Others think its tone of rejoicing over the fall of the great empire is a better fit to the time when Assyria was losing its grip on the provinces, and would be a prophetic explanation of its breakup as the work of Yahweh. There is no additional evidence to enable us to date the book accurately within this period, but that need not impede our investigation of its theology.

Ashurbanipal's death in 627 coincided with the rise of serious threats to Assyria. The Medes, in northern Iran, had gained control of Persia (southern Iran), and were moving toward the west. In 625 their king, Cyaxares, besieged Nineveh, but was repulsed. To the south, Nabopolassar had made himself king in Babylon in 626, and soon the Medes and the Chaldeans (the ruling class in Babylonia) became allies in the effort to overthrow the Assyrians. Cyaxares took the old capital, Ashur, in 614, and Nineveh fell in 612 after a two-and-one-half-month siege. What was left of the Assyrian army fled west to Haran, under the leadership of Ashuruballit. Nabopolassar and his army seem to have arrived just in time to share in the division of the spoils, with the Medes claiming the northern part of the empire, and the Chaldeans the southern part. Nahum's description of the attack on Nineveh and of its fate is so powerful and so detailed that some have even suggested he must have been an eyewitness to the event, but the poetry can be explained in another way. Since Judah had been under the rule of Assyria for a long time, some first-hand information about the capital city would probably have been readily available to people who had never left their homeland, and there had been enough attacks on cities near Judah in the seventh century that it would not be hard for a great poet to reproduce very accurately the effects of siege and fall. It is more than a great piece of war poetry, however, and its value for our study of the prophetic tradition is to be found almost entirely in the materials of the first chapter, because of their relationship to Nahum's predecessors and to the Jerusalem cult.[10]

Rex Mason has written of Nahum, "We shall not read it properly unless we see it as part of 'The Book of the Twelve,' . . . the 'Prophets' as a whole, and, indeed, the entire canon,"[11] exactly what I have set out to do with respect to all the prophets. It is of special importance for Nahum, however, since it is a single-subject book. He stands in continuity with Isaiah and Zephaniah, for they also condemned the arrogance and cruelty of Assyria (Isa. 10:7–19; 37:22–29; and Isa. 14:4–21 if originally addressed to a king of Assyria; Zeph. 2:13–15). Assyria's world-dominating power had raised two serious theological issues for Judeans. The first was power itself. What good did it do them to have a God who could not protect them from a foreign king who did as he pleased with them? Isaiah's effort to explain that was to say that Yahweh was in charge after all, and that it was he who was sending the Assyrians as his instruments of judgment for the sins of Israel and Judah (e.g., Isa. 5:25–30; 7:17–25; 8:5–8; 10:5–6). But that raised an issue as serious as the former one, if not more so. Assyria was certainly no better than Israel and Judah, and all the evidence indicated that the conqueror also ought to stand under Yahweh's judgment. How could Assyrian domination be accepted as the will of the God they believed to be just and righteous? Can both the power and the goodness of Yahweh be believed when Assyria rules the world?

The answer given in the texts from Isaiah and Zephaniah noted above was emphatically reaffirmed by Nahum. God has used Assyrian power for his own purposes, but that by no means justifies Assyrian cruelty. They will be held responsible for their use of the power given them, and will inevitably be judged as harshly as they have treated their victims. Habakkuk will accept that as a partial answer, but will recognize that it does not deal adequately with the second issue, the goodness of God. He will offer a very different kind of answer to that question.

Nahum begins with a theophany, and the theophanic tradition plus his original contributions to it contain the entire theological message of the book. Since it is traditional language and the rest of the book is highly original poetry, earlier scholars tended to downgrade its importance, and many assumed it must have been added to the prophet's work at a later time. Without the theophany, however, the book is just a war poem and would scarcely qualify as a prophetic work. Until recently the poem in ch. 1 drew the attention of scholars more because of its form than its content. It appears to be a fragmentary acrostic, containing in vv. 2–8 lines beginning with each of the first eleven letters of the alphabet. It requires some ingenuity to find it, and those who believe it is there have tried to account for its fragmentary form in various ways.[12] Most of those efforts need not concern us greatly, but the evidence suggests an explanation, accepted in several recent works, that will correspond well with the function the poem now serves. Nahum may be using a theophanic poem that already existed in acrostic form, quoting it freely and adding his own emphases to it (especially in vv. 2–3). The acrostic form was apparently of no great interest to him, so he modified it as he pleased, and dropped it completely after v. 8, perhaps because the remaining subject matter was not as useful to him. If this seems a likely explanation, then it will be clear that his choice of theophany and his distinctive use of it will be keys to the theology of the book.

"Theophany" in the Old Testament refers to those texts that speak of the coming of Yahweh from a definite place and the tumult in nature resulting from his nearness. The place is most often Sinai or the southern desert, although at least once it is Zion (Ps. 50:2). What makes these poems distinctive ways of talking about the nearness of God is their extensive use of imagery drawn from the most terrifying of natural phenomena: the quaking of the earth, the melting of mountains, windstorms, clouds, rain, fire, and darkness. The classic theophany was the appearance of God above Mount Sinai, as described in prose in Exodus 19, but the others in the Old Testament are found in poems of great power. Efforts to explain them have often assumed they were evidence that in early times Yahweh was a nature god. Most of the phenomena that appear are the kind that accompany volcanic eruptions, leading some scholars to suggest Yahweh was originally a God associated with a volcano. The nearest volcanoes to be active in historic times are in northern Arabia,[13] so one may feel unsure how much impact such impressive events would have had on Judeans. There is more support for associating Yahweh with the thunderstorm, as was done with Baal and Hadad in neighboring cultures, although that does not account for all the imagery, either. The home of theophanic language in Israel appears to have been the Jerusalem cult, for it appears in longer or shorter forms in several of the psalms.[14] J. H. Eaton has proposed that these poems originated in the cult not as a result of some direct experience with nature, but as prophetic speech, the expression of a personal encounter with God.[15] If so, this would both explain their appearance in the books of the prophets and the otherwise puzzling references to natural phenomena. The inspired person would be expressing, as best he or she could, how it feels to be in the immediate presence of God.[16] The immediate sense is that of being overpowered, as indicated in Isa. 6:5; Ezek. 1:28; Dan. 10:9–10. That feeling may thus have been put into words by alluding to the most awe-inspiring natural phenomena imaginable, including things no one is likely to have seen, such as the melting of mountains and the drying up of the sea.

These efforts to discover the original setting of theophanic language are relevant to our work because although there is continuity between the Psalms and the prophetic books there is a difference in the way the theophanies have been used in those two parts of the Old Testament. The most impressive example in the Psalter is in Psalm 18, which is a thanksgiving psalm. After describing the trouble he had been in (vv. 4–5) and his cry for help (v. 6) the psalmist provides a terrifying description of the coming of the Lord (vv. 7–15), but this is the God who had come to save (vv. 16–19) and who is now being praised at length in the remainder of the psalm. Here, as in Rudolf Otto's description of the Holy One, the *tremendum* is always accompanied by the *fascinans*:

> . . . he delivered me, because he delighted in me. . . .
> With the loyal you show yourself loyal;
>   with the blameless you show yourself blameless;
> with the pure you show yourself pure. . . .
> This God—his way is perfect;
>   the promise of the LORD proves true;
> he is a shield for all who take refuge in him.
>   (Ps. 18:19b, 25–26a, 30)

Elsewhere in the Psalter, these descriptions of the terrifying effects of the coming of the Lord also speak of the God who comes to save. Psalm 29 celebrates the kingship of the Lord, concluding with "May the LORD give strength to his people! May the LORD bless his people with peace!" (Ps. 29:11). Psalm 68:7–10 praises the God who appeared in theophany to provide for his people in the wilderness. Psalm 77 is a lament, but in the section that probably functions as the expression of confidence the psalmist recalls the wonders of old, disruptions of nature which he associates not with disaster but with God's guidance of his people through the wilderness (vv. 11–20). Psalm 97 is a hymn praising the kingship of Yahweh, exalting his power over the other gods with theophanic language. The function of the brief passage in Psalm 50 does appear to be somewhat different (vv. 2–3), for this is a psalm in which God comes to distinguish those who are truly faithful among his people from those who think all he asks of them is sacrifice. It recalls the making of the covenant at Sinai, and that probably accounts for the allusions to "devouring fire and a mighty tempest."[17]

The theophanies in the prophetic books take on a much more judgmental tone, and Nahum may have been the first to make a very extensive use of one, although Micah does include a brief passage of this type to begin his judgment of Samaria:

> For lo, the LORD is coming out of his place,
>> and will come down and tread upon the high places of the earth.
> Then the mountains will melt under him
>> and the valleys will burst open,
> like wax near the fire,
>> like waters poured down a steep place.
>
> (Micah 1:3–4)

It is an impressive theophany, although not an extended one, and there seems no good reason to deny it to Micah as a new use of the genre. No more will the Lord come to save his people, but to judge them. Amos had used similar language in the same kind of setting, but without making an explicit move from theophany to judgment (Amos 9:5–6). In Isaiah theophany is used to proclaim judgment, but of Assyria rather than Judah, in a passage that thus appears to be a predecessor of Nahum (Isa. 30:27–33). In its present form it is associated with a festival celebrating the deliverance (vv. 29, 32), however, so this may be a use of the theme which should be dated later than Nahum. We have seen close relationships between Isaiah and Nahum, with reference to their attitude toward Assyria, so it does not matter a great deal which text comes first. The Isaiah passage does introduce something that is not characteristic of theophanies in the Psalter and that is greatly emphasized in Nahum, so one is inclined to give the latter prophet credit for it. That is the theme of the wrath of God (Isa. 30:27).

Wrath would scarcely play an appropriate role in the theophanies of the Psalms, where God comes to save, and Nahum may be the first among the prophets to introduce it (unless Isa. 30:27 is earlier). He does so in a most emphatic way:

A jealous and avenging God is the LORD,
   the LORD is avenging and wrathful (*ba'al ḥemah*);
the LORD takes vengeance on his adversaries
   and rages (*noṭer*) against his enemies.

(Nahum 1:2)

Who can stand before his indignation?
   Who can endure the heat of his anger (*ḥăron 'appo*)?
His wrath (*ḥămatho*) is poured out like fire,
   and by him the rocks are broken in pieces.

(Nahum 1:6)

He has used four of the synonyms for anger in these two verses, and the wrath of God appears elsewhere in theophanies only in Habakkuk 3 and Isaiah 13, both later than this book. Theophany has been moved to a new level in Nahum. That is made all the more apparent by his unusual use of two other terms in v. 2: jealous (or "zealous," *qanno'*) and avenging (*noqem*). Note that the latter occurs three times in the verse. These are unusual terms for the early prophets. Isaiah uses the root *qana'* in a positive sense twice, in the formula "the zeal of the LORD of hosts will do this" (Isa. 9:7; 37:32). Zephaniah uses it twice of God's destructive zeal (Zeph. 1:18; 3:8). Other uses in the prophets are later. The root *naqam* occurs only three times in books ascribed to prophets earlier than Nahum, Isa. 1:24; 34:8; and Micah 5:14, but the last two passages are likely to be later in date, and that may also be true for Isa. 1:24.

We know the former root best from the Sinai tradition, for the Second Commandment reads in part, "for I the LORD your God am a jealous God, punishing children for the iniquity of parents, to the third and the fourth generation of those who reject me, but showing steadfast love to the thousandth generation of those who love me and keep my commandments" (Exod. 20:5–6). God's "jealousy," a poor choice of words in English for a divine attribute, is his zeal for the maintenance of the relationship established with his people. He made them his own when he brought them out of Egypt, and his zeal extends both to keeping them safe from their enemies (as in Isa. 26:11; Joel 2:18–19) and to making sure they are fit to be his partners, which can lead to chastisement. As to the second word, "vengeance" in the hands of God is not irrational or unjust revenge, but is the exact meting out of justice when it has failed to be upheld at the human level.[18] In other words, Nahum claims the time has finally come for God to make right a situation in the world that has gone terribly wrong. Suffering under the Assyrians has gone on for so long, and human efforts have not succeeded in breaking their power, that God's reaction must now be called his wrath and the heat of his anger. Nineveh is the "city of bloodshed, utterly deceitful, full of booty—no end to the plunder!"(Nahum 3:1). "Who has ever escaped your endless cruelty?" (Nahum 3:19). Nahum took from the Jerusalem cult the most powerful way of describing the coming of God to save his people, the theophany, and made it depict how the warrior, motivated by anger against oppression, comes to set things right by destroying the enemy.

He has not thereby said the character of the God of Israel has changed, however. This sometimes dangerous zeal (*qin'ath*) was an aspect of the God who revealed himself at Sinai, but he also made himself known as "Yahweh, Yahweh, a God merciful and gracious, slow to anger, and abounding in steadfast love and faithfulness, keeping steadfast love for the thousandth generation, forgiving iniquity and transgression and sin, yet by no means clearing the guilty, but visiting the iniquity of the parents upon the children and the children's children, to the third and the fourth generation" (Exod. 34:6–7). Part of that is quoted in the Second Commandment, concerning not clearing the guilty, and Nahum has used both the commandment's reference to the zeal of the Lord and to his not clearing the guilty in Nahum 1:2–3. He also knows and uses the great, divine self-affirmation of Exodus 34, however, for v. 3 begins, "The LORD is slow to anger but great in power." It is a brief reference, and surprising in the midst of all the wrath vocabulary, but there can be no question that it alludes to God's merciful character. It is qualified here by "but great in power," probably because of the possible misunderstanding of all the words about compassion and patience in Exodus 34; for some might then think that God puts up with too much and never gets around to doing anything about iniquity. "Justice delayed is no justice," someone said, and Nahum insists God will wait no longer. Familiar hymnic language appears just at the end of the theophany, as it does in the Psalter, as further evidence that Nahum's message, focused narrowly on God's destruction of the enemy, does not supersede or ignore completely the rest that Israel believed about God's true character:

> The LORD is good,
>   a stronghold in a day of trouble;
> he protects those who take refuge in him,
>   even in a rushing flood.
>   (Nahum 1:7–8)

Zephaniah and Nahum revived parts of the message of Isaiah, applying it to their time. Both reaffirmed Isaiah's insistence that Assyria, in spite of apparently invincible power, was ultimately responsible to Yahweh and would be judged for its arrogant cruelty. Zephaniah also reformulated the message of his predecessors, that the people of Yahweh were supposed to be different from the nations, but they had failed, and radical changes lay ahead. Shortly after these two prophets another, Habakkuk, tackled for the first time flaws in the traditional prophetic message, raised by the claim that it was God who sent foreign armies to punish the wicked. How did that make things any better? One kind of answer would finally become evident in the exile, but earlier Habakkuk found another kind.

3.3 Habakkuk

This book is different from all the other prophetic books, but when one reads through the canon of the prophets recognizing that this collection came into being because each of the books contributed to the understanding of what God was doing in the death and resurrection of his people, then it will be seen to play an appropriate, perhaps a necessary role. It asks what would appear to be a modern question about the way earlier prophets had interpreted the actions of the armies that had invaded their country: What does an army of occupation do that can properly be understood as fulfilling the will of a just and righteous God?[19]

Habakkuk is the first to be designated "the prophet" (*hannabi'*) in the superscription to his book. Elsewhere the title is used only of the postexilic prophets Haggai and Zechariah, whose work was closely associated with the reestablishment of the temple. This has led a good many scholars to suggest Habakkuk may have been a professional prophet, active in the Jerusalem cult. Support for this has been found in his use of a psalm of lament in Hab. 1:2–4, 12–17, the introit in 2:20, and the theophany in ch. 3. We have found that nearly every prophetic book contains materials that had their origins in worship, however, so no firm conclusions can be drawn about Habakkuk's profession. There are also close associations between the vocabulary and themes of wisdom literature and this book, but that should not lead to the claim he was really one of the professional sages of the Jerusalem court.[20] It reminds us, rather, that the language of the sages had a widespread influence on the literature of the Old Testament,[21]

The central theme, the basic structure, and the choices of genres in Habakkuk and Job are remarkably similar. Both deal with suffering and the justice of God. Both make a prominent use of the lament genre, contain dialogue, and conclude with a theophany.[22] But the special characteristics of this book do not put Habakkuk outside the ranks of the prophets whose canonicity depends on what they contributed to the understanding of the death and resurrection of Israel. The prominence of the prophetic "I" in this book brings those events that affected the life of the *nation*, as other prophets saw it, down to the level of the individual Judean. What was to become of him or her as all that had once seemed dependable was collapsing? We first saw Zephaniah choosing a term—the humble—to designate some people whose present faithfulness might be the basis for a better future (Zeph. 2:3; 3:12–13). Habakkuk also makes a distinction at the individual level, unlike other prophets who thought almost entirely of the death of the nation. His term was "the righteous" (*tsaddiq*, 1:4, 13; 2:4), used in ch. 1 in one of its primary senses, as the innocent, but with broader overtones in 2:4.

Although there is no biographical detail for Habakkuk except for "the prophet" in 1:1, the person of the prophet is more prominent in this book than any other except for that of his contemporary, Jeremiah. The prophetic "I" does not appear very often within the canonical books, and the fact that it is usually found in an expression of dismay of some sort casts a ray of light on what it must have been like to be one of those prophets:

> Woe is me! I am lost, for I am a man of unclean lips, and I live among a
> people of unclean lips; yet my eyes have seen the King, the LORD of hosts!
> (Isa. 6:5)

Then I said, "How long, O Lord?"
(Isa. 6:11)

> Ah, Lord GOD! Truly I do not know how to speak, for I am only a boy. (Jer. 1:6)

O LORD, you have enticed me,
  and I was enticed.
(Jer. 20:7; and see the other so-called confessions of Jeremiah)

> Ah Lord GOD! I have never defiled myself. (Ezek. 4:14)

O Lord GOD, forgive, I beg you!
  How can Jacob stand?
  He is so small!
                              (Amos 7:2)

There are some exceptions:

> Here am I; send me! (Isa. 6:8)

The spirit of the Lord GOD is upon me,
  because the LORD has anointed me;
he has sent me to bring good news to the oppressed,
                              (Isa. 61:1)

The most remarkable exception to the expressions of dismay is Hab. 3:17–19.

Unlike most prophetic books this one has a simple outline. It begins with dialogue between the prophet and God (1:2–17), leading to the report of a vision (2:1–5). A sequence of woe (*hoy*) oracles follows, concluding with "But the LORD is in his holy temple; let all the earth keep silence before him!" (2:6–20). A psalm, with its own superscription and concluding rubric, completes the book. Whether the psalm may have been a later addition to chs. 1—2 has been widely discussed, largely because of its liturgical notes, and when the Habakkuk Pesher from Qumran was found to deal only with the first two chapters, that was momentarily thought to settle the matter.[23] On second thought, however, it may be that the commentator did not include the psalm because it was not as useful for his purpose, and most contemporary interpreters now agree that whether or not the two parts of the book once had a separate existence, the psalm now forms an appropriate conclusion to the book.[24]

Some time ago one scholar admitted that Habakkuk has suffered more from literary criticism than any other prophet,[25] and although some of the excesses of the past have been rejected, the "improvements" to the book that are being suggested are still extensive.[26] The text is very difficult in places, and new emendations continue to be proposed. The lack of specific historic references has led to a great number of hypothetical situations for the book, most of which need not concern us here. We shall accept the one historical reference in the book, to the Chaldeans in 1:6, as authentic, and noting that there is no hint that Jerusalem has fallen, will agree with the majority of scholars that Habakkuk's message is a reaction to the abuses perpetrated in Judah during the reign of Jehoiakim (608–598 B.C.E.; 2

Kings 23:34–24:6) and to the appearance in Syria/Palestine of the Chaldean army under Nebuchadnezzar (the beginning of the Neo-Babylonian empire).

Josiah had been killed at Megiddo by Pharoah Necho (2 Kings 23:29) and was succeeded by his son Jehoahaz, who reigned only three months before he was taken by Necho to Egypt where he died (2 Kings 23:31–34; Jer. 22:10–12). Necho placed Jehoahaz's brother Jehoiakim on the throne, and the latter remained loyal to Egypt until sometime after Nebuchadnezzar defeated the Egyptian army at Carchemish in 605. He then transferred his loyalty to Nebuchadnezzar (2 Kings 24:1; Jer. 46:2), but rebelled after the failure of the Babylonian effort to invade Egypt, leading Nebuchadnezzar to lay siege to Jerusalem (2 Kings 24:7–11). Jehoiakim apparently died during the siege and was succeeded briefly by his son Jehoiachin, who was exiled to Babylonia after the city fell in 597 B.C.E. (2 Kings 24:12–17; *ANET*, 564). Jehoiakim gets a bad report in both 2 Kings and Jeremiah, and the conditions in Judah that Jeremiah reports at length seem to have been the basis for Habakkuk's lament in 1:2–4.

In keeping with the rest of the prophetic tradition, the most natural reading of 1:2–4 is to take it as Habakkuk's complaint about the kinds of injustice within Judah that his predecessors had condemned. Instead of proclaiming a word from God announcing the judgment of the wicked, however, Habakkuk takes the unique course of addressing his own word to God, asking why there is still no evidence of divine judgment. Isaiah also had lamented the sinfulness of his people, in Isa. 1:4–9, but he addressed them, not God. Habakkuk's words take the same form as the psalms of lament, when sufferers in Israel took their distress to God in prayer (cf. Pss. 13:1–2; 22:1; 74:10; 88:1, 13; 89:46). What follows, in 1:5–11, is clearly a word from God, but is not an oracle of deliverance, as some readers have assumed, creating serious problems for understanding the book. It is God's traditional response to wickedness among his people, as we have heard it from Amos through Zephaniah: "For I am rousing the Chaldeans, that fierce and impetuous nation" (Hab. 1:6). Amos had said, "An adversary shall surround the land, and strip you of your defense; and your strongholds shall be plundered" (Amos 3:11). Isaiah had said, "He will raise a signal for a nation far away, and whistle for a people at the ends of the earth; here they come, swiftly, speedily!" (Isa. 5:26). Zephaniah had recently taken up again the old message of the "day of trumpet blast and battle cry against the fortified cities and against the lofty battlements" (Zeph. 1:16). There had been time enough to reflect on the results of the coming of the Assyrians, however, and Habakkuk was not as ready as Zephaniah to accept God's message that he was using enemy armies to accomplish his purpose for his people.

Indeed, Habakkuk has heard from the earlier prophets (e.g., Isa. 10:5–6), and now from God himself, "You have marked them for judgment; and you, O Rock, have established them for punishment" (Hab. 1:12), but how is greater violence the solution to violence?

> Your eyes are too pure to behold evil,
>   and you cannot look on wrongdoing;

that is what he has been taught and tries to go on believing, *but*

why do you look on the treacherous,
   and are silent when the wicked swallow
those more righteous than they?
(Hab. 1:13)

Has the entire prophetic interpretation of history been a mistake? They have been maintaining that God acts to uphold or restore justice on earth, but Habakkuk looks in vain for evidence of it. He may have been the earliest in Israel to demand better evidence for God's justice, and it appears to have been the work of the earlier prophets that led to his dilemma. The only other prophet to challenge God is Jeremiah, but his complaints concern his own personal misfortune.

Habakkuk's report of the vision that followed is a tantalizing one, for we had hoped for more. Indeed he records not a vision but a word, and it is brief and cryptic. There are two as yet unresolved problems; the meaning of the second word in 2:4, and the question whether v. 5 should be understood as somehow reinforcing that verse, or is actually the introduction to the verses that follow. The word 'uppĕlah in v. 4 occurs only here in the Hebrew Bible, and may mean something like "puffed up." The structure of the verse suggests it should stand in contrast to "righteous" in v. 4b, so it might be used metaphorically to mean "presumptuous," but that is guesswork, like every other attempt at translation.[27] For our purposes the three words in v. 4b, which are not problematic, are of great importance and we shall concentrate on them. They promise life, and in a collection of books whose main theme so far has been death that is remarkable in itself. The theme of life is so rare that even the word "life" (hayah) occurs only a few times in the earlier prophetic books. The only significant uses are in Amos:

Seek me and live;
   but do not seek Bethel, . . .
Seek the LORD and live,
   or he will break out against the house of Joseph with fire, . . .
Seek good and not evil, that you may live.
(Amos: 5:4, 6, 14)

In the last reference seeking good is then defined as establishing justice in the gate, and the promise of life is qualified by "it may be that the LORD, the God of hosts, will be gracious to the remnant of Joseph" (Amos 5:15). Amos was echoing a cultic formula here, as the parallels in the Psalms reveal (Pss. 24:6; 27:8; 34:10 [MT 11]), and putting it to his own, new use. For him it contained a very modest promise, and functioned primarily as a warning. The only other occurrences of hayah in prophetic literature earlier than Habakkuk are in Hosea:

After two days he will revive us;
   on the third day he will raise us up,
   that we may live before him.
(Hos. 6:2)

This is probably a statement of the people, which Hosea doubts. In Hos. 14:7 [MT 8] a promise for the future reads, "They shall again live beneath my shadow."[28] The fact that *hayah* is a truly rare word in the preexilic prophets already points to the uniqueness of the promise in Hab. 2:4b. Amos's use of "live" in a borrowed cultic formula and Habakkuk's uses of cultic material elsewhere in his book will be helpful clues to what he meant by "live."

The noun "righteous" (*tsaddiq*) is almost as rare in Habakkuk's precursors. In Amos 2:6; 5:12; Isa. 5:23; 29:21 the righteous are the innocent people who are oppressed by those in power, and this is exactly the way Habakkuk uses the word in 1:4, 13. It is a common term in the wisdom literature and appears in proverbial form in Hosea:

> For the ways of the LORD are right,
> > and the upright (*tsaddiq*) walk in them,
> > but transgressors stumble in them.
> > > (Hos. 14:9 [MT 10])

The only other occurrence is in a promise, in Isa. 3:10: "Tell the innocent (*tsaddiq*) how fortunate they are, for they shall eat the fruit of their labors."[29]

The third word, *ĕmunah*, best translated "faithfulness," is not used of humans by any prophet earlier than Habakkuk. It specifically means "truth" as his contemporary Jeremiah uses it, and is not used at all by Ezekiel.[30]

Shortly after the book of Habakkuk was produced, Ezekiel (who could have been a contemporary) associated "life" with the "righteous" in a very emphatic way (Ezek. 3:21; 18:5–9, 24; 33:12–13). He was a priest, and it has been shown that the way he uses these words depends on his cultic background. "Live" is a declaration that God has accepted the worshiper and intends to bless him or her with all that "life" implied in Hebrew usage.[31] Merely existing did not count as living in Hebrew thought. When sick, weak, in danger, or one's reputation was hurt, one was in the grip of death and not fully alive. To be alive was to have vigor, honor, and security. The parallel in Ezekiel thus helps us to understand Habakkuk's association of righteousness with life. He speaks of those whom God declares to be innocent and thus intends to bless.

The instrumental and thus crucial "by his faithfulness" is original with Habakkuk, however. For Ezekiel what was instrumental was walking in God's statutes and observing his ordinances (e.g., Ezek. 18:9), and that surely would be part of what Habakkuk meant by it. In the context of this book, however, there must be more to it.[32] There is no evidence of blessing for the righteous now, and the temptation to doubt God's power to do good (or do anything, recall Zeph. 1:12) is very strong, as Habakkuk 1 indicates. If one gives in to that (as Hab. 2:1 shows us the prophet did not do), then there would be no reason to continue walking in God's statutes. In other words, without faith there would be no reason for faithfulness, and faith is "the assurance of things hoped for, the conviction of things not seen" (Heb. 11:1)—exactly Habakkuk's situation. This book, which expresses doubt concerning the purposes of God as no other prophetic book does, moves toward life as no predecessor had done. There is no "perhaps" here, but instead a promise of a way for the individual facing disaster to endure it, and more: to achieve a personal triumph over it.

The earliest prophetic book, Amos, considers the possibility that there may be a few survivors of the national disaster, and has a tentative bit of hope to offer them (Amos 5:14–15). Hosea and Isaiah looked for a basis to say more about what God would bring out of the coming calamity (e.g., Hosea 2; Isa. 1:24–28), and Zephaniah also hoped for more than mere survival for a few (Zeph. 2:3; 3:11–13). In Habakkuk's time there was still no evidence God was doing anything for the faithful. He had nothing to say about national destiny, but did receive a new promise for the righteous, the innocent who still were deprived of justice. It was still a modest promise, for it called upon them to remain faithful during the present time when there were no visible supports for faithfulness, but it offered them life, if they persevered. The emphasis on waiting, in Hab. 2:3, very likely sheds light on the kind of faithfulness called for in such a time.

The truly skeptical would call this no answer, for it calls for one to go on believing while God has still apparently done nothing. So, the remaining two parts of the book are essential to its message. Few scholars have agreed with my suggestion that the woe oracles in Hab. 2:2–19 were intended as a mock funeral song, but there is some evidence to support it, and if that is true, the song takes on great power, and makes a remarkable fit into its surroundings.[33] As argued in connection with Amos 5:18, 6:1 the cry *hoy* originally carried strong overtones of grief. Most of the uses of the word in the prophets have been taken to have the effect of a curse, and it is true that there is no indication of grief in some of them, but frequently enough they appear in contexts of death and lamentation (e.g., Jer. 22:18; 30:7; 34:5). In Habakkuk, the emotion is clearly joy, but it is joy because a tyrant is dead (2:10). The principal theme that runs through the first four stanzas is the reversal of fortune—power turned to weakness—and this is one of the major themes of funeral songs. "How the mighty have fallen!" are the words David used to lament the deaths of Saul and Jonathan (2 Sam. 1:19, 25). The same theme reappears in the song of rejoicing over a tyrant's death in Isa. 14:4–21: "How the oppressor has ceased! . . . Your pomp is brought down to Sheol. . . . Is this the man who made the earth tremble?" (vv. 4, 11, 16). As in Isaiah 14, Habakkuk may be seen as using the language and themes of a funeral song, but for a brutally new purpose. Amos had already transformed the dirge long before, mourning the death of Israel in advance (Amos 5:1–2). The emotion expressed there seems truly to be one of grief, but in Habakkuk everything has been reversed. God authorizes a suffering people to sing a mock funeral song over the tyrant who has oppressed them —in advance. If so, there is a dramatic contrast in the chapter. The prophet had just spoken of life, but death immediately reappears as he speaks of the arrogant who "open their throats wide as Sheol; like Death they never have enough" (Hab. 2:5). But it is the arrogant who will die.

The book concludes with one of the most impressive theophanies in the Old Testament. Its language is exceptionally violent in places, but it corresponds well with the terror that would soon befall Judah, with Jerusalem besieged and destroyed. When theophanies are described in the Psalms, they typically lead to words of praise for the God who has come to deliver the one (or ones) in need (cf. Psalms 18; 68; 97). Habakkuk's response, in 3:16, takes the unusual form of describing the physical effects on him of God's presence. Similar features occur in accounts of visionary experiences elsewhere (Ezek. 1:28; Dan. 10:9).[34] Then Habakkuk's words of praise appear, but like much else in his book they take a most unusual course. While the psalms often praise God for deliverance from death (e.g., Ps. 116:3, 8), Habakkuk now calmly contemplates the possibility of death (3:17–18). Consider the economy of Judah in his time. The important fruit crops were olives, grapes, and figs:

> Though the fig tree does not blossom,
> and no fruit is on the vines;
> though the produce of the olive fails

They raised grain crops; barley and wheat:

> and the fields yield no food;

The domesticated animals we know of were cattle, sheep, and goats:

> though the flock is cut off from the fold
> and there is no herd in the stalls,

What is left to eat? Invading armies lived off the land they occupied, and if there was not enough left for the population still alive after the battle, starvation could be their fate. But something has happened to the prophet that has left him certain of being able to cope with whatever may come, and to do more than cope; to rejoice:

> yet I will rejoice in the LORD;
> I will exult in the God of my salvation.

What he has told us is that God has come near to him in daunting power and irresistible attractiveness, and that has changed things for him.

There are a few parallels to this in the Old Testament; especially in Psalms 49 and 73. In brief and almost cryptic language they speak of having found a relationship with God that transcends trouble and even death, bringing to life a kind of joy that no tribulation can destroy (Pss. 49:15; 73:23–26). Judaism would need such an assurance when martyrdom became the world's reward for faithfulness ("in my soul I am glad to suffer these things because I fear him," 2 Macc. 6:30). Habakkuk's insight surely also corresponds with the "peace that passes understanding" of which Paul spoke (Phil. 4:7).

Habakkuk's message to the individual came at a time when communities would soon be broken up and the survivors would be left to their own devices more than ever before. From some of those survivors God would eventually create a new community, but the need for this prophet's wrestling with the problems the disintegration of society made for faith is demonstrated by the ways Jeremiah and especially Ezekiel addressed the individual—a significant shift from the work of their predecessors. Major decisions by individuals would be called for, and righteousness would certainly not be immediately rewarded, but the possibility of a personal experience with God would make survival, and more than survival, possible.

3.4 Jeremiah

Jeremiah lived through the second moment that brought forth the work of the canonical prophets—the fall of Jerusalem. His book and that of his younger contemporary Ezekiel point forward to the third moment—the achievement of God's aim in all of this, the creation of a new people via the experience of exile. The brief period of hope for national independence because of the collapse of Assyria came to a bitter end with the death of Josiah in his futile attempt to head off the Egyptian army under Pharaoh Necho as it moved north in an effort to aid the remnants of the Assyrian army (609 B.C.E.; 2 Kings 23:29). Necho's aim was evidently to preserve a weak Assyria as protection against the Neo-Babylonian army, so as to enable him to take control of Syria/Palestine. After Josiah's death there apparently was reaction to the religious reforms he had instituted (2 Kings 22—23), for there is no evidence of them in Jeremiah or Ezekiel. His son Jehoahaz succeeded him briefly, but after only three months Necho deposed him and took him into exile in Egypt (2 Kings 23:30–33; Jer. 22:11; Ezek. 19:1–4), where he died. His brother Eliakim, renamed Jehoiakim, was enthroned as a puppet king (2 Kings 23:34–37).

Nebuchadnezzar had assumed command of the Neo-Babylonian army and in 605 inflicted a decisive defeat on the Egyptian army at Carchemish.[35] In 604 he succeeded his father Nabopolassar as king and received tribute from Jehoiakim, who had recognized that it would be wise to change his allegiance (2 Kings 24:1). When Nebuchadnezzar's efforts to invade Egypt in 601 were unsuccessful, however, Jehoiakim made the mistake of tryng a bid for independence. It took some time for Nebuchadnezzar to rebuild his army, but in 598 he marched into Judah to put down the rebellion. Jerusalem was besieged and it fell in March 15/16, 597 (2 Kings 24:10–17; Wiseman, 72–73). Jehoiakim had died before the defeat and had been replaced by Jehoiachin, his son, so once again it was a king who had ruled only a few months who suffered for the mistakes of his predecessor. Jehoiachin, members of the upper classes, and skilled craftsmen were taken into exile in Babylonia.[36] His uncle, Mattaniah, was installed as puppet king, with his name changed to Zedekiah (2 Kings 24:17–19). One incipient rebellion by a coalition including Judah, Edom, Moab, Ammon, Tyre, and Sidon was averted in 595/4 (Jer. 27:1–3), but in 598 Zedekiah was persuaded by his advisers to declare independence. Judah was immediately attacked, many cities were destroyed, and in 587 Jerusalem fell again (2 Kings 25:1–21).[37] This time there was extensive destruction, with the walls breached so that they were useless (until repaired under Nehemiah more than a century later). The temple itself was destroyed and its treasures taken as booty. More people were taken into exile. Galilee and Samaria seem not to have been involved in the rebellion, for the archaeological evidence does not reveal destroyed cities there, as it does in Judah.[38] The author of 2 Kings says that only the poorest of the land were left in Judah (2 Kings 25:12), and the last evidence we have for events in Judah before the restoration began in 538 is to be found in Jeremiah 40—42.

The book of Jeremiah looks back at the reigns of Josiah, Jehoahaz, Jehoiakim, and Jehoiachin (ch. 22), and the narratives concerning events in the life of the prophet involve Jehoiakim and Zedekiah (e.g., chs. 25—28, 34—38) in addition to recounting the events after the fall of Jerusalem just alluded to. His call is dated early, in the thirteenth year of Josiah (627/26), but the book itself is largely a commentary on the events from 609 on, so we shall not find it necessary to debate the date of his call, or the question of what relationship, if any, he may have had with Josiah's reform.[39] The themes of the book fit the period of the reigns of Jehoiakim and Zedekiah, and shortly after.

Unresolved Issues in Jeremiah[40]

The interpreter of the book of Jeremiah faces a unique question for Old Testament study: Which book? The Septuagint translation is about one-eighth (about 2700 words) shorter than the Masoretic Text, with words, phrases, and whole paragraphs missing. The oracles against the nations, chs. 46—51 in the Masoretic Text, are located following ch. 25:13, and the nations appear in a different order.[41] Arguments for the priority of the Septuagint, as having been based on a Hebrew text earlier than the Masoretic, have been persuasive to many, although the standard commentaries still follow the Masoretic Text.[42] Fortunately, the differences between the two texts do not represent significant theological differences, so the textual problem is not a major issue for this book. Other questions, however, cannot be so easily put to one side.

Unlike the earlier prophetic books, Jeremiah contains a great deal of prose. Many incidents from his life are recorded, and some of his messages are in a prose form strongly reminiscent of the language of Deuteronomy, and very different from the passionate character of his poetry. The extended discussions of these features have found it convenient to use Sigmund Mowinckel's designations:[43]

> A—The poetic oracles
> B—The "biographical" material
> C—The prose sermons

Some have followed Mowinckel in omitting the oracles against the nations (chs. 46—51) from this analysis (as coming from a later source); others consider at least some of them to come from the same period.

There are both stylistic and theological differences between the oracles (A) and the sermons (C). Efforts to ascribe them both to Jeremiah have claimed he used the prose form when attempting to persuade the people to change their ways.[44] Other explanations have described them as a rewriting of his messages by his disciples (Baruch or others),[45] or as a reapplication of Jeremiah's ideas to the situation of the Babylonian exiles by preachers in later generations.[46] A major point of discussion has been the apparently close relationship betweeen the style of the sermons and that of the book of Deuteronomy and other Deuteronomistic literature (especially material about the prophets in 1 and 2 Kings). Many scholars believe the style is definitely Deuteronomistic; then the question is whether Jeremiah would sometimes have spoken this way.[47] A few claim it is just the normal prose style of the late seventh and early sixth centuries.[48] For our purposes the issue is not the biographical one—who wrote what?—but whether the book contains two significantly different theologies. We shall find that on one subject—repentance—the oracles are fully in keeping with the earlier prophetic tradition, but some of the sermons contain exhortations like those in Deuteronomy and the Deuteronomistic literature, unusual for the prophetic books. Without trying to solve the question whether these two bodies of material came from the same person, we will have to consider two points of view on the subject of repentance. On most other matters the theology of the two types of literature does not differ as much as some authors have suggested.

Only recently has the authenticity of the narratives about Jeremiah's experiences (Mowinckel's B) been challenged. Most studies of the book have attempted to use them as the framework into which the oracles and sermons are inserted in order to provide as complete an account of his career as possible.[49] Some assume that the scribe Baruch must have been responsible for both the sermons and the "biography," and that cannot be proved impossible, but a current trend questions the historical value of all this material.[50] This study of prophetic theology has taken the position that it is unnecessary to try to reconstruct the lives of the prophets, but given the large amount of material about Jeremiah himself in this book, the question of its meaning must obviously be taken seriously. Earlier, it was claimed that incidents from the lives of the prophets were preserved only when, and because, they contained an important message from God to Israel. The same claim can be made for Jeremiah. Only the latter years of his life are recorded, and that is very likely because they were also the last years of the life of Judah. He was the prophet who experienced personally the failures of leadership during those years and the horror of the fall of Jerusalem and its aftermath. The partial recording of Jeremiah's story can thus be understood as the work of survivors who understood that his story comprehended and explained the story of his people.[51]

My approach to the book will be similar to that of several recent authors; that it is a message from and concerning Jeremiah, directed to the community of Jews in exile. Peter Ackroyd said of the book of Jeremiah, "we are concerned less with portraying individuals and their thought, and more with understanding the mind of a period and its significance."[52] The approach taken by Ronald Clements in his commentary is: "On the basis of what the prophet had preached, a book intended to be read by persons in ancient times of recorded sayings, reminiscences, and reflections has been compiled. . . . My aim therefore has been to try to enable the modern reader to sense how this remarkable book would have been read in ancient Israel and to discern the situation to which it was addressed."[53] James Ward speaks of the entire book as "an interpretation of the fall of the kingdom of Judah, for the benefit of surviving Judeans and their descendants."[54] Since the book shows no knowledge of the surrender of Babylon to the Persians in 539 B.C.E., it is likely that most of the work on it took place prior to that date. This would mean that most of the the promissory passages represent true promises, issued before there was any obvious evidence that they might come true. The shift from judgment prophecy to promise of future blessing will thus be a major subject in the study of Jeremiah.

Judah Is Dying

Jeremiah's oracles put less emphasis on predicting the end of the kingdom of Judah and more emphasis on lamenting its desecration and desolation.[55] A pall of death hangs over the entire book. The most dominant literary type is lament—of the prophet, of the people, and even of God. The lament sometimes anticipates what is to come, but often bewails what has already happened to Judah.[56] Jeremiah struggles with the inability of his people to change and knows nothing can avert what still lies ahead.

> Is Israel a slave? Is he a homeborn servant?
> Why then has he become plunder?
> The lions have roared against him,
> they have roared loudly.
> They have made his land a waste;
> his cities are in ruins, without inhabitant.
> (Jer. 2:14–15)

> Besiegers come from a distant land;
> they shout against the cities of Judah.
> They have closed in around her like watchers of a field,
> because she has rebelled against me,
> says the LORD.
> Your ways and your doings
> have brought this upon you.
> This is your doom; how bitter it is!
> It has reached your very heart.
> (Jer. 4:16–18)[57]

From the beginning of the book the oracles are typically expressions of distress at what is happening and is about to happen in his country. In the earlier prophets the closest parallel is Isa. 1:4–9. Lamentation is especially prominent in chs. 8—14. The scene of community mourning envisioned by Amos reappears in Jeremiah (Amos 5:16–17; Jer. 9:17–22 [MT 16–21]):

> Consider, and call for the mourning women to come;
> send for the skilled women to come;
> let them quickly raise a dirge over us,
> so that our eyes may run down with tears,
> and our eyelids flow with water.
> For a sound of wailing is heard from Zion:
> "How we are ruined!
> We are utterly shamed,

because we have left the land,
　　because they have cast down our dwellings." . . .
"Death has come up into our windows,
　　it has entered our palaces,
to cut off the children from the streets
　　and the young men from the squares."
(Jer. 9:17–19, 21)

It will soon be seen that the personal involvement of the prophet with the fate of the people on one side and with God on the other side is one of the most striking features of this book, and that appears in the laments. The language of distress is sometimes his, sometimes the people's, and sometimes God's:

My grief is beyond healing,
　　my heart is sick within me.
Hark, the cry of the daughter of my people
　　from the length and breadth of the land:
"Is the LORD not in Zion?
　　Is her King not in her?"
"Why have they provoked me to anger with their graven images,
　　and with their foreign idols?"
"The harvest is past, the summer is ended,
　　and we are not saved."
For the wound of the daughter of my people is my heart wounded,
　　I mourn, and dismay has taken hold on me.
Is there no balm in Gilead?
　　Is there no physician there?
Why then has the health of the daughter of my people
　　not been restored?
O that my head were waters,
　　and my eyes a fountain of tears,
that I might weep day and night
　　for the slain of the daughter of my people!
(Jer. 8:18–9:1 [MT 8:23], RSV)

The first and third sets of quotation marks in the RSV assist the reader to identify two quotes from the people, and the second set indicates a question from God, but who is it that speaks of "the daughter of my people" four times—Jeremiah or God, or both? The prophet clearly speaks for God when he says,

I have forsaken my house,
　　I have abandoned my heritage;
I have given the beloved of my heart
　　into the hands of her enemies.
(Jer. 12:7)

In another passage Jeremiah is clearly expressing his own, physical distress at the beginning, but by the end it is God speaking once again:

My anguish, my anguish! I writhe in pain!
  Oh, the walls of my heart!
My heart is beating wildly;
  I cannot keep silent;
for I hear the sound of the trumpet,
  the alarm of war.
Disaster overtakes disaster,
  the whole land is laid waste.
Suddenly my tents are destroyed,
  my curtains in a moment.
How long must I see the standard,
  and hear the sound of the trumpet?
"For my people are foolish,
  they do not know me;
they are stupid children,
  they have no understanding.
They are skilled in doing evil,
  but do not know how to do good."
                (Jer. 4:19–22)

Note the frequent occurrence of questions in the passages quoted thus far. Jeremiah's accusations are familiar ones, repeating what the prophets before him had found wrong, but they take on distinctive forms with him, and appear especially as the impassioned question, Why?

Why then has this people turned away
  in perpetual backsliding?
They have held fast to deceit,
  they have refused to return.
                (Jer. 8:5)

What wrong did your ancestors find in me
  that they went far from me,
and went after worthless things, and became worthless themselves?
                (Jer. 2:5)

Why do you complain against me?
  You have all rebelled against me,
  says the LORD.
                (Jer. 2:29)

Ask among the nations:
  Who has heard the like of this?
. . . my people have forgotten me.
                (Jer. 18:13, 15)

For a century and a half the prophetic testimony had been in the air, to no effect. Jeremiah's reuse and elaboration of Hosea's theme of the unfaithful wife is well known and has been widely discussed (Jeremiah 2—3 and elsewhere), but his book also contains echoes of Amos and Isaiah.[58] Like Hosea and Micah he cites the leaders in his community as bearing the guilt for much that has gone wrong. Scribes, the wise, prophets, and priests are condemned again and again (8:8–12 and elsewhere). The familiar charges of unjust gain (6:13), oppression and deceit (9:5–6), and shedding the blood of innocents (19:14) are repeated, but a key word for Jeremiah is "falsehood" (or "lie," usually *sheqer*). The prophets speak lies in the name of God, and the ways of other leaders are false, leading to destruction (e.g., Jer. 23:16–40; chs. 27—29).[59] This question of truth probably took on such prominence in the book of Jeremiah because he was repeating an old message that had not been accepted, it was a demoralizing message at a time when the threat to Jerusalem was very real, and those who opposed it were the people in power.[60]

A special scandal for Jeremiah is the prevalence of Baal worship in Judah, which he considers to be apostasy. Only Hosea, in the Northern Kingdom, had attacked the worship of Baal in a similar way.[61] This, and Jeremiah's tendency to speak of Judah's other sins in general terms, may be accounted for by noting that for him the heart of the problem was the breaking of a relationship between God and the people that God had intended to be everlasting. Relational terms appear with a prominence matched, again, only by Hosea, and they are to be found in sermons (C) and oracles (A) alike. The father-son relationship is used as Hosea 11 did, to speak of God's intention to care for and bless a people (the Northern Kingdom!) who have rejected him and not responded to his love for them:

I thought
  how I would set you among my children,
and give you a pleasant land,
  the most beautiful heritage of all the nations.
And I thought you would call me, My Father,
  and would not turn from following me.
(Jer. 3:19; cf. 3:4, 14, 22; 4:22; 10:20; 31:19–20)

The breaking of that relationship between God and the Northern Kingdom is described in terms of husband and wife in the verse following the one just quoted: "Instead, as a faithless wife leaves her husband, so you have been faithless to me, O house of Israel, says the LORD" (Jer. 3:20). Jeremiah's frequent uses of the verbs "forsake" (*'azab*), "forget" (*shakah*), and "be faithless" (*bagad*) show that Abraham Heschel was right in saying "God's pain and disappointment ring throughout the book."[62]

Hosea had also used the term "covenant" more than other prophets, and the broken covenant relationship is the basis for the threats in Jer. 11:1–13, a passage filled with typically Deuteronomistic language (cf. also 22:9). The prominence of relational language in the book is thus to be found in both the poetic and prose parts, although the choice of terminology may vary. There should have been an exclusive bond between God and Israel, and that is why the worship of other gods along with Yahweh is such a scandal for Jeremiah. Like his predecessors since the time of Amos, he does not speak of a theoretical monotheism, but he is a "practical monotheist"; that is. it matters not whether other gods may exist; for Israel, Yahweh is the only God.[63]

Although Jeremiah's message has been read as one calling for repentance, most of the book reflects the attitude of the earlier prophets, and puts it even more strongly: It is too late for change now; the sentence has been passed and judgment is near. Jeremiah expresses his, at best, faint hopes for change in various ways, and finally declares it to be impossible.[64] The desperateness of Judah's sinfulness is emphasized in both the poetry and prose of the book:

> In vain I have struck down your children;
>> they accepted no correction.
>>> (Jer. 2:30)

> Run to and fro through the streets of Jerusalem,
>> look around and take note!
> Search its squares and see
>> if you can find one person
>> who acts justly
>> and seeks truth—
> so that I may pardon Jerusalem.
>>> (Jer. 5:1)

> See, their ears are closed,
>> they cannot listen.
> The word of the LORD is to them an object of scorn;
>> they take no pleasure in it.
>>> (Jer. 6:10)

> Can Ethiopians change their skin
>> or leopards their spots?
> Then also you can do good
>> who are accustomed to do evil.
>>> (Jer. 13:23)

> The heart is devious above all else;
>> it is perverse—
> Who can understand it?
>>> (Jer. 17:9)

In the oracles, the most extreme statements of the present hopeless state of God's people come near to the Calvinist doctrine of total depravity (Jer. 6:10; 13:23; 17:9). Most Old Testament writers assume that humans have the ability to obey if they only try. The appeals that run through Deuteronomy are classic examples of this point of view (e.g., Deuteronomy 4–11; 30). True pessimism about human potential, of the kind that appears in the New Testament in Paul's writings, scarcely appears outside of Jeremiah and Ezekiel.[65] There are clearly historical reasons for their disillusionment about the human ability to obey God. Nothing has worked, and all is now lost. People have not changed, they do not change no matter what the prophets do, and finally Jeremiah concluded they cannot change.

Although the prose sermons (C) do contain suggestions that repentance might be possible, as will be noted shortly, they also speak of inevitable judgment, and in a most severe way. Apparently one of the traditional functions expected of prophets was intercession on behalf of their people. Amos interceded successfully twice, before learning it was too late (Amos 7:1–6). Abraham and Moses were very likely thought to have been performing a prophetic role in their intercessory prayers (Gen. 18:22–33; Exod. 32:11–14; Num. 14:13–19), but Jer. 15:1–4 says that even though Moses and Samuel stood before God (to pray for Judah), God would not turn toward "this people." Intercession will not be accepted, and so twice in the prose material Jeremiah is forbidden to pray for his people (7:16; 14:11–12), and God says, "I will not pity or spare or have compassion when I destroy them" (Jer. 13:14). As the heart, which in Hebrew thought represents the ability to think and make decisions, is "devious above all else" and "perverse" in the oracle at 17:9, so in prose passages the heart is "stubborn":

> This evil people, who refuse to hear my words, who stubbornly follow their own heart and have gone after other gods . . . (Jer. 13:10, RSV)

> We will follow our own plans, and will every one act according to the stubbornness of his evil heart. (Jer. 18:12, RSV)

When the book offers promises of a better future, then, human nature itself, the heart, the ability to make decisions, will have to be transformed, as we shall see later (Jer. 24:7; 31:33; 32:39).

Many interpreters of Jeremiah have argued that early in his career he believed repentance was still possible for Judah, and that only after years of failure did his message harden to the position just described.[66] A survey of the key occurrences of the word *shub*, "turn, return," then metaphorically "repent," suggests another reading of the few places where repentance seems to be taken as a real possibility.[67] Three times Jeremiah is quoted as saying, "It may be . . . ," but that is the work of the biographer, who knows very well it did not happen, and who does not in fact quote any actual appeals from Jeremiah (26:3; 36:3, 7). The conditional promises that appear a few times reflect the optimism of Deuteronomy, and stand in sharp contrast with everything in the oracles (18:8; cf. 7:3–7, which uses "amend," *hetib*). The passage in 3:1–4:4, in which the root *shub* appears sixteen times, is composed of a variety of materials, and its structure is very difficult to understand,[68] but significant parts are addressed to the exiles of the Northern Kingdom (e.g., 3:12–13, 19–23). Although most scholars claim that some of the appeals to return to Yahweh are addressed to Judah (e.g., 3:14; 4:1–4), it may be that the whole passage speaks to exiles from the Northern Kingdom, who had already experienced the judgment and to whom a promise for a better future is now appropriate. This would correspond with the point of view found in the rest of the book. The promises of the book can follow judgment, not avert it (e.g., Jer. 24:4–7; 29:10–14; 32:25–44; 33:5–16).

"You Shall Be a Sign"

God did not say this to Jeremiah, but Isaiah and Ezekiel were said to have been signs to their people (Isa. 8:18; 20:3; Ezek. 12:6, 11; 24:24, 27), and the book of Jeremiah offers the most extended example of the fact that for some of the prophets, life itself became a part of the message.

> One of the most important factors affecting the prophets of this time is the way in which their office increasingly invaded their personal and spiritual lives. . . . The very forms which he [Jeremiah] uses proclaim this—he expands his message into lyrics into which a new element enters: in these poems the prophet opens up a dimension of pain. It is a twofold suffering, the suffering of those upon whom judgment has come, but at the same time also God's grief over his people. And then—and this is the really important thing—Jeremiah himself enters into this twofold suffering; it weighs upon him, and he speaks of it as his own personal affliction.[69]

The book moves without introduction, comment, or modification from a passionate expression of the prophet's grief over the deaths he has witnessed (14:17–18) to a quotation of a lament of his people, in which they confess their sin and ask for God's help (14:19–22). Both have become words of Jeremiah. God had made him the tester and refiner of his people, who has found them to be stubbornly rebellious, rejected by the Lord (6:27–30), but Jeremiah is one of those people. He had just cried out,

> O daughter of my people, gird on sackcloth,
>   and roll in ashes;
> make mourning as for an only son,
>   most bitter lamentation;
> for suddenly the destroyer
>   will come upon us.
>
> (Jer. 6:26)

Note the first person plural at the end; Jeremiah will experience it all. He will not only feel what the condemned people feel ("But if you will not listen, my soul will weep in secret for your pride; my eyes will weep bitterly and run down with tears, because the LORD's flock has been taken captive," 13:17), he will endure it physically as well, according to the biographical sections, to be noted shortly.

As a prophet he makes the astounding claim to have felt what God feels as well, however. "But I am full of the wrath of the LORD; I am weary of holding it in" (Jer. 6:11), he will say at one point, but elsewhere the expression of intense physical and emotional pain that he experienced because of the destruction around him merges without a seam into a word from God (Jer. 4:19–22). Since he spoke both for the people and for God, Jeremiah is also depicted as one who found both the people and God to be his enemies, so in addition to participation a part of his work led to isolation. This aspect of the prophetic role appears with the greatest prominence in the passages traditionally called the "confessions of Jeremiah," but more accurately designated complaints (Jer.

11:18–12:6; 15:10–12, 15–21; 17:14–18; 18:19–23; 20:7–18). The form is that found in the psalms of lament. Most of the language is traditional, for complaints about the plots of enemies, questions why the wicked prosper, and challenges to God to intervene with justice are regular parts of the laments in the Psalter. This has led some to question whether the Jeremiah passages contain any personal information about him, but parts of the complaints have no parallels in the Psalms and make sense only as words of a prophet (e.g., Jer. 15:16–18; 20:8–9).[70] Jeremiah was remembered as one who had shared the distress of his people but had been seen by them as an enemy because of his words of judgment. The complaints speak of plots against him, against his very life, and by members of his own family (11:11; 20:10). The loss of reputation, for an Israelite, was almost as troublesome as physical danger (15:15, 17; 20:7). Jeremiah protested to God that it was not his will to bring harm to his people, but God had forced him into that role:

Remember how I stood before you
  to speak good for them,
  to turn away your wrath from them.
                    (Jer. 18:20)

But I have not run away from being a shepherd in your service,
  nor have I desired the fatal day.
You know what came from my lips;
  it was before your face.

                         (Jer. 17:16)

He had fulfilled the divine call:

Your words were found, and I ate them,
  and your words became to me a joy
  and the delight of my heart;
for I am called by your name,
  O Lord, God of hosts.

                    (Jer. 15:16)

The eventual result, however, was as offensive to him as it was to his people:

For whenever I speak, I must cry out,
  I must shout, "Violence and destruction!"
For the word of the Lord has become for me
  a reproach and derision all day long.
If I say, "I will not mention him,
  or speak any more in his name,"
then within me there is something like a burning fire
  shut up in my bones;
I am weary with holding it in,
  and I cannot.

                         (Jer. 20:8–9)

So he turned against the people who have become his enemies (18:21–23), attacks God, who is no help (20:7), and finally curses the day he was born (20:14–18). With that, the complaints come to an end. There is no indication that his faith in God, which he had confessed before (e.g., 17:14; 20:11), ever alleviated his bitterness, nor is there another promise of divine help (as in 15:19–21). Jeremiah lived to see the fall of Jerusalem, and experienced involuntary exile—and that is all we know. The complaints thus reflect the course of his life, and his life reflected the disaster that overtook Judah. His questions about where God was to be found in his experiences echo the questions in the book of Lamentations about where God was to be found in the ruins of Jerusalem.

"With Jeremiah and Ezekiel at least, the prophetic 'I' suddenly becomes very much more prominent."[71] The books of only these two prophets begin with the account of a call, representing a claim of divine authority for their words based on an experience that set them apart from the rest of humanity.

> Before I formed you in the womb I knew you,
>   and before you were born I consecrated you;
> I appointed you a prophet to the nations. . . .
> Do not be afraid of them,
>   for I am with you to deliver you,
> says the LORD.
>
>   (Jer. 1:5, 8)

The promise "I am with you to deliver you" will be needed by Jeremiah, for the role of prophet, as we have begun to see, includes more than simply speaking the words God puts into his mouth (as in 1:7). Only the book of Jeremiah contains complaints like those just surveyed, extended descriptions of what it was like for a human being to participate in the judgment he had to pronounce over others. The participation involved carrying out symbolic actions that were more than just "object lessons."[72] There are probably seven passages in Jeremiah dealing with symbolic acts, although some interpreters find more. Several of them function as analogies to what will actually happen, and need not be dealt with at length here. As the waistcloth was spoiled, so will God ruin the pride of Judah and Jerusalem (Jer. 13:1–11); as the flask was smashed, so will the people and the city be broken so that they can never be mended (Jer. 19:1–14); as Jeremiah bore a yoke on his shoulders, so should Zedekiah and the people of Jerusalem be willing to accept the yoke of Nebuchadnezzar (Jeremiah 27—28). Others seem to have been intended as effective acts, putting in motion the events represented: the setting of stones on which Nebuchadnezzar's throne will be placed (Jer. 43:8–11), and the sinking of a book of words against Babylon in the Euphrates (Jer. 51:59–64).

Of greater interest and importance, however, are the actions like Hosea's marriage and Isaiah's barefoot and naked walk (Hosea 1; Isaiah 20), which changed the life of the prophet. These become more than mere symbols. Four such events are recorded for Jeremiah, and there are more in Ezekiel. One passage (Jer. 16:1–13) reveals perhaps more effectively than any other how the prophet's life and message became intertwined. It contains three prohibitions: (a) Jeremiah is not to marry and have children (16:1–4). The day will soon come when others' children will be dead, and because others will be childless, God's prophet must be childless. Given the Israelite conviction that to die without offspring meant one was truly dead (cf. the earlier comments on Amos 5:1–2), scarcely anything worse could have been asked of Jeremiah. (b, c) He must also not participate in funerals or weddings, for the day will soon come when the proper care for the dead will no longer be possible, and when there will be no opportunity to rejoice at a wedding feast (16:5–9). The prophetic call thus does not raise one above the people who stand under judgment; this one who is closer to God than any other must stay with the people. The implications of this will become clearer in Ezekiel, where we shall see that they point toward the concept of the Servant of the Lord in Isaiah 53.

Jeremiah was also made a sign of hope when there was no reason to hope, when he redeemed the field at Anathoth that was in danger of being lost to his family (Jeremiah 32). The Babylonian army was camped on it at the time, not an auspicious moment for investment in real estate, but the transaction was made with attention to all the legal details (32:9–14), as a different sort of sign—that God had plans for people and land after the inevitable judgment had come to pass. The act changed Jeremiah's life only by reducing his capital—he never occupied that field—but this is an important passage for the book's transition from judgment to promise, for it connects hope with an anticipatory experience of the prophet himself.

We have been largely concerned so far with the poetic oracles in the book (A), and have made use of the sermons (C) when they expressed the same outlook, noting one significant difference. In sermons such as those in chs. 7 and 26 the possibility that Jerusalem might be saved if Judeans change their ways is held out, in contrast with the message of the oracles. This point is in keeping with the theology of Deuteronomy and adds support to the linguistic evidence that the sermons are a reapplication of Jeremiah's message by Deuteronomistic authors. Other tensions within the book appear when the "biographical" material (B) is considered. It is not biography proper, since only selected incidents in Jeremiah's life are recorded, and Jeremiah himself does not appear in some sections (Jer. 39:1–10; 40:7–41:18). Chapters 37—45 have sometimes been called Jeremiah's "passion story," but his sufferings are not their sole theme.[73] Early in this chapter I suggested that this material has been included in Jeremiah because it preserved memories of the fall of Jerusalem that were important to the exiles. Jeremiah is the central character in most of it because he was the prophet directly involved, whose words offered ways to understand it.

Four themes may be detected in the prose material (both B and C),[74] that partly reinforce and partly stand in tension with one another. It should not be surprising that an event so devastating and apparently final as the fall of Jerusalem, destruction of its temple, and exiling of its king would lead to more than one explanation in the effort to know what to do next.

1. Jeremiah is depicted as one who announced inevitable doom, in line with the tradition begun by Amos. For example, the prose account of his symbolic act of breaking a flask in the Hinnom valley is interpreted as a sign of certain death for the people of Jerusalem, who already stand under judgment (ch. 19). Such a mes-

sage led to beating and imprisonment by the order of Pashhur the priest (20:1–6), who was then threatened with exile as the message of doom was reiterated. The theme of resistance to the prophetic message that first appeared in Amos 7:10–17 thus reappears, with an increased emphasis on the danger that created for the prophet.

2. A related theme, revealing a stronger Deuteronomistic influence, has Jeremiah offering Jerusalem one more chance, which is rejected, with the rejection once again endangering the prophet. It is thought that ch. 26 provides information about the results of the temple sermon recorded in ch. 7, since both contain the unusual reference to the temple that once stood at Shiloh (7:12; 26:6, 9). Even though threat in this sermon is conditional, the reaction was more violent than Pashhur's, and Jeremiah's life was threatened (26:11). Some of the leaders took his side and saved his life by appealing to a precedent from the prophetic tradition: Micah had predicted the destruction of Jerusalem and he was not executed (26:16–19). An important example of the rejection of a message that was intended to lead to repentance is contained in the account of Jeremiah dictating a scroll containing his earlier messages (ch. 36).[75] It makes King Jehoiakim personally responsible for an attempt to destroy the word of God, but unsuccessfully, since all of it is rewritten, with additions. For the survivors of the disaster, the memory of these incidents served to justify God. These stories insisted that what happened was deserved, and could have been avoided. Whether or not the modern reader can fully accept that reasoning, the exiles did accept it, and doing so changed history.

3. Another way of averting disaster appears in other narratives. The act of wearing the yoke to represent submission to Babylon was not interpreted as a threat, but as a way of saving Jerusalem from destruction:

> I spoke to King Zedekiah of Judah in the same way: Bring your necks under the yoke of the king of Babylon, and serve him and his people, and live. Why should you and your people die by the sword, by famine, and by pestilence, as the LORD has spoken concerning any nation that will not serve the king of Babylon? (Jer. 27:12–13)

Such a message made Jeremiah seem to be a traitor, if not a Babylonian agent, to the patriots in Jerusalem (37:11–15). He was imprisoned as a result, but insisted on repeating the same message to King Zedekiah (38:17–23): Surrender is the only way to avoid complete disaster. He was thrown into a muddy cistern with the intention of putting him to death, but was rescued from there by the Ethiopian, Ebed Melech, and then remained incarcerated until the city fell (38:1–13, 28).

These passages stand in some tension with the first two themes, in that they contain political advice rather than moral judgment, but they may represent a realistic evaluation of the options available to the weak King Zedekiah. Jerusalem might have been saved in 597 and 587 if Jehoiakim and Zedekiah had not rebelled. Nebuchadnezzar dealt with the Philistine cities on his way toward invading Egypt, but Judah was off the beaten track and he probably would not have invaded if those kings had been willing to accept vassal status and continue to pay tribute. This part of the Jeremiah tradition was thus preserved in order to insist that the judgment need not have been as severe as his oracles suggested. Jeremiah is said to have understood how it might have been averted, and to have recognized that among the worst of the sins of Judah's leaders was the willingness to risk all in a foolish bid for independence.

4. The fourth theme associating the fall of Jerusalem with events in Jeremiah's life involves the aftermath: Jeremiah's decision to remain in Judah and his involuntary exile in Egypt. Having insisted (according to prose materials we shall consider later; chs. 24 and 29) that there would be a future for God's people, but among the exiles, not in Judah, he surprises us by choosing to stay in Judah when the Babylonians give him an option (40:1–6). Why would he not have gone to Babylon to provide leadership there? Did his prophetic role as one who must share in his people's experiences include staying with those who had no future, or was the decision a practical one, to support a new government under Gedaliah? We are not told, but we are told that when forced to accompany refugees to Egypt he found himself at the end still in the midst of a people he believed to be under divine judgment (42:1–44:23).

A Prophet to the Nations

Jeremiah was given this unique title as part of his call (Jer. 1:5) and the exact reason for it is still not altogether clear. What could it have meant to the survivors of 587 that this prophet was given such a title, and more: "See, today I appoint you over nations and over kingdoms, to pluck up and to pull down, to destroy and to overthrow, to build and to plant" (Jer. 1:10)? The prominence of these references to the nations certainly suggests that careful attention should be given to what this book says about the nations at the time of the fall of Jerusalem. They appear in roles that are familiar from the other prophetic books, but several passages specifically fit the time of Jeremiah, when the prophetic message shifted to announcements of what God intended to do after the judgment had been inflicted.

Traditional themes: (a) A foreign nation, now Babylon, will be used by Yahweh as his agent of judgment (Jer. 25:9; 27:7–8). Babylon now takes the role played by Assyria in earlier prophetic books. More must be said about the place of this nation and of Nebuchadnezzar a bit later. (b) The nations in general will be witnesses of what Yahweh will do to Judah, first in judgment (Jer. 6:18; 22:8–9; 26:6; 44:8), then in restoration (Jer. 31:10; 33:9). This is a very prominent theme in Ezekiel, who speaks of these events as evidence that will lead the nations to "know that I am Yahweh," but it plays a lesser role in Jeremiah. (c) In due time the nations will be judged for their excesses (Jer. 10:25; 25:15–38). This theme is less prominent in Jeremiah than in some of the other prophetic books. In the collection of oracles against the nations the only abuses against Israel that are mentioned are with reference to Moab once (Jer. 48:27) and Ammon once (Jer. 49:1–2), until we come to the oracles against Babylon (chs. 50—51), whose sins against Israel and the other nations are frequently condemned.

Interspersed with this familiar material are some unusual passages expressing hopes for the other nations. Except for Isa. 2:2–4 (Micah 4:1–4) and Isa. 19:18–25 we have seen little of this in the earlier books. Most commentators have shown little interest in these passages in Jeremiah except for the question of date and authorship,[76] but they have something to contribute to our understanding of the theology of the book. A promise inserted into the passage offering repentance to the Northern Kingdom speaks of a time when Jerusalem (not the ark of the covenant, which had disappeared, with no record of when or how) will be called the throne of Yahweh. Then both Israel and Judah will return from exile, and the nations will come in pilgrimage (Jer. 3:15–18). This is a hope for Jerusalem similar to the one found in Isa. 2:2–4. At the end of the "repentance section," comes a surprising promise: If they really do return to Yahweh, "then nations shall bless themselves in him, and in him shall they glory" (Jer. 4:2, RSV). This is an echo of the promise to Abraham (Gen. 22:18) and is a most remarkable motive for repentance if addressed to the obdurate people of whom Jeremiah speaks: Change so that the nations may be blessed! Hope for the nations takes the form of a prayer followed by a short oracle, in Jer. 16:19–21. The prayer anticipates the time when the nations will understand that their idols are nothing. This book, like Isa. 19:18–25 and Ezek. 29:9b–16 (cf. Isa. 23:13–18), also assumes that the history of Yahweh's dealings with the nations will follow the same pattern as Israel's history: judgment for their sins, leading to exile, then eventual restoration to their homelands (Jer. 12:14–17; 46:25–26; 48:46–47; 49:5–6, 34–39). Clearly, then, the book assumes that the role of the prophet is not only to declare the will of Yahweh for the covenant people, but to be responsible for explaining world history as the working of Israel's God.

This happened at a time when the ordinary observer could see no evidence of that, for the people of Yahweh were drawing ever nearer to extinction. Jeremiah's time was the time when Judah ceased to be one of the nations, and the individuals who survived lived on as sojourners among other nations or were a remnant in the Babylonian province that had once been their kingdom. Within Jeremiah's lifetime there would be no Judah left to be the recipient of his words, like the words of earlier prophets. The nations were no longer "out there." Those who might remain of the people of God were now part of the nations, and that may account for his being called "prophet to the nations."

Jeremiah makes a remarkable claim for Nebuchadnezzar, going beyond the earlier prophets' designation of a foreign nation as Yahweh's agent of judgment. He calls Nebuchadnezzar Yahweh's "servant" (Jer. 25:9; 27:7; 43:10), a term reserved for the prophets elsewhere in Jeremiah (e.g., 7:25; 25:4; 26:5).[77] According to these passages Yahweh has, for the time being, turned over the nations to the dominion of the Babylonian king:

> Now I have given all these lands into the hand of King Nebuchadnezzar of Babylon, my servant, and I have given him even the wild animals of the field to serve him. All the nations shall serve him and his son and his grandson, until the time of his own land comes; then many nations and great kings shall make him their slave. (Jer. 27:6–7)

There are two practical lessons to be drawn from this. In ch. 27 the message is to King Zedekiah: Do not rebel, for submission to Nebuchadnezzar is the will of

Yahweh. The second lesson is addressed to the exiles taken to Babylonia in 597: Do not expect to return to Judah in your lifetime, for it is Yahweh's will that you live and prosper there. Seek the welfare (*shalom*) of Babylon, your enemy! (Jer. 29:4–7). The ambiguity in the references to Babylon forms a natural transition to the promissory passages in Jeremiah, and thus ch. 29 will be one of the passages with which the next section will begin. For the time being Babylon is doing God's will, the above texts claim, but eventually the excessive suffering inflicted on the world by Nebuchadnezzar's armies will rebound on Babylon, as it did on Assyria (Jer. 50:17; 51:34–37, 49). The location and order of the oracles against the nations in the Masoretic Text (unlike the Septuagint), at the end of the book (chs. 46—51) and with Babylon last (chs. 50—51), make them function in the book of Jeremiah as Isa. 10:5–19 functioned in the book of Isaiah. "Penultimately, the purposes of Yahweh converge with the interests of Babylon. Ultimately, God's purposes converge with no earthly arrangement, and certainly not with Babylon."[78] Whether or not both points of view originated with Jeremiah, both were needed to complete his book, as Isaiah 10 was needed at the end of the eighth century.

Restoration

There was little left. Yahwism of some sort did continue to be practiced in the territory of the old Northern Kingdom, for a group of unfortunate pilgrims from Shechem, Shiloh, and Samaria is mentioned in Jer. 41:4–5. The reaction to Josiah's attempted reform late in the seventh century seems to have been fairly extreme, according to Jeremiah 44 and Ezekiel 8, for the Judean form of Yahwism was highly syncretistic. Jeremiah had some friends who intervened on his behalf, but there is no evidence preserved of a faithful group who recognized the special character of Yahwism as the prophets had taught it. Judah might have survived without the extensive destruction wrecked by Nebuchadnezzar, if Jehoiakim and Zedekiah had been more astute politicians, but it did not. The end, predicted from Amos through Jeremiah, had come, but no one could find satisfaction in that. What more could be said? What reason would there be to say more?

We cannot be sure that it was Jeremiah who made the transition from judgment to promise. There is no reason why he could not have done so, since the question whether there would be any future for the people of Yahweh became a critical one during his lifetime. Most of the promissory material in the book is in the prose parts, however, and the relationship of Jeremiah himself to those materials remains an open question.[79] For our purposes the question of authorship is less important than the recognition that the promises make a highly creative theological move. If not from Jeremiah, they come from another prophet who was at least as original as Jeremiah, if not as skilled a writer. The transition was made from judgment to promise with specific reference to Babylon, in the passages cited in the previous section. Babylon was identified as God's chosen agent for the judgment of sinful Judah, in accordance with long-standing prophetic tradition. Exile, as the climax of that judgment, could be spoken of as an apparently absolute end:

I will scatter them among nations that neither they nor their ancestors have known; and I will send the sword after them, until I have consumed them. (Jer. 9:16 [MT 15]; cf. Jer. 20:4; 27:10, 15)

But in two passages dated between 597 and 587, a new move is made. In ch. 24, Jeremiah sees two baskets of figs. The figs themselves apparently mean nothing, but their condition is the basis for a message from God concerning the relative futures of the 597 exiles, and those left in Judah. Popular theology may very well have applied the prophetic message to those exiles, deducing that their fate had proved them guilty, while those still left in the homeland must have been justified. That conclusion is challenged here, with the good figs compared with the exiles and the rotten figs with those left in Judah. Does this mean the prophet considers the exiles to be morally superior? He does not say that. Presumably the basis for the distinction is that they have already suffered the maximum punishment—exile.[80] The nature and the order of the promises are remarkable: "I will set my eyes upon them for good" (Jer. 24:6a). They are not declared to be good; God's intention for them is good. "I will bring them back to this land. I will build them up, and not tear them down; I will plant them, and not pluck them up. I will give them a heart to know that I am the LORD; and they shall be my people and I will be their God" (vv. 6b–7a). Restoration to their homeland is the most frequently repeated promise in the prophetic books. Added to it will be anthropological change, necessary for a new world, given the desperateness of the human situation as it is described in Jeremiah. God now promises to give the exiles a heart to know that he is Yahweh. This is far more than intellectual awareness. Zimmerli's study of the expression concluded that it means "adoration that kneels because of divinely inspired recognition, an orientation toward the one who himself says, 'I am Yahweh.'"[81] Finally, "for they shall return to me with their whole heart" (v. 7b). "Return," that is, repentance, seems here to be the result of God's action to restore them physically to their land and to change them internally in order to make obedience possible. The order is different from Deut. 30:1–5, where restoration is dependent on the human decision to return, and probably deliberately so, for this is not the only place in the prophets that says repentance is possible only after an act of divine grace.[82]

The second passage dealing with the future of the 597 exiles is the letter from Jeremiah, advising them to make Babylonia their home, for they need not expect to return. The words "build" and "plant," familiar from Jer. 1:10, occur here also, but in a new way:

Build houses and live in them; plant gardens and eat what they produce. Take wives and have sons and daughters; take wives for your sons, and give your daughters in marriage, that they may bear sons and daughters; multiply there, and do not decrease. But seek the welfare (*shalom*) of the city where I have sent you into exile, and pray to the LORD on its behalf, for in its welfare you will find your welfare. (Jer. 29:5–7)

Eventual restoration to the homeland is promised, and once again that precedes the reference to people seeking the Lord (vv. 10–14), but they are not to expect restoration until seventy years have passed. The temptation to calculate with the seventy-year figure has seldom been resisted, beginning already with Dan. 9:2, 24–27, but it is most likely to be explained with reference to Ps. 90:10: "The days of our life are seventy years, or perhaps eighty, if we are strong." Seventy years was the hoped-for, long life span (actually achieved by few at that time), so the point of citing that number was to say to the exiles, "You are not going back," thus emphasizing the importance of building houses, planting gardens, and having children. In these two chapters exile has thus taken on a radically new meaning. Prior to this it had been wholly negative, but Babylon now becomes a place of waiting, from which something new and transformed will come.

Babylon is thus both the enemy, bringing terrible suffering, and the place from which a better future will be created. As the enemy, whose power apparently cannot be challenged, Babylon is also a threat to the prophetic claim that Yahweh is Lord, and so the traditional oracles of judgment of the foreign conqueror must also appear in Jeremiah's book (chs. 50—51; 25:12–26). The fall of Babylon was expected to lead to a return from exile (e.g., 50:4–5, 17–20), even including those who had gone into exile in Assyria from the Northern Kingdom in the eighth century (see also Jer. 31:2–6, 15–22).[83] Two of the most frequent themes of the poetic oracles of Jeremiah reappear in the form of a promise in Jer. 23:1–8. This passage immediately follows a long sequence dealing with the recent kings of Judah (21:11–22:30), and after a general condemnation (23:1–2) moves to promises of restoration of exiles to their land and of the gift of a righteous king to rule over them (vv. 3–8). The "new exodus" will so far surpass the former one that the original will be forgotten:

> Therefore, the days are surely coming, says the LORD, when it shall no longer be said, "As the LORD lives who brought the people of Israel up out of the land of Egypt," but "As the LORD lives who brought out and led the offspring of the house of Israel out of the land of the north and out of all the lands where he had driven them." Then they shall live in their own land. (Jer. 23:7–8; also in 16:14–15)

The promise of a new king is equally striking because it is the only expectation of a righteous king in Jeremiah (repeated, with elaborations, in 33:14–26):

> The days are surely coming, says the LORD, when I will raise up for David a righteous Branch, and he shall reign as king and deal wisely, and shall execute justice and righteousness in the land. In his days Judah will be saved and Israel will live in safety. And this is the name by which he will be called: "The LORD is our righteousness." (Jer. 23:5–6)

The term "branch" and the emphasis on justice and righteousness may be compared with the promise in Isa. 11:1–5, and note that both Judah and Israel are expected to be ruled again by a Davidic king. His name, *Yahweh Tsidqenu*, may be an ironic comment on the name of Judah's last king, Zedekiah, *Tsidqiyah*, which means almost the same thing: "Yahweh is our righteousness" or "Yahweh is my righteousness." As always in these prophetic passages which were later called

Messianic prophecies, the hope is for the coming of a human figure, a king who will rule justly once God has established peace on earth.

Chapters 30—31 contain the most extended collection of promises in the book, and restoration to the land is once again the most prominent theme. That God intends to turn the sorrow of his people to joy is a motif that runs throughout. The desolation of the land, which Jeremiah had lamented, will be replaced with abundant fertility (e.g., 31:5, 12). David (30:9) and Zion (30:17; 31:6, 12, 38–40) are mentioned in passing, but are not prominent themes. The need for an internal change in the human recipients of these material blessings once again appears, in the promise of a new covenant (31:31–34). It also will be with both Israel and Judah, and the change that is promised clearly refers to the covenant made at Sinai: "It will not be like the covenant that I made with their ancestors when I took them by the hand to bring them out of the land of Egypt—a covenant that they broke" (v. 32). The change will not be in the contents of the covenant, however, but in the recipients: "I will put my law within them, and I will write it on their hearts; and I will be their God, and they shall be my people" (v. 33). The heart, the seat of the rational will, as Israelites understood it, by which one could decide whether to obey or not, had become "devious above all else; and perverse" (Jer. 17:9). If there was to be any hope for a better future that would not be perverted immediately by human sinfulness, people themselves will have to be transformed, and this prophet believed that was God's intention.[84] Finally, "for I will forgive their iniquity, and remember their sin no more" (31:34b) promises forgiveness without demanding prior repentance. The message of the book concerning the present human condition is consistent in claiming that hope depends entirely on the promise that God will make it possible for us to change. This book speaks more explicitly of an eschatological forgiveness than any other; that is, not just of a willingness to let us start over, but to change humans so that they will not sin again:

> In those days and at that time, says the LORD, the iniquity of Israel shall be sought, and there shall be none; and the sins of Judah, and none shall be found; for I will pardon the remnant that I have spared. (Jer. 50:20)[85]

Ezekiel took up the human dilemma from a similar point of view, and the outlook of these two prophets with respect to human potential and divine intention clearly lies behind the theology of Paul.

3.5 Obadiah

There is a great variety of opinion concerning the date and unity of the book of Obadiah, but for thematic reasons it is useful to discuss it just after Jeremiah.[86] Many date at least parts of it shortly after the fall of Jerusalem, and whatever its date, it provides a helpful basis for considering the effects on Judeans of the loss of territory after 587. The book identifies itself as a vision concerning Edom, calling for the nations to rise up against it in battle because of its pride (vv. 1–5), then describes its crimes explicitly as the mistreatment of Edom's brother Jacob in the day of his calamity (vv. 6–14). The second and last major unit of the book then speaks of the coming of the Day of the Lord against all nations, concluding with a promise that Israelites will once again possess the lands they have lost, and more (vv. 15–21). What little we know of the history of the Edomites in the period after 587 reveals that these two parts possess a thematic unity, for Edom came to occupy a large portion of what had once been Judah.

During the final years of the kingdom of Judah, the Edomite kingdom extended from the River Zered (at the southeast end of the Dead Sea) southward along the east side of the Arabah, as far as the Gulf of Akabah. Its eastern border was the Arabian desert. The earlier history of troubled relations between Edom and Judah need not be surveyed here.[87] Important for understanding Obadiah are references to the ways the Edomites took advantage of the defeat of Judah by Nebuchadnezzar. Ezekiel 25 contains a series of oracles condemning the neighboring nations for their treatment of Judah at that time, and the oracle against Edom says, "Because Edom acted revengefully against the house of Judah and has grievously offended in taking vengeance upon them . . . ," but adds no specifics (Ezek. 25:12). Psalm 137 seems to make them participants in the fall of Jerusalem: "Remember, O LORD, against the Edomites the day of Jerusalem's fall, how they said, 'Tear it down! Tear it down! Down to its foundations!'" (Ps. 137:7). Both of these texts were probably produced shortly after the fall of the city. There is no record of Edomite activity during the last years of Judah in 2 Kings, Jeremiah, or in Neo-Babylonian documents.[88] We find only these bitter memories of their participation in the destruction of Jerusalem. They are expressed most fully in Obad. 10–14.

Obadiah makes use of the patriarchal traditions equating Edom with Esau, Jacob's twin brother (Genesis 25, 27—28, 32—33), in order to emphasize the seriousness of the crime: "For the slaughter and violence done to your brother Jacob, shame shall cover you, and you shall be cut off forever" (Obad. 10). There had been periodic conflicts between the neighboring countries, and Judah had been guilty of mistreating Edom in the past (2 Sam. 8:13–14),[89] but the issue in Obadiah is clearly the fall of Jerusalem:

On the day that you stood aside,
   on the day that strangers carried off his wealth,
and foreigners entered his gates
   and cast lots for Jerusalem,
     you too were like one of them.

(Obad. 11)

Then follows a series taking the grammatical form of prohibitions. Literally they read, "Do not . . . ," but since v. 11 refers to something that has already happened there is general agreement that the NRSV reproduces the force of the accusations appropriately:[90]

But you should not have gloated over your brother
   on the day of his misfortune;
you should not have rejoiced over the people of Judah
   on the day of their ruin;

you should not have boasted
    on the day of distress.
You should not have entered the gate of my people
    on the day of their calamity;
you should not have joined in the gloating over Judah's disaster
    on the day of his calamity;
you should not have looted his goods
    on the day of his calamity.
You should not have stood at the crossings
    to cut off his fugitives;
you should not have handed over his survivors
    on the day of distress.

(Obad. 12–14)

The details and the emotional force of this poetry suggest that at least this part of the book was produced not long after 587.[91]

This indictment forms the center of the book. Two announcements of judgment precede it. There are significant parallels between vv. 1b–5 and the oracle against Edom in Jeremiah 49 (vv. 9–16). There is no way of determining whether one prophet was quoting the other, and the general opinion among scholars now is that both passages probably use stock phrases that had been used more than once, perhaps in oracles against enemy nations produced for use in the cult.[92] The quotation of an oracle against Moab, Edom, and Philistia in Psalm 60 provides some support for these theories of cultic prophecy, but it should be noted that we have no description anywhere in the Old Testament of liturgies such as those suggested to be the setting for the kind of prophecy found in Obadiah.

A peculiarly intense hatred of the Edomites persisted for a long time (cf. Mal. 1:2–5), and that was probably due more to the loss of territory than to a single event, the Edomites' behavior in 587. Ezekiel 35 makes that explicit:

> Because you said, "These two nations and these two countries shall be mine, and we will take possession of them,"—although the LORD was there—therefore, as I live, says the Lord GOD, I will deal with you according to the anger and envy that you showed because of your hatred against them; and I will make myself known among you, when I judge you. You shall know that I, the LORD, have heard all the abusive speech that you uttered against the mountains of Israel, saying, "They are laid desolate, they are given us to devour." (Ezek. 35:10–12)

Although the Babylonians deported a relatively small number of Judeans, according to the figures given in 2 Kings and Jeremiah,[93] the population was also depleted by deaths and by flight to neighboring countries. We have no evidence to indicate how the Babylonians governed the Judean territory after the death of Gedaliah (Jeremiah 41), but the southern part was evidently open to incursions by the Edomites from the east. The Edomite monarchy was apparently brought to an end by Nabonidus (556–539 B.C.E.), who campaigned in the Transjordan and southward as far as the oasis Tema, in the Arabian desert.[94] In the next century,

Edom is not mentioned in the book of Nehemiah and seems to have been part of the province of Arabia. Diodorus Siculus reports that by 312 B.C.E. an Arabian tribe called the Nabateans had occupied Edom (*Bibliotheca Historica* 19.94). These sketchy bits of evidence, plus indications from archaeological surveys that former Edomite sites were unoccupied during the Persian period, suggest that Edom had been under pressure by Arabian tribes migrating northward for some time.[95] As early as the sixth century there is archaeological evidence for the presence of some Edomites in the Negev, so it appears likely that migration across the Arabah into former Judean territory that could no longer be defended began at that time, and continued because of pressure from the Nabateans until eventually the Edomites dominated the region from Beth-zur southward.[96] During the Hasmonean period, John Hyrcanus conquered the region, now known by the Greek name Idumaea (derived from "Edom"), and carried out forced conversions of its inhabitants to Judaism (Josephus, *Antiquities* xiii 9.1 [255–58]).

The loss of this large portion of what had once been Judah, including Hebron, with its associations with Abraham and David, forms the likely basis for the eschatological text that concludes the book of Obadiah (vv. 15–21). It begins with an announcement that the Day of the Lord is near, as in Zeph. 1:14, but now the Day is for the judgment of the nations, not of Israel. Indeed, the house of Jacob will now be the agent used by Yahweh to punish Edom for its crimes (v. 18). The cup of judgment, which Jeremiah was to force upon Jerusalem first, then all the nations (Jer. 25:15–29), will in the near future be given only to the nations (v. 16; cf. Lam. 4:21). The book reaches its climax with the promise that Israelites will once again inhabit the lands from which they have been expelled, using the root *yarash*, "possess, dispossess" five times in vv. 17–20. This most often repeated part of prophetic eschatology, the promise of return to the land, is the single promise offered by Obadiah.

The land promised to Abraham extended further than any Israelite king ever succeeded in mastering: "To your descendants I give this land, from the river of Egypt to the great river, the river Euphrates" (Gen. 15:18). The boundaries described to Joshua were at least as extensive: "From the wilderness and the Lebanon as far as the great river, the river Euphrates, all the land of the Hittites, to the Great Sea in the west shall be your territory" (Josh. 1:4). Obadiah does not think of territory as far north as the Euphrates, but he also extends the boundaries of the land given to Israelites beyond anything they had occupied before: into Phoenicia, Philistia, and Edom. He foresees "those of the Negeb," an area probably occupied by Edomites in his day, as extending their territory eastward into what had formerly been Edom. Those of the Shephelah, the region between the hill country of Judah and Philistia, will take over the former Philistine territory. The former Northern Kingdom (Ephraim and Samaria) will become Judean territory, and Benjamin will occupy Gilead, in the Transjordan, so the new land will extend unbroken from the Transjordan in the east to the Mediterranean in the west (Obad. 19). The northern border will be at Zarephath, between Tyre and Sidon, and the southern border in the Negeb (v. 20).[97]

Obadiah's hope for justice in the future is based on the theme of reversal of fortune, or perhaps one should say, retribution; those who have brought suffering to Judah will in the future suffer the same kind of distress. "As you have done, it shall be done to you; your deeds shall return on your own head" (v. 15; cf. vv. 10, 16, 17). This certainly represents an insistence on justice, and an expectation that God's justice will one day be manifest on earth, and that is an important part of eschatology, but it is not the highest level of theology. It is a starting point beyond which most of the other prophets made considerable progress. The last line of Obadiah shows that the book is not unaware of Israel's more fully developed prophetic theology: "The kingdom shall be the LORD's."[98]

3.6 Ezekiel

Ezekiel faced a different challenge from the prophets who preceded him. He was one of the Judeans who did lose everything and found themselves in exile. He experienced the judgment to the fullest—except for death itself—and the question whether anything lay ahead for a people of Yahweh was a personal matter for him. But he was called to be a prophet to the exiles and as such he had to be a creative theologian, doing far more than reinterpreting the prophetic tradition for his own time. Elsewhere I have said that his ministry was a pastoral one, in that we find him responding to the needs being expressed by his people in ways we do not find in the earlier books.[99] Much of the theology of the book can thus be traced by noting the issues to which he responded.

The book is more neatly organized than others, with a consistency about it that is not to be found in Isaiah or Jeremiah. It is mostly prose, with a good many of the oracles dated, and with a clear, three-part structure. Most of chs. 1—24 focus on a single message: The fall of Jerusalem is inevitable, and will be the just judgment of Yahweh.[100] Chapters 25—32 contain a collection of oracles against other nations, with special emphasis on Tyre and Egypt. Chapter 33 makes the transition from judgment to promise, with news that Jerusalem has fallen (in 587 B.C.E.), and chs. 34—48 deal with restoration.[101] A series of dates (not all of them in order) provides an additional indication that the book as a whole has a plan, of a sort that can scarcely be found in any other prophetic book.[102] They indicate that Ezekiel's ministry began in 593 B.C.E. (ch. 1:2) and extended at least until 571 (29:17; out of chronological order; the date previous to this is in 40:1, 573). The book also locates him among the exiles by the river Chebar (near Nippur, in Babylonia; 1:1, 3), at the site called Tel-abib (3:15), so he was among those upper classes who were deported in 597. He was a priest (1:3), and his priestly training shows clearly in his choice of vocabulary.

The book of Ezekiel is thus almost our only source of information about the early years of exile in Babylonia (except for a few fragments in Jeremiah 29). After Ezekiel we have no data until Second Isaiah begins to speak, and the audience addressed by the latter prophet—essentially the second generation in exile—seems to have been very different from those to whom Ezekiel was sent. Remarkable things happened during those years, and so Henry McKeating appropriately begins his book, "The importance of Ezekiel can hardly be overstressed."[103] His message moves from death to resurrection, and those terms are realistic assessments of what did happen in his generation and the generations that followed. At the beginning of his ministry he had to insist on the completeness of the death of the people of God, and to be a part of it. The awfulness of the experience and the message that had to correspond to it led him to use language that surpasses, if possible, the brutality of his predecessors. This has led to unenthusiastic, if not negative judgments of him by some interpreters, but he and his people had been affected by suffering as others have not, so if we take their experiences seriously, we may appreciate the reasons for his language.

> The context of exile suggests that weariness is an experience of the collapse of everything secure and precious, the jeopardizing of one's historical identity, submission to forces and powers which are hostile or at least indifferent and the absence of any support or assurance of rescue. . . . Exile was not simply displacement from the land but it was the experience of the end of creation, the exhaustion of salvation history, the demise of king, temple, city, land and all those supports which gave structure and meaning to life.[104]

Ezekiel and his fellow exiles knew what it was like to be bottled up inside a walled city, with an enemy army camped outside, had participated in caring for people wounded in the early fighting and had seen them die, had seen the food supplies becoming smaller and had experienced hunger. With surrender, families were separated, some people escaped, some just disappeared. Eventually the Chaldeans selected those to be taken into exile, they were rounded up into camps, and finally marched away. Many must then have been isolated individuals, still in shock from seeing their loved ones die, or frantic with anxiety because they did not know what had become of husband or child, wife or parent. And they walked, day after day, for months. The route from Jerusalem to Babylonia is about 700 miles. They walked, and more died, and then found themselves in a strange and forbidding land, not hilly and wooded like Palestine, but a flat alluvial plain, marked only by great rivers and an extensive network of canals watering fertile fields; and here and there what seemed to them to be immense walled cities, with temple towers looming into the heavens. At the site of an old, ruined city, Tel-abib, Ezekiel and some of the exiles had found their new home. It was in that alien place that Ezekiel encountered the God of Israel.

When Ezekiel uses language such as that in 5:15, 17, "You shall be a mockery and a taunt, a warning and a horror, to the nations around you, when I execute judgments on you in anger and fury, and with furious punishments. . . . I will send famine and wild animals against you, and they will rob you of your children; pestilence and bloodshed shall pass through you; and I will bring the sword upon you," he is not *imagining* a wrathful, vengeful God, nor expressing his own anger. He speaks of things he and his audience have already seen, and like the other prophets he claims they deserved it. God described Ezekiel's congregation at the time of his call, and they were no *faithful* remnant:

> Son of man, I send you to the people of Israel, to a nation of rebels, who have rebelled against me; they and their fathers have transgressed against

> me to this very day. The people also are impudent and stubborn: I send
> you to them; and you shall say to them, "Thus says the Lord GOD." (Ezek.
> 2:3–4, RSV)

> But the house of Israel will not listen to you; for they are not willing to lis-
> ten to me; because all the house of Israel are of a hard forehead and of a
> stubborn heart. (Ezek. 3:7, RSV)

There was a community of sorts at Tel-abib, with a prophet living in their midst.
But what future did they have? Was there any likelihood that they could achieve
and maintain an identity that could preserve the uniqueness of the Yahwistic faith
under these conditions? How could one expect it, when even in their homeland—
where tradition, culture, language, government, and custom were unified in telling
them who they were—the essence of Yahwism remained constantly in jeopardy,
and as practiced it was a mishmash of elements drawn from several religions?
Now they lived in an alien culture that denied the truth of their ancestral faith. Any
judgment of their future based on purely human factors would have to expect them
to assimilate to the predominant culture within a few years, leaving nothing but a
few vague recollections of Yahweh and Israel. The Yahwistic faith did survive,
however, and it did more than survive. It is the book of Ezekiel that reveals to us
the severity of the crisis, and it must have been the prophet's own work that laid
some of the foundations for a new "house of Israel." He responded to a faith built
on sand, to unbelief, and to despair, and at significant points in the book the challenges he faced are revealed by quotations of what the people were saying. Those
"proverbs" serve very well to introduce much of the theology of Ezekiel.

The Attack on Complacency: Jerusalem Will Fall

> The word of the LORD came to me: "Son of man, what is this proverb that
> you have about the land of Israel, saying, 'The days grow long, and every
> vision comes to nought'? Tell them therefore, 'Thus says the Lord GOD: I
> will put an end to this proverb, and they shall no more use it as a proverb
> in Israel.' But say to them, The days are at hand, and the fulfilment of
> every vision." (Ezek. 12:21–23, RSV)

"Complacency" may seem a strange word to choose for these circumstances,
but it will serve to describe two attitudes Ezekiel dealt with, one of them among
the exiles and the other among those left in Jerusalem after 597. The complacency was based on the conviction Jeremiah also fought against, that Jerusalem
was invulnerable. For the exiles, that provided a basis for hope that their sojourn
in Babylonia would be brief. Surely Yahweh would intervene soon, and they
would return to their homes in triumph. Ezekiel understood that was hope built on
sand and sought in a variety of ways to convince them of its futility, but they
found a way to resist hearing him, as the proverb quoted above shows: Yes, he is
a prophet, and his words may come true someday, but these words of doom have
nothing to do with us. Ezekiel makes their wishful thinking more explicit later in
the same chapter:

> Again the word of the LORD came to me: "Son of man, behold, they of the house of Israel say, 'The vision that he sees is for many days hence, and he prophesies of times far off.'" (Ezek. 12:26–27, RSV)

That complacency could survive under those circumstances is remarkable, but it is wishful thinking that keeps most people going. Ezekiel's task—to convince those exiles that Jerusalem would certainly fall—was critical because when wishful thinking is all you have, and that is suddenly done away with, what will you do then? So he tried every means to get them to face the reality that they could not base their hope on Jerusalem, and that they were not going home.[105]

He devised new rhetorical techniques in order to try to get the attention of that "rebellious house," and his methods were a part of his message. One of the most prominent features of the book is the presence of numerous allegories, a genre that seldom appears elsewhere in the Old Testament. Ezekiel took familiar metaphors —the vine, lions, trees, and the unfaithful wife already found in Hosea and Jeremiah—and spun them out into elaborate stories. They are all highly offensive, for various reasons, and that was certainly intentional. As stories, they got one's attention; as offensive stories their aim was to force one to think about the unacceptable. Chapter 16 makes of Jerusalem, that city chosen by Yahweh to be his dwelling place, a foundling child of dubious parentage:

> Thus says the Lord GOD to Jerusalem: Your origin and your birth were in the land of the Canaanites; your father was an Amorite, and your mother a Hittite. As for your birth, on the day you were born your navel cord was not cut, nor were you washed with water to cleanse you, nor rubbed with salt, nor wrapped in cloths. No eye pitied you, to do any of these things for you out of compassion for you; but you were thrown out in the open field, for you were abhorred on the day you were born. (Ezek. 16:3–5)

Ezekiel makes new uses of his people's history. Here he reminds them that Jerusalem was a Canaanite city until the time of David, a latecomer into their history. He accepts the prevailing belief that Yahweh chose it to be the place where he could be found; in the allegory, God saved the child's life and when she grew up chose her to be his wife. But the rest of Jerusalem's history is judged in the most severe way possible. She became a wanton woman, a harlot, and not even a respectable harlot because her lovers didn't pay her; she bought them. So Ezekiel dragged the holy city, the one last hope of his people, down to become the subject of a filthy story.[106] He used the same theme again in ch. 23, now giving God two wives, which should remind us not to take metaphor too literally. The wives are Samaria and Jerusalem, so the history of the Northern Kingdom is introduced in order to make a point opposite to that in 1 Kings 17: The sins of Jerusalem are even worse than those of Samaria.

Closely associated with the election of Jerusalem was the election of David (cf. Psalm 132), and Ezekiel also dealt with kingship in his own, original way. He called one of his allegories a riddle, because none of it makes much sense until one knows the key—which he then provided:

A great eagle, with great wings and long pinions,
    rich in plumage of many colors,
        came to the Lebanon.
He took the top of the cedar,
    broke off its topmost shoot;
he carried it to a land of trade,
    set it in a city of merchants.

(Ezek. 17:3–4)

The eagle represents Nebuchadnezzar, and the shoot carried away is the young king Jehoiachin, who was exiled in 597 (17:12). The story continues with the appointment of Zedekiah as vassal king and his attempts to get aid from Egypt, then moves to the prediction of his death. This passage contains both allegory and its literal interpretation, so that no one might misunderstand, but a second text concerning the kings is metaphorical throughout (ch. 19). It is introduced as a lamentation, a genre more likely to be chosen by Ezekiel to speak of kings than by earlier prophets, for he no longer had to suffer under those inept rulers.[107] Every story had an unhappy ending.[108] The result? "Then I said, 'Ah Lord GOD! they are saying of me, "Is he not a maker of allegories?"'" (Ezek. 20:49). He had gained a reputation as a good storyteller, but the exiles did not accept the point of his stories.

He retold Israel's history in plain language, as well. In 20:1–31, he depicts the classic period, from oppression in Egypt to the gift of the land, in three scenes, each of them with two themes: Israel's disobedience and God's patience. Ezekiel even accuses the ancestors of practicing idolatry in Egypt, something Exodus never mentions (v. 7). Of the wilderness period, only the traditions of rebellion are recalled. But the punishment they deserved throughout their history had been forestalled, for the sake of God's name, "that it should not be profaned in the sight of the nations" (vv. 9, 14, 22). The divine motive, "for the sake of my holy name," is a central part of Ezekiel's theology, and it will be examined in the next section of this chapter. Here, it functions as the motive for God's patience in bearing with a rebellious people throughout their history, from Egypt to the promised land, but the point of the recital is to insist that patience cannot be counted on anymore (vv. 27–31).[109] This highly original reworking of the traditional history is then used as the basis for an extended promise concerning a new exodus and settlement in the land (20:32–44). Like Ezek. 17:22–24, this is probably a reworking of the pre–587 prophecy, after the fall of Jerusalem, when a new kind of message was called for. We shall return to it later in this chapter.

Ezekiel heard about an opposite kind of complacency enjoyed for a short time by those left in Jerusalem after 597. They seem to have concluded that the prophetic threat had come to pass, the guilty had suffered the judgment due them, by death or exile, and claimed that history had vindicated the remnant in Jerusalem, as the true people of God. Jeremiah countered that attitude with his word about the good and rotten figs (Jeremiah 24), and Ezekiel also deals with it at the end of his longest vision-account (chs. 8—11). His supernatural trip to Jerusalem has been explained in many different ways. It is not necessary to debate the phenomenology of Ezekiel's paranormal experiences in a book on prophetic theology, so the reader is referred to the commentaries for that discussion. We cannot prove that Ezekiel did not have second sight, so as to be able to know what was going on in Jerusalem from his place in Babylon, but it may also be that in a visionary experience he saw things he had already learned about from more normal sources. At any rate, he knew that people in Jerusalem were saying of the exiles, "They have gone far from the LORD; to us this land is given for a possession" (11:15). Remarkably, this futile hope is countered in the present context not by another message concerning the inevitable fall of Jerusalem, the theme that dominates chs. 1—24, but by a promise for the 597 exiles. It thus functions the way the promises in Jeremiah 24 and 29 do, as an insistence that the future lies with the exiles, not with those left in Jerusalem. It is tempting to think this passage must also have been added to an earlier vision after 587, but it may also be that the nature of the issue—claims of Jerusalemites—called for a promise to exiles. There is a parallel text in 33:23–29, taking up the same claim to the land by those left behind, but responding in the expected way, with condemnation of their sins.

The participatory nature of the prophetic symbolic act reaches its climax with Ezekiel. Some of them functioned as "object lessons," like Jeremiah's yoke (Jeremiah 27—28). Ezekiel was told to tie up some of his belongings so that he could carry them on his back, then to dig a hole through a wall with his hands and to crawl through it with his baggage as if he were setting off on a journey (Ezek. 12:1–7). He was to make sure he had an audience, and when they asked him what he was doing he was to answer: "This oracle concerns the prince in Jerusalem and all the house of Israel in it. . . . I am a sign for you: as I have done, so shall it be done to them; they shall go into exile, into captivity" (12:10–11). He was to eat his bread with quaking and drink his water with trembling and with fearfulness, for the day would soon come when the people of Jerusalem would "eat their bread with fearfulness, and drink their water in dismay, because their land shall be stripped of all it contains, on account of the violence of all those who live in it" (12:18–19).

In ch. 4 he is instructed to make a model of the city of Jerusalem, build a siege wall around it and make tiny siege engines so as to act out the attack on the city, which he knows is coming soon. But he also had to experience the siege, in a more intense way than the acted-out escape in ch. 12. He was put on siege rations. "And you, take wheat and barley, beans and lentils, millet and spelt; put them into one vessel, and make bread for yourself" (Ezek. 4:9). This was no new health food recipe; the idea was that he had to eat small quantities of this and that, just as people in a besieged city would have to make do with whatever they could find. "The food that you eat shall be twenty shekels a day by weight; at fixed times you shall eat it. And you shall drink water by measure, one-sixth of a hin; at fixed times you shall drink" (4:10–11). He was eating about eleven ounces of food a day, and drinking about a quart of water. Only once did Ezekiel protest something God ordered him to do. He was a priest and had always carefully followed the rules of ritual cleanliness, but God told him to bake his little loaf of bread on human dung (as others would have to do, because of a shortage of fuel). When Ezekiel protested, God permitted him to use cow's dung instead (4:12–15). The prophet and his group were safe in exile at this point, not threatened by the army that would soon threaten Jerusalem again, but as a man of God he had to share what God's people anywhere would suffer. God made the reason for all of this clear: "Son of man, behold, I will break the staff of bread in Jerusalem; they shall eat bread by weight and with fearfulness; and they shall drink water by measure and in dismay. I will do this that they may lack bread and water, and look at one another in dismay, and waste away under their punishment" (4:16–17, RSV). His mission was not only to announce judgment, and not only to justify God's treatment of them by spelling out in accurate detail all that they had done wrong, but as a man of God he must also experience the punishment with them.

This accounts for one of the symbolic acts that has puzzled readers most. He was told to lie on his left side for 390 days, equal to the 390 years of Israel's punishment, then on his right side for 40 days, corresponding to the 40 years of Judah's punishment (4:4–8). Questions about whether this is physically possible have led several interpreters to claim none of the so-called symbolic acts were performed, but all were actually parables.[110] We cannot be sure how the act was carried out, or whether it was a parable, but the explanation of lying on his side is of great theological importance: "You shall bear their punishment for the number of days that you lie there. . . . So you shall bear the punishment of the house of Israel . . . and bear the punishment of the house of Judah" (vv. 4, 5, 6). Here is explicit language showing that interpreting the symbolic actions as prophetic participation in the sufferings of their people is not reading a theology into these texts that they were not intended to convey. The terms here are the verb *naśa'* (lift, bear, carry) and the noun *'awon* (iniquity, guilt) and Baruch Schwartz has shown that in the priestly vocabulary of the Old Testament when one bears one's own iniquity that means one is guilty, but when one (usually God) bears someone else's iniquity it means that person is released from guilt.[111] Schwartz does not discuss Ezekiel 4, but it scarcely seems possible that the passage intends to say the prophet's suffering lifted the burden of sin from his people, even though the book is strongly influenced by priestly language. It seems more likely to be saying that although he did not commit the sins of which his people are guilty, he bears their guilt with them. "He brings together in his symbolic bondage the guilt of Israel as a burden in his own life."[112] To ask the prophet to bear the guilt of others has reached the limit of what a human can do. This passage makes Ezekiel the predecessor of the servant of the Lord in Isa. 52:13–53:12. The same terminology is used there, in ways that seem to surpass what is possible for any human.

The last of his recorded symbolic acts involves participation in the effects of Jerusalem's fall in 587.

> "Son of man, behold, I am about to take the delight of your eyes away from you at a stroke; yet you shall not mourn or weep nor shall your tears run down. Sigh, but not aloud; make no mourning for the dead. Bind on your turban, and put your shoes on your feet; do not cover your lips, nor eat the bread of mourners." So I spoke to the people in the morning, and at evening my wife died. And on the next morning I did as I was commanded. (Ezek. 24:16–18, RSV)

Once again we hear from his audience, puzzled as usual by his behavior, not able to draw the appropriate conclusion because it is a message they cannot think about: "Then the people said to me, 'Will you not tell us what these things mean for us, that you are acting this way?'" Ezekiel's response was to tell them that the delight of their eyes, Jerusalem, was about to die, as his wife had died. On that day the exiles will be innocently going about their daily activities by the River Chebar, working and eating and chatting as usual. They will have lost the rest of their families that day, and the temple will be in flames, but the dead will not be mourned. Because that is true, then God's prophet may not mourn his dead either!

Something more must be said about the symbolic acts of the prophets at this point, because of the added meaning provided by this book. What is said of the lives of Jeremiah and Ezekiel seems to be claiming that in the prophet the divine and the human were somehow trying to come together. God's way of approaching his people was not to stand over against, as the messages of the earlier prophets suggest, pronouncing judgment. The strangeness of the lives of these later prophets suggest a divine move toward participation in the lives of God's people, including the sharing of the just punishment he had to inflict. In the sufferings of these men of God are hints that God also intends to experience the sufferings himself, although as humans the best they could be was a sign of what God was up to. Christians may thus see in the symbolic acts, bizarre as some of them may be, intimations of the incarnation.

The Sovereignty of God

The God revealed in Ezekiel is one who acts with terrifying and unrelenting anger against a sinful people, a God whose will cannot be swayed by any appeal (note Ezek. 14:12–23). Even the prophets of that God get no special privileges, for they must suffer along with their condemned people. Yet we have just seen a hint that the prophets may be suffering along with God, as well. The God revealed in Ezekiel is also one who longs to forgive and who has the power to do so. Eventually Ezekiel will claim that God will one day forgive, renew, and restore, not because of anything anyone deserves, but solely because it is God's nature to do so. Both messages, judgment and forgiveness, thus fall under the heading, "sovereignty," a term frequently applied to the God of Ezekiel.

Key phrases for this theme are "I am Yahweh," "Then you/they will know that I am Yahweh," "for the sake of my holy name," and perhaps also "son of man." The last is included because God's regular address of Ezekiel in this unusual way may be intended to remind him (and the readers) of the radical difference between humanity and God, a difference also denoted in the Old Testament by the word "holy."

The "otherness" of God is expressed in a wide variety of ways in this book. Ezekiel's inaugural vision (ch. 1) represents God's power and freedom in imagery drawn from the new environment in which he found himself. It is a theophany, but very little of the traditional language is used. Compare Ezek. 1:4 with Psalm 18 or Habakkuk 3. The vision of the throne chariot shows the influence of Babylonian art on the prophet's subconscious, as Othmar Keel has shown in his collection of parallels to the living creatures, the throne with wheels, and so on.[113] Most important is the impression made by the presence of fire and the quick and untrammeled motion of the throne. Irresistible energy is the point of it all. The extremely difficult Hebrew text may not be due entirely to textual corruption, but rather to the impossibility of expressing in human language a vision of the God who is wholly other. So, at the end, Ezekiel very carefully tells us what he did not see, using a series of qualifications of what he saw: "This was the *appearance* of the *likeness* of the *glory* of the LORD" (1:28, italics added). The effect of the experience left him prostrate, and the fact that he felt it possible even to stand only with the help of the divine spirit (2:1–2) introduces us to the view of human potential—useless without divine intervention—that runs through the book. There was a specific message for Ezekiel and his people in that vision of the freedom and energy of God, for it revealed that Yahweh was by no means confined to the temple or the land of Israel. In another vision Ezekiel saw the glory of the Lord leave Jerusalem (10:4–19; 11:22–23), but the importance of the inaugural vision was to show the prophet that Yahweh was active there among the exiles.[114]

Divine freedom is a major part of what Ezekiel needs to affirm about God, but it stands in tension with a certain vulnerability. One key term is, "for the sake of my holy name," as the motive for God's action. It is self-motivated, and not dependent on any human qualities or deeds. But the other term is "profane my holy name." There is tension between the two, for the name of the sovereign God is said to be vulnerable to human activity, after all. How could anything a human being did "profane" God's name—understanding "name," as it is used in the Old Testament, to mean one's character, one's essential nature (e.g., Pss. 9:10; 109:21).[115] It seems to be possible because God in his freedom has chosen to make himself intimately associated with a group of people who bear his name, who may take his name in vain, who may bring shame on his name by their behavior. "Name" thus includes reputation, since God is concerned that his name has been profaned in the sight of the nations, but Ezekiel expresses a concern deeper than that. In the formula that occurs, with variations, nearly eighty times, "Then you/they will know that I am Yahweh," it is the revelation of God, that is, knowledge of the true character of the one called Yahweh, that is the central concern.

God is thus related to Israel as more than a sovereign who enforces justice. Indeed, the sufferings that have befallen and will befall the Judeans are God's just punishment for their sins (e.g., Ezek. 5:6; 6:4–6; 18:10–13), but there is more to it than that. The nations have learned something about Yahweh from what they have seen of Yahweh's people, and what they have learned thus far is false. This is how God's name has been profaned among the nations. Ezekiel thus has introduced new understandings of the relationship between Israel and Yahweh, and between Yahweh and the nations. He thinks of the world as a kind of theater in the round: "This is Jerusalem; I have set her in the center of the nations, with countries all around her" (5:5). The nations are witnesses, first of Israel's rebellion against their God (5:6), then of their resultant distress (36:20–21), and finally of the truth about Yahweh when he restores and re-creates them (36:23–36). Ezekiel did not yet move to the ethical principle taught later by the rabbis, that a Jew should do nothing that would lead the nations to speak ill of their God, but the roots of that principle are probably to be found here.[116] It would eventually be understood that to be the people of God calls for lives that are reflections of the true character of God.[117] Ezekiel has also moved in a direction that more would be made of later in his concern for knowledge of Yahweh by the nations. In the future Yahweh should no longer be their anonymous sovereign, as he is in the earlier prophetic books, for when they see what he does with and for Israel, then they will know that he is Yahweh.

Walther Zimmerli's detailed studies of that frequently repeated expression, "Then you/they will know that I am Yahweh," have shed light on a rather mysterious statement.[118] Why not, "Then they will know me"? The answer begins with the use of "I am Yahweh" in the Old Testament. It is a formula of self-introduction (cf. especially Exod. 6:2, 6), uttered by one who cannot be sought and found by any human means, but who in his own freedom comes and announces his presence. His presence involves action and calls for recognition and obedience from humans.[119] Although the name is associated with the verb "to be" in Exod. 3:14, nowhere in the Old Testment is it suggested one can learn anything about God from the meaning of his name. It is simply a name, making it possible for humans to address God and identifying God when he speaks, but no more. Ezekiel's concern about knowledge maintains that distance. One does not *know Yahweh*, but it will become possible to "know that I am Yahweh."[120]

History, Ezekiel announces, will bring that knowledge even to the nations. They play the original and regular role of witnesses throughout the book, and appear in two other ways that are characteristic of Ezekiel. Earlier prophets announced God's future judgment of Assyria (and Babylonia, in Jeremiah 50—51) for the abuses committed against Israel, but oracles against other nations often did not judge them for being Israel's enemies (recall Amos 1—2; exceptions, e.g., Obadiah; Zeph. 2:8). Ezekiel 25:1–26:6; 29:6b–9 contain a series of oracles dealing specifically with the way those nations treated Judah at the time of her fall to the Babylonians. After the fall, then, prophets began to speak of Yahweh taking Judah's side over against the nations that had mistreated her, unlike the typical message prior to the exile, when all stood under judgment.

The theme of *hybris*, which appeared with some prominence in Isaiah (e.g., 2:6–22; 10:15; 14:4–21; 37:23–29), is elaborated at length by Ezekiel in a series of oracles against Egypt and Tyre. As Isaiah reused a familiar mythological theme in 14:4–21, so Ezekiel makes use of myths that enable him to speak of the power and wealth of foreign kings in extravagant ways, then to destroy the original meaning of the myth by announcing the future death of those kings. Egypt drew special attention because Pharaoh Hophra's troops briefly forced Nebuchadnezzar to lift the last siege of Jerusalem (Jer. 37:5–11), and that very likely aroused false hopes that with Egypt's help Judah might regain freedom. Tyre was a special case; the main city was on an island and held out against the Babylonian army for thirteen years, finally coming to terms without having been conquered (cf. Ezek. 29:17–20). Their ability to resist for so long may also have been appealed to as the basis for hope. Ezekiel found it necessary to counteract these sources of wishful thinking also, as he tried to prepare his fellow exiles to face reality. His ability as an allegorist enabled him to depict Tyre as one of the merchant ships for which the city was famous, and to sink the ship (ch. 27), but it is his use of mythological themes that is of greatest theological importance.[121] He equated the king of Tyre with the first man in the garden of God (the only Old Testament parallel to Genesis 2—3), thus extolling his riches and wisdom, but then does something the ancient Near Eastern myths of the first man did not do. Because of his pride he is driven out of the garden and dies (Ezek. 28:1–19). Ezekiel was willing to exalt the king of Egypt also, by identifying him with the cosmic tree, source of life and security for the whole world, a widespread mythological theme, but then has the tree cut down because of its overweening self-exaltation (ch. 31). Twice he equates the Pharaoh with an aquatic monster, perhaps the crocodile since it was a sacred animal in Egypt, and the great beast is killed (29:1–5; 32:1–16). Ezekiel acknowledged human accomplishment in these texts, freely using myth to speak of power, wealth, and wisdom, but then destroying the original meaning of those myths by drawing a line between humanity and deity. He understood that the power of the state (the king) can become so great that it can virtually deify itself, but knew that is folly, for his God Yahweh is the only God. The end of each story is death—the final proof that those kings (those states) were no gods after all.[122] There is still no theoretical monotheism in Ezekiel, but these passages in their own distinctive way make the claim that there is no God but Yahweh. The death of Israel and the death of the nations will accomplish the same end: "Then they will know that I am Yahweh" (cf. 25:7, 11, 17; 26:6; 29:6; 28:23).

We found elements of universalism in Amos's claim that the Philistines and Arameans had also experienced an exodus (Amos 9:7), and the designation of Egypt and Assyria as "my people" and "the work of my hands" in Isa. 19:24–25. A similar assumption that God's way with other nations is like his way with Israel appears in Ezek. 29:9b–16. He predicts a forty-year exile for the Egyptians, followed by a restoration. It will not be the glorious restoration promised Israel, for Egypt will then be a lowly kingdom, but there were practical reasons for that: "The Egyptians shall never again be the reliance of the house of Israel; they will recall their iniquity, when they turned to them for aid. Then they shall know that I am the Lord Yahweh" (v. 16).[123]

The book of Ezekiel adds a new act to the promise of Israel's restoration, one not found elsewhere. The account of the attack and destruction of Gog and his allies in chs. 38—39 seems to interrupt the context, for 37:27–28 would form a good introduction to the vision of the new temple in chs. 40—48. The story of Gog introduces a situation that would not seem to be relevant to Ezekiel's contemporaries—another invasion of the promised land after the restoration had succeeded (cf. 38:8–9)—so many scholars consider these chapters to be a later addition. No matter what their date, they do represent a reaffirmation of a major theme of Ezekiel—Yahweh's power over the nations and the vindication of his holy name, no matter what threat may come from human sources (38:16, 23; 39:7, 21).

What had happened so far was no proof of Yahweh's holiness for some of the exiles, however, and we conclude this section with another of those proverbs that brought forth a response from Ezekiel. "The parents have eaten sour grapes, and the children's teeth are set on edge" (Ezek. 18:2), adding, "The way of the Lord is unfair" (18:25). Some of the exiles, at least, would admit that their history was a history of rebellion, as the sacred traditions told it, but then asked what that had to do with them. "Why should we suffer for the sins of our ancestors?" they were asking. Ezekiel took up the issue, using his knowledge of the priestly tradition, citing the law, which had always punished individuals—and no one else— for their own crimes. Since they were blaming their fate on their ancestors, he takes the cases through three generations to make his point: "A child shall not suffer for the iniquity of a parent, nor a parent suffer for the iniquity of a child; the righteousness of the righteous shall be his own, and the wickedness of the wicked shall be his own" (18:20). His declaration, "He is righteous; he shall surely live," is drawn from the priestly vocabulary and refers to one who has met the basic requirements of harmonious community relationships and is thus worthy to participate in the life of the worshiping community.[124] So far there was nothing new in that; it laid the responsibility for their misery on their own shoulders, as the prophet had been doing in various ways throughout his ministry.[125] But how can one bear such responsibility? He understood that to be the real question, and so his "case law" is just preliminary to the real point of his message: Change is possible, and the past need not dictate what the future must be. That is true only because there is a God who has the power, in effect, to erase the past, by forgiveness. "But if the wicked turn away from all their sins that they have committed and keep all my statutes and do what is lawful and right, they shall surely live; they shall not die" (18:21).

As the book is structured, the mystery of forgiveness has been included in the midst of the judgment passages of Ezekiel, and I have taken it up in the section on the sovereignty of God rather than with the promises. Certainly ch. 18 contains a major promise, but it involves an explanation of the judgment in which they find themselves and speaks very directly about the character of the God who has imposed such a severe punishment. In spite of what the exiles have seen and experienced, Yahweh is not a God of death, but of life. If the ferocity of the judgment Ezekiel has proclaimed is really the will of God, why not turn to some other god, or no god at all? The answer must be to reaffirm the other side of God's character, and here God actually pleads with his people not to choose anymore the way of death: "Why will you die, O house of Israel? For I have no pleasure in the death of anyone, says the Lord GOD. Turn, then, and live" (18:31b–32). Here Ezekiel speaks as if they really can turn of their own volition, and he has God plead with them to get themselves a new heart and a new spirit (v. 31a). This also must be an ad hominem argument and not to be taken as optimism concerning human nature, for Ezekiel reveals no more hope for human potential elsewhere than Jeremiah did. Elsewhere the new heart and new spirit will have to be the gift of God, and even true repentance will be the result, not the basis, for restoration (ch. 36). This chapter, which focuses so much on the human will, thus does belong in the section on the sovereignty of God, for at the end the subject is not justice, as the exiles thought, but forgiveness, and only God has the power to forgive.[126]

Accepting responsibility for their situation would prove to be crucial for the exiles' future, for it would eventually enable them to recognize and accept their unique role as the people of Yahweh. The moral character of the exiles would determine (humanly speaking) whether a people of Yahweh could endure. But the book of Ezekiel does not reveal that happening yet.

> As for you, son of man, your people who talk together about you by the walls and at the doors of the houses, say to one another, each to his brother, "Come, and hear what the word is that comes forth from the LORD." And they come to you as people come, and they sit before you as my people, and they hear what you say but they will not do it; for with their lips they show much love, but their heart is set on their gain. And, lo, you are to them like one who sings love songs with a beautiful voice and plays well on an instrument, for they hear what you say, but they will not do it. When this comes—and come it will!—then they will know that a prophet has been among them. (Ezek. 33:30–33, RSV)

There was more to be done.

Restoration—Resurrection

Ezekiel's quotations of what he heard his fellow exiles saying reveal not only wishful thinking and criticisms of God's justice; they might also express deep despair, and we use two of that kind to introduce this last section. One appears in a chapter (33) that has been composed so as to make the transition between the prophet's words prior to the fall of Jerusalem in 587 and the message that came after. He heard them saying, "Our transgressions and our sins weigh upon us, and we waste away because of them; how then can we live?" (33:10). "How then can we live?" may very well be taken as the theme of chs. 33—48. The very word "life" (or live) appears eight times in the first of those chapters, in addition to two occurrences of the formula, "As I live." Chapter 33 is perhaps the clearest example of editorial work to be found in the prophetic books. It reprises three themes that have appeared earlier in the book, connecting them now with the arrival of a messenger with the news that Jerusalem had fallen (33:21–22). The effect is to recall for readers three of the messages that had seemed appropriately located in Ezekiel's message before 597, and now to use them to introduce the promises that were forthcoming after Jerusalem's fall. His role as watchman (sentinel, NRSV), which had been introduced as part of his call to prophecy (3:16–21), reappears, in what seems a more appropriate location, for upon him is placed the heavy responsibility of defining for the exiles the way of death and the way of life. In ch. 18 the assurance that the way of life was not closed to them had been developed at length; the same message reappears more briefly in 33:10–16. Before Jerusalem fell, Ezekiel had responded to the optimism of those left in Judah, who thought the land was now their own (11:14–21), with the message that the future lay with the exiles. Now he responds to a similar claim from "the inhabitants of these waste places in the land of Israel" with severe words of judgment (33:23–29). Three major texts (chs. 34; 35—36; 37) then move from the desolation and death that had been his earlier message, now come true, to a plan for the future.[127]

The despair that followed the news that Jerusalem had been destroyed took its classic form in another proverb: "Our bones are dried up, and our hope is lost; we are cut off completely" (Ezek. 37:11). In spite of what Ezekiel had been saying, the exiles' only hope had been the integrity of Jerusalem, and now that was gone. Israel is dead, they said, and this time Ezekiel's vision of the dry bones does not correct the exiles' idea, but acknowledges that they are right: "These bones are the whole house of Israel." The prophetic message first spoken by Amos had come true. The question for the exiles was not whether Israel was dead, nor whether God can raise the dead ("Can these bones live?" "O Lord GOD, you know," 37:3). The question was, Does God *intend* to raise the dead? The vision declared that he did, and spoke of it as a new creation, an important point for understanding the promises of a glorious future that follow.[128] Details are not provided in this text except for the association of new life with restoration to their land. This is a powerful assertion with a single message: There is a basis for hope after all, and that is solely to be found in the will of God.

This book contains a virtual plan for the restoration, unlike the piecemeal promises that appear in the other prophetic books. Certain themes reappear in several passages, and rather than discuss each text in turn, it will be possible to use ch. 36, the most complete of them, as a base, with references to the others. Chapters 40—48, which do not parallel the other visions of the future, will have to be dealt with separately. Three passages from the first section of the book will be included: 11:17–20; 16:53–63; 20:33–44. Since their promises would be meaningful to the exiles only after their hopes based on Jerusalem had been destroyed, it is likely that they represent a reworking of those chapters (especially 16 and 20) so as to make them move from judgment to promise, as chs. 34 and 36 also do.

There is a single motive for restoration, and it has nothing to do with any virtue that might be found in the exiles. They will be re-created as a new people solely because that is the way the true character of Yahweh can be manifested on earth, to the new Israel and to the nations. Chapter 36 puts it most bluntly: "It is not for your sake, O house of Israel, that I am about to act, but for the sake of my holy name, which you have profaned among the nations to which you came. I will sanctify my great name" (36:22–23a; see 20:41; 39:25, 27). New Testament language would say they will be saved by grace alone, but Ezekiel's language is less gracious. He never uses *'ahab*, "love," *hesed*, "steadfast love," or *hanan*, "have mercy," and *raham*, "have compassion," appears only in 39:25. But this prophet's stern way of speaking does declare that it is the will of Yahweh to create a people whom he can bless, and who can live in harmony with him.

The most frequently repeated promise is, "I will take you from the nations, and gather you from all the countries, and bring you into your own land" (36:24, 28; 11:17; 20:34; 28:25; 34:11–13; 37:15–22; 39:27–28). Even though Jews would learn how to be the faithful people of Yahweh in the diaspora, wherever in the world they might live, they did not develop a theology that fully accounted for their existence apart from some reference to the promised land. Materials such as the stories of faithful exiles in Daniel 1—6 suggest what might have been done, but was not. As the first of the exilic theologians, Ezekiel might have begun to work on a theology that did not depend on the promised land, but there is no trace of it in his book.

Other passages speak of an intermediate state before the land can once again be occupied. There will be a new exodus, and that will involve a new wilderness experience, interpreted in accordance with some of the original wilderness traditions as a time of purging (Ezek. 20:35–38; cf. 34:17–22, which speaks of judgment after bringing them into the land). The Israel of the future must be a purified people, and one relatively superficial way to do that would be to sort out those still uncommitted to the true Yahwistic way of life. More thoroughgoing measures will be needed, however. Ezekiel's priestly heritage had led him to speak of sin as producing uncleanness, as defiling the land and the people. Now he speaks of future cleansing as a metaphor for forgiveness and more—for the transformation of the human will. "I will sprinkle clean water upon you, and you shall be clean from all your uncleannesses, and from all your idols I will cleanse you" (36:25; 37:23; in 11:18 the returnees will cleanse the land). But more than the negative work of cleansing will be needed. Their hearts, that is, the ability to make right decisions and act on them, have become "petrified," unable to function as God had made them, and so he will give them a new heart and a new spirit. Then they will be able to obey him (36:26–27; 11:19–20). Ezekiel, like Jeremiah, had concluded human beings had lost the very ability to make the right choices, but having given up on humans, he had not given up on God.

The aim of making changes in human nature itself was to establish a permanent, close relationship of harmony between God and his people. The term *bĕrith*, "covenant," is not used in ch. 36, but 16:60 and 37:26 speak of an everlasting covenant. "Covenant of peace" is used in 34:25 and 37:26, and 20:37 has the expression "bond of the covenant." Elsewhere, he uses what has been called the "covenant formulary": "You shall be my people, and I will be your God" (36:28; 11:20; 37:23, 27).[129] Worship, which had been intended to assure Israel of God's presence in their midst and his acceptance of them, but which had been hopelessly corrupted by their idolatrous practices (recall chs. 8—11), will be restored.

> For on my holy mountain, the mountain height of Israel, says the Lord
> GOD, there all the house of Israel, all of them, shall serve me in the land;
> there I will accept them, and there I will require your contributions and
> the choicest of your gifts, with all your sacred things. As a pleasing odor
> I will accept you, when I bring you out from the peoples, and gather you
> out of the countries where you have been scattered; and I will manifest my
> holiness among you in the sight of the nations. (Ezek. 20:40–41)

God's presence with his people in the future is promised with the "I am with you" formula in 34:30, and both covenant language and promise of presence are combined with the restoration of the sanctuary itself in 37:26–28.

At the material level, restoration to the promised land will include the blessing of nature itself, and the assurance of security (36:33–38; 34:25–31). "And they will say, 'This land that was desolate has become like the garden of Eden; and the waste and desolate and ruined towns are now inhabited and fortified'" (36:35).[130] Kingship is a somewhat ambiguous subject in these texts. In 20:33 Yahweh says, "I will be king over you," and in 34:15, "I myself will be the shepherd of my sheep," using one of the most familiar metaphors for kingship in the ancient Near East.[131] But a few verses later God promises a human shepherd: "I will set up over them one shepherd, my servant David, and he shall feed them: he shall feed them and be their shepherd. And I, the LORD, will be their God, and my servant David shall be prince among them; I, the LORD, have spoken" (34:23–24). Given the theocentricity of Ezekiel's theology and his negative view of kingship in the present (chs. 17; 19), it may be asked whether these verses have been added to the original oracle. The fact that the new David is called "prince" and not "king" may be in keeping with Ezekiel's conviction that only Yahweh is the true king, however. The new David reappears in 37:25 as prince, but is called king in 37:24. Whether the title would have been ascribed to him by Ezekiel remains questionable, but it is clear that the human ruler played a very small role in his hopes for the future. Ezekiel, like Jeremiah (chs. 3—4, 30—31), hoped also for the reunion of the Northern and Southern Kingdoms, and expressed it in the form of another symbolic action (Ezek. 37:15–23).

Finally—and it is important that it is "finally" rather than initially—the people will recognize their guilt and acknowledge that they have been rebels. Ezekiel's view of the future is not the logical result one would expect from his appeals for repentance in ch. 18, but is like Jeremiah's ordering of things (Jer. 24:4–7), with repentance the result of God's work on the human heart. That may be because his appeals had not been successful, for we do not find a reference to the beginnings of a truly faithful community in this book. In four places Ezekiel speaks of the future results on people's minds and feelings of God's unmerited work of restoration. "Then you shall remember your evil ways, and your dealings that were not good; and you shall loathe (*qut*) yourselves for your iniquities and your abominable deeds. . . . Be ashamed (*bosh*) and dismayed (*kalam*) for your ways, O house of Israel" (Ezek. 36:31, 32b). Once he speaks of self-loathing (*qut*) as a result of the exile experience (6:9), but elsewhere this feeling, expressed by one or more of the three verbs that occur in 36:31–32, is the result of being blessed by God. In ch. 16 it comes after the restoring of fortunes of Sodom (i.e., Jerusalem) and Samaria (vv. 53–54), and after he establishes his everlasting covenant with them (vv. 60–63). Nothing that they must do, or can do, is prescribed as a requirement for the establishment of the covenant, not even repentance. These terms seem to be Ezekiel's way of speaking of repentance (rather than *shub* "turn," as in Jeremiah and elsewhere), for in 20:43, after restoration to the land they will loathe themselves for all the evils they had committed, in 36:31 they loathe themselves for their iniquities and abominable deeds, and in 39:26 they will bear their shame for all their treachery, once God has restored their fortunes and brought them back to their land.[132] In 16:63 it is God who makes atonement (*kipper*) for all that they have done (NRSV "forgive"). Although the Old Testament frequently speaks of repentance as the precondition for forgiveness, the order in these passages in Jeremiah and Ezekiel does correspond to a part of the reality of the experience of forgiveness. That is, only when one is offered and can accept forgiveness is it possible to see one's life without apology and to take full responsibility for what one has done. We need not be as surprised at these texts as some readers have been. Ellen Davis has expressed it nicely:

Only God's *prior* act of deliverance from the effects of sin makes it possible for Israel to stand at some critical distance from its own conduct. Encouraged by the demonstration of God's undeserved favor, the nation can begin to make proper use of its memory by entering into an honest assessment of the past and assuming full responsibility for what it has done.[133]

The final section of Ezekiel also speaks of the future, at considerable length, but for the most part has a quite different character from the passages just discussed. It is introduced as a vision, but its visionary quality is lost when new regulations for the life of the restored community are introduced (chs. 43—46). Ezekiel saw a new temple (chs. 40—42) located in a newly divided land (47:13–48:35), where a purified cult would be practiced. Whether this section, or parts of it, can be ascribed to Ezekiel himself has been widely debated.[134] We shall deal with it briefly. It fits the priestly theology of the rest of the book, with its concern for the holiness of the temple as the place where Yahweh can dwell in the midst of his people. The eschatology of chs. 1—39 shows little interest in the Jerusalem of the future, however, and in chs. 40—48 the holy city is the focus of all the interest, although it may be significant that neither the word "Jerusalem" nor "Zion" is used. The theological significance of that holy city can be summed up by referring to two passages. In 47:1–12, the prophet says he saw a miraculous stream of water flowing from below the threshold of the temple, moving eastward through the wilderness of Judea, growing deeper as it went, and bringing life to the Dead Sea itself. He is saying that in the natural world also, it is God's intention to bring life out of death, and the source of that life will be the place where his presence can be known at all times. The city will thus need a new name: The LORD Is There (Ezek. 48:35).

In the generation after Ezekiel there would be a return of some exiles to the land and a temple rebuilt, but the restoration of the sixth and following centuries would not lead to the ideal future he and the other prophets hoped for. The question whether what did happen can appropriately be called resurrection will be taken up in the final chapter of this book. But the end forecast by the prophets had come true so completely in Ezekiel's time, and the potential for the development of a faithful community among the exiles looked so hopeless that one can see why a new creation by a God who refused to be defeated by anything humans did was the only way Ezekiel could speak of hope for the future. Without some basis for hope after 587 there would have been no point to his messages of judgment, or those of his predecessors. The exiles would rightly have said, "Our bones are dried up, our hope is lost, we are clean cut off," and it would have been the end.

3.7 Jonah

The book of Jonah cannot be dated, so the location of this chapter, at the end of the section on the Neo-Babylonian period, is somewhat arbitrary. Several themes have been proposed as the keys to understanding the purpose of the book, and there is no agreement among scholars as to which, if any, should be taken as central,[135] but it is for thematic reasons that discussion of the book has been located here. One of the possible readings takes Jonah as a reflection on the shift from judgment to promise that occurred during the exilic period.[136] That makes the book a useful basis for our reflection on that phenomenon.

Jonah has been expounded as a "missionary tract" many times. He is depicted as a narrow nationalist who resists going to preach repentance to the Gentiles. The book is then associated with Ruth as two appeals for openness in postexilic Judaism, contrary to the exclusivism of those who followed the programs of Ezra and Nehemiah.[137] There are other readings of the book, but this one needs to be disposed of before proceeding because of its widespread popularity.[138] Jonah is not a preacher of repentance. He is an "Amos," with a single message of doom: "Forty days more, and Nineveh shall be overthrown!" (Jonah 3:4). His reason for resisting the mission to Nineveh cannot, therefore, be that he did not want the Ninevites to be converted, for he did not resist calling for repentance. He resisted announcing certain judgment. The book has been misread because it has been approached with the same assumptions we have found in the readings of other prophetic books: Readers have insisted they must fit the pattern set forth in 2 Kings 17:13 ("Yet the LORD warned Israel and Judah by every prophet and every seer, saying, 'Turn from your evil ways and keep my commandments and my statutes'"), and must have really been preaching repentance, no matter what their words say.

Once that assumption has been dismissed, the reading of the book becomes more straightforward, despite its many subtleties. It is widely recognized as a masterpiece of literature,[139] filled with allusions to other parts of the Old Testament, and making abundant use of irony. Only some of those features will be noted here as they contribute to the theology of the book, and the reader is urged to turn to other thorough studies for a full appreciation of its artistry.[140] It is a short story, quoting only one brief oracle, and thus it differs from the other books in the prophetic canon. It was identified as a prophetic book by those responsible for making that collection, however, and that probably means it originated in prophetic circles. Two other facts lead us to identify it as "prophetic."[141] Its author has chosen for his antihero a prophet briefly mentioned in 2 Kings 14:25: "He restored the border of Israel from Lebo-hamath as far as the Sea of the Arabah, according to the word of the LORD, the God of Israel, which he spoke by his servant Jonah son of Amittai, the prophet, who was from Gath-hepher." The book also begins with a call story, leading the reader from the first sentence to expect to learn something about the work of a prophet. Expectations are continually disrupted with strange twists and turns as the story continues, however, and it will be suggested here that these are the result of some puzzlement within prophetic circles as to the course God's work in history was taking, expressed in the form of an ironic and at times humorous narrative.

The usual "call story" moves directly from a divine commission to an objection from the one called that he cannot undertake the mission (cf. Exodus 3—4; Judg. 6:15; Jer. 1:6), but Jonah says nothing, and simply leaves. He set out for Tarshish (in the far west) to flee "from the presence of the LORD." How did he expect to do that? By sea? He himself will shortly identify his God as the one "who made the sea and the dry land" (Jonah 1:9). His flight provoked a strong reaction from God, who hurled a great storm on the sea, but even at this point, Jonah was a contrary soul. Instead of reacting as a normal person would, he was sound asleep, and this prophet of God had to be urged by pagans to pray. The storm made converts out of the sailors, and perhaps it did lead Jonah to his finest moment, for he offered to let them throw him overboard that the storm might be stilled. Even then, however, we cannot be sure of his motive; whether he did it to save the sailors' lives or just to escape God by dying.

Normally, to be swallowed by an animal would be a horrible fate, but not in this book. It was God's none-too-dignified way of saving Jonah's life. And in the fish's stomach he sang a hymn. It is one of the traditional hymns of thanksgiving, using, as many of the psalms do, water imagery and references to the threat of drowning as vivid metaphors for peril of any kind, but for the first time in history such a psalm is actually sung under water.[142] Finally Jonah is vomited out on to dry land.

The story begins again, in ch. 3, with the same commission in almost the same words, and this time Jonah did as he was commanded. He did not call for repentance, but delivered a message like that of most of the preexilic prophets: "Forty days more, and Nineveh shall be overthrown!" (3:4). The result is completely unexpected, except that as an afterthought we realize it is parallel to the sailors' conversion in ch. 1. The whole city repented, of its own volition, and the act of repentance included even the animals! And the king of Nineveh's theology fits the theology of the whole book, with his question, "Who knows? God may relent and change his mind; he may turn from his fierce anger, so that we do not perish" (3:9), for the freedom of God is one of the book's major themes.[143]

God did change his mind, and the city was saved. So, when Jonah did obey God he became a false prophet, for his words did not come true. Finally he reveals why he ran away. He did not want to be forced to proclaim judgment when he knew God would probably change his mind and thus ruin Jonah's reputation (4:2). At the end God dealt with him by means of an object lesson that left him feeling both miserable and foolish. He made a vine to shade Jonah and then a worm to destroy the vine. Then he said, "You are sorry that the plant died; should I not be sorry for 12,000 ignorant people and their animals?" (cf. 4:10–11). The abrupt ending and the reference to the animals are in keeping with the author's style, but he leaves it to us to decide why the book should end this way.

He has withheld revealing the motive for Jonah's strange behavior until near the end of the story. The storm and the fish had scarcely suggested that a major theme would be God's graciousness and compassion. Once Exod. 34:6 is quoted in Jonah 4:2, however, we realize that the change of God's mind in Jonah 3:10 was also an allusion to the same context in Exodus, when God changed his mind about destroying the Israelites after the sin of the golden calf. Only in the book of Jonah is the classic statement of God's merciful character presented as a problem, and the best explanation for that is to recognize that the repentance of Nineveh and God's decision not to destroy the city had made Jonah a false prophet. Not quoted, but clearly hovering near in the background is the definition of true and false prophecy in Deut. 18:21–22: "You may say to yourself, 'How can we recognize a word that the LORD has not spoken?' If a prophet speaks in the name of the LORD but the thing does not take place or prove true, it is a word that the LORD has not spoken. The prophet has spoken it presumptuously; do not be frightened by it." Deciding who spoke truly and who spoke falsely seems to have become a serious issue near the end of the Judean monarchy, from the evidence in the books of Jeremiah and Ezekiel, and Jeremiah is quoted as having made his own variation on the Deuteronomic criterion: "The prophets who preceded you and me from ancient times prophesied war, famine, and pestilence against many countries and great kingdoms. As for the prophet who prophesies peace, when the word of that prophet comes true, then it will be known that the LORD has truly sent the prophet" (Jer. 28:8–9). Jeremiah seems to assume the truth of judgment prophecy and to believe that no peace prophet had yet been validated. In this story, Jonah stands in the tradition Jeremiah appeals to, but something goes wrong. He had come to Nineveh as a judgment prophet, commissioned by Yahweh to deliver a single, straightforward message, and his message did not come true. This explains his behavior at the end of the book, sitting in his booth east of the city, waiting to see what will happen—an episode that has been puzzling when the book is read differently.[144] His only hope of vindication is that something will happen leading to the judgment of the city, and so he waits.[145] He is angry at God for not keeping his word and for sending him on a mission that had destroyed his reputation—angry enough to die. That was not mere petulance, for in the culture of the ancient Near East what good would life be without reputation?

If Jonah's behavior after his message proved untrue is understandable, his resistance to the original commission still remains to be explained, however. Jonah does that by quoting scripture back at the God who sent him on that mission: "O LORD! Is not this what I said while I was still in my own country? That is why I fled to Tarshish at the beginning; for I knew that you are a gracious God and merciful, slow to anger, and abounding in steadfast love, and ready to relent from punishing" (Jonah 4:2). He makes a claim no other judgment prophet made; namely, that he knew from the first that God could not be trusted to follow through on a threat to destroy. He knew it, he says, because of what Israel had long believed about the true character of Yahweh. (Israel is never mentioned in the book, but readers have always known that Jonah 4:2 quotes Exod. 34:6.) This is a radical shift in the prophetic tradition begun by Amos, which had emphasized the inevitability of judgment and had considered the possibility of averting it only with caution, as in the hopeful passages of Hosea. We have seen that appeals for repentance, joined to conditional promises, are very rare, and Jonah himself made no such appeal. Repentance happened spontaneously in this book, however, and among pagans who knew nothing of Yahweh, and could at best say, "Who knows . . . ?" (Jonah 3:9).

Yahweh not only responded to repentance (3:10), but Jonah claims he knew all along that the character of Yahweh is such that he is far more inclined to be gracious than to judge and that no message of judgment can thus be counted on.[146] This is an astonishing point of view, even though based on an old, creedal formula, given the reality that judgment did fall upon Israel and Judah with unmitigated severity.[147] Could this have been a last appeal to Judah, prior to 587, claiming it is still not too late to change? It seems unlikely, for one would think that if that was its intent the point would have been made explicit. There is no way to demonstrate that an exilic setting corresponds to the situation that really produced the book, but it may be that some highly skilled and sensitive author in that period took this way of asserting that no longer are the peace prophets the ones whose messages are suspect. Now, judgment prophecy is likely to become false prophecy. The book may thus be an ironic reflection on the kind of change found so prominently in the books of Jeremiah and Ezekiel. Once judgment had fallen, a new message began to be heard, words of promise, and that may have been disturbing at first. Had they now, willy-nilly, joined that suspect group of peace prophets?

With this reading of the book we now see that although on the surface it is a story about prophecy, the deeper theme is the character of God. Yahweh is the same mysterious deity who appears elsewhere in the Old Testament, but what is said here seems to take on its greatest significance when read in the light of the prophetic discovery that there was to be another chapter in Israel's story, following the judgment: that new life was Yahweh's ultimate intention for them.

The sovereignty of the creator God who does as he pleases with nature is the theme, running all through the book, that the author uses to undergird what he says about God's treatment of human beings.[148] Jonah confessed that his God was the maker of sea and dry land (ironically, since he was trying to escape from God by sea), making creation theology explicit early in the story. A distinctive verb, "appoint" (*manah*, piel), is used to designate God's uses of nature for any purpose he may choose: the fish, to save Jonah (1:17), the plant, to give him comfort (4:6), and the worm, to kill the plant (4:7). His sovereignty over all is revealed, as elsewhere in the Old Testament, both by destructive and saving acts. He threatens the lives of sailors by a great storm because one man has displeased him, and he destroys a plant as quickly as he made it grow. But he saves the life of his rebellious prophet, and will not destroy Nineveh when repentance is found there, even though it means not keeping his own word. Even the lives of the cattle are a concern to him (4:11). The abrupt ending of the book is thus not meaningless, for it is a final reminder that the whole of creation belongs to Yahweh.[149]

Jonah thus found himself forced by the sovereign God, whose will cannot be resisted, to proclaim a message that would not come true. That not only made Jonah a false prophet, but seemed to reveal a rather arbitrary God who does not even have to keep his own word.[150] Behind this rather unflattering picture of God surely lies the conviction found elsewhere in the Old Testament that it is more important to God to save than to judge. That is the presupposition of Abraham's argument over the fate of Sodom in Gen. 18:23–33, and in Moses' citation of Exod. 34:6 in his intercession on behalf of rebellious Israel, in Num. 14:18–19. It provided assurance to the psalmist who quoted the same text in Psalm 103. That had not been the thrust of the prophetic tradition begun by Amos, but in the exile it took on new life.

In conclusion, it should be reemphasized that it cannot be demonstrated that Jonah was written in the exilic period, or that it was produced within prophetic circles. That has been assumed here because it provides a logical basis for one of several possible readings of the book, and because the reading offered makes the book useful as a transition between prophecy dominated by messages of judgment, and that which consists largely of oracles of promise. Jonah—the judgment prophet who proved to be a false prophet—may be taken as a highly ironic reflection on that radical change in a long-standing tradition.

PART TWO

RESURRECTION: 538 B.C.E. AND THE POSTEXILIC PERIOD

4

THE MID-SIXTH CENTURY AND LATER: RESTORATION TO THE PROMISED LAND

Nebuchadnezzar died in 562 B.C.E. and was succeeded by a series of weaker kings: Amel-marduk (called Evil-merodach in 2 Kings 25:27; 562–560 B.C.E.), Nergal-sharusur (or Neriglissar, 560–556 B.C.E.), and Labishi-marduk. The last of these was displaced by a usurper, Nabonidus (556–539 B.C.E.), who became unpopular because of his intense interest in the sanctuary of the moon god, Sin, in Haran, which led him to ignore the official cult of Marduk, god of Babylon. He spent nearly ten years of his seventeen-year reign at the oasis of Tema, in north Arabia, probably in order to bring in new revenue from caravan trade in that area, but this meant that for several years the New Year's festival could not be celebrated in Babylon, since the king had to be the central figure in the ritual.[1] The Babylonian priests' opinion of this is expressed in the "Verse Account of Nabonidus" (*ANET*, 312–15), a violent attack on him followed by praise for Cyrus the Persian who delivered the Babylonians from their hated king.

Cyrus was also a usurper, but his grasp for power marked the beginning of an empire rather than the end. Western Asia had been ruled for a half-century by two great powers: the Neo-Babylonians in the Fertile Crescent and the Medes in eastern Asia Minor, Armenia, northern Assyria, and Iran. The Median capital was in northern Iran, at Ecbatana, and southern Iran (Persia proper) was ruled at this time by Cyrus as a vassal to Astyages, king of the Medes. Sometime between 559 and 550 B.C.E. Cyrus rebelled against his overlord, but the army Astyages sent against him defected and joined Cyrus, probably because of the king's mistreatment of his general. A second army, led by Astyages himself, showed a similar respect for him; they mutinied and turned their king over to the Persian rebel. With relative ease, Cyrus thus was able to proclaim himself king of the Medes and the Persians.

In order to consolidate his claim to the former Median empire, Cyrus then began a lengthy series of campaigns, moving from Iran through north Mesopotamia and Armenia into Asia Minor. In 543, Nabonidus returned from Tema to Babylon, probably recognizing a potential threat, but between 545 and 539 Cyrus's armies campaigned far to the east, through what is now Afghanistan, the part of Russia east of the Caspian Sea, and Pakistan, as far as the Indus Valley. Only then did he turn against Babylonia, and once again the unpopularity of a king smoothed the way for him. Two battles were fought along the Tigris as the Persians approached, and after that all Babylonian resistance failed. Nabonidus fled, and Cyrus's general Gubaru (Gobryas) entered Babylon without a fight on October 13, 539. The people were treated as having been liberated rather than conquered, and Cyrus made his entry into the city in that spirit two weeks later.

Cyrus's own inscriptions produced for Babylonian benefit describe him as a devotee of Marduk, chosen by that deity to restore his cult as it had been before the impious Nabonidus came to power, and Cyrus did exactly that for Marduk as well as for numerous other Mesopotamian deities (*ANET*, 315–16). These attitudes and activities were the results of a totally different approach to conquered peoples from that used previously by the Assyrians and Babylonians. Cyrus aimed to control his empire not by terror and wholesale deportations but rather by appearing as liberator, restorer, and protector. This is the tolerant attitude reflected in the decree quoted in Ezra 1:2–4 and 6:3–5, permitting the return of Jewish temple treasures to Jerusalem. The picture of him in the work of the exilic prophet now called Second Isaiah (Isaiah 40—55) thus corresponds very well with Cyrus's own publicity about himself.

Second Isaiah's messages suggest that the exiled Jews may have had something in common with the priests of Marduk in finding life to be less agreeable under Nabonidus than it had been earlier. At any rate this prophet, unlike Jeremiah or Ezekiel, expresses strong anti-Babylonian sentiment (e.g., Isa. 43:14; 47:1–15). Isaiah 40—55 provides no details about the lives of the exiles, but part of the rejoicing expressed there may be accounted for if their lot was exacerbated by the rule of Nabonidus, and his son Belshazzar, who governed Babylon in his father's absence.[2]

If a sociologist of religion such as Peter Berger had been able to study the community of Jewish exiles in Babylonia, he surely would have found them to be a classic example of what he calls a *cognitive minority*. This is "a group of people whose view of the world differs significantly from the one generally taken for granted in their society."[3] The exiles lived in a culture dominated by the great temples of the cities of Babylonia. The temples owned large estates and thus played a major role in the economy of the region, overseeing the irrigation canals and the production, transport, and sale of agricultural goods.[4] The temple Eanna, at Uruk (Erech), in the far south, had been a major center of religion since the Sumerian era. Many of the Jewish exiles may have been settled near Nippur, home of another of the most important Sumerian deities, Enlil, king of the earth. By the Neo-Babylonian period, the city of Babylon had become the center of the worship of Marduk, now exalted to the position of leader of the pantheon,[5] whose temple Esagila was greatly enlarged and enriched by Nebuchadnezzar.[6] Marduk was celebrated as creator of heaven and earth, establisher of order, and maker of human beings, whose duty it was to serve the gods.[7]

Living in the vicinity of the great walled Babylonian cities, the cities themselves dominated by gigantic stepped temple towers—the ziggurats—the exiles must have found it hard to see any continuing relevance in the religion of their homeland, the worship of Yahweh, God of Jerusalem, who had not even been able to protect his own temple, let alone save his people. Southern Mesopotamia was a fertile agricultural area, with a highly developed economic system based on the use of canals for irrigation. Nebuchadnezzar's victories made available a captive labor force, timber, stone, and treasures from throughout the empire, so that Babylon could be enriched far beyond anything ever seen in Israel. The Babylonian theology explained all this. How long would it be before the exiles, who had found a new life there, began to believe what everyone around them believed?

Peter Berger's studies of contemporary cognitive minorities help us to understand how remarkable it is that Yahwism survived at all:

> The status of a cognitive minority is thus invariably an uncomfortable one —not necessarily because the majority is repressive or intolerant, but simply because it refuses to accept the minority's definitions of reality *as* "knowledge." At best, a minority viewpoint is forced to be defensive. At worst, it ceases to be plausible to anyone.[8]

Berger finds that those whose beliefs find no support in the dominant culture that surrounds them have three options. They may eventually surrender; accepting as truth what everyone else claims to be true, leading to the "self-liquidation of theology and of the institutions in which the theological tradition is embodied."[9] Experiment has shown how difficult it is not to surrender under such conditions. The opposite reaction is "defiance," which for all but a few very strong individuals requires the support of a countercultural community, that is, a sect.[10] Instead of either extreme, however, a kind of cognitive bargaining process may ensue, by which the minority carefully accept aspects of the majority beliefs that are found not to be destructive to the essentials of their faith. If circumstances allow, in a tolerant culture, they may also seek ways to convince the majority that at least some of their peculiar views are not nonsense, after all.[11]

We have no written records of life in exile from the time of Ezekiel until shortly before 538 B.C.E., when Cyrus's decree made return to the homeland possible. From Ezekiel's description of the despair and lack of faithfulness among the people to whom he ministered, we would have expected little resistance to the temptations to assimilate to the victorious Babylonian culture that surrounded them. The tensions appear in one of the few psalms that can certainly be associated with the exile: "How could we sing the LORD's song in a foreign land?" And yet, "If I forget you, O Jerusalem, let my right hand wither!" (Ps. 137:4, 5). The first evidence that a community of faith did survive is to be found in Isaiah 40—55.

4.1 Isaiah 40—55

Among the exiles, about a generation after the time of Ezekiel, there lived a person with a sense of divine calling, whom we now call Second Isaiah (or Deutero-Isaiah), the author of the materials in Isaiah 40—55. This prophet's major mission was the battle against cognitive surrender.[12] It has been shown that the poems in these chapters make use of themes taken from the religion of Babylon, but in ways that can scarcely be called cognitive bargaining. Is this retrenchment, then? The word does not seem quite appropriate, for the prophet is not merely reaffirming and insisting on the truth of old beliefs. He (or she) is making new claims

(43:18–20; 48:6–7). With apologies to Berger, then, it may be said that Second Isaiah was engaged in a "cognitive offensive."

"Therefore, Deutero-Isaiah had not only to announce the coming salvation but also like a wisdom teacher to explain and to convince the exiled people of God by the power of argument."[13] The poetry of the book is written in a flowing, argumentative, highly rhetorical style, in the effort to convince the exiles that Yahweh is God, Yahweh *can* do something about their predicament, and Yahweh *intends* to do it in the immediate future.[14]

> Have you not known? Have you not heard?
>> Has it not been told you from the beginning?
> Have you not understood from the foundations of the earth?
> It is he who sits above the circle of the earth,
>> and its inhabitants are like grasshoppers;
> who stretches out the heavens like a curtain,
>> and spreads them like a tent to live in;
> who brings princes to naught,
>> and makes the rulers of the earth as nothing.
>> (Isa. 40:21–23)

The style echoes that of the psalms and of disputation language, with little use of traditional prophetic genres. No other book devotes so much effort to the attempt to persuade, with so little detail concerning the situation being addressed, or so little detail about what God intends to do. The major theme is a simple one, but clearly one that called for powerful speech, if the prophet was to be believed:

> Why do you say, O Jacob,
>> and speak, O Israel,
> "My way is hidden from the LORD,
>> and my right is disregarded by my God"?
> Have you not known? Have you not heard?
> The LORD is the everlasting God,
>> the Creator of the ends of the earth.
> He does not faint or grow weary;
>> his understanding is unsearchable.
>> (Isa. 40:27–28)

Nothing certain is known about the author of Isaiah 40—55 except for the prophet's beliefs about God. There may be one personal reference: "Draw near to me, hear this! From the beginning I have not spoken in secret, from the time it came to be I have been there. And now the Lord GOD has sent me and his spirit" (Isa. 48:16).[15] Neither are there any very explicit details provided about the lives of those addressed. We cannot even be sure of the prophet's gender, so complete is the anonymity,[16] but the date and place of his or her words can be established with fair certainty. The anonymous prophet is called Second Isaiah because from ch. 40 on, the setting is clearly not the one reflected in the first 39 chapters of Isaiah. It is not the eighth but the sixth century B.C.E., and the enemy is not Assyria but Babylon, and Judeans are in exile. One personal name appears, that of Cyrus, and his approach is said to be imminent, but there is no hint that the fall of Babylon has occurred as yet. This places the date between 550 and 540 B.C.E. The good news that return from exile will soon begin seems to locate the prophet and his constituency in Babylonia.[17] Once the evidence of date and place has made it clear that the author of these chapters was not the Isaiah of eighth-century Jerusalem, one then may add more subjective arguments: differences of vocabulary, style, and themes.[18] These chapters, with their strikingly different message from that of the preexilic prophets, thus mark the beginning of something new in the history of the people of God. Eventually we shall need to consider seriously whether it seems appropriate to say that Ezekiel's term "resurrection" is a fitting way to designate what follows.

The message of Second Isaiah can be summarized in one paragraph: (a) Yahweh has raised up Cyrus to bring the Babylonian empire to an end. (b) He has done this because the time of punishment (exile), which Israel deserved, is over. They are still God's elect, and he has forgiven their sins. (c) He can do this because he is the only God, and has created everything there is. (d) He will lead Israel back to their homeland, and Jerusalem will be rebuilt in splendor. (e) The nations will bow down to Israel, recognizing they are the favorites of the only God. (f) All this is so that Yahweh shall be glorified in all the earth.[19] The following sections will elaborate on each of these six themes.

a. Yahweh has raised up Cyrus to bring the Babylonian empire to an end.

We read a good many lines of poetry before the key to Second Isaiah's good news becomes evident; namely, that the conquests of Cyrus the Great of Persia are in fact being used by Yahweh, God of Israel, in order to restore and renew his people. There is a hint early, but without an identification of the conqueror:

Who has roused a victor from the east,
    summoned him to his service?
He delivers up nations to him,
    and tramples kings under foot;
he makes them like dust with his sword,
    like driven stubble with his bow.
He pursues them and passes on safely,
    scarcely touching the path with his feet.
                (Isa. 41:2–3)[20]

This might have been said by the first Isaiah about Sennacherib, or by Jeremiah about Nebuchadnezzar, but now the empire builder is said to be coming for the salvation, not the judgment, of God's people. In 44:24–45:7 a long passage moves, as the prophet frequently does, from the affirmation of Yahweh as creator of all things to the promise of the restoration of Jerusalem and Judah, and then gets explicit about how this shall be done. Cyrus is named twice (44:28; 45:1; and again later in 45:13). He is given exalted titles; he is God's shepherd (a familiar metaphor for "king," Isa. 44:28), and is even called Yahweh's "anointed" (*mashiaḥ*, "messiah," 45:1) another royal designation, but used only here of a foreign king. Yahweh has grasped Cyrus's right hand, a sign of appointment to kingship (45:1), has chosen him to carry out his purpose (44:28), and has called him by name (45:4). It is the God of Israel who will make his victories possible (45:2–3a), and it will all be done for the sake of Israel (45:4a, 13), although the prophet knows very well that Cyrus has in fact never heard of Yahweh (45:4–5). This is a new use of an old prophetic tradition; the insistence that Yahweh uses the foreign nations, without their knowledge, as his agents to carry out his purpose. Only the purpose has changed.

b. Yahweh has done this because the time of punishment (exile), which Israel deserved, is over. They are still God's elect, and he has forgiven their sins.

So the book begins:

Comfort, O comfort my people,
    says your God.
Speak tenderly to Jerusalem,
    and cry to her
that she has served her term,
    that her penalty is paid,
that she has received from the LORD's hand
    double for all her sins.
                (Isa. 40:1–2)[21]

There is no quarrel with the message of the earlier prophets, who had said Israel's present distress would happen as the result of their sins, and would be the work of Yahweh. "Who gave up Jacob to the spoiler, and Israel to the robbers? Was it not the LORD, against whom we have sinned, in whose ways they would not walk, and whose law they would not obey?" (Isa. 42:24).[22] But that is past tense, now. There are a few other references to sinfulness, as reminders of why their present plight is deserved, but those references now move to promises of a better future, rather than to threats of judgment, as in preexilic prophecy.[23] Ordinarily, the prophet accuses them not of the list of sins familiar to us from Amos through Ezekiel, but only of an inability to believe that Yahweh is really able and ready to deliver them:

Listen, you that are deaf;
    and you that are blind, look up and see!
Who is blind but my servant,
    or deaf like my messenger whom I send?
Who is blind like my dedicated one,
    or blind like the servant of the LORD?
He sees many things, but does not observe them;
    his ears are open, but he does not hear.
                (Isa. 42:18–20)[24]

They are still God's elect, and the prophet piles up vocabulary in order to emphasize that:

> But you, Israel, my servant,
>> Jacob, whom I have chosen,
>> the offspring of Abraham, my friend;
> you whom I took from the ends of the earth,
>> and called from its farthest corners,
> saying to you, "You are my servant,
>> I have chosen you and not cast you off";
> do not fear, for I am with you,
>> do not be afraid, for I am your God;
> I will strengthen you, I will help you,
>> I will uphold you with my victorious right hand.
>> (Isa. 41:8–10)

"Servant" and "chosen" are used twice here, and Jacob/Israel is also called the offspring of Abraham, the friend of God. They have been called by God, and have been offered the assurance given to Moses, Gideon, and Jeremiah: "I am with you" (cf. Exod. 3:12; Judg. 6:16; Jer. 1:8). Another group of terms appears in Isa. 43:4: "Because you are precious in my sight, and honored, and I love you, I give people in return for you, nations in exchange for your life." Even more emotion is attributed to God in Isaiah 54:

> For a brief moment I abandoned you,
>> but with great compassion (*raḥămim*) I will gather you.
> In overflowing wrath for a moment
>> I hid my face from you,
> but with everlasting love (*ḥesed*) I will have compassion on you,
>> says the LORD, your Redeemer (*go'el*).
>> (Isa. 54:7–8)

"Redeemer" is a term that specifically refers to family relationships, so this is yet another way chosen by Second Isaiah to emphasize the closeness of the relationship between Yahweh and Israel.[25] "Do not fear, for I have redeemed you; I have called you by name, you are mine" (Isa. 43:1b). There had been estrangement, but that was over. Second Isaiah claims that the forgiveness Jeremiah promised as part of the future new covenant had now become reality:

> I, I am He
>> who blots out your transgressions for my own sake,
>> and I will not remember your sins.
>> (Isa. 43:25)

> I have swept away your transgressions like a cloud,
>> and your sins like mist;
> return to me, for I have redeemed you.
>> (Isa. 44:22)

Note that the understandings of forgiveness found in Jeremiah and Ezekiel reappear in Second Isaiah. There is a single basis for it; the character of God: "for my own sake." And, as in the earlier books (cf. Jer. 24:7; Ezek. 36:22–27), forgiveness is what makes repentance possible: "Return to me, for I have redeemed you." Except for a brief statement such as this, however, the prophet does not speak of the individual life, of the need for change in human nature, or of the possibility of obedience in the future, as Jeremiah and Ezekiel did.[26] Most of these messages speak of the people of God as a whole, in broad, sweeping terms, with little specificity. The author feels the need to be very specific on one subject, however, and that is the nature of God.

c. Yahweh can do this because he is the only God, and has created everything there is. (So, the other so-called gods can be ridiculed.)

This was the point of attack of Second Isaiah's cognitive offensive, and it must have been formulated by a truly remarkable mind. Only a few people can believe in something that seems to be completely discredited by events in the real world.[27] This prophet, one of a small group of displaced persons from a defeated nation, had the audacity to claim that his God was in control of everything, and in fact was the only God there is.[28] As far as anyone could see, Marduk was in charge, and had an abundance of gods to assist him, each of them with a temple and a flourishing cult. Yahweh did not even have a temple, and had lost the war, but Second Isaiah is far from defensive. He makes a frontal attack on everything claimed as truth in the religion of Babylonia.

It is Yahweh (not Marduk) who created the heavens and the earth, and everything in them:

> Thus says the LORD, your Redeemer,
>   who formed you in the womb:
> I am the LORD, who made all things,
>   who alone stretched out the heavens,
>   who by myself spread out the earth.
> (Isa. 44:24; cf. 40:12–17, 21–31; 41:17–20)

> For thus says the LORD,
> who created the heavens
>   (he is God!),
> who formed the earth and made it
>   (he established it;
> he did not create it a chaos,
>   he formed it to be inhabited!):
> I am the LORD, and there is no other.
>   (Isa. 45:18)

Why should anyone believe such a claim? The usual proof of claims about a god's power was the fact of victory, and Yahweh had lost. So, Second Isaiah offers a different argument, echoing Deuteronomy's definition of true prophecy: It can predict the future (Deut. 18:21–22). Second Isaiah says repeatedly, Yahweh tells in advance what he will do, and it happens. No other so-called god can do that:

> Set forth your case, says the LORD;
>   bring your proofs, says the King of Jacob.
> Let them bring them, and tell us
>   what is to happen.
> Tell us the former things, what they are,
>   so that we may consider them,
> and that we may know their outcome;
>   or declare to us the things to come.
> Tell us what is to come hereafter,
>   that we may know that you are gods;
> do good, or do harm,
>   that we may be afraid and terrified.
> You, indeed, are nothing
>   and your work is nothing at all;
>   whoever chooses you is an abomination.
>   (Isa. 41:21–24, cf. vv. 25–29)

Second Isaiah offers this as the proof that there is no other god but Yahweh:

> Thus says the LORD, the King of Israel,
>   and his Redeemer, the LORD of hosts:
> I am the first and I am the last;
>   besides me there is no god.
> Who is like me? Let them proclaim it,
>   let them declare and set it forth before me.
> Who has announced from of old the things to come?
>   Let them tell us what is yet to be.
> Do not fear, or be afraid;
>   have I not told you from of old and declared it?
>   You are my witnesses!
> Is there any god besides me?
>   There is no other rock; I know not one.
>   (Isa. 44:6–8)

The implicit or practical monotheism that we found in the earlier prophets, who did not deny the existence of other gods, but considered Yahweh to be the only power to reckon with, has now become explicit in Second Isaiah.[29] Only one other passage in the Old Testament makes such a forthright claim that Yahweh alone is God: "So acknowledge today and take to heart that the LORD is God in heaven above and on the earth beneath; there is no other" (Deut. 4:39, cf. v. 35).[30]

The idolatrous cults of Babylonia are a temptation for the exiles, and the prophet warns them against idolatry more than once (e.g., 48:3–5), but for Second Isaiah personally the other gods are no threat, and he can just make fun of them. They are statues and nothing more. In 46:1–4 he points out that Bel and

Nebo have to be carried around by their people, but Yahweh, in contrast, carries his people. In a prose passage that may be an addition by a disciple of Second Isaiah, but which is fully in keeping with the spirit of the rest of the book, idol worship is ridiculed by describing the making of a wooden image (Isa. 44:9–20). Half of the piece of wood the carpenter burns in order to cook his meal; the other half he makes into an image, bows down to it, and says, "Save me, for you are my god!" (v. 17). There were probably very few among the exiles with faith as strong as this prophet's, and these attacks on idol worship were no doubt an essential part of his arsenal of weapons as he attempted to convince them that a God they could not see was in fact the only God there is, and a God who loved them.

d. Yahweh will lead Israel back to the homeland, and Jerusalem will be rebuilt in splendor.

The theme of a new highway through a transformed wilderness, over which the exiles may return in a triumphal procession to the promised land, appears at the beginning and end of the book (Isa. 40:3; 55:12–13). Its prominence in ch. 35 raises the question whether this chapter may have been the work of the same prophet. Once Cyrus took control of Babylon, he did in fact permit exiled peoples to return to their homeland, but Second Isaiah anticipated this before the fact. These passages were certainly not written up after the restoration began, for the prophet gets most of it wrong. There was no highway, the desert did not bloom, and Jerusalem did not become the glory of the earth. Only the prediction that return would become possible did come true. The basis for it was not to be found in the realities of history, but in the traditions of the exodus and of Zion theology, projected into the future.[31] Awareness of the desert that lay between Judea and Babylonia made it possible to use the old tradition of God's guidance of his people through the wilderness. The return would thus not follow the Fertile Crescent northwest through Assyria and Syria, then southward to the land of Israel, but would involve a march straight west across the desert:

> Go out from Babylon, flee from Chaldea,
>> declare this with a shout of joy, proclaim it,
>> send it forth to the end of the earth;
>> say, "The LORD has redeemed his servant Jacob!"
> They did not thirst when he led them through the deserts;
>> he made water flow for them from the rock;
>> he split open the rock and the water gushed out.
>> (Isa. 48:20–21; cf. 49:7–12)

No sea needed to be crossed, as in the exodus from Egypt, but the notion of a new exodus led to a double use of water imagery:

> Thus says the LORD,
>> who makes a way in the sea,
>> a path in the mighty waters,

who brings out chariot and horse,
 army and warrior;
they lie down, they cannot rise,
 they are extinguished, quenched like a wick:
Do not remember the former things,
 or consider the things of old.
I am about to do a new thing;
 now it springs forth, do you not perceive it?
I will make a way in the wilderness
 and rivers in the desert.
         (Isa. 43:16–19)

Like Jeremiah, Second Isaiah declares that the second exodus will so far over-shadow the first that the exodus from Egypt will be forgotten (Jer. 16:14–15).[32] The crossing of the sea had taken on such an important place in Israel's worship that some of the psalms had incorporated the theme of a god's conflict with the sea from Canaanite myth (e.g., Ps. 74:12–18). Second Isaiah takes up this hymnic language and makes it part of his promise that return is imminent:

Awake, awake, put on strength,
 O arm of the LORD!
Awake, as in days of old,
 the generations of long ago!
Was it not you who cut Rahab in pieces,
 who pierced the dragon?
Was it not you who dried up the sea,
 the waters of the great deep;
who made the depths of the sea a way
 for the redeemed to cross over?
So the ransomed of the LORD shall return,
 and come to Zion with singing;
everlasting joy shall be upon their heads;
 they shall obtain joy and gladness,
 and sorrow and sighing shall flee away.
         (Isa. 51:9–11)

As in the other prophets, the expectation is for a return of everyone in the diaspora, no matter where they have been scattered:

Do not fear, for I am with you;
 I will bring your offspring from the east,
 and from the west I will gather you;
I will say to the north, "Give them up,"
 and to the south, "Do not withhold;
bring my sons from far away
 and my daughters from the end of the earth—
everyone who is called by my name,

> whom I created for my glory,
> whom I formed and made."
> (Isa. 43:5–7)

The second half of the book, chs. 49—55, devotes special attention to Jerusalem-Zion, although the promise of rebuilding is not missing from the earlier chapters, for it is said to be God's reason for raising up Cyrus (Isa. 44:26–28; 45:13). Zion is introduced in highly poetic forms later, however. In 49:14–21 she is the childless woman, who thinks, "The Lord has forsaken me, my Lord has forgotten me." Then God is compared with a mother: "Can a woman forget her nursing child, or show no compassion for the child of her womb? Even these may forget, yet I will not forget you." Now the city as a woman is forgotten for a moment; it is a place with walls, but a map is inscribed on the very palms of God's hands, so he can never forget it (v. 16). Next, Zion is a bride (v. 18), and she is promised an abundance of children.

The theme of the barren wife reappears in ch. 54:1–3, followed immediately by widowhood (vv. 4–5) and divorce (vv. 6–7) as other ways of expressing the grief of Judeans over the destruction of their city, but now in the context of promises that all will be made right again.[33] But soon the mind of the poet has moved to another realm, and the divine builder of the city is more a jeweler than an architect:

> O afflicted one, storm-tossed, and not comforted,
>   I am about to set your stones in antimony,
>   and lay your foundations with sapphires.
> I will make your pinnacles of rubies,
>   your gates of jewels,
>   and all your wall of precious stones.
> (Isa. 54:11–12)

And now God has become a teacher: "All your children shall be taught by the Lord, and great shall be the prosperity of your children" (54:13).

Zion theology, which Jeremiah and Ezekiel opposed because it had created a false sense of security, and which had apparently been completely repudiated by the destruction of Jerusalem, has been revived a generation later, among the exiles. All is different now, Second Isaiah claims, for the justly deserved punishment is complete, forgiveness is a reality, and the old promises preserved in both the exodus and Zion traditions will soon become effective. This was clearly not an easy message to get across, given the extended argument the prophet makes in order to try to persuade his audience that better days really were coming. Since his words were added to the earlier collection of the words of the eighth-century prophet Isaiah, they must have had their desired effect.

e. The nations will bow down to Israel, recognizing they are the favorites of the only God.

The foreign nations had been a concern of the prophets from early times. One of the traditional roles of a prophet was to give oracles assuring victory before a battle.[34] That old tradition reappeared in the canonical prophets, used in new ways from Amos on. The oracles against the nations in Isaiah 1—39, Zechariah, Jeremiah, and Ezekiel promised that a time of peace for Israel would become possible once Yahweh intervened and defeated the nations that had troubled them again and again. The same kind of oracle appears in Isaiah 47, addressed to Babylon. The city is accused of *hybris*, the sin that formed the central theme of Isa. 14:4–21; Ezek. 28:11–19; 29:1–12; and 31:1–18.

> You felt secure in your wickedness;
>> you said, "No one sees me."
> Your wisdom and your knowledge
>> led you astray,
> and you said in your heart,
>> "I am, and there is no one besides me."
>>> (Isa. 47:10; cf. v. 8)

Babylon was in fact not destroyed in the sixth century, but these words were accepted by the Jewish community without correction, presumably thinking that the significant change in their fortunes brought about by the successes of Cyrus was "close enough."

The nations in general appear in a new way, as the prophet elaborates on the promise of return to the homeland and restoration of Jerusalem. There is no hint of the near equality of Israel and the other nations found in Isa. 19:19–25, or of the parallel histories of Israel and Egypt in Ezek. 29:13–16. Israel's future supremacy is emphasized by Second Isaiah.

> I give Egypt as your ransom,
>> Ethiopia and Seba in exchange for you.
> Because you are precious in my sight,
>> and honored, and I love you,
> I give people in return for you,
>> nations in exchange for your life.
>>> (Isa. 43:3–4)

So, when the restoration comes, the nations not only will have to assist Israel, but they will remain subservient in the future:

> I will soon lift up my hand to the nations,
>> and raise my signal to the peoples;
> and they shall bring your sons in their bosom,
>> and your daughters shall be carried on their shoulders.
> Kings shall be your foster fathers,
>> and their queens your nursing mothers.
> With their faces to the ground they shall bow down to you,
>> and lick the dust of your feet.
>>> (Isa. 49:22–23; cf. vv. 24–26)

Unlike some of the other prophetic books, in which Israel is declared to be no better than the nations, if not worse, in Second Isaiah the fact that Yahweh is the only God is extended to mean that the people chosen by Yahweh, Israel, must be superior to all others (cf. Isa. 45:14; 54:3). And yet, this is the prophet who has been said to have a missionary message that is more explicit than any other. It is true that Israel is said several times to be a witness (Isa. 43:10, 12; 44:8; cf. 55:4). What is not so clear is what form the witness will take, and that has led to debate. Some claim that Israel's "vocation is to convert all the nations," that is, there is in the book a true call to be missionaries to the world.[35] Others will say, "Second-Isaiah is actually responsible for the narrow and exclusive attitude of postexilic days."[36] A middle course, as represented by the well-balanced treatments of Martin-Achard and Gelston (although they do not come to identical conclusions), seems more likely.[37]

"Turn to me and be saved, all the ends of the earth!" (Isa. 45:22) certainly sounds like a missionary appeal, when read in isolation, and the idea is supported by the promise, "To me every knee shall bow, every tongue shall swear" (45:23). In context, however, this does not appear to be a reference to conversion of Gentiles. The passage is addressed to "you survivors of the nations" (45:20), and they are most likely to be the exiles, to whom the prophet has been speaking all along. The point is a familiar one: Yahweh alone is God, and the appeal to turn and be saved is most naturally read as being addressed to Jews in every part of the earth. That every knee shall bow to Yahweh may indeed refer to his rule over all the earth. That the concern of the passage throughout is Israel, however, is shown by the conclusion: "In the LORD all the offspring of Israel shall triumph and glory" (45:25).

Self-identification, "I am the LORD's," in 44:5, may refer to proselytes, as has often been claimed,[38] but may also simply refer to the descendants of the exiles (44:3), who will firmly maintain their identity in the future.[39] Two other texts that might be taken as offers of universal salvation are also more likely to refer to God's work on behalf of Israel, when read in context. "All the ends of the earth shall see the salvation of our God" is connected with the redemption of Jerusalem (52:9–10), so it is Israel's salvation that they will see. David, alluded to as a witness in 55:3–5, was a witness to the power of Yahweh over the nations, so the promise that "nations shall run to you" (v. 5) is associated with the glorification of Israel.

The prophet does expect that the nations will come to know that Yahweh alone is God as a result of what he does for Israel (cf. 45:6; 49:26b), and in that sense we can speak of universalism.[40] At least two passages may express a more generous hope for the Gentiles. God says of the servant that "it is too light a thing that you should be my servant to raise up the tribes of Jacob and to restore the survivors of Israel" (49:6). He has an additional charge: "I will give you as a light to the nations, that my salvation may reach to the end of the earth." That will lead kings and princes to prostrate themselves (49:7). No additional content is added to the "salvation" offered in v. 6, so the promise of justice on earth offered elsewhere appears to be the most positive word for the nations, since it is not said how they will otherwise benefit by their recognition that Israel's God is the only God:

> Listen to me, my people,
>> and give heed to me, my nation;
> for a teaching will go out from me,
>> and my justice for a light to the peoples.
> I will bring near my deliverance swiftly,
>> my salvation has gone out
>> and my arms will rule the peoples;
> the coastlands wait for me,
>> and for my arm they hope.
>> (Isa. 51:4–5; cf. Isa. 42:1–7)

Martin-Achard's summary seems to be a very fair evaluation of the prophet's understanding of Israel's relationship to the nations:

> *It is by granting life to His people that Yahweh makes it the light of the world.* Deutero-Isaiah's message is not a missionary message in the usual sense of the term; there is no question of proselytism in his preaching. The prophet does not invite Israel to scour the globe in order to call the heathen to conversion. The Chosen People's business is to exist: its presence in the world furnishes proof of Yahweh's divinity; its life declares what He means for Israel itself and for the universe. The mission of Israel consists in reflecting the glory of God by accepting His gifts and His judgment alike.[41]

f. All this is so that Yahweh shall be glorified in all the earth.

Second Isaiah reflects Ezekiel's theology in significant ways. The divine motive for saving Israel from exile is the same: "For my own sake, for my own sake, I do it, for why should my name be profaned? My glory I will not give to another" (Isa. 48:11; cf. Isa. 42:8; Ezek. 36:22–23). Israel was created for the glory of its God (Isa. 43:7), and the restoration from exile will reveal that to all: "Then the glory of the LORD shall be revealed, and all people shall see it together, for the mouth of the LORD has spoken" (Isa. 40:5; cf. Ezek. 43:1–5). Since Yahweh is God of the whole earth, the whole earth should know it, as noted in the previous section. He has raised up Cyrus in order to bring his people back home, "so that they may know, from the rising of the sun and from the west, that there is no one besides me; I am the LORD, and there is no other" (Isa. 45:6; and Cyrus also is expected to know it, 45:3). Nature itself will join in, once Yahweh begins to be given the praise he deserves:

> Sing to the LORD a new song,
>> his praise from the end of the earth!
> Let the sea roar and all that fills it,
>> the coastlands and their inhabitants,
> Let the desert and its towns lift up their voice,
>> the villages that Kedar inhabits;
> let the inhabitants of Sela sing for joy,

let them shout from the tops of the mountains.
Let them give glory to the LORD,
    and declare his praise in the coastlands.
(Isa. 42:10–12)

The wild animals will honor me,
    the jackals and the ostriches;
for I give water in the wilderness,
    rivers in the desert,
to give drink to my chosen people,
    the people whom I formed for myself
so that they might declare my praise.
(Isa. 43:20–21)

The Servant of the Lord

Except for the commission to be a light to the nations, the four passages identified since the work of Duhm as discrete "Songs of the Suffering Servant of the Lord" (Isa. 42:1–4; 49:1–6; 50:4–9; 52:13–53:12) have contributed little to the preceding six-point summary of the message of Second Isaiah. Although there are challenges to the isolation of those songs from the rest of the book,[42] there are few close thematic relationships except for the concept of servant.[43] The word is a favorite term in Isaiah 40—55, used of Israel thirteen times outside the four passages just listed and six times within the songs. This stands in contrast to the uses of the word in Isaiah 1—39 and 56—66, where it may be found only four times. The identity of the servant described in the songs has been discussed at least since the incident recorded in Acts 8, when the Ethiopian eunuch asked Philip, "About whom, may I ask you, does the prophet say this, about himself or about someone else?" (v. 34). The history of interpretation has been thoroughly surveyed by Christopher North, and need not be repeated here.[44] Indeed, it will be claimed here, with Claus Westermann and others, that the identity of the servant is not the key issue for understanding these texts.[45] As Curt Lindhagen has shown in his detailed study of the use of the term in the Old Testament, it points away from the servant and toward the master whose will the servant must carry out, and who in return offers protection and support.[46] What God accomplishes through the servant is the important subject, although the traditions used to depict that person will be of help in understanding his work.

The first of the songs has few significant relationships with the others. The imagery is largely drawn from royal traditions, for the servant's task is to bring forth justice. The parallels with the description of the work of the righteous king in Isa. 11:1–5 are evident.[47] Royal imagery is not prominent in the other songs, however, and much of their language is reminiscent of the earlier prophetic books. The passages in 49:1–6 and 50:4–9 are in the first person singular, and the natural reading of them would be to take them as two of the very few references Second Isaiah may have made to himself. The second song speaks of being called "before I was born"

(49:1), an echo of Jeremiah's report of his call (Jer. 1:4–10), and it continues with complaint reminiscent of the laments of Jeremiah (Isa. 49:4; cf. Jer. 15:15–18). Jeremiah was to be a prophet to the nations, and the servant will be given as a light to the nations (Jer. 1:5; Isa. 49:6). In the third song, the lamentation becomes more intense, with a description of physical suffering which has been the result of faithfulness to the Lord's work (Isa. 50:4–6). As in the psalms of lament, this song continues with words of confidence (vv. 7–9). The Deuteronomistic Historical Work and the prose parts of Jeremiah speak regularly of God's "servants the prophets," and this idea of the prophetic servant appears to have been taken up by Second Isaiah as a special theme, in songs two through four. This enabled him to make some use of the earlier prophetic message about death and new life.

I take the key to the meaning of the fourth song, Isa. 52:13–53:12, to be Second Isaiah's several references to the prophetic tradition in general, along with the expressions "laid on him the iniquity of us all" (Isa. 53:6), "bear their iniquities" (53:11), and "bore the sin of many" (53:12). These clauses are not identical to the term used of Ezekiel, when he was ordered to lie on his side to bear the iniquity (*naśa' 'awon*) of his people, but they are very close. That was the symbolic act which was most explicitly interpreted as participation by the prophet in the judgment pronounced over his people. Second Isaiah shows evidence of knowing the tradition (found especially in Jeremiah and Ezekiel) of the suffering prophet whose obedience necessitated carrying in his own body the punishment deserved by his people. These songs may then represent his realization, near the end of the exilic period, that what those prophets said and did was responsible for the ability of the exilic community to maintain their faith and identity—for Israel to live on and not truly die. This prophet does not make much of the themes of death and life, except in ch. 53. Here he seems to speak of the death and resurrection of the servant, which may be a reflection of Israel's discovery that, having died with the fall of Jerusalem, they had indeed been raised to new life, as Ezekiel had promised.

Was the servant Israel or an individual?[48] The effort to provide a collective interpretation of Isa. 52:13–53:12 stumbles over the highly personal language used therein. Efforts to identify the servant with any known individual (e.g., Moses, Jeremiah, Second Isaiah) encounter statements that could scarcely have been made about any human by a sixth century author. So, von Rad says such extreme language could not be applied to any living person—or even one recently dead, but believes the imagery used is that of the suffering prophet.[49] Von Waldow agrees that the servant is described as a prophet, and asserts that neither the corporate nor the individual identification is satisfactory. Rather, he finds "Israel as a community represented by an individual, and conversely as an individual described with the characteristics of a community of which he is an extension."[50] The explanation offered earlier, in the sections on Jeremiah and Ezekiel, of the symbolic acts as participative, and the term "bearing the iniqity," which moves to the very limits of (if not beyond) what any human being could do, offer support to Paul Hanson's reading of the fourth song: "This is a daring plunge into the heart and mind of a God who suffers so intensely with the people as to lead to a course of action that breaks all conventions of justice."[51] God had laid the sins of their people upon his faithful servants, Jeremiah and Ezekiel, who had been thought little of in their own time. Now that the crisis brought about by the loss of everything had led some, at least, of the exiles to take the earlier prophetic message seriously, they recognized the righteousness of those figures, and understood that the prophets' faithful words and actions had shown them the way to a new life. If this is the way Second Isaiah's thinking went, then the language of the fourth song, which speaks of events that go beyond any conceivable human experience, may be understandable. He speaks of an idealized righteous person who suffers because he is righteous, challenging all the normal concepts of justice, and claims that was both God's intention ("it was the will of the LORD to crush him," 53:10) and the servant's own choice ("he poured out himself to death," 53:12). He claims that those who were truly guilty finally came to the realization that they had been healed, forgiven (vv. 5b, 11b, 12b), because of what he suffered. Those sufferings led to death itself (vv. 8–9), and apparently to life beyond death (vv. 10–12).

This may be the prophet of the future, carrying the work of his predecessors far beyond anything one of them could do—suffering worse and accomplishing more because God is present in him to an extent never before imagined. Vicarious suffering of this sort is not spoken of elsewhere in the Old Testament, or in later Judaism, but nowhere else is there a poem quite like this. The belief that Yahweh could resuscitate individuals who had died, if he wished (e.g., 2 Kings 4:32–37; Ezek. 37:3), had been the basis for Ezekiel's vision of the corporate resurrection of Israel in exile. The resurrection of the ideal prophet, as God's vindication of his righteousness, is thus not something beyond the understanding of Second Isaiah or his audience.[52] We cannot be sure what such a poem would have meant to Jews in the sixth century, but without introducing the fullness of Christian theology into the passage, its relationship to what is said about the prophets elsewhere, and to the concept of the suffering of God in the Old Testament does suggest that this is an intimation of the necessity of incarnation.

Prophecy in Exile

The most important and lasting message of the exilic prophet concerned the true nature of God. Yahweh is the only God, in charge of all that is and all that happens, and with the will to deliver his people Israel. Yahweh is Holy One, Creator, Judge, and King, but also Redeemer, Savior, Comforter, and Teacher. The power of this prophet's language made the message about God persuasive and enduring, in spite of the fact that it came from a visionary within a minority group, who could point to little in the world around them to justify such a belief.

There was, in fact, much that called Second Isaiah's message into question. It is ironic that the prophet who insisted so strongly that the evidence that Yahweh alone is God is the ability to announce beforehand what will come to pass was a prophet who promised many things that did not come true. So Whybray points out that the failure of the hopes raised by Second Isaiah seems to have created many of the problems later prophets (Haggai, Zechariah, Third Isaiah) had to cope with, and asks, "Was Deutero-Isaiah, then, a false prophet?"[53] We should not let the beauty and power of the poetry blind us to those problems, for they were real ones for the postexilic community. Even so, the Jews did not reject this prophecy, for it became part of the canon of holy scripture. Some promises were fulfilled: Cyrus brought the Neo-Babylonian empire to an end (although Babylon was not destroyed). His decree did make it possible for exiles to return to their homeland, and some of them did go back (but only a few). The temple was rebuilt, but without the richness of Solomon's building. Jerusalem was repopulated, but its walls were not restored for another hundred years, and the city certainly was not glorified with the wealth of nations.

For the returnees, then, Second Isaiah's message could be affirmed as having partly come true, but at the same time it raised serious questions. Was this, in fact, really the fulfillment of what the prophet had promised, or was this return a meaningless event? At any rate, Ezekiel's concept of the restoration as a resurrection of deceased Israel was certainly not the obvious way to think of what had happened so far. The beauty and power of the poetry of Second Isaiah thus mask a troublesome ambiguity. He proclaimed the truth about who God really is, and what God is really like, and the believing communities have agreed, since then, that he was right. But this prophet no more knew exactly what the future will be like than any other human (inspired or not), and the enthusiastic poetry depicting a glorious future meant that Second Isaiah could not be the end of prophecy. God's work with and for his people in this new era was not as clear as it needed to be, and it is hard to say what their future might have been without the work of the postexilic prophets of the sixth and fifth centuries.

4.2 Haggai and Zechariah

Cyrus was succeeded by his son Cambyses (530–522 B.C.E.), who was able to add Egypt to the Persian empire, but died while campaigning there. His death led to a period of uncertainty over who would succeed him, leading to several years of unrest until Darius (522–486 B.C.E.) established himself in control of the entire empire.[54]

According to Ezra 1:2–4 (Hebrew) and 6:3–5 (Aramaic), Cyrus had issued a decree permitting exiled Jews to return home, allowing the temple to be rebuilt, and restoring the temple furnishings that Nebuchadnezzar had taken. The Old Testament record is similar enough to the decree found on the Cyrus Cylinder (*ANET*, 316) that there is no good reason to doubt that Persian policy did treat the exiles this way. The temple was rebuilt between 520 and 515, and Haggai and Zechariah were involved in that activity, but the record of life in Judah between 538 and 520 is sketchy and confusing.[55] Fortunately for our purposes, it is not essential to have all the historical, sociological, and economic details clarified in order to understand the theology of these books, for the modern literature on Judaism in the Persian period is more filled with theories than with facts.[56] Much that remains uncertain about the period need not be discussed here: Who was Sheshbazzar (Ezra 1:8)? What became of him? Did temple reconstruction begin shortly after 538? Did Haggai and Zechariah come to Judah from Babylon? How many returns and returnees were there? Was Zerubbabel removed from office during Zechariah's time?

We can be reasonably certain of other things. The decree recorded in Ezra 1:2–4 is in consonance with the policy found on the Cyrus Cylinder. The appointment of Zerubbabel as governor and Joshua as high priest, with rebuilding of the temple at the same time, make a logical fit with the actitivies and policies of Darius I. Judah existed as a small and rather poor province of the Persian empire. Without a native king, the role of the high priest in Jerusalem became more important. The second temple became a spiritual center for world Judaism. Since most Jews continued to live in the diaspora, that spiritual center became a matter of great and lasting importance. Since Haggai's sole concern was the rebuilding of the temple, it is appropriate at this point to turn to his work.

Haggai

The speeches of Haggai, who is explicitly identified as a "prophet" in the superscription to the book,[57] are dated with reference to the reign of Darius I, and they fall between August 29 and December 18, 520.[58] Since the book differs from most books of the preexilic prophets in containing no social critique and in focusing on building a center for worship—a subject sharply criticized by his predecessors—Haggai has been considered one of the least of the prophets by those inclined to make such value judgments. Recent studies make a fairer estimate of his contribution, based on awareness of what was needed at that time, rather than comparing him with those of an earlier period.

Without question Haggai's primary concern was the rebuilding of the temple. The social and political implications of that have been widely discussed elsewhere, and are not our central concern. The theology of Haggai presumably must have involved a revival of something of the old Zion theology, which had been challenged by Jeremiah and Ezekiel, but revived by Second Isaiah. The reasons for such a revival and the effects of the appearance of a temple with its cult on Jewish theology from this time on are important for our purposes.

Haggai reaffirmed very little of the triumphalist, overly optimistic Zion theology of the Psalms or Second Isaiah. Only in Hag. 2:6–9 is the cosmic and international dimension of the temple proclaimed, as in Psalms 46; 48; 76; and 87. He probably could assume, since it is never argued, that the destruction of the first temple had shown Jeremiah and Ezekiel to be correct in their insistence that the presence of the temple was no guarantee of security for them. He did associate two hopes with the restoration of the place of worship, however. For the present it could become the center for the creation of a new people, in whose midst Yahweh intended to dwell (Hag. 1:8; 2:5). He also reaffirmed the eschatological hope found in Micah 4:1–4, Isa. 2:2–4, and elsewhere, for the coming of a new era (Hag. 2:5–9, 22).

The first issue raised by Haggai was the question whether the temple should be rebuilt at that time. "Thus says the LORD of hosts: These people say the time has not yet come to rebuild the LORD's house" (Hag. 1:2). The reasons may have been partly lack of resources or selfish attention to their own needs, as Hag. 1:4–7 suggest, but there may also have been a theological issue, created by the extravagant promises of Second Isaiah. A glorious restoration had been promised, associated directly with the exploits of Cyrus. The promises had begun to come true—apparently—for Cyrus conquered Babylon and some exiles did return, but the return was nothing like what Second Isaiah had said. The desert did not bloom, the diaspora did not all come home, Zion was not glorified, and the nations did not bow down in subjection.[59] It must have seemed perfectly legitimate to ask whether they had misunderstood, and to think their return to the homeland was premature and not part of the fulfillment of the divine promises, after all. If so, then to try to restore the temple would surely be a futile effort.[60] This would seem to have been a perfectly reasonable interpretation of current events, but Haggai, like earlier prophets, read things differently. He was convinced they were in fact in the early stages of Yahweh's creation of a new era, and that they had something to contribute. As several commentators have recently noted, his reasoning was not simply cause and effect—no temple: no prosperity; build the temple and you will be rewarded. He does use that as an ad hominem argument in 1:5–6, 9–10; 2:16–19, but his concern is more than crops. It is hope for the divine presence among a purified people. Twice the potent divine promise "I am with you" is offered to assure leaders and people that this is what God wants of them (Hag. 1:13; 2:4), and "my spirit abides among you" is added to the second one. The initial promise concerning the building of the temple, "that I may take pleasure in it" (Hag. 1:8), may also include God's presence in glory, as in RSV, although that expression may also be translated "and be honored," as in NRSV.

Rather than accusing Haggai of abandoning the high standards of the preexilic prophets and giving in to a focus on temple, cult, and priesthood, recent scholars have found his concern to be the right response to the needs of his time and the years to come.[61] Elizabeth Achtemeier's evaluation is reflected in other commentaries: "When Haggai, 'the messenger of the Lord' (1:13), calls for temple rebuilding, it is therefore an announcement that the Lord of Hosts yearns to give himself again."[62]

> Because at the Exile the nation died, the Return was interpreted as its revival from the grave after doing full penance for its guilt; and this made it possible from thenceforward to regard the prophetic message of judgment and new creation as in essentials fulfilled, and to direct the irrepressible energy of men's hopes to removing the remaining obstacles to the worldwide realization of God's dominion. The understanding of the covenant as an eternal and unalterable relationship of grace could now be revived in all its force; and the restoration of the Temple, by affording a pledge of Yahweh's unceasing covenant favour, prepared the ground for the community of the Law, which was to find its vocation in the realization of God's sovereignty on earth, and to live in the confidence generated by its own daily experience of his righteousness and loving-kindness.[63]

From our perspective, there is more to be said about the success of Haggai and Zechariah in restoring the temple. Carol Meyers and Eric Meyers consider the social and political life of the community in Judea from this time on and point out that the temple was the key to the establishment of a new, largely ecclesiastical community under Persian rule.[64] Carroll Stuhlmueller emphasizes the restoration of worship: "Haggai realized that God's great redemptive acts for the chosen people Israel could have been forgotten had they not been celebrated with each new generation at temple liturgy."[65] Beyond this, the restoration of a religious center in Jerusalem, with sacrifice being offered daily on behalf of the Jewish people, no matter where they lived, provided a mental (spiritual) way of unifying a scattered people.[66] From that time on, one of the ways Jews have identified themselves is with the sense of having a special relationship to Jerusalem.[67] The need to have a *center*, toward which one relates oneself as an important part of one's identity, seems to be basic to most human beings.[68] The Jewish identification with Jerusalem has been the source of great political problems, without question, but Haggai is not to be blamed for that. It is also one of the factors that has enabled Judaism to survive throughout a troubled history.

Probably more has been written about the last verse of the book than is necessary. Haggai expected the divine intervention which would bring war to an end to occur very soon (2:21–22), and declared that at that time Zerubbabel would be made "like a signet ring (*kaḥotham*), for I have chosen you, says the LORD of hosts" (2:23). Zerubbabel was a member of the Davidic family, presently governor of Judea by Persian appointment, and this cryptic verse may mean that Haggai expected the Davidic dynasty to be restored at the time of divine intervention. "Make you like a signet" is a unique expression, however. Its closest parallel is in Jer. 22:24, in which the Lord says that even though Coniah (Jehoiachin, Zerubbabel's grandfather) were like a signet ring on his right hand, God would tear him off and give him over to Nebuchadnezzar, as did happen. If it was Haggai's hope that Coniah's fate would be reversed in his time, it did not come true, but it should be noted that only one verse is dedicated to the subject. Wolff comments, "the promise is couched in extremely muted terms."[69] Theories that Haggai supported a futile move toward Judean independence, with Zerubbabel as a new king, have no evidence to support them, and run counter to the prophet's words that make God's choice of Zerubbabel the consequence of divine intervention that overthrows the armies of the earth.

Zechariah 1—8

The book of Zechariah contains three dates that locate his work during the period of temple rebuilding, supporting the references in Ezra 5:1 that make him and Haggai the prophetic motivators of that work. Haggai's dates fall in the sixth, seventh, and ninth months of Darius's second year; Zechariah's in the eighth and eleventh of that year and the ninth of his fourth year (Zech. 1:1, 7; 7:1). This locates Zechariah's earliest words after temple construction had begun, which may explain why temple building does not appear as an issue, as it did in Haggai, and why it plays a smaller role in his book. Zechariah undertook a more comprehensive mission: He understood himself to be in the service of Yahweh in order to assist in bringing about the new community fit for the new age promised by the earlier prophets. He believed that when the enemy nations were overcome, and came to join Yahweh in Jerusalem, when the temple was rebuilt and Yahweh dwelt in their midst, then "you will know that the LORD of hosts has sent me to you" (Zech. 2:9, 11 [MT 2:13, 15]; 4:9; 6:15).

The book contains many difficult passages, and there are questions that cannot be answered, but for our purposes we can work with several widely accepted conclusions. The differences between chs. 1—8 and chs. 9—14 strongly suggest that they come from different sources. The latter part of the book has been dated as late as the Hellenistic period, and the present trend is to locate it in the Persian period between the times of Zechariah and Nehemiah, but there is very little in it that is useful for dating.[70] The visions in chs. 1—6 may have undergone editing a few years after Zechariah's time, but the differences between the theology of the visions and that of the editorial additions are not significant enough to affect our work.[71] The major historical issue that has concerned interpreters of the book has to do with the roles of the high priest Joshua and the governor Zerubbabel, and what Zechariah's position toward them was, as it is reflected in Zech. 3:1–10; 4:6–10a; and 6:9–15.[72] As we consider the roles of these two leaders in Zechariah's theology, the mystery of what became of Zerubbabel, which hovers above these passages, will be seen to be not as critical for us as it is for the historian.

With reference to the three critical moments in Israel's history around which this book is organized, it is clear that Zechariah has in fact come to proclaim the third "moment," which we have identified as beginning with Cyrus's decree in 538 B.C.E.[73] He looks back at an earlier era, the time of the former prophets (Zech. 1:2–6; 7:4–14; 8:9), understands the exile to have been the fulfillment of their words, and declares that he and his fellow Jews now stand at the threshold of the new era. With this in mind, the visions in chs. 1—6 may be seen to be less cryptic than they appear to be on first reading, and to contain a rather straightforward message concerning what God has already begun to do in the new age that is at hand.[74] The first (Zech. 1:8–17) raises the question of the delay of the promise that we found underlying Haggai's work: "How long will you withhold mercy from Jerusalem and the cities of Judah, with which you have been angry these seventy years?" (v. 12). The answer is a forceful one: "I have returned to Jerusalem with compassion" and the temple will be rebuilt (v. 16). The renewed form of Zion theology that we found in Second Isaiah will appear throughout Zechariah in a less rhapsodic form than the earlier prophet used. Part of the restoration of Jerusalem and of the exiles, in this theology, always involves the judgment of the nations who had inflicted a surplus of suffering on God's people. That appears in v. 15 of the first vision, and is the main subject of the second (Zech. 1:18–21 [MT 2:1–4]). The third (Zech. 2:1–5 [MT 2:5–9]) speaks of the repopulated Jerusalem as a city without walls, protected by God himself, and this leads to an oracle calling upon the exiles to return and promising that God will dwell in their midst in Zion (2:6–13).

The fourth and fifth visions (Zech. 3:1–10 and 4:1–4, 10b–14), with an interpolated oracle (4:6–10a), deal with leadership in the new community in a way more specific than earlier prophets had done. Isaiah, Micah, and Jeremiah had spoken of the coming of a righteous king (e.g., Isa. 11:1–5; Micah 5:2–5; Jer. 23:5–6) and Ezekiel promised a new David (Ezek. 34:23–24), but these were hopes for some indefinite future. Zechariah believed that the time of blessing was at hand, and that the men chosen by God to lead his people were present. So, he saw a cleansing of the high priest Joshua, symbolic of the cleansing of the people (Zech. 3:4; cf. 3:9), accompanied by the commission, "If you will walk in my ways and keep my requirements, then you shall rule my house and have charge of my courts, and I will give you the right of acccess among those who are standing here" (3:7). The fifth vision is difficult, and seems to be interrupted by an oracle declaring that Zerubbabel will succeed in building the temple (4:6–10a), but its conclusion, "These are the two anointed ones who stand by the Lord of the whole earth" (4:14) suggests that Zechariah thought in terms of two equal leaders, the priest and the governor, as representing the will of Yahweh for his people, now that they no longer had a native king. Whether he had hopes that Zerubbabel might become king, restoring the Davidic line, as Haggai may have indicated in Hag. 2:23, is uncertain. The cryptic title "the Branch" appears in Zech. 3:8 and 6:12. He appears to be an eschatological figure in 3:8–10, but in 6:12–13 the term would seem to refer to Zerubbabel, although his name is not mentioned. This has led to theories of the possible revision of ch. 6 as a result of a failed attempt to make Zerubbabel king, but we have no evidence to support or refute that. It is clear enough that Zechariah considered his role as a prophet to include guidance for those now ruling his people, analogous to the ways earlier prophets dealt with kings before the exile.

Visions six and seven (Zech. 5:1–4 and 5–11) use mysterious language to speak of a familiar prophetic theme, the need for righteousness among God's people. Zechariah's flying scroll brings an end to stealing and false swearing, and wickedness itself is, in the sixth vision, exported to Babylon. He will take up the theme of the character of God's people in more straightforward language in chs. 7—8. The point of the final vision (Zech. 6:1–8) is less obvious than the others, but probably refers to the coming of general peace on earth.

A group of oracles has been associated with an event that occurred two years after the rebuilding of the temple had begun (chs. 7—8, dated Dec. 7, 518 B.C.E.). They may not all have been originally delivered at the same time, but together they form one of the most interesting prophetic comments on exile and restoration that we have. As the rebuilding of the temple was in progress, a delegation from Bethel came to Jerusalem with a question about a custom that had been followed since the destruction of the city in 587 (Zech. 7:3). Should we continue to fast in mourning of that tragic event, now that restoration has begun? The issue taken up by Haggai, whether the present events were to be understood as the fulfillment of the promises of earlier prophets, had not yet been settled for them. The question provided the occasion for Zechariah to bring together an understanding of the past, present and future of God's people. He reminded them of the law of God: "Render true judgments, show kindness and mercy to one another; do not oppress the widow, the orphan, the alien, or the poor; and do not devise evil in your hearts against one another" (7:9–10). He repeated the now generally accepted explanation of the disasters that had befallen them; that they were the result of their ancestors' failure to live according to God's will (7:12–14; 8:14). His summary of the message of the earlier prophets now becomes his own message, and the gist of it becomes the basis for life in the new era in 8:16–17: "These are the things that you shall do: Speak the truth to one another, render in your gates judgments that are true and make for peace, do not devise evil in your hearts against one another, and love no false oath; for all these are things that I hate, says the LORD."

They are now at the turning point between judgment and blessing: "Thus says the LORD: I will return to Zion, and will dwell in the midst of Jerusalem; Jerusalem shall be called the faithful city, and the mountain of the LORD of hosts shall be called the holy mountain" (8:3). The result is described in terms that represent a fairly complete example of the eschatology of the Old Testament.[75] God's people will be restored to the promised land (8:7–8). No king is mentioned, somewhat remarkable given the interest in leadership in chs. 4–6, but the king is also missing from Isaiah 40–55 and 56–66. The nations will no longer mock and scorn (8:13), but they will instead come voluntarily to Jerusalem to "entreat the favor of the LORD and to seek the LORD of hosts" (8:20–23). The people of Zion will make it possible to characterize Jerusalem as the "faithful city" (8:3). Disobedience is not considered an option for the people of the city of the future. Peace and security will be enjoyed by all: old men and old women, boys and girls. No one will be left out (8:4–5). The curse on nature that had resulted in fruitless work in the past will be lifted: "For there shall be a sowing of peace; the vine shall yield its fruit, the ground shall give its produce, and the skies shall give their dew; and I will cause the remnant of this people to possess all these things" (8:12). The good life that Zechariah projects for the inhabitants of Jerusalem is a mixture of the material and the spiritual, of the work of Yahweh and the obedient response of the people. When that day comes, the answer to the question about fasting will be that fasts will be turned into days of rejoicing (8:18–19). That beautiful picture of the future God had in mind for his people was more realistic and less extravagant than the one Second Isaiah had offered, and it seems to have encouraged the people of Judah during those difficult times, for the temple was rebuilt, and a purified cult under the direction of a series of high priests was established. Complete fulfillment still remained out of reach, however, and the chapters added to Zechariah's work seem to reflect the tensions that affected the community during succeeding generations.

Zechariah 9—14

It is generally acknowledged that the prophetic canon is concluded with three short collections, each introduced by the Hebrew word *maśśa'*, traditionally rendered "burden," but represented by "an oracle" in the NRSV (Zechariah 9—11; 12—14; Malachi 1—4). There is little explicit evidence for the date of these materials, but the current trend is to locate at least most of the contents of these three units in the first half of the fifth century B.C.E. Much of Zechariah 9—14 seems to reflect a time of unrest, perhaps the effects of the war between Persia and Greece (beginning around 460 B.C.E.), which led to the construction of a series of Persian forts on both sides of the Jordan, in the hill country, and on the coast.[76] There is some evidence of continuity between chs. 1—8 and 9—14. Mason lists the following: use of the Zion tradition, concern for the cleansing of the people, universalism, use of earlier prophetic traditions, and concerns about leadership, but it should be noted that these are general themes that occur widely.[77] Some of the items in Stuhlmueller's list of differences seem more significant: no personal names are used, there are no explicit references to the temple, strongly negative opinions of leaders are expressed, and there is a strongly militaristic tone.[78] It seems likely that these latter chapters contain a collection of materials from more than one author, for not only are there differences from the first eight chapters, but there also appear strong tensions within 9—14.

Paul Redditt has discerned six collections within these chapters, an analysis that helps to summarize their main themes:[79] (1) a vision of the restoration of the Davidic kingdom, to include Damascus, Phoenicia, and Philistia (Zech. 9:1–10); (2) the promise of restitution of the peoples of Ephraim and Judah to their home-land (Zech. 9:11–10:1; 10:3b–12); (3) shepherd materials (Zech. 10:2–3a; 11:1–17; 13:7–9); (4) a vision of Jerusalem under attack (Zech. 12:1–4a, 5, 8–9); (5) supplements to collection 4, concerning the elevation of Judah (12:6–7) and the cleansing of Jerusalem (12:10–12; 13:1–6); (6) a second vision of Jerusalem un-der attack (Zech. 14:1–13, 14b–21). Redditt believes that the more optimistic ma-terial in collections 1–2, 4, and 6 represent an original collection that was redacted with the addition of collections 3 and 5, representing a more negative point of view, critical of the leadership and dubious about the restoration of Ephraim. It is difficult to know how many of the contrasts represent conflicting attitudes, and how many are the reuse of traditional prophetic themes. A brief survey of the themes in these chapters will illustrate the problem.

Zion theology reappears, especially in chs. 12 and 14. In both, the old theme of a great attack on Jerusalem appears, to be repulsed by the intervention of Yahweh himself. This is a reuse of cultic material known from the psalms (e.g., Psalm 48) and elaborated by other prophets (e.g., Ezekiel 38—39). The same may be said of the glorification of Zion, which reaches its most extravagant form in Zech. 14:8–11: no cold nor frost, no night, living waters flowing to the Dead Sea (cf. Ezek. 47:1–12) and the Mediterranean, and the whole land turned into a plain except for Jerusalem, which will remain exalted.

The judgment of the nations reappears, with more militaristic language than is apparent in chs. 1—8 (cf. 9:1–8, 11–17; 12:1–9; 14:1–5). This material, plus the re-working of the theme of attack on Jerusalem, may reflect the political unease of the fifth century. The king that is promised in 9:9–10 is a man of peace, however, whose description stands in striking contrast with its warlike setting: "humble (or afflicted) and riding on an ass [the animal of peace, in contrast to the horse, the animal of war], . . . and he shall command peace to the nations."[80] He is the king promised by the ear-lier prophets, who will rule in peace after Yahweh has defeated the enemy nations, thus a truly eschatological figure. A hope for the conversion of the nations reappears in 14:16–19 (cf. Zech. 8:20–23), showing that the implications of belief in one God were not ignored, even in times when the nations were a threatening entity.

Contemporary rulers are dealt with as brusquely as the preexilic prophets had spoken of earlier kings. The familiar royal imagery of shepherd is used, leading some interpreters to think of 10:2–3; 11:3–17; and 13:7–9 as references to earlier kings, but others find in these texts a sharp criticism of current leadership, with hope for something better to come from the descendants of David in their midst (cf. 10:3b–5; 12:7–12; 13:1).[81]

The return of exiles from both kingdoms is promised, recalling that both Jeremiah and Ezekiel also expressed hopes for the remnant of the Northern Kingdom (Jer. 3:15–4:2; Ezek. 37:15–23; cf. Zech. 9:12–17; 10:6–12). A strikingly different opinion of the future appears in one of the most puzzling passages of the book, however. In Zech. 11:4–17 we seem to encounter the last of the prophetic symbolic acts. He plays the role of a worthless shepherd, whose task is to annul the family ties between Judah and Israel (11:14). For the details of this passage the commentaries must be consulted. It is one of the most obvious examples of the mixture of hope and disillusionment within the early postexilic community, however.

There are hints of other disturbing elements. Superstition was still a problem (as it is to this day). There is one reference to the use of techniques of divination, reminding us of the "psychics" in our midst (Zech. 10:2) and a reference to idols (13:2). The latter is linked with a condemnation of prophecy as it was practiced at that time, associating it with "the unclean spirit" (13:2b–6). When this text was written the title "prophet" was evidently associated with those other forms of divination mentioned in 10:2. In spite of the problems which these chapters reveal to have existed in the postexilic community—danger from without, inadequate leadership, and the continuation of some of the practices condemned by the earlier prophets—there is no widespread condemnation of the religious practices or the ethical standards of the people at large, as in the preexilic period. The issues that concern these authors do not lead them to cite the law, as in Zech. 7:8–10; 8:16–17, but only to express the hope that in the day to come all will be cleansed of sin and uncleanness (Zech. 13:1) and that all of Jerusalem will be holy (Zech. 14:20–21).

4.3 Isaiah 56—66

The theology of Isaiah 56—66 is distinct enough from that of the rest of Isaiah that it deserves a separate section. There are similarities with Isaiah 40—55, but the setting and the issues that concern this prophet are significantly different, so for the past century most scholars have designated these chapters Third Isaiah.[82] Agreement on the use of that title is not a reflection of any consensus on the nature of the materials contained in these chapters, however. Since many of the debated issues affect one's interpretation of the theology (or theologies) of Isaiah 56—66, the point of view to be adopted in this section must be explained at the outset.

Judah is clearly the setting of these chapters, and the temple has been rebuilt. Potentially, the prophet who produced Isaiah 40—55 might have returned from exile and have continued his ministry in Jerusalem, but there is general agreement that Third Isaiah represents the work of a disciple or disciples of the exilic prophet. There are apparent inconsistencies in the message, leading to the widespread opinion among scholars that multiple authorship is involved. Some passages have been dated in the preexilic period, because of their similarity to the messages of earlier prophets (Isa. 56:9–12; 57:3–6, 7–13a), and others are so much like Lamentations that they have been dated shortly after the fall of Jerusalem (Isa. 59:1–15; 63:7–64:12).[83] Whether these are reuses of older material or newly created texts based on old forms will be of less importance to us than the question what these materials meant when used within a document addressing the problems and hopes of the Judean community early in the restoration period. The chapters cannot be dated with any accuracy, but several factors suggest that they were produced between the time of Haggai and Zechariah and that of the fifth-century reforms carried out by Nehemiah and Ezra. The temple and its cult have been restored, but the local leadership has become corrupt, and the cult has not yet been purified of all the practices that had been condemned by the preexilic prophets. Two texts (Isa. 61:4 and 64:10–11) have been cited as evidence that at least part of the prophet's (or prophets') work preceded the rebuilding of the temple, but this is poetry, and if not taken literally may simply reflect the distress of the people at the inadequacy of the restoration that had taken place thus far. They may be compared with Daniel's prayer, which speaks of the desolation of Jerusalem in the sixth century as a way of lamenting what was happening in the second century (Dan. 9:2–19).

Third Isaiah speaks of internal dissension in the Judean community that surpasses in severity anything reflected in Haggai or Zechariah, and that subject has produced an equal amount of dissension among contemporary scholars. Paul Hanson's reading of Third Isaiah as the production of a group of visionaries, followers of Second Isaiah, out of power because they disagreed with the program of the priestly establishment, whose views are to be found in Haggai and Zechariah 1—8, has gained few followers, but continues to be discussed.[84] A recent rereading of Third Isaiah by Brooks Schramm will be followed here, since it offers a convincing explanation of the tensions evident in these chapters.[85]

The community described in Isaiah 56—66 scarcely seems to fit Ezekiel's term "resurrection." Eventually we shall need to consider critically whether there is any reason to use that term justly of postexilic Judaism. Third Isaiah represents a significant move in a new direction that is relevant to this question. He redefines "Israel," now to include only those who are faithful to the true character of Yahwism, as found in the messages of the preexilic prophets and accepted by the exilic community.[86] His theology has been formed by the experience of exile, and especially by the insights of Second Isaiah. It will become evident that this is the theology that eventually triumphed as Judaism continued to mature in the second temple period, but these chapters were produced at a time when the survival of that theology was by no means certain. The early years of restoration produced what seemed to be the beginnings of the fulfillment of Second Isaiah's promises, but most of it seemed to be delayed, and the difficult circumstances of life in Judah produced severe morale problems. The prophet's role changed during this period. The message still contained an announcement of what God was about to do with his people, but no longer was it assumed that every member of the community qualified to be God's people. The prophet now offers a definition of the "true Israel," with the traditional blessings now restricted to them, while judgment will befall not the people as a whole (as in preexilic prophecy), but only the unfaithful.[87] Third Isaiah does not emphasize the uniqueness and power of Yahweh, as Second Isaiah does, but there are some echoes of the insights of the earlier prophet. The titles "Holy One of Israel," "your Savior and your Redeemer, the Mighty One of Jacob" appear in Isa. 60:9, 14, 16. The transcendence and mercy of God are emphasized in Isa. 57:15:

> For thus says the high and lofty one
>> who inhabits eternity, whose name is Holy:
> I dwell in the high and holy place,
>> and also with those who are contrite and humble in spirit,
> to revive the spirit of the humble,
>> and to revive the heart of the contrite,

and in Isa. 64:4:

> From ages past no one has heard,
>> no ear has perceived,
> no eye has seen any God besides you,
>> who works for those who wait for him.

No temple could contain the maker of heaven and earth:

> The heavens are my throne and the earth is my footstool.
> Where will you build a house for me,
>> where will my resting place be?
> These are all of my own making,
>> and all belong to me.
>> (Isa. 66:1–2, REB; cf. 1 Kings 8:27)

It is best not to take this as indicating opposition to the temple, as many have done, but as a way of extolling the greatness of God.

Second Isaiah's message that the exile was a deserved punishment for Israel's sins, but that the time of punishment has been replaced by a time of forgiveness is reiterated in these chapters.

> Because of their wicked covetousness I was angry;
>> I struck them, I hid and was angry;
>> but they kept turning back to their own ways.
> I have seen their ways, but I will heal them;
>> I will lead them and repay them with comfort,
>> creating for their mourners the fruit of the lips.
> Peace, peace, to the far and the near, says the LORD;
>> and I will heal them.
>> (Isa. 57:17–19; cf. 60:10)

Once again, forgiveness is entirely the result of the divine initiative, without an insistence on prior repentance.

The return of exiles to the promised land had begun, but was far from complete, so this promise of Second Isaiah's was also repeated:

Your sons shall come from far away,
    and your daughters shall be carried on their nurses' arms.
For the coastlands shall wait for me,
    the ships of Tarshish first,
to bring your children from far away,
    their silver and gold with them.

(Isa. 60:4b, 9a)

Thus says the Lord GOD,
    who gathers the outcasts of Israel,
I will gather others to them
    besides those already gathered.

(Isa. 56:8)

The glorification of Zion will be a necessary part of that final restoration, as in the other prophets. Most of chs. 60 and 62 elaborate on that subject. The temple will become "a house of prayer for all peoples" (Isa. 56:7b).

As to "all peoples," Third Isaiah partly follows the rather negative view of the nations found in Second Isaiah, but departs from it in several places to advocate an openness toward membership in the faithful community surpassing even that noted in Zech. 2:15; 8:20–23; 14:16–19. As in chs. 40—55, it is expected that foreigners will become subservient to Israel, enriching Zion by their labors (Isa. 60:10–12, 14; 61:5). This prophet's intention to define the people of God according to their faithfulness, rather than ancestry, leads to the conclusion that the barriers to membership found elsewhere in the Old Testament need not apply (contrast Deut. 23:1–8; Ezek. 44:4–16). This is a remarkable move away from the national/ethnic understanding of religion that prevailed in the ancient world, but it is a logical conclusion to draw from the explicit monotheism of Second Isaiah. The Priestly Code, which took its final form in the exilic or early postexilic period, shows a considerable interest in the absorption of sojourners, resident aliens, into the Jewish community (e.g., Exod. 12:48–49; Num. 15:14–16). Third Isaiah moves beyond the resident alien (*ger*) to claim that the "foreigner" (*ben hannekar*) and the eunuch, who are faithful to Yahweh, are not to be excluded from the worshiping community in Jerusalem (Isa. 56:3–8). Like other prophets, he also looks forward to the day when all peoples and nations will worship the one God (Isa. 66:18–21).

Finally, as we compare chs. 56—66 with 40—55, neither section shows any interest in the restoration of the monarchy, in contrast with Isaiah 1—39. Second Isaiah had democratized the covenant with David, extending it to Israel (Isa. 55:3), and Third Isaiah claims royal attributes for himself, as will be noted later (Isa. 61:1–4).

The differences between Second and Third Isaiah become apparent immediately, as one turns to ch. 56. Justice and righteousness are primarily attributes of God in Isaiah 40—55, and the promises offered by that prophet are unconditional, but 56:1 begins immediately with the subject of human responsibility: "Maintain justice, and do what is right, for soon my salvation will come, and my deliverance be revealed." These standards are by no means new, for they pervade the entire Old Testament, but beginning with this chapter they serve to divide one part of the community from another.[88] The definitive character of justice and righteousness is next put in its most striking form with the insistence (noted above) that even the foreigner and the eunuch can qualify for membership in the people of God, if they fulfill this criterion, described now in other terms: joining oneself to the Lord (56:3, 6), choosing the things that please God (56:4), holding fast his covenant (56:4, 6), and keeping the sabbath (56:2, 4, 6), a distinguishing mark for the Jew that became especially important in the postexilic period (cf. Ezek. 20:12–13). As the book begins with a concern for the acceptance of foreigners, so it ends, with 66:18 declaring, "I am coming to gather all nations and tongues; and they shall come and see my glory," and later, "From new moon to new moon, and from sabbath to sabbath, all flesh shall come to worship before me" (66:23).

The prophet's intention to redefine Israel then leads him immediately to those who do not qualify, beginning with leaders of the community, who are condemned in some of the harshest language to be found anywhere in the prophetic books (Isa. 56:9–57:13). They are called wild beasts and are accused of a series of cultic practices, including idol worship, that are reminiscent of the preexilic period. The theme reappears in Isa. 65:1–12 and 66:3–5. These texts have been variously explained, but the most natural reading seems to be the one advocated by Schramm.[89] The syncretism that was typical of worship in Israel and Judah before the exile had probably not been purged from the practices of the people of the land, as it apparently had been in the Babylonian exile. Once the restoration began, the new form of Yahwism brought back to Judah by the returnees did not immediately prevail, so the old issue of the proper way to worship Yahweh had not yet been settled. This accounts for aspects of the work of Third Isaiah, Malachi, Nehemiah, and Ezra, but the evidence from post-Old Testament literature indicates that from the time of the latter two reformers that victory had largely been won.[90]

In contrast to the coming judgment of the unfaithful in their midst, God promises to dwell "with those who are contrite and humble in spirit" (Isa. 57:14–21). The lamenting question concerning God's delay in fulfilling his promises, "Why do we fast, but you do not see? Why humble ourselves, but you do not notice?" (Isa. 58:3) is answered at length with a redefinition of fasting, in ethical terms:

> Is not this the fast that I choose:
>   to loose the bonds of injustice,
>   to undo the thongs of the yoke,
> to let the oppressed go free,
>   and to break every yoke?
> Is it not to share your bread with the hungry,
>   and bring the homeless poor into your house;
> when you see the naked, to cover them,
>   and not to hide yourself from your own kin?
>
>   (Isa. 58:6–7)

The ethical dimensions of Yahwism, which played lesser roles in the messages of Second Isaiah, Haggai, and Zechariah, thus reappear with great prominence in Third Isaiah. He must deal with complete unconcern for the insights gained by the exilic experience on the part of those he condemns, and with very low morale on the part of those who would be faithful, but do not understand why God is inactive, since they are suffering from poor economic conditions and from oppression by their leaders. The depth of the problem is revealed by the laments he quotes in 59:1–15 and 63:7–64:12. The form and contents of these laments are familiar to us from the laments of the community in the Psalter, but it is not clear whether these are quotations of traditional material, or whether the prophet formulated these speeches, acting as a spokesman for the people. Their function in this context is clear, however. The prophet cites them so as to offer a response, and where necessary, a correction. The former lament is followed by a description of theophany, the coming of the savior God, but now God's coming involves a division; he will come to redeem "those in Jacob who turn from transgression" (Isa. 59:15b–20). The latter lament is answered sharply with the condemnation of syncretistic practices:

> I was ready to be sought out by those who did not ask,
>> to be found by those who did not seek me.
> I said, "Here I am, here I am,"
>> to a nation that did not call on my name.
> I held out my hands all day long
>> to a rebellious people,
> who walk in a way that is not good,
>> following their own devices;

and then those devices are described (Isa. 65:1–7). On the other hand, there are some who are God's servants, his chosen ones (v. 9), and the different fates of the servants and the unfaithful are described in a striking series of contrasts, in vv. 13–16.

Both laments are then followed by a series of eschatological promises, unconditional in nature, and emphasizing the glorification of Zion (chs. 60–62 and 65:17–25). The former section has been identified as the nucleus of the book, around which other materials have been arranged in concentric fashion.[91] It is the passage most closely related to Second Isaiah, in that it addresses Israel as a single unit without divisions, and offers unconditional promises. As the book now reads, it functions the same way as 65:17–25, as an eschatological answer to the community's laments. Since the latter passage is shorter and simpler, we shall begin with it. The prophet promises that God is about to begin creating again, a new heaven and a new earth, a tacit acknowledgment that radical changes are needed before the will of God can fully be experienced on earth. But everything the prophet needs to say about the new heaven and earth can be said with reference to Jerusalem. This apparent inconsistency has troubled commentators who have not noticed that Jerusalem is the center around which all of prophetic eschatology is organized.[92] In the new Jerusalem, which certainly represents the new earth, weeping will be replaced by joy, there will be no more premature deaths, the land will be fertile, and work will not be futile. Finally, there will be no more hurting or destruction, quoting a portion of Isa. 11:6–9.

The future Zion is described in equally glorious terms, but at greater length in chs. 60 and 62, with an additional emphasis on the return of the exiles and the reversal of fortune of Jerusalem and the Jews. The middle of the section, 61:1–11, contains a unique, personal statement by the prophet:

> The spirit of the Lord GOD is upon me,
>   because the LORD has anointed me;
> he has sent me to bring good news to the oppressed,
>   to bind up the brokenhearted,
> to proclaim liberty to the captives,
>   and release to the prisoners;
> to proclaim the year of the LORD's favor,
>   and the day of vengeance of our God;
>   to comfort all who mourn.
>
> (Isa. 61:1–2)

Among the canonical prophets, only Micah and Ezekiel claim to have the gift of the spirit: "But as for me, I am filled with power,with the spirit of the LORD, and with justice and might, to declare to Jacob his transgression and to Israel his sin" (Micah 3:8). Micah's commission was to announce judgment; Third Isaiah may have thought of himself as fulfilling another role, that of the servant proclaimed by Second Isaiah: "I have put my spirit upon him; he will bring forth justice to the nations" (Isa. 42:1b), since his message is good news. He claims to have been anointed, probably metaphorically, since anointing had been the way kings were designated (cf. 1 Sam. 10:1; 16:13, where anointing and the gift of the spirit are combined). There are no more kings in Israel, and the prophet seems to have taken up the role of the ruler who once could have set captives free, along with that of the herald who went through the land to declare that the Jubilee year had come: "you shall proclaim liberty throughout the land to all its inhabitants" (Lev. 25:10). The ideals contained in the priestly legislation for the jubilee year, when everyone would be given a second chance (Lev. 25:8–17), are now declared to be God's intention for the restored community from this time on. Those now in mourning will be called oaks of righteousness (Isa. 61:3), they will build up the ancient ruins (v. 4), "for I the LORD love justice, I hate robbery and wrongdoing; I will faithfully give them their recompense, and I will make an everlasting covenant with them" (v. 8). So the passage closes with a hymn of praise (vv. 10–11), "for as the earth brings forth its shoots, and as a garden causes what is sown in it to spring up, so the Lord GOD will cause righteousness and praise to spring up before all the nations."

Third Isaiah is evidence for the major religious issue that faced the restored community in Judah—putting into practice the insights into the true character of Yahwism that had been gained in exile. Religion as practiced in Judah still preserved the syncretism of the preexilic period, and that was not eliminated during the early years of the restoration. The role of the prophet, with respect to the abuses that prevailed—cultic and social—was different from before. The restoration prophets did not see their situation as hopeless. They were convinced this was the beginning of the new era of God's favor. They believed the radical changes in history brought about by the Persians were signs that God was at work to bring the world into harmony with his will. They could identify a faithful group of Jews who accepted the responsibility to live in accordance with the new world that was coming into being. But they needed instruction, admonishment, and encouragement. These prophets differed from their predecessors in that they did offer appeals for repentance coupled with promises, for there was time to repent, God was ready to forgive, and repentance would make a difference. The future was in God's hands, but humans had something essential to contribute, so Third Isaiah begins with the call for justice and righteousness, and defines his mission as being sent to the oppressed, the broken-hearted, captives, and those who mourn—with good news for them.

Earlier we pondered the remarkable fact that the Yahwistic religion survived the destruction of Israel and Judah. At the human level, it can be partly explained by noting that the exiles in Babylonia became willing to accept responsibility for what had happened, and that they received from some of the prophets promises of a better future (to be the work of that same Yahweh) and believed them. As we consider the early years of restoration and the contrast between what the exiles had hoped for and what really transpired, the survival of the religion once again becomes a matter for wonder. Another factor, besides the work of the prophets, will enter in, about which more must be said in the final chapter of this book. That is scripture, written texts containing the law of God which were accepted as definitive for the nature of the community and for the life of the individual believer. The next prophet to be discussed, Malachi, contains some evidence of that.

4.4 Malachi

There are no historical references in this book, but there is no reason to doubt that it originated in Judah fairly early in the postexilic period. It may be anonymous, for the word *mal'achi* means "my messenger," and the identical form appears in Mal. 3:1, where it cannot be understood as a proper name. Since the book begins with the same words found also in Zech. 9:1 and 12.1, "An oracle. The word of the LORD," it has been suggested that three anonymous texts were added at the end of the scroll of the minor prophets. Eventually "my messenger" was taken to be the name of a prophet, so these chapters were identified as a separate book, but the other two short units were added to Zechariah 1–8, producing a total of twelve prophets, a highly symbolic number. This is possible, but some commentators do argue for Malachi as a personal name, and at any rate, these theories have no effect on the way one interprets the book. It is clearly a self-contained unit, distinguished by a unique form, called variously disputation, diatribe, or lawsuit.[93] There are six of these disputations, Mal. 1:2–5; 1:6–2:9; 2:10–16; 2:17–3:5; 3:6–12; 3:13–4:3 [MT 3:13–21], plus two brief appendixes (3:22–24), considered by most scholars to be additions to the collection of the twelve prophets rather than originally part of Malachi. The book addresses a series of problems within the

Judean community in an argumentative way, citing what people believe, quoting questions they are asking—or may ask, challenging them with rhetorical questions, and attempting to motivate them with threats and promises. Few of the typical prophetic genres are used, but the author clearly assumes prophetic authority.

The arguments make it possible for us to deduce a good bit about the situation that concerned this prophet. There was a governor in Judah (Mal. 1:8), no doubt a Persian appointee, but his activity was not Malachi's concern. Internal affairs were clearly under the control of the priesthood, and Malachi had a high view of that, as an institution. The problem was that those in charge during his time were not living up to the ideals of the institution as he understood them, were seriously neglecting their duties, and since they were the leaders who were supposed to be defining the character of the community, this was a critical matter. Challenges to the priests thus occupy most of Mal. 1:6–2:9 and 3:2b–4.

Throughout the book we are given a picture of priests and laypeople who are discouraged and disillusioned, even to the extent of questioning whether God does anything for his people. No major crisis is in view; Malachi says little about oppression or economic difficulty. Rather, he quotes general complaints: "How have you loved us?" "All who do evil are good in the sight of the LORD, and he delights in them." "Where is the God of justice?" "It is vain to serve God" (Mal. 1:2; 2:17; 3:14). Other than these skeptical attitudes, there are no false beliefs challenged by Malachi, and he does not speak of idolatry or syncretistic practices, as Third Isaiah did.[94] The problem seems to be one of generally low morale that has led to neglect of the unique way of life that should characterize the people of Yahweh.

This attitude has led to a priesthood that goes through the motions, accepting any kind of sacrifice—lame, blind, and sick animals (Mal. 1:7–14). They were to be the teachers who kept their people informed of the will of God for them, but they have neglected that essential duty (Mal. 2:6–9). The institution of marriage is being violated in a way that Malachi finds deeply offensive (Mal. 2:10–16). Unfortunately, this is the most difficult part of the book, and there are many opinions as to the issue or issues condemned in these verses. The first problem is in v. 11: "Judah has profaned the sanctuary of the LORD, which he loves, and has married the daughter of a foreign god." This has been taken both literally, meaning marriage to foreign women, and metaphorically, meaning apostasy.[95] The translation of vv. 15–16 is very uncertain. The first two words of v. 16 are simply "hate" and "send away," so it is by no means clear who hates, or who or what is hated, and it can be disputed whether "send away" means divorce, although it has usually been taken that way. A common reading takes the problem to be divorce of one's Jewish wife ("your companion and your wife by covenant," (v. 14b) in order to marry a foreigner.[96] Since Malachi shows no concern elsewhere about syncretism or apostasy, it seems safest to think the problem here does have to do with marriage and to disruption of the home in some way because of marriage to a foreign woman. Since a man could have more than one wife, if he could afford it, it remains uncertain whether Malachi was speaking specifically about divorce.

The tithe, which was an important part of the income of priests and Levites (Lev. 27:30–33; Num. 18:21–32; Deut. 14:22–29), was being neglected, a problem that evidently occurred more than once in Jewish history, as Neh. 13:10–12 indicates. Malachi does not cite that as a reason for the priests' neglect of their duties, but considers the failure to tithe to be robbing God (Mal. 3:8–12). In addition to these problems, there appears one familiar list of sinners who will be punished when the "messenger of the covenant" appears: sorcerers, adulterers, those who swear falsely, and those who oppress hired workers, widow, orphan, and alien (Mal. 3:5). These are problems that occur in every generation. We get the impression that Malachi worked during a time when the temple-centered community in Judah was living in relative peace—he shows no interest in political affairs—and had somehow resolved many of the problems that faced Third Isaiah. We can learn more about the people of his time by asking what Malachi assumes they knew, and what he can assume they believe. Then we shall look for the bases for the claims he makes over against the ways his people are living.

They know the story of the rivalry between Jacob and Esau, and of the way that story claims Yahweh favored Jacob (Mal. 1:2; cf. Genesis 25—27, 32—33). They have been told that God loves them, the first indication in Malachi of his very close relationship with the theology of the book of Deuteronomy (Mal. 1:2; cf. Deut. 7:8). They know of rules indicating that animals for sacrifice must be perfect, or Malachi could not have insisted on it (Mal. 1:8, 14; cf. Lev. 22:20–25; Deut. 15:21). He can allude to the priestly blessing (Num. 6:23–27) saying it will become a curse (Mal. 2:2). He assumes that they know about a covenant with Levi —more than we know, in fact, for Levi is given a central position beyond anything found elsewhere in the Old Testament (Mal. 2:4–6).[97] They know that instruction is one of the responsibilities of priests (Mal. 2:7; Lev. 10:10–11; Deut. 31:9–13), and Malachi's reference to the law of tithing would not have been news to them (Mal. 3:8–10).

There are certain beliefs that Malachi takes for granted and assumes he can use in his arguments. The people are used to calling God "father" (Mal. 1:6; 2:10), and we found that term used also in Third Isaiah (Isa. 63:16; 64:8). Second Isaiah's insistence that there is only one God apparently can now be appealed to as a common belief: "Have we not all one father? Has not one God created us?" (Mal. 2:10).[98] God is Israel's creator. They believe justice should be an attribute of God, although some now question it (Mal. 2:17). That the Day of Yahweh would be a day of judgment is something they would have heard from the tradition of the earlier prophets, and it probably had become a part of popular belief by now (Mal. 3:2; 4:1). In addition to the covenant with Levi, "covenant" is used in two other ways (Mal. 2:14; 3:1), and since covenant is an important term in Deuteronomy, this is another indication that the theology of that book was generally known.[99]

It is not surprising, then, that most of Malachi's claims over against the practices he deplores are based on what we now know as the Pentateuch. He may not have been responsible for 4:4, "Remember the teaching of my servant Moses, the statutes and ordinances that I commanded him at Horeb for all Israel," for this is the first of the "appendixes" that many scholars think was added when the complete collection of the twelve prophets was made. His work indicates, however, that the transition from dependence on tradition and the living words of inspired persons to the use of written scripture as definitive for the faith and life of the Jewish community was well under way. In two ways he assumes for himself the freedom and authority of the older prophets. He claims to be able to interpret what God is doing in a current event, namely, that the devastation of Edom is in fact the work of God to fulfill the judgment predicted by earlier prophets (Mal. 1:3–5). And he claims to know the future, with his proclamation that the Day of the Lord is coming soon (Mal. 3:1–5; 4:1–3).

Given the interests of Second and Third Isaiah, Haggai, and Zechariah, it is remarkable that Zion theology plays a very small role in Malachi. He by no means rejects it, since the holiness of the temple is a major concern, but the return of exiles and the glorification of the city are themes that are pervasive in other prophetic books, but missing from Malachi. His monotheism has affected his attitude toward the nations in ways similar to what we found in Zechariah and Third Isaiah. Once Judah recognizes that Yahweh has fulfilled his threats against Edom, Malachi expects they will exclaim, "Great is the LORD beyond the borders of Israel!" (Mal. 1:5). He gives Yahweh the title assumed by human empire builders, "Great King," for Yahweh's name is feared among the nations (Mal. 1:14). Whether he thought Gentiles had already come to revere the God of Israel, or is thinking of the worship of Yahweh among the Jewish diaspora, is not made explicit, but the latter seems more likely. Much debated is an earlier saying in the same unit (Mal. 1:11): "For from the rising of the sun to its setting my name is great among the nations, and in every place incense is offered to my name, and a pure offering; for my name is great among the nations, says the LORD of hosts." This has been given two different eschatological interpretations: (a) In the Roman Catholic Church it was taken to predict the worldwide offering of the Mass. (b) Others have taken the verse to refer to Malachi's expectation that soon all the nations would worship Yahweh.[100] Two present-tense readings ascribe to Malachi at least a qualified acceptance of other religions: (c) He accepts worship of the high god in other religions as acceptable to Yahweh. (d) It is hyperbole; even pagan sacrifice is superior to what is presently being offered in Jerusalem. Of these interpretations, only b is in keeping with the traditions Malachi knew and used. A fifth explanation is also possible, although there is a problem with it, as with the other four: He refers to the fact that Yahweh is being worshiped faithfully by other Jews, throughout the diaspora. The question this one raises is whether incense and offerings were being used in worship elsewhere, or whether Malachi might have been using the words metaphorically.[101]

There is one bit of narrative in the book, Mal. 3:16–18, suggesting that Malachi's words gained a positive response from some in his community. If those who "revered the LORD" in v. 16 were some of those who had said, "It is vain to serve God. What do we profit by keeping his command or by going about as mourners before the LORD of hosts? Now we count the arrogant happy; evildoers not only prosper, but when they put God to the test they escape" (3:14–15), then a significant change must have occurred.[102] Others see v. 16 as introducing a distinct group of righteous Jews, not identified elsewhere in the book.[103] The narrative says that they have been written in a "book of remembrance" before the Lord,[104] and promises that they shall be the Lord's special possession, on the day when he acts.

Malachi's eschatology focuses on the day of Yahweh as a day of judgment, when the distinction between the righteous and the wicked will become evident (Mal. 3:2–5, 17–18; 4:1–3). His special contribution is the promise that God's messenger (*mal'achi*) will prepare the way. Elsewhere, the messenger plays a positive role (Exod 23:23; 32:34; Isa. 42:19; 44:26); but in Mal. 3:1–4 he is a mysterious figure, whose exact relationship to God is not completely clear. A messenger is to prepare the way before Yahweh (3:1), then the Lord (not Yahweh, in Hebrew, but the word meaning "lord," *ădonay*) will suddenly come to his temple, next we are told the "messenger of the covenant" is coming. It is natural to think that *ădonay* must refer to God, but is the messenger of the covenant God, or the messenger of 3:1? We cannot be certain.[105] The messenger's role is a distinctive one, for Old Testament eschatology, in that he, like a refiner's fire and fuller's soap, will purify the Levites (rather than punishing them), so that pure offerings may be made in the future.

This prophet puts a heavy emphasis on responsibility, on the need for leaders and people to commit themselves to faithfulness to what they know and believe. The spiritual stagnation of their time had led to carelessness and worse—to serious skepticism about the truth of some of what they had been taught. Like his model, Deuteronomy, Malachi challenged his people to live what they had been taught, assuring them that they will then see the difference. His saying, "Return to me, and I will return to you, says the LORD of hosts" (3:7, quoted also in Zech. 1:3), reverses the order of eschatological forgiveness promised in Jeremiah, Ezekiel, and Isaiah 40—66; agreeing instead with Deuteronomy 30, which makes forgiveness dependent on repentance. In exile, when the situation seemed hopeless, the promise that God would take the initiative was essential if anyone was to have hope. ("For I the LORD do not change; therefore you, O children of Jacob, have not perished," Mal. 3:6.) Now, God had given them a new start, but it would amount to nothing if they did not embrace their responsibilities with enthusiasm, and so Malachi calls for initiative on their part. The problems he deals with and the approaches he takes have often been compared with those found in the books of Ezra and Nehemiah,[106] and the sketchy evidence we have for the fifth century B.C.E. suggests that these three books represent the movement toward the establishment of Judaism based on a growing collection of books accepted as the definitive statement concerning who God really is, and what God wants for the people he has chosen, and for the world.

4.5 Joel

The book of Joel has been dated as early as the ninth century B.C.E. and as late as the second.[107] There are strong indications that it originated in the postexilic period, but beyond that nothing certain can be said about its date. I have placed it last in the sequence partly because to locate it anywhere else might suggest we know more about its setting than we really do. Another reason for this position is the significant difference between the message of this book and the others in the prophetic canon.

There is much about the book that remains mysterious. Mason comments about the "bewildering variety of scholarly interpretations of the book, which seem to differ more and more and to become more and more speculative as time goes on, and further and further away from consensus."[108] About certain features there is general agreement among contemporary scholars, however, and these can be noted briefly here as background to our primary concern with the message of the book. Its unity, which had been challenged earlier in this century, was convincingly defended by Hans Walter Wolff, and is now generally accepted.[109] Allusions to or direct quotations of material found in other Old Testament books are a prominent feature of Joel, leading, of course, to discussion of who is quoting whom, but clearly giving this book an "anthological" character that sets it apart from the other prophets.[110] That chs. 1—2 are strongly influenced by the genre of the psalms of lament is also generally recognized, and some read the whole book with reference to laments.[111]

The book has a clear outline. It begins with a description of the devastating effects of a locust plague, together with calls to the Judean community to lament and fast (Joel 1:2–20). Next an invasion, called the Day of Yahweh, is described in terms that some take to be a reference to a human army, others to the locust plague, and still others to an eschatological event (Joel 2:1–17). This section includes a call to the people to return to the Lord with fasting and weeping, reminding them of the true character of Yahweh as expressed in Exod 34:6. The third part of the book begins with a clear turning point, describing now the blessings God has in store for his people, with the renewal of the fertility of the land, and the gift of the spirit, which will make access to God possible for everyone (Joel 2:18–32 [MT 2:18–27; 3:1–5]). The fourth section continues with promises, emphasizing God's judgment of Judah's enemies, so that security in their land will be possible (Joel 3:1–21 [MT 4:1–21]).

There have been many attempts to associate Joel with a specific life situation, but none has been persuasive to many. Debate has raged over the relationship between chs. 1 and 2.[112] How many disasters are alluded to? At the most, locusts, drought, fire, and invasion have been listed. I am inclined to agree with those who see the plague of locusts as the basis for both chapters, with the first focusing on their effects on the land, and the second describing their activity in vividly poetic terms.[113] Another point of difference among contemporary scholars is the meaning of Joel 2:12–14. In the past it was assumed to be a call to national repentance, and most still read it that way. Joel says nothing about any sins Judeans may have committed, however, and never refers to Yahweh's ethical demands on his people. This has led to creative efforts to identify the sin that must have concerned the prophet,[114] but a few have proposed understanding the verb *shub* by its basic meaning of "turn," that is, turn to God for help, rather than "return," that is, return to God in repentance.[115] I shall read the book in that way.

Evidence for the unity of the book, as shown by Wolff, plus the difficulty in identifying the life setting to which it might have been directed suggest that it should be read more as a "treatise" than as a collection of oracles originally delivered by a prophet in order to interpret a specific situation. Like the psalms of lament (e.g., Psalms 44; 60; 79; 80) Joel seems to use the destruction caused by locust plagues, by drought and fire, and by invading armies as powerful metaphors that might be used by the community at any time of severe distress.[116] He uses them in order to make a generally applicable point: Disaster can be averted by turning to God, for God's ultimate goal for his people is abundant blessing.[117]

There is only one God for Joel; the threat of syncretistic cults is never considered. He uses a form of Ezekiel's "recognition formula" combined with Second Isaiah's explicit monotheism in 2:27: "You shall know that I am in the midst of Israel, and that I, the LORD, am your God and there is no other." This is a God whose compassion and intention to bless his people will be emphasized by the prophet, but who is also responsible for disaster (cf. 1:15; 2:1–2, 11), and Joel leaves that unexplained. He associates all the destruction described in 1:2–2:11 with the Day of Yahweh.[118] That apparently had been originally understood in Israel to be the day when Yahweh came out to battle against their foes, as their deliverer. Amos had reversed its meaning, declaring that Israel had now become the enemy (Amos 5:18–20), and Zephaniah used the theme in the same way (Zeph. 1:2–18). For other prophets, the original sense, Yahweh's intervention to save Israel from the enemy nations, was retained, and the theme will reappear in that way in the latter part of Joel (Joel 3:14; cf. Isaiah 13; Ezekiel 30). In the first two chapters of Joel, however, the Day of Yahweh is a time of disaster for Judah (Joel 1:15; 2:1–2, 11), but without the explanation provided by Amos and Zephaniah. The earlier prophets emphasized that this was Yahweh's just judgment of his people for their sins, but no reason of any kind is offered by Joel. Instead, his words are reminiscent of the psalms of lament in which part of the complaint involves a lack of understanding why God should let such terrible things happen to his people, although Joel does not offer an explicit claim of innocence, as in Ps. 44:17–18: "All this has come upon us, yet we have not forgotten you, or been false to your covenant. Our heart has not turned back, nor have our steps departed from your way." Joel simply assumes that disaster of any kind must come from Yahweh, and does not discuss how that could be. Given his monotheism, what other source could there be? This does not lead him to despair, however, for he believes that Yahweh's ultimate intention is to bless his people, and that assurance appears at the center of the book (Joel 2:12–14), then becomes the entire subject of the last half.

The fact that Joel says nothing of sin or even of the wrath of God (contrast Zephaniah 1–2) in the first half of the book strongly suggests that the correct way to read Joel 2:12–14 is not as a call to repentance, but as a call to turn to God for help in time of trouble, coupled with the assurance that Yahweh is compassionate and merciful, slow to anger, and abounding in steadfast love, who relents from doing harm. Joel takes the positive part of the classic statement of the attributes of God, found in its full form in Exod. 34:6–7, and reinforces it by alluding to God's willingness to relent even when punishment was deserved, found in the same context, Exod. 32:12–14. Jonah makes the same combination (Jonah 4:2); whether one author was influenced by the other or both used Exodus in the same way is not a subject that need concern us here.[119] Joel's insistence on the freedom of God not to be coerced even by fasting, weeping, and mourning, with his "Who knows whether he will not turn and relent, and leave a blessing behind him?" also appears in another way in Jonah, as a word of the king of Nineveh (Jonah 3:9). "Who knows?" corresponds to the "Perhaps" attached to other promises in the prophets (Amos 5:15; Zeph. 2:3; and, again, Exod. 32:30). Joel clearly believes in the importance of public worship, given his calls to the priests and the people in 1:13–14 and 2:15–17, but he knows prayer and fasting will not produce automatic results. Having begun with a lengthy and terrifying description of disaster, he has come in 2:12–14 to the point of his work, however, which is that in spite of the terrible reality of those times he identifies as the Day of Yahweh, Yahweh's true intention for his people is to bless them. He is the source of help to whom they must turn.

The turning point of the book is introduced with a bit of narrative, in Joel 2:18–19a: "Then the Lord became jealous [or zealous] for his land, and had pity on his people. In response to his people the Lord said . . . ." The imperfects with waw consecutive normally indicate past tense and should be translated that way here in spite of the questions that raises. Perhaps we find here another influence from the Psalms, recalling how psalms of thanksgiving repeat the complaints and petitions that had been uttered in laments, then affirm that God has answered the prayer (e.g., Psalms 30; 116; 118). The prophet has chosen two more verbs, to add to those used in 2:13, in order to emphasize God's true intentions for his people: words designating jealousy or zealousness, and pity. The remainder of the book contains promises following a repertoire typical of the prophetic books. The blessings of nature will be restored (2:19, 21–26a), leading finally to an eschatological picture of abundance (3:18). There is no ambiguity about the nations in this book, as there is in other parts of the Old Testament. They are Judah's enemies, and peace and security will come only when they are defeated by the intervention of the Divine Warrior (Joel 3:1–16, 19). Joel's view of future peace differed sharply from that found in some of the prophets, as he emphasized by reversing the saying found in Isa. 2:4 and Micah 4:3: "Beat your plowshares into swords, and your pruning hooks into spears; let the weakling say, 'I am a warrior'" (Joel 3:10). He does not show the interest in peace among the nations found elsewhere; his concern is only for security for Judah.[120]

One of the most remarkable passages in the prophetic books appears in Joel 2, for it promises a "democratization" of the gift of prophecy:

> Then afterward
>   I will pour out my spirit on all flesh;
> your sons and your daughters shall prophesy,
>   your old men shall dream dreams,
>   and your young men shall see visions.
> Even on the male and female slaves,
>   in those days, I will pour out my spirit.
>   (Joel 2:28–29 [MT 3:1–2])

Direct access to knowledge of the will of God had always been thought to be a special gift afforded only to a few. Certain people had been set apart for a specific work by the gift of the divine spirit. It might be the gift of artistic and technical ability, as in the case of Bezalel (Exod. 35:31), of the power to act as a great warrior, as with Saul and David (1 Sam. 11:6; 16:13), or it could be directly identified with wisdom (Deut. 34:9; Isa. 11:2). Among the other prophetic books, Isa. 61:1, Micah 3:8, and Ezekiel (e.g., Ezek. 3:24; 11:5) speak of prophetic powers as gifts of the spirit, and that claim had been associated with the precanonical prophets (e.g., 2 Kings 2:9, 15). A single parallel to Joel 2:28–29, another hope for an outpouring of the spirit that would make prophets of *all* of God's people, appears in Numbers 11. The Lord had instructed Moses to choose seventy elders to assist him in the managing of daily affairs in the wilderness. He took them to the tent of meeting, where the spirit rested on them and they prophesied, on that one occasion. For some reason, Eldad and Medad had not joined the others, but they also received the spirit and prophesied. When Joshua protested this irregularity, Moses responded, "Would that all the LORD's people were prophets, and that the LORD would put his spirit on them!" (Num. 11:29). A thin line of tradition thus runs from Moses' hope to Joel's promise to Peter's claim that the promise had been fulfilled at Pentecost with the gift of the spirit on all believers (Acts 2:14–21, 33).

A similar hope does appear elsewhere in the prophets, however, using different terminology. For Hosea, knowledge of God—the lack of it—was a major issue (e.g., Hos. 4:1, 6; 6:6). Jeremiah's promise of inner change—law written on the heart—claimed God intended to correct that deficiency: "For they shall all know me, from the least of them to the greatest, says the LORD" (Jer. 31:31–34). Knowledge of God as a future gift was a major theme of Ezekiel: "Then you/they will know that I am Yahweh" is a regular theme. His promise of anthropological change also includes the gift of a new spirit (Ezek. 36:26–27; cf. 37:14; 39:29). Both Jeremiah and Ezekiel include forgiveness as an essential step in the creation of the new humanity. It is striking, but in keeping with the rest of the book of Joel, that he saw no need to include that in his vision of the future. Perhaps he believed that the way of repentance and atonement for sin in the cult was functioning as it should.

The results of the future outpouring of the spirit, for Joel, would be prophecy, dreams, and visions—three of the typical means God made his will directly known, as Israel understood it. Joel thus expected that sometime in the future ("afterward") everyone in Israel would enjoy a direct, not mediated access to God. Commentators generally agree that for him "all flesh" (Joel 2:28) meant all Israel, not all humankind. Note that he says *your* sons and daughters, old and young. Even so, the extent of his democratization is not to be overlooked. He thought of a time when male and female alike would prophesy—no distinction based on sex, and when the old and the young alike would receive God's revelation—no distinction based on age. In a culture where slavery was permitted, neither would he exclude male or female slaves. On them also, God will pour out his spirit, Joel announced, and although he does not say so, many of them were probably Gentiles. Paul did not quote Joel when he wrote that in Christ there is "no longer Jew or Greek, there is no longer slave or free, there is no longer male and female" (Gal. 3:28), but he had a remarkable forerunner in Joel.

Joel's concern about access to God takes another form that also appears significantly in Ezekiel. The people of God need to be in the presence of God. The priestly theology of the tabernacle located it in the center of the camp (Exodus 35—40), and Ezekiel's vision of the new Jerusalem located it in the middle of the promised land (Ezekiel 48). These were the places where God could, when he chose, dwell in the midst of his people. Ezekiel's new city was to have a new name, in case anyone missed the point of its location: *Yahweh Shammah*, "Yahweh Is There" (Ezek. 48:35). Joel offered the same promise:

> So you shall know that I, the LORD, your God,
>   dwell in Zion, my holy mountain.
>   (Joel 3:17)

> . . . for the LORD dwells in Zion.
>   (Joel 3:21)

The book of Joel was produced at a time when the temple and its cult were a central part of life in Judah. This prophet finds nothing in the cult itself to criticize; neither the corruption of Yahwism by syncretistic variations found in preexilic worship nor the carelessness criticized by Malachi. He considers faithful cultic activity to be essential to the health of the community. Suggestions that the book may have been a liturgical piece intended to be used in worship have not met with general favor, but there is no question that it is very much a cult-oriented piece, using especially the language of the psalms of lament, and combining it with typically prophetic speech.

Two subjects of great interest to other prophets are missing from the book. Joel has no interest in the government, either present or future, so there is no criticism of contemporary leaders; neither is there an expression of hope for the coming of the righteous king in his eschatology. More surprising is his failure to say anything about Judah's social responsibilities. His only imperatives have to do with worship. That makes the book a very incomplete reflection of the character of postexilic Judaism, but its focus on worship does serve as an important reminder of the centrality of the temple in the lives and thought of Jews during the second temple period.

Joel agrees with the other prophets in recognizing a need for change in human beings, but here also it is access to God rather than obedience to the law so as to maintain justice and righteousness in daily life that concerns him. With this exception, he uses and takes for granted most of the theological insights of the earlier prophets, such as the sovereignty of the one God over all that exists, the merciful and compassionate nature of God, and the special relationship he has established with Israel. The fact that he does not explain the Day of Yahweh as judgment for Israel's sins does leave a large theological issue untouched. The earlier prophets accounted for the death of Israel by making it God's just judgment for their sins, but nothing of that theology appears in Joel. He contemplates disasters of various kinds with the conviction that there is a remedy—lament and fasting, calling on Yahweh for help—and that seems to have satisfied him. Natural disasters and harm done by other nations were thus no longer theologized as the signs of radical change in the relationship between Yahweh and Israel, as they had been in the past. Presumably, the three key moments—the deaths of the Northern and Southern Kingdoms and the beginning of restoration to the promised land—had happened, and the time had come when life in the land could once again be lived in a normal way. The normal way was far different from what it had once been, however, and some reflection on that will conclude our study of the theology of the prophetic books.

5

THE CONTINUING INFLUENCE OF
OLD TESTAMENT PROPHECY

5.1 The "End of Prophecy"

By 200 B.C.E. Judaism was using four scrolls containing the works of the prophets. Sirach's retelling of the history of Israel includes references to Isaiah, Jeremiah, Ezekiel, and "the Twelve Prophets" (Sir. 48:20, 23; 49:6, 8, 10). Soon the term "the Law and the Prophets" would become a standard way of referring to the books considered to be the authoritative word of God by most Jews.[1] At some point in the postexilic period the process of editing the prophetic books had been brought to an end.[2] Unfortunately, there is no explicit evidence as to how early that happened, the process by which those large scrolls were compiled, or the conditions that led to the general acceptance of those books as "inspired Scripture."[3]

The completion of this collection of prophetic writings has often been associated with the assumption that from a certain point on there were no more prophets functioning within Judaism—thus the "end of prophecy." A few texts seemed to state that explicitly. Psalm 74 was sometimes dated late, and "We do not see our emblems; there is no longer any prophet, and there is no one among us who knows how long" (v. 9) was taken to refer to the end of prophecy, but it may well come from early in the sixth century, contemporary with Jeremiah and Ezekiel, and be lamenting the end of cultic prophecy in the now destroyed temple. The Prayer of Azariah 15 (added to Daniel 3 in the LXX) also laments the end of all the sacred institutions: "In our day we have no ruler, or prophet, or leader, no burnt offering, or sacrifice, or oblation, or incense, no place to make an offering before you and to find mercy." The setting is the exile, but it is probably an explicit reference to the persecutions of the Jews by Antiochus IV Epiphanes in the second century B.C.E. Those tragic years and the ensuing success of the Maccabean revolt also led to references to the absence of a prophet when one was needed. Judas Maccabeus decided that the altar which had been profaned by pagan offerings should be torn down and the stones stored "until a prophet should come to tell what to do with them" (1 Macc. 4:46). When Judas's brother Simon took on himself the offices of king and high priest, part of his justification was "until a trustworthy prophet should arise" (1 Macc. 14:41). The idea that Jews of the second century believed that there were no more prophets among them seems to be solidly confirmed by 1 Macc. 9:27: "So there was great distress in Israel, such as had not been since the time that prophets ceased to appear among them." These texts and others from the later rabbinic writings have led to extensive discussions of the reasons for the decline and presumed disappearance of prophetic activity in Judaism, but recent studies have shown conclusively that charismatic figures claiming divine inspiration never ceased to appear, and in that sense prophecy never ended.[4] The texts just cited are probably more properly to be understood as saying that at the time when an authoritative voice was needed, none was to be heard, rather than as general statements.

The focus of this book on the message of the figures whose work appears in the collection we call the canonical prophets leads us to take the title of this section—The "End of Prophecy"—in the narrow sense of the completion of this collection and its acceptance as the word of God to his people rather than in the much-discussed broader sense: the appearance in history of charismatic figures claiming divine inspiration. In that sense, prophecy never ended, and continues to this day. This collection of prophetic words, identified as having originated with a limited number of persons chosen by God to reveal his will to Israel was "closed," however. A popular theory to account for that makes it the result of the triumph of the priestly class in Jerusalem over those who would have still claimed charismatic gifts.[5] This is related to the older claim that in the second temple period the law triumphed over and stifled the freer forms of religion practiced in Israel earlier.[6] These reconstructions have some validity, but the emphasis of this book on exile and restoration as the themes that run right through the entire prophetic canon suggests another explanation. The materials that were eventually collected into the four scrolls were those that provided explanations of the unbelievable fact that their God had allowed Samaria and Jerusalem to fall and his people to be exiled from the promised land, together with the unprecedented good news that the time had come when new life could begin on that same land. The last of the canonical prophets provided the assurance that in spite of all disappointments, the restoration that had begun was the beginning of that new era willed by God, and they provided further definition of the true character of God's new people. Once their messages had been accepted as true, the work of this kind of prophet was completed. Three radical, divine interventions into human history had occurred, a series of unique speakers had announced and explained them, and now the time had come for Judaism to maintain and strengthen its identity—finally understood clearly by all who had survived the trial—by continual reference to its definitive documents, the Law and the Prophets. Note the uses of this term in the Prologue to Sirach, 2 Macc. 15:9; 4 Macc. 18:10; Matt. 5:17; 7:12; 11:13; 22:40; Acts 13:15; 28:23. It may be claimed, then, that books of this kind ceased to be produced because this kind of work was completed. Israel had passed through the crises, had finally accepted what it meant to be the people of God. The two foundations for its further growth were in place: Jerusalem as its spiritual center, and a body of literature—Law and Prophets—accepted as the revelation of God's will for them. Other scholars may not speak as positively about this accomplishment, however, and will speak of the failure of prophecy, or of the triumph of law over prophecy, so a good deal more must be said on that subject.

5.2 Did the Prophetic Mission Succeed or Fail?

In the past, Christian scholars could seldom resist the temptation to make judgments about the quality of postexilic Judaism as a religion, and they were almost always negative. These value judgments were less the result of careful scholarship than they were the continuation of traditional Christian polemic against the Jews, and expressions of personal bias. Fortunately, recent scholarship tends to present a much fairer and more accurate picture of second temple Judaism, and that has revealed how subjective and inappropriate were the negative judgments of the past. Since progress has been made, most of that unfortunate material can now be relegated to a footnote. The work of Peter Ackroyd,[7] Klaus Koch,[8] E. P. Sanders,[9] and Joseph Blenkinsopp,[10] among others, may be cited as important correctives to the anti-Jewish bias that corrupted most earlier treatments of the second temple period.[11]

Apart from the value judgments, there has been widespread agreement that the exile brought about radical changes, to the extent that two different terms have been regularly used. Most scholars speak of the "religion of Israel" when dealing with the period before 587 B.C.E., and of "Judaism" for the period after the exile. That the exile was the "death" of Israel, as this book has claimed, has thus been widely accepted.[12] A series of representative quotes will illustrate the general acknowledgment that radical change occurred as a result of the fall of Jerusalem and the Babylonian exile. Whether the change can appropriately be called "resurrection" will call for further discussion.

> Had the people of Judah remained in peaceful possession of their land, the reformation of Josiah would hardly have penetrated to the masses; the threads uniting the present with the past were too strong. To induce the people to regard as idolatrous and heretical centres of iniquity the Bamoth, with which from ancestral times the holiest memories were associated, and some of which, like Hebron and Beersheba, had been set up by Abraham and Isaac in person, required a complete breaking-off of the natural tradition of life, a total severance of all connection with inherited conditions. This was accomplished by means of the Babylonian exile, which violently tore the nation away from its native soil, and kept it apart for half a century,—a breach of historical continuity than which it is almost impossible to conceive a greater. . . . From the exile there returned, not the nation, but a religious sect,—those, namely, who had given themselves up body and soul to the reformation ideas.[13]

> The pages of the Old Testament bear witness to an early and a late religious stage, which we may call, respectively, the religion of Israel and Judaism. The first was national, the second universal; an ancient Israelite worshiped the God of his people, but a Jew worshiped the sole God in existence; an Israelite was the member of a nation, a Jew the member of a religious congregation; Israel had a moral code based on custom, Judaism's moral law was revealed by God, through his prophets, in inspired Scriptures.[14]

It is a stupendous paradox that a god does not only fail to protect his chosen people against its enemies but allows them to fall, or pushes them himself, into ignominy and enslavement, yet is worshipped only the more ardently. This is unexampled in history and is only to be explained by the powerful prestige of the prophetic message. This prestige rested, as we saw, externally on the fulfillment of certain predictions of the prophets, or more correctly, on the construction of certain events as the fulfillment of prophecies.[15]

It is understandable that Jewish authors emphasize the positive changes brought about by the exile:

When the prophets preached in Israel before and immediately after the destruction of the Temple, they were only a small minority. Against them stood the majority of the people, addicted to a creed and mode of life which seemed sheer idolatry. But now the people were physically decimated and socially run down, threatened with national extinction, living, so to speak, without firm ground under their feet. Nevertheless, in this condition they actually came nearer the goal set by the prophets than ever before. The leading groups in the Babylonian Exile gradually developed the characteristics of holiness on a national scale, rather than in a few representative men. The faith of the prophets became a democratic possession; it spread and encompassed the whole ethnic group.[16]

With the fall, Israelite religion was uprooted from the land which had nurtured it and given it life, the land to which it was bound by countless threads of rite and custom and culture. The fateful question was: Could Israel stand this separation; could they endure apart from the seedbed of their culture? The lesson of history is that they not only endured, but that it was precisely in exile that the full stature of Israelite religion began to manifest itself.[17]

I am by no means the first Christian scholar to apply Ezekiel's "death and resurrection" theme to the exile and restoration experiences, although this has remained a minority position and resurrection may still be considered too strong a word even by those who have achieved an appreciation of the Jewish accomplishment. Early in the twentieth century, in a popular book on the Old Testament, J. C. Todd began his work as follows:

The Old Testament is the epos of the Fall of Jerusalem. From the first verse of Genesis to the last of Malachi there rings through it the note of the Capture, the Sack, and the Destruction of the City by the Babylonian Army in 586 B.C. That terrible event is the key to the book. . . . Nor was the disaster confined to these two cities [Jerusalem and Samaria]. It included the whole Western Semitic area. . . . To all these nations save one it was practically the full end. . . . Judah alone preserved her life, though in an altered form. Syria, Phoenicia, Israel, Philistia have disappeared as living factors in the world's history. Judah lives; and the Old Testament is the record of what was practically her death and resurrection, and from it we learn how it came to pass that in that deluge of destruction she escaped the annihilation which overtook her neighbors.[18]

He is blunt in expressing his opinion of the negative judgments of postexilic Judaism that were current:

The whole fantastic conception of moral decline must be thrown to the moles and the bats. . . . Each generation of Israel shows a falling short of its own standard: but the standard was constantly rising, and the final ethics of Israel have practically become the ethics of the world.[19]

Studies of the religion of preexilic Israel as it was actually practiced (in contrast to the understanding of how it should be practiced expressed by the Old Testament writers) show that it was syncretistic, a largely uncritical conglomeration of elements from primitive Yahwism and Canaanite religions.[20] Occasional efforts at reform are reported, as in the times of Hezekiah and Josiah (2 Kings 18:1–6; chs. 22—23). The descriptions of what those reforms tried to abolish, and the acknowledgments that the reforms failed are confirmations of the prophetic judgment that there were standards associated with the worship of Yahweh that were neither understood nor practiced by the majority of the people (cf. Jeremiah 44; Ezekiel 8).

In contrast to this, the acknowledgment of any god but Yahweh is out of the question for the majority of Jews during the second temple period. There is scattered evidence of syncretistic practices during the early years of the restoration,[21] and there were individuals who became apostates, as happens in every religion, but monotheism and the rejection of idolatry clearly prevailed from this time on. The acceptance of the Torah as the law of God, defining one as a Jew no matter where on earth one might live, made it possible for the religion to thrive in the diaspora, in spite of its focus on Jerusalem and the promised land. Jewish exclusivism, so much criticized by Christians and others, was accepted as a sociological necessity, in order to preserve Jews' unique identity.[22] It was assumed that the distinctiveness of their beliefs and way of life would lead to suffering, so the literature of the time created heroic characters as role models (Daniel 1; 3; 6; Mordecai, in Esther 3—4; Tobit 2).

Jeremiah had promised that one day God would write the law on his people's hearts (Jer. 31:33)—we would say the law would be internalized—and the literature of the second temple period provides an abundance of evidence that this had become true for many. People whose ancestors never quite caught on to what the prophetic message was all about are now willing to die rather than give up their belief in the One God and their faithfulness to his law. When Antiochus IV Epiphanes attempted to wipe out the Jewish religion in 167–165 B.C.E., many of them did die for their God (1 and 2 Maccabees). It is no sterile, priestly dominated, formalism (as Wellhausen and successors described Judaism) that produces martyrs.[23] The prophets had failed in their own lifetimes, but through the experience of exile as they interpreted it a new people did come into being, who were able to bring to life the faith of the prophets and to preserve it even under the worst of circumstances.

5.3 New Manifestations of the Prophetic Message

If the work of the prophets had finally been accomplished, with the appearance of the new religion of Judaism and its survival through the persecutions of 167–165 B.C.E., and the fall of Jerusalem in 70 C.E., did their documents then become merely records of the past? Judaism had survived the three crucial moments of 722, 587, and 538 B.C.E., but the past still needed a great deal of accounting for. The fall of Jerusalem and the exile remained matters of present concern. The temple had been restored, but exile was still a reality in two different ways. The diaspora continued; more Jews lived outside of Palestine than within it. Even in the homeland, when it was ruled by foreigners, as it was continuously except for the era of the Hasmonean kings (c. 165–63 B.C.E.), there was a sense that exile was not yet over. The difficulty of maintaining the uniqueness of Judaism when surrounded by alien cultures seems to have become more intense during the Hellenistic and Roman periods. New disasters occurred, and 587 became the archetype used to account for them all, as Jews applied to each of them the prophetic message of judgment and hope for salvation. Although the Torah and its interpretation in the *halakah* of the sages became the guide for daily life, the message of the prophetic books influenced Judaism, and later, Christianity in a variety of ways.

Apocalyptic Literature

The latter part of the second temple period was a turbulent one for the Jews in Palestine. The Persian period (539–333 B.C.E.) and most of the century when Palestine was ruled from Egypt by the Ptolemies were relatively peaceful, but Morton Smith has estimated that about two hundred campaigns were fought in the area between 232 and 63 B.C.E., when the Romans took over.[24] The period of persecution during the years 167–165 B.C.E., which threatened the very existence of the Jewish religion in Palestine, has already been referred to. The rule of Herod the Great (37–4 B.C.E.) gave the Jews about thirty years of peace, but in the first century C.E. the misrule of prefects and procurators led finally to open revolt against Rome.[25] In 70 C.E. Jerusalem was completely destroyed, but another revolt erupted under the leadership of Simon bar Kochba in 132–135. When it failed, the Romans built a new city, Aelia Capitolina, on the site of Jerusalem, forbidding Jews to enter it on pain of death. The center of rabbinic activity moved first to Jamnia, on the coast, then to Galilee. The terrible events of these years, approximately 200 B.C.E. to 100 C.E., led to the production of a new type of literature, called apocalyptic (from the Greek root meaning "reveal").

Apocalyptic literature is not a direct descendant of Old Testament prophecy, but the writers of those books did make use of a good many prophetic themes. The books are appropriately called apocalypse—revelation—because they claim to be able to reveal various secrets: the meaning of history—including its culmination, the reason for the power of evil on earth, and even the nature of heaven and hell. They are responses to issues different from those dealt with by the Old Testament prophets, so they are a different kind of literature, but the claims of their authors to have received revelations from God were bound to lead to similarities with the prophetic books.

There are many unsettled issues in the study of these works, including the very definition of what should be called apocalyptic. Most of these need not take up space here, except for the question of the relationship between the canonical prophets and the books generally classified as apocalyptic literature: Daniel 7—12, 1 Enoch, Sibylline Oracles 3—5, Assumption (Testament) of Moses, 2 Enoch, Apocalypse of Abraham, 2 Esdras (4 Ezra), 2 Baruch, and 3 Baruch.[26] It has been commonplace to think of these works as having developed out of the prophetic tradition, and there are good reasons for that, but these are very eclectic works, using materials from the wisdom tradition and probably showing some influences from Zoroastrianism and from Hellenistic thought. They are learned works, and a great variety of lore may be found within them. Although they share certain common features, they are also highly individualistic, each one differing from the rest in significant ways, and this is responsible for most of the difficulties in defining what should be called apocalyptic literature, let alone apocalyptic theology or eschatology.

The "seers" who produced these books shared with the prophets the claim of divine inspiration. Rather than pronouncing oracles, the word of God to his people, however, they presented their messages most often in the form of descriptions of visions. The books of Ezekiel and Zechariah may have influenced this choice of genre. Whether the apocalyptic writers were true visionaries, or were using this simply as a traditional form is something we cannot now determine. The writers regularly spoke of an interpreter, who explained the visions, as in Zechariah (cf. Dan. 8:15–26; chs. 10—11), for they did not want to leave their readers unsure of the meaning of the symbolic vision, and the use of an interpreter enabled them to make sure it was understood. Like the prophets, the seers also believed they understood what God was doing in history, and announced what was to come in the immediate future. They differed in several ways: They broadened their interests to include at times all of history from creation to the eschaton (e.g., 1 Enoch 85—90; 2 Baruch 53—74), or all of Israel's history (1 Enoch 93; 91:12–17; Assumption [Testament] of Moses 2—10). History could take on a cosmic scope, as the battle between the forces of good and evil ranged through heaven and hell, in addition to earth. The coming judgment announced by the prophets was thus magnified to become a great, final battle against the forces of evil, in which God would be triumphant and would save his faithful people. Israel as a whole thus no longer stood under judgment, but it was to be reserved for the nations (who have become unambiguously associated with the powers of evil), and the apostates among the Jews. The great battle in which God defeats the coalition of nations led by Gog of Magog (Ezekiel 38—39) provided a pattern for the last judgment in the apocalyptic books (cf. also Zechariah 12; 14). The prophetic interest in the foreign nations is thus continued in apocalyptic, but no longer do they serve as God's agents of judgment.

The immediate future was emphasized in a way not found in the prophetic books, which speak in vague terms of "that day" or "days are coming." For apocalyptic eschatology, the end of tribulation is very near.[27] As messages of hope addressed to suffering people, a promise of divine aid sometime in the indefinite future would have been of little help. One way of emphasizing the nearness of the end was by the periodizing of history. Daniel speaks of four periods in chs. 2 and 7. The Apocalypse of Weeks in 1 Enoch 83—90 divides history into ten "weeks" of unequal length, each marked by an important event. The Testament of Abraham speaks of seven world periods, while twelve is the number preferred by the Apocalypse of Abraham, 2 Esdras, and 2 Baruch. In each case, the reader could find that the last period of history was just ahead. The prophetic focus on the fall of Jerusalem and the exile has influenced most of these retellings of history, for 587 regularly appears as a turning point, and the seers differ in their evaluations of the restoration period.[28] The exile influenced the writers of some apocalypses in other ways. All these books are pseudonymous, and there are two periods from which the pen names have been chosen. Many are ascribed to characters from the period between Adam and Moses, but another group focuses on the fall of Jerusalem and the exilic period: Daniel, Jeremiah's scribe Baruch (2 and 3 Baruch are apocalyptic works), and Ezra (2 Esdras, or 4 Ezra). Daniel 9 contains a prayer concerning the sorry state of Jerusalem, ostensibly lamenting its post-587 condition, but actually speaking of the devastation wreaked by Antiochus IV Epiphanes in the second century B.C.E. Both 2 Baruch and 2 Esdras contain laments over the fall of Jerusalem, again set in the sixth century, but actually referring to the disaster of 70 C.E. This is an example of the eclectic character of this literature: Daniel is depicted as a wise man (especially ch. 2), Baruch and Ezra are scribes, but their work as they are depicted in these books has them take up issues raised by the prophetic interpretation of the fall of Jerusalem and the exile.

The writers of apocalyptic literature thus appear to have been learned people, convinced because of visionary experiences or their scholarly work that they understood the meaning of their people's sufferings and knew that God was still in charge and would soon bring history to a meaningful conclusion. Unlike the pre-exilic prophets they identified within Jewish society a faithful group whom they were convinced God was about to save. Like the prophets, they issued no fervent calls to action, but for a different reason. For the prophets it was too late; for apocalyptic the power of evil was so strong only divine intervention could be expected to triumph over it. Because they affirmed God's sovereignty over nature and history, as the prophets did, it was natural for them to draw themes and symbols from that earlier literature, but they freely used materials from a great variety of sources. The situation they addressed and their answers to it were different enough from Old Testament prophecy that it seems best to consider apocalyptic literature as a phenomenon in its own right, rather than as the "child" of prophecy. It is certainly evidence for the continuing influences of the work of the prophets, however.

Exile as a Continuing Theme

O come, O come, Emmanuel,
And ransom captive Israel,
That mourns in lonely exile here.
(Latin hymn, 12th century)

At the human level, Jerusalem fell because Nebuchadnezzar had the better army and the Judean rulers were foolish enough to rebel against him. For those who believed that God is active in the world a theological explanation was also called for, however, and there were several options available. Some may have concluded that the gods of Babylon were stronger than Yahweh, others that Yahweh was an uncaring or cruel God. The prophets' claim, that Yahweh was punishing his people for their disobedience, was not an original idea. Mesopotamian laments also explain defeat as being the result of displeasing one's god. What was original was the fact that the prophetic advocacy of that explanation was not only accepted by those who went into exile, but that they maintained their identity in spite of the loss of everything, and even made the exile experience a part of their self–identification. The true people of God, they would claim, were those who had been exiled. Remarkably, exile was not only accepted as a just punishment; it also was identified as the mark of being God's elect.[29] The book of Ezra indicates that those who returned from Babylonia, noting the differences between their practice and that of the Yahwists who had never left the land, made it clear that they possessed the truth (Ezra 4:1–3; 6:16–21). Jacob Neusner describes the exile, at this point, as the answer to the question, "Who is Israel?":

> It follows that it is Scripture—and Scripture alone—that says that what happened was that Israel died and was reborn, was punished through exile and then forgiven, and therefore—and this is critical—to be Israel in a genealogical sense is to have gone into exile and returned to Zion.[30]

The move from judgment to promise in the prophetic books, and the insistence by the postexilic prophets that the early events of restoration were in fact the beginning of the fulfillment of those promises must have been major contributors to this remarkable conclusion: that exile did not mean God's final repudiation of those involved, and neither did it mean a divine vindication of the ways of those who never left the land (cf. Ezek. 11:15–21).

Evidence for the way the Jewish religion was practiced from roughly the time of Ezra and Nehemiah on shows that with reference to the changes in faith, worship, and ethics brought about by the exile, its results can be called theologically a death and resurrection. The physical condition of the Jewish people was another matter. For the most part it was far different from what the prophets expected, and so exile has remained an issue in Judaism to this day.[31] Return to the land was only partial, contrary to what the prophets had said, and that has remained so. During the second temple period and after, the sufferings of Jews within the land continued, and this was understood as the continuance of the conditions of exile, even though they had come home. Ezra's prayer in Neh. 9:6–37 recalls Israel's history as a continual repetition of the pattern, sin-suffering-deliverance, and concludes with reference to the restored community: "Here we are, slaves to this day—slaves in the land that you gave to our ancestors to enjoy its fruit and its good gifts" (Neh. 9:36). The concept of exile continued to be used in speaking of new disasters. The distress brought about by the persecution of the Jews by Antiochus IV Epiphanes was described in laments that show the influence of the book of Lamentations, for the fall of Jerusalem in 587 had become the archetypal calamity.

> Jerusalem was uninhabited like a wilderness;
>> not one of her children went in or out.
> The sanctuary was trampled down,
>> and aliens held the citadel;
>> it was a lodging place for the Gentiles.
> Joy was taken from Jacob;
>> the flute and the harp ceased to play.
>> (1 Macc. 3:45; cf. 1:38–40; 2:7–13)

The prayers in Daniel 9:4–19 and Prayer of Azariah 3–22 are put in the setting of exile, lament the fall of Jerusalem in 587, and accept the prophetic judgment that it was deserved because of Israel's sins, but their actual setting in history was the second century B.C.E. These authors thus took the pattern of sin and judgment and used it to account for their present distress, moving then to appeals to the grace and forgiving mercy of God. The book of Baruch in the Apocrypha (1 Baruch) is written with reference to the Babylonian exile, but is probably to be dated around 100 B.C.E. The continuing problems of Judaism are once again dealt with in terms of the familiar pattern: confession of sin which accounts for the exile (1:15–3:8), appeals to God's mercy, and promises of salvation which echo the words of the earlier prophets (3:9–5:9). It thus serves as a "general purpose" book suitable for any time of trouble. Neusner says the exile and return formed the pattern Israel chose as its history. Exile was identified with everything people find wrong with their life, and return with what people hope will happen to set things right.[32] "Judaism took shape as the system that accounted for the death and resurrection of Israel, the Jewish people, and pointed for the source of renewed life toward sanctification now and salvation at the end of time."[33]

When Jerusalem and its temple were destroyed again, by the Romans in 70 C.E., it was thus natural to take up the theological problems associated with that devastating loss with reference to the archetype, 587 B.C.E. Two apocalyptic books, 2 Esdras (4 Ezra) and the Syriac Apocalypse of Baruch (2 Baruch), were written within a decade or so after 70, claiming Baruch and Ezra (who is anachronistically located in the sixth century) as their authors. Both lament the fall of Jerusalem, supposedly in 587, and ask why God's people should suffer so (e.g., 2 Esd. 3:28–36; 2 Baruch 3). For Baruch, the familiar explanation of judgment for sin is given (ch. 1), but the author of 2 Esdras is not so easily satisfied. "Are the deeds of those who inhabit Babylon any better? Is that why it has gained dominion over Zion?" (3:28, and vv. 29–36). Theodicy is a major issue for this author, more so than for the author of 2 Baruch, but the answer given to the questions of both is an eschatological one. Baruch is promised that in the days of the Messiah all the blessings found in the prophetic books will be fulfilled (chs. 72—74). For Ezra, the promise takes an unusual turn, for in 14:27–35 the familiar survey of history with emphasis on sin and judgment then leads to a conditional promise: "If you, then, will rule over your minds and discipline your hearts, you shall be kept alive, and after death you shall obtain mercy" (v. 34). An otherworldly hope has replaced the usual expectation of blessings on earth. All of this is really a way of trying to cope with the fall of Jerusalem in 70 c.e., but 2 Esdras shows us that there were some who could not accept the familiar explanation—we deserve this because of our sins.[34] Another way of working with the problem is found in the Midrash to Lamentations. These grieving poems, the results of 587, provided the basis for wide-ranging rabbinic discussion of the new situation in which they found themselves after 70. Lamentations gave them a place to start, for it reminded them that the situation was not actually new, after all.[35]

For the writers of the New Testament, the dispersion of the Jews and their hopes for return to the promised land were nonissues, so this major prophetic theme does not reappear. They had their own, original way of dealing with scripture, beginning with their experiences with Jesus and moving to the Old Testament to search for texts that would account for what had happened, most of which they found in the Prophets and the Psalms, rather than taking an interest in the original message of the prophets.[36] Jerusalem was important to Christians, however. Matthew depicted Jesus in a prophetic role in chs. 23—24, first delivering a new series of "woe oracles," then predicting the fall of the holy city. The prophetic focus on Jerusalem as the center of their eschatological hopes reappears in the book of Revelation, chs. 21—22, which are strongly dependent on Ezekiel 40—48 and Isaiah 56—66. Exile is given a new sense in Hebrews, using Abraham and Sarah as the archetypes, rather than Israel as a whole. Their sojourn in Canaan has become the type of life on earth for Christians, and the land promised them has now become a heavenly home (Heb. 11:8–16). That home is still described as a city, but the original themes have been individualized and spiritualized.[37]

The most important contribution of the prophets to the message of the New Testament is not to be found in the writers' quotations from them or reuses of their themes. It lies in their understanding of the true nature of the human condition on earth, and their message concerning the extent to which God will go in order to create a people who can live in harmony with him and with one another. Beginning with Amos, a series of prophets insisted that the Creator of all that lives intended to put his people to death. That was a way of speaking about a change in history—the end of national existence of two little kingdoms—terrible enough physically since it involved pain and death for uncounted individuals. Theologically it seemed worse. As an explanation, was it anything better than an expedient? The empire builders came; the little nations fell before them. Were not they the authors of death, and the prophetic word that this was God's doing no more than a desperate effort to find some place for him in the world where kings and armies determine human destiny? One might well be content with that if it had not been for the unexpected and still not adequately explained fact that survivors of one of those little kingdoms became a people with a unique faith and way of life that has survived, for twenty-five hundred years, every cataclysm that could afflict a human being. The later prophets had claimed this would be the result; death would not be the end: "I will open your graves and raise you up, O my people" (Ezek. 37:12).

God's own people died, and from death came new and better life. According to the New Testament writers, God's own Son died, and once again God raised the dead. In the earliest interpretations, Jesus' resurrection was seen primarily as God's vindication of one whose death would have been thought to be evidence he was wrong, but soon the early Christians found that it had produced not only life for Jesus, but new life for themselves as well. What might have been explained simply as the result of the uncaring exercise of power—the Romans doing what the Assyrians and Babylonians had done before them—required more explanation when death, which should be the end, resulted once again in a beginning of something unprecedented: first Judaism; now the church. In both cases, vitality and a step forward toward the fuller realization of what it should mean to be a human being was the outcome of failure and an end.

Paul explains why something must come to an end, and in that he agrees with the estimates of human potential in Jeremiah and Ezekiel, although he does not quote them (Romans 1—3; 7; cf. Jer. 13:23; 17:9). The prophets had touched on one of the deepest mysteries of human life—our inability to do what will lead to health and peace, using our powers instead to destroy and kill. The gospel proclaimed by the prophets acknowledged that God does not prevent the killing, for there is much that needs to be brought to an end, but they insisted that God has the power and the intention to bring something better out of what is done away with. That does not explain it all, for there is a greater mystery. The good also suffer and die. What is health-giving and peacemaking also is violently brought to an end. That mystery remains unexplained, but the gospel of the New Testament says that God does something about it—dying with and for both good and evil, becoming a personal participant in the death that leads to new life. Earlier, I suggested that the symbolic acts of Jeremiah and Ezekiel, plus Isaiah 53, may be taken by Christians as intimations of the need for incarnation. They suggest that there is a God who moves toward identification with those who fall under his righteous judgment. Reflection on the meaning of the death of Jesus led early Christians to conclude that in him God had done more than die with the guilty, but had died for them. But another death is still needed, as Paul explained it, for the human predicament will not be resolved by good teaching and example—of Torah or Jesus. Something in us must die that we may be raised to new life in Christ. "For if we have been united with him in a death like his, we will certainly be united with him in a resurrection like his," Paul writes, emphasizing the need to die to sin (Rom. 6:5; see the whole chapter). "I want to know Christ and the power of his resurrection and the sharing of his sufferings by becoming like him in his death, if somehow I may attain the resurrection from the dead" (Phil. 3:10–11; cf. 2 Cor. 4:10–12). Death to sin and resurrection to a new life, already in this world as well as in the future, had become part of a creedal formula in the church by the time it was quoted in 2 Tim. 2:11: "The saying is sure: If we have died with him, we will also live with him."

Can we be that bad, that hopeless when left to depend entirely on our own wills and efforts? Let me suggest an answer, briefly. The prophets' words had little effect, and the reforming kings accomplished nothing. Jesus taught and healed, and was executed for his trouble. Paul was a man committed to doing right, but admitted, "I do not do the good I want, but the evil I do not want is what I do" (Rom. 7:19). Improvement comes at great cost, but "for God all things are possible" (Matt. 19:26). Death of a nation, death of the Son of God, death of something in the self—from each of them, scripture insists, God brings a resurrection.

NOTES

Chapter 1: The Prophets as Theologians

1. Joseph Blenkinsopp, *A History of Prophecy in Israel*, rev. and enl. (Louisville, Ky.: Westminster John Knox Press, 1996); R. E. Clements, *Prophecy and Covenant*, SBT 43 (London: SCM Press, 1965); R. E. Clements, *Prophecy and Tradition* (Atlanta: John Knox Press, 1975); Abraham J. Heschel, *The Prophets* (New York: Harper & Row, 1962); Klaus Koch, *The Prophets, vol. 1, The Assyrian Period* (Philadelphia: Fortress Press, 1982); Klaus Koch, *The Prophets, vol. 2, The Babylonian and Persian Periods* (Philadelphia: Fortress Press, 1984); Johannes Lindblom, *Prophecy in Ancient Israel* (Oxford: Basil Blackwell, 1962); James M. Ward, *Thus Says the Lord: The Message of the Prophets* (Nashville: Abingdon Press, 1991).

2. These are the books called Latter Prophets in the Hebrew Bible. Daniel is included among the Writings, and although the book has been placed among the prophets in Christian Bibles, it will not be dealt with here, for it is a different type of literature, with chs. 1—6 composed of short stories and chs. 7—12 including apocalyptic-style visions.

3. John Barton, *Oracles of God: Perceptions of Ancient Prophecy in Israel after the Exile* (Oxford: Oxford University Press, 1986).

4. Cf. ibid, 13–23.

5. Lindblom, *Prophecy in Ancient Israel*, 1–219.

6. Henning Graf Reventlow, *Das Amt des Propheten bei Amos*, FRLANT 80 (Göttingen: Vandenhoeck & Ruprecht, 1962), *Wächter über Israel. Ezechiel und seine Tradition*, BZAW 82 (1962); J. D. W. Watts, *Vision and Prophecy in Amos* (Grand Rapids: Wm. B. Eerdmans Publishing Co., 1958); Ernst Würthwein, "Kultpolemik oder Kultbescheid?" in *Tradition und Situation: Studien zur alttestamentliche Prophetie, Artur Weiser zum 70. Geburtstag*, ed. E. Würthwein and O. Kaiser (Göttingen: Vandenhoeck & Ruprecht, 1963), 115–131.

7. For a useful survey, see Clements, *Prophecy and Covenant*, ch. 5.

8. For example, see the commentary on Amos by Douglas Stuart in *Hosea—Jonah*, WBC (Waco, Tex.: Word Books, 1987).

9. For a survey of research on the covenant, see Ernest W. Nicholson, *God and His People: Covenant and Theology in the Old Testament* (Oxford: Clarendon Press, 1986).

10. For a survey and evaluation, see R. N. Whybray, "Prophecy and Wisdom," in *Israel's Prophetic Tradition: Essays in Honour of Peter R. Ackroyd*, ed. R. Coggins, A. Phillips, M. Knibb (Cambridge: Cambridge University Press, 1982), 181–99.

11. A good survey of this work appears in Lester L. Grabbe, *Priests, Prophets, Diviners, Sages: A Socio-Historical Study of Religious Specialists in Ancient Israel* (Valley Forge, Pa.: Trinity Press International, 1995), 85–98.

12. For a skeptical evaluation of these efforts, see Robert P. Carroll, "Prophecy and Society," in *The World of Ancient Israel: Sociological, Anthropological and Political Perspectives*, ed. R. E. Clements (Cambridge: Cambridge University Press, 1988), 203–25.

13. Still affirmed by Gerhard von Rad in the 1960s: "The reason for their isolation was therefore this—as they listened to and obeyed a word and commission of Jahweh which came to them alone and which could not be transferred to anyone else, these men became individuals, persons. They could say 'I' in a way never before heard in Israel." *Old Testament Theology*, vol. 2 (New York: Harper & Row, 1965), 177.

14. Grabbe, *Priests, Prophets, Diviners, Sages*, 106, 107.

15. A. Graeme Auld, "Prophets Through the Looking Glass: Between Writings and Moses," *JSOT* 27 (1983): 3–23.

16. Clements, *Prophecy and Tradition*, 34–39.

17. William Rainey Harper's commentary is a classic example of this procedure: *A Critical and Exegetical Commentary on Amos and Hosea*, ICC (Edinburgh: T. & T. Clark, 1905).

18. Hans Walter Wolff's discovery of six stages in the growth of the book of Amos is a good example of the application of this method: *Joel and Amos*, Hermeneia (Philadelphia: Fortress Press, 1977).

19. Cf. Brevard S. Childs, "Retrospective Reading of the Old Testament Prophets," *ZAW* 108 (1996): 362–77.

20. According to Carroll, if there was a "historical Jeremiah" we can learn nothing of him from the present book: Robert P. Carroll, *Jeremiah, a Commentary*, OTL (Philadelphia: Westminster Press, 1986), 55–64. Lemche moves without proof from the likelihood that the books contain some postexilic material to the assumption that they are entirely the creations of postexilic authors: Niels Peter Lemche, "The God of Hosea" in *Priests, Prophets and Scribes: Essays on the Formation and Heritage of Second Temple Judaism in Honour of Joseph Blenkinsopp*, JSOTSup 149 (Sheffield: JSOT Press, 1992), 241–47.

21. "It is remarkable that men should read the prophets and suppose that their call to Israel was: 'Repent, come back to God, and he will forgive you all your sins.'" G. A. F. Knight, *A Christian Theology of the Old Testament* (London: SCM Press, 1959), 230. See the thorough study of the subject by A. Vanlier Hunter, *Seek the Lord! A Study of the Meaning and Function of the Exhortations in Amos, Hosea, Isaiah, Micah, and Zephaniah* (Baltimore: St. Mary's Seminary and University, 1982).

22. Klaus Koch, "Das Profetenschweigen des deuteronomistischen Geschichtswerks," in *Die Botschaft und die Boten: Festschrift für Hans Walter Wolff zum 70. Geburtstag*, ed. J. Jeremias and L. Perlitt (Neukirchen-Vluyn: Neukirchener Verlag, 1981), 115–28. 2 Kings 17:23 and 25:21 may, however, be allusions to Amos 7:17. See Donald E. Gowan, "The Beginnings of Exile-Theology and the Root *glh*," *ZAW* 87 (1975): 204–7. For another effort to explain the silence of the History with reference to the canonical prophets, see Christopher Begg, "The Non-mention of Amos, Hosea and Micah in the Deuteronomistic History," *BN* 32 (1986): 41–53.

23. See the discussions of the prophets in Brevard S. Childs, *Introduction to the Old Testament as Scripture* (Philadelphia: Fortress Press, 1979), 305–498.

24. Lindblom, *Prophecy in Ancient Israel*, 311–312.

25. von Rad, *Old Testament Theology*, 2:178

26. Clements, *Prophecy and Covenant*, 43.

27. Hans Walter Wolff, "Prophecy from the Eighth through the Fifth Century," *Int* 32 (1978): 23; repr. in *Interpreting the Prophets*, ed. J. L. Mays and P. J. Achtemeier (Philadelphia: Fortress Press, 1987), 20.

28. John Barton has questioned whether these books were recognized as a distinct group as early in the history of Judaism as has been regularly claimed, pointing out that "prophets" was used in a broad sense, and may have referred to any of the books of scripture outside the Torah until the Talmudic period. *Oracles of God*, 35–95. However, Sirach works Isaiah, Jeremiah, and Ezekiel into his recital of Israel's history, then adds a reference to "the Twelve Prophets"; strong evidence that there existed in his time (c. 190 B.C.E.) four scrolls containing the completed collection of these works (Sir. 48:22–25; 49:6–10).

29. James Ward called attention to this in his *Hosea: A Theological Commentary* (New York: Harper & Row, 1966), xiii–xiv, but does not seem to have made much use of it in his published work.

30. John Barton offers such an explanation, although he does admit Amos may perhaps be dated before the international threat became obvious. "History and Rhetoric in the Prophets," in *The Bible as Rhetoric: Studies in Biblical Persuasion and Credibility*, ed. Martin Warner (London: Routledge, 1990), 51–64.

31. I am well aware of the problems associated with trying to speak of God's acts in history, as delineated in Langdon Gilkey's influential article, and will try to formulate what I say about history in a way that will not make it subject to the same criticisms he made of the work of G. Ernest Wright and Gerhard von Rad. My work will remain subject to criticism based on materialist readings of history, and that must be. See Gilkey, "Cosmology, Ontology, and the Travail of Biblical Language," *JR* 41 (1961): 194–205.

32. Albert Schweitzer, quoted in Edgar H. S. Chandler, *The High Tower of Refuge* (New York: Praeger, 1959), 26.

33. The anthology edited by John Simpson, *The Oxford Book of Exile* (Oxford: Oxford University Press, 1995), is an interesting resource, but deals almost entirely with individuals.

34. Frederick A. Norwood produced a massive study of the history of the exiling of people for religious reasons, *Strangers and Exiles: A History of Religious Refugees*, 2 Vols. (Nashville: Abingdon Press, 1969).

35. Much of what follows depends on the most thorough study of the subject to this date: Bustenay Oded, *Mass Deportations and Deportees in the Neo-Assyrian Empire* (Wiesbaden: Reichert Verlag, 1979).

36. Treaty of Esarhaddon with Baal of Tyre (7th century B.C.E.), *ANESTP*, 534.

37. Inscription of Sargon II, who carried out the deportation of Israelites mentioned in 2 Kings 17:22–23. Daniel David Luckenbill, *Ancient Records of Assyria and Babylonia*, (Chicago: University of Chicago Press, 1927), II, p. 155, #351.

38. E.g., Luckenbill, I, p. 173, #489, p. 228, #617, p. 258, #723.

39. Archibald Paterson, *Assyrian Sculptures: Palace of Sinacherib* (The Hague: Martinus Nijhoff, 1915), plates 15, 17–18, 39, 52, 79, 91.

40. "Tarhunazi, their ruler, together with his warriors, I threw into fetters of iron. His wife, his sons, his daughters, with 500 of his captive fighters, I carried away to my city of Assur." Luckenbill, II, p. 12, #26.

41. A letter probably written to King Sargon II. Leroy Waterman, *Royal Correspondence of the Assyrian Empire* (Ann Arbor: University of Michigan 1930) I:167.

42. A letter to King Ashurbanipal. Waterman, 2:792.

43. I. M. Diakonoff, "*mdy 'ry*: The Cities of the Medes" in *Scripta Hierosolymitana* 33 (Jerusalem: Magnes Press, 1991), 13–20. The various fictions about the "Ten Lost Tribes of Israel" came into being because of the lack of records of the fate of the exiles from the Northern Kingdom, but in fact they were never lost. A few bits of evidence are now available, showing the continuing existence of people with Hebrew names in Assyria. Ran Zadok, *The Jews in Babylonia during the Chaldean and Achaemenian Periods according to the Babylonia Sources*, Studies in the History of the Jewish People and the Land of Israel; Monograph Series 3 (Haifa: University of Haifa Press, 1979), 35–38.

44. Luckenbill, II, p. 211, #527.

45. Luckenbill, I, p. 271, #766. Cf. I, p. 173, #489, p. 270, #764; II, p.12, #26.

46. Oded, *Mass Deportations*, 46–48. Cf. Luckenbill, II, p. 29, #57: "Kibabe, governor of Harhar, I besieged, I captured; himself, together with the people of his land, I counted as spoil. That city I restored, peoples captured by my hand I settled therein, and set my official as governor over them."

47. C. J. Gadd, "Inscribed Prisms of Sargon II from Nimrud," *Iraq* 16 (1954): 181.

48. Luckenbill, II, p. 102, #183.

49. Sennacherib (704–681 B.C.E.): "The people of Chaldea, the Arameans, the Manneans, (the people of) the lands of Kue and Hilakku, (of) Philistia and Tyre, who had not submitted to my yoke, I deported (from their lands), made them carry the headpad and mold bricks." Luckenbill, II, p. 166, #383.

50. Luckenbill, II, p. 120, #240.

51. Oded, *Mass Deportations*, 93–95.

52. The most thorough study of this evidence, to date, is the monograph by Ran Zadok; see n. 43.

53. Luckenbill, I, p. 276, #772.

54. For lists of place-names, see Jacob Neusner, *A History of the Jews in Babylonia, vol. 1, The Parthian Period*, Studia Post-Biblica 9 (Leiden: E. J. Brill, 1965), 10–14.

55. Lawrence of Arabia noted that even the Arabian desert is divided by landmarks into tribal territories. T. E. Lawrence, *Seven Pillars of Wisdom* (New York: Dell Publishing Co., 1963), 86.

56. The ancient Egyptians had a good deal to say about their land, glorying in it as the best place on earth, but they assumed their right to it. Cf. H. and H. A. Frankfort, John A. Wilson, Thorkild Jacobsen and William A. Irwin, *The Intellectual Adventure of Ancient Man: An Essay on Speculative Thought in the Ancient Near East*, (Chicago: University of Chicago Press, 1946), 33–42.

57. Walter Brueggemann, *The Land* (Philadelphia: Fortress Press, 1977), Norman C. Habel, *The Land Is Mine: Six Biblical Land Ideologies* (Minneapolis: Augsburg Fortress, 1995); Moshe Weinfeld, *The Promise of the Land: The Inheritance of the Land of Canaan by the Israelites* (Berkeley: University of California Press, 1992); Christopher J. H. Wright, *God's People in God's Land* (Grand Rapids: Wm. B. Eerdmans Publishing Co., 1990).

58. Cf. Claus Westermann, *The Promises to the Fathers: Studies on the Patriarchal Narratives* (Philadelphia: Fortress Press, 1980); Brueggemann, *The Land*, 15–27; Habel, *The Land Is Mine*, 115–133.

59. For covenant in the Old Testament, see Delbert R. Hillers, *Covenant: The History of a Biblical Idea* (Baltimore: Johns Hopkins University Press, 1969); David Noel Freedman, "Divine Commitment and Human Obligation: The Covenant Theme," *Int.* 18 (1964): 419–31.

60. Jože Krašovec, "Two Types of Unconditional Covenant," *HBT* 18 (1996): 55–77.

61. For a full study of these texts, see Götz Schmitt, *Du sollst keinen Frieden schliessen mit den Bewohnern des Landes*, BWANT 91 (1970).

62. Numbers 33:55 does not contain *moqesh*, but is similar to and probably dependent on Josh. 23:12–13, speaking as it does of "thorns in your sides."

63. For the two views of the covenant, see Moshe Weinfeld, "The Emergence of the Deuteronomic Movement: The Historical Antecedents" in *Das Deuteronomium: Entstehung, Gestalt und Botschaft*, ed. N. Lohfink, BETL 68 (Louvain: Leuven University Press, 1985), 76–97.

64. Because of this apparent inconsistency, the translation "be carried off from" has been suggested for *'bd* in Deut. 4:26; 11:17; Josh. 23:13, 16.

65. Cf. Donald E. Gowan, "The Beginnings of Exile-Theology and the Root *glh*," *ZAW* 87 (1975): 204–7.

66. Adam Cleghorn Welch, *Post-Exilic Judaism* (Edinburgh: Wm. Blackwood, 1935), 19; H. Louis Ginsberg, *The Israelian Heritage of Judaism* (New York: Jewish Theological Seminary of America, 1982), 19–24; Foster R. McCurley Jr., "The Home of Deuteronomy Revisited: A Methodological Analysis of the Northern Theory," in *A Light unto My Path*, ed. H. N. Bream et al. (Philadelphia: Temple University Press, 1974), 295–317; Weinfeld, "Deuteronomic Movement."

Chapter 2: The Eighth Century:
The Assyrian Threat and the Death of Israel

1. Gösta Ahlström, *The History of Ancient Palestine from the Palaeolithic Period to Alexander's Conquest*, JSOTSup 146 (Sheffield: Sheffield Academic Press, 1993), 618–20.

2. William W. Hallo and William Kelly Simpson, *The Ancient Near East: A History* (New York: Harcourt Brace Jovanovich, 1971), 287–89.

3. Damascus was defeated by Adad Nirari III in 796, *ANET*, 281–82.

4. Ahlström, *History of Ancient Palestine*, 612; Hallo and Simpson, *Ancient Near East*, 131.

5. Donald E. Gowan, "Prophets, Deuteronomy, and the Syncretistic Cult in Israel," in *Transitions in Biblical Scholarship*, ed. J. Coert Rylaarsdam (Chicago: University of Chicago Press, 1968), 93–112.

6. The RSV reads "Assyria" in Amos 3:9, following the LXX, but the MT's "Ashdod" is almost certainly correct.

7. For other readings of the theology of Amos, see Koch, *The Prophets*, 1: 36–76; James L. Mays, *Amos, A Commentary*, OTL (Philadelphia: Westminster Press, 1969). The best thorough commentary: Shalom Paul, *Amos*, Hermeneia (Philadelphia: Fortress Press, 1991).

8. For details, see Donald E. Gowan, "Amos," *NIB* 7 (Nashville: Abingdon Press, 1996), 385–86.

9. The NRSV translates *niham* "relent," which is appropriate. Older translations and even recent scholarly literature use "repent," which is misleading since it suggests turning away from evil, and that is not what is meant by the Hebrew word, when God is the subject. For a full study, see Francis I. Andersen and David Noel Freedman, *Amos: A New Translation with Introduction and Commentary*, AB (Garden City, N.Y.: Doubleday & Co., 1989), Excursus: When God Repents, 638–79.

10. Benno Landsberger, "Tin and Lead: The Adventures of Two Vocables," *JNES* 24 (1965): 285–96; William L. Holladay, "Once More, 'ᴀNAK = 'Tin,' Amos VII 7–8," *VT 20* (1970): 492–93.

11. This is a minority position, explained in my commentary on Amos, but the majority reading, "plumb line," seems without adequate support in spite of the recent efforts of H. G. M. Williamson, "The Prophet and the Plumb-Line: A Redaction-Critical Study of Amos vii," *OTS* 26 (1990): 101–21.

12. There are two roots *glh*, one with the general sense of "uncover," the other with the sense of "depart," hence "go into exile." The dissertation by R.E. Price shows that the roots also occur in Assyrian and Aramaic, with the meaning "exile" first appearing in eighth-century texts, thus about the same period as the book of Amos. "A Lexico-graphical Study of *glh*, *sbh*, and *swb* in Reference to Exile in the Tanach" (Ph.D. dissertation, Duke University, 1977), 33.

13. For my effort to account for this, "Beginnings of Exile-Theology," 204–7.

14. John Barton sees the prophets' message to be based on political considerations. They saw their people threatened by a great power and sought some way to justify it by accusing them of crimes for which they were about to be punished, even though the crimes they could cite scarcely deserved so severe a punishment. This reading first appeared in his *Amos's Oracles Against the Nations: A Study of Amos 1.3–2.5*, SOTSMS 6 (Cambridge: Cambridge University Press, 1980), 48, and was developed further in "History and Rhetoric in the Prophets," 51–64.

15. For an elaboration of the characteristics of that relationship, see Donald E. Gowan, *Theology in Exodus: Biblical Theology in the Form of a Commentary* (Louisville, Ky.: Westminster John Knox Press, 1994), 173–96.

16. In Amos 2:6 the pair of sandals for which the needy were sold is not a good parallel to silver. "Sandals" may have been used symbolically in a legal process involving property of some value (cf. Ruth 4:7–8; Deut. 25:9–10), but we cannot be sure of that. Verse 7 is mostly unclear. NRSV: "They who trample the head of the poor into the dust of the earth" probably gets the sense of the line, although the grammar of the Hebrew text is difficult. The Hebrew of the latter part reads, "a man and his father go to the girl." Most interpreters take this as a reference to sexual intercourse, although the usual verb for that is *bo'* "go in" rather than *halak*, "go", which is used here. This may refer to a son and father sexually involved with one of their slave girls, but certainty is not possible.

17. We cannot be sure whether "cows of Bashan" was an insult or a compliment in the eighth century. See Gowan, "Amos," *NIB* 7.

18. For these groups, see Donald E. Gowan, "Wealth and Poverty in the Old Testament: The Case of the Widow, the Orphan, and the Sojourner," *Int* 41 (1987): 341–53.

19. The international ethic theory: Barton, *Amos's Oracles against the Nations*. The Davidic empire theory: Max Polley, *Amos and the Davidic Empire: A Socio-Historical Approach* (New York: Oxford University Press, 1989). For a critique of both, see Paul Noble, "Israel among the Nations," *HBT* 15 (1993): 56–82.

20. Gowan, "Amos," *NIB* 7:353–58, 392–93.

21. The reference to Ethiopia (*kush* in Hebrew; more likely Nubia and the Sudan) should not be taken as downgrading Israel, as others have done. The region is not spoken of in negative terms elsewhere in the Old Testament (Job 28:19; Ezek. 30:4), and Amos probably chose it because it was the most distant place known in Africa (Isa. 18:1; Ezek. 29:10; Zeph. 3:10), so all nations are Yahweh's, to the farthest reaches of the earth.

22. See the commentaries for various efforts to solve the problems of the structure of ch. 5.

23. "Remnant" is for Amos a threat, not a promise. He has defined it twice. In 5:3 any army that goes out will lose 90 percent of its men. In 3:12, the remnant is like the remains of a sheep "rescued" from a lion—two legs or a piece of an ear.

24. Stanley N. Rosenbaum, *Amos of Israel: A New Interpetation* (Macon, Ga: Mercer University Press, 1991).

25. See the commentaries for discussion of Amos 7:14. The Hebrew sentence contains no verbs, leaving the reader to supply the verb "to be" where needed. The problem for us is then to decide whether he said, "I *am* no prophet, . . ." or "I *was* no prophet, . . ." If the former, he rejected the label *nabi'*, even though he used the verb form of the same root when he said the Lord told him to go prophesy. If the latter, he was saying once I was not a prophet but since the Lord's call, now I am. To complicate matters, Amaziah had called him a seer (*ḥozeh*), not a *nabi'*. On either reading, the issue seems to have been how Amos made his living; he was not a professional prophet, as Amaziah had assumed.

26. Help with the many difficulties of the book may be found in the excellent commentaries by Hans Walter Wolff, *Hosea*, Hermeneia (Philadelphia: Fortress Press, 1974), and James Luther Mays, *Hosea, A Commentary*, OTL (Philadelphia: Westminster Press, 1969).

27. See the recent histories, and a useful survey of opinions by Gershon Galil, "The Last Years of the Kingdom of Israel and the Fall of Samaria," *CBQ* 57 (1995): 52–65.

28. Shalmaneser: A. K. Grayson, *Assyrian and Babylonian Chronicles*, Texts from Cuneiform Sources 5 (Locust Valley, N.Y.: J. J. Augustine, 1975), 73. Sargon: *ANET*, 284–85.

29. *ANET*, 284–85.

30. Wolff, *Hosea*, xxvii: "The end of the ancient saving history now has actually begun." Cf. Martin J. Buss, *The Prophetic Word of Hosea: A Morphological Study*, BZAW 111 (Berlin: Verlag Alfred Tîpelmann, 1969), 128–29.

31. For a survey of the many theories, see H. H. Rowley, "The Marriage of Hosea," *BJRL* 39 (1956/57): 200–233; reprinted in his *Men of God* (Edinburgh and London: Thomas Nelson & Sons, 1963), 66–97. The meaning of "wife of harlotry," "children of harlotry," and "the land commits great harlotry" in 1:2 will be discussed in the next section.

32. For "promiscuous" as a translation of the root *zanah*, see Francis I. Andersen and David Noel Freedman, *Hosea*, AB (Garden City, N.Y.: Doubleday & Co., 1980), 163–70.

33. It seems doubtful that Hos. 1:7, with its assurance that Judah would be saved, was part of the earliest form of this message. The promises in vv. 7, 10, and 2:1 will be taken up in a later section.

34. For discussion, resulting in the rather desperate expedient, "possess the land" (adopted by NRSV), see Wolff, *Hosea*, 28; and "Der grosse Jesreeltag (Hosea 2,1–3)," *EvTh* 12 (1952–53): 78–104.

35. This reading would support those who find Hos. 1:7, 10, and 2:1 to be additions to the original text. Thus 1:11 would be the conclusion of the original, following 1:9, with "Jezreel" in vv. 4 and 11 bracketing the passage. A redactor then later reversed each of the threats, adding v. 7 after "Not pitied," v. 10 after "Not my people," and 2:1 after the final threat in 1:11.

36. "To me" is not in the MT and has been supplied by the translator. Note two uses of *shuv* in the verse, first in the literal sense of returning, then in the metaphorical sense of repenting and changing one's ways.

37. For specialized studies, see Walter Brueggemann, *Tradition for Crisis: A Study in Hosea* (Atlanta: John Knox Press, 1968); Else Kragelund Holt, *Prophesying the Past: The Use of Israel's History in the Book of Hosea*, JSOTSup 194 (Sheffield: Sheffield Academic Press, 1995).

38. Also Isa. 10:31; 21:14–15; 33:3; Jer. 49:5.

39. Note also the carrying of the calf away to Assyria in Hos. 10:5–6, reminiscent of Amos 5:26–27.

40. Peter C. Craigie, *Ugarit and the Old Testament* (Grand Rapids: Wm. B. Eerdmans Publishing Co., 1983); J. C. L. Gibson, *Canaanite Myths and Legends* (Edinburgh: T. & T. Clark, 1978); John Gray, *The Legacy of Canaan: The Ras Shamra Texts and Their Relevance to the Old Testament*, VTSup 5 (Leiden: E. J. Brill, 1957).

41. What is metaphorical and what is literal is often hard to determine. Hosea 4:14 appears to be the strongest evidence for cultic prostitution. Cf. Phyllis Bird, "'To Play the Harlot': An Inquiry into an Old Testament Metaphor," in *Gender and Difference in Ancient Israel*, ed. Peggy L. Day (Minneapolis: Fortress Press, 1989), 75–94.

42. Koch, *The Prophets*, 1:81. Von Rad acknowledges that the references to the partner shift between land (1:2; 2:3) and Israel (2:14); *Old Testament Theology*, 1:141.

43. Cf. the relationship between Baal and Anat in *ANET*, 139–42.

44. Note Hosea's concerns for the land in 2:18–22; 4:3.

45. Cf. Bird, "'To Play the Harlot,'" 75–94.

46. Gale A. Yee, "Hosea," *NIB* 7, 200–203.

47. For knowledge in Hosea, see Mays, *Hosea*, 63.

48. The judgment of "your mother" along with priest and prophet in Hos. 4:5 has ordinarily been taken to be a reference to the allegory in ch. 2, but since the other two are obviously cultic officials the question should be asked whether there was an office filled by women called "mothers," which Hosea also found to be leading the people astray. There is no other reference to such an office in ancient Israel, so if it did once exist, it must have been done away with at an early period. See Margaret S. Odell, "I Will Destroy Your Mother: The Obliteration of a Cultic Role in Hosea 4.4–6," in *A Feminist Companion to the Latter Prophets*, ed. Athalya Brenner (Sheffield: Sheffield Academic Press, 1995), 180–93. The possibility leads to further reflection. Perhaps first the role of the mothers was eliminated from the cult, then after the exile the prophets fell by the wayside, and after the fall of Jerusalem in 70 C.E. there was no longer any function for the priests. The rabbis were left, teachers of the Torah, advocates of the knowledge of God Hosea called for.

49. Margaret Odell, "Who Were the Prophets in Hosea?" *HBT* 18 (1996): 78–95.

50. Albrecht Alt, "Das Königtum in den Reichen Israel und Juda," *VT* 1 (1951): 2–22; trans. in his *Essays on Old Testament History and Religion* (Garden City, N.Y.: Doubleday & Co., 1968), 239–59.

51. I write this as if we knew that it all comes from the same source. A hundred years ago, writers on Hosea assumed he should have been consistent with his judgment message, and assigned the promises to a later source. Recent commentaries are more inclined to try to understand the tensions in the book as the work of the same prophet. When I speak of "Hosea" I am referring to the message of the book, rather than claiming to know what one individual may have said.

52. "I have loved Jacob but I have hated Esau" in Mal. 1:2–3 refers to God's choice of Jacob for the covenant relationship. Cf. "love" in Prov. 8:36; 21:1; Micah 3:2; 6:8; Zech. 8:19.

53. This is probably the original location for the change of names. The insertion of promises in Hos. 1:7, 10, and 2:1 [MT 1:7; 2:1, 3], contradicts the judgmental tone of the passage, and seems premature. They were probably added by an editor. For my reading of 1:11 as part of the judgment passage, see above, pp. 40–41.

54. For example, on Hos. 11:7, which seems relatively simple, Harper listed ten suggested translations and concluded, "The case is certainly a desperate one." Harper, *Amos and Hosea*, 368.

55. Compare H. Schüngel-Straumann, "God as Mother in Hosea 11," *TD* 34 (1987): 3–8, with Siegfried Kreutzer, "God as Mother in Hosea 11?" *TD* 37 (1990): 221–26.

56. R. J. Coggins, *Samaritans and Jews* (Atlanta: John Knox Press, 1975); J. Macdonald, *The Theology of the Samaritans* (Philadelphia: Westminster Press, 1964).

57. For a recent study of these materials see Grace I. Emmerson, *Hosea: An Israelite Prophet in Judean Perspective*, JSOTSup 28 (Sheffield: JSOT Press, 1984).

58. Magen Broshi, "The Expansion of Jerusalem in the Reigns of Hezekiah and Manasseh," *IEJ* 24 (1974): 21–26.

59. For a good survey, see K. Jeppesen, "New Aspects of Micah Research," *JSOT* 8 (1978): 3–32.

60. Examples of commentaries representing the two extremes: Only chs. 1—3: James Luther Mays, *Micah, A Commentary*, OTL (Philadelphia: Westminster Press, 1976); Hans Walter Wolff, *Micah: A Commentary* (Minneapolis: Augsburg, 1990). Most of the book: L. C. Allen, *The Books of Joel, Obadiah, Jonah and Micah*, NICOT (Grand Rapids: Wm. B. Eerdmans Publishing Co., 1976); Delbert R. Hillers, *Micah*, Hermeneia (Philadelphia: Fortress Press, 1984).

61. The Assyrian invasion of 701 B.C.E. will be discussed at greater length in the section on Isaiah 1—39.

62. W. E. Barnes, "Dr Karl Budde on Mic. ii, iii," *JTS* 25 (1924): 79–84; Gershon Brin, "Micah 2.12–13: A Textual and Ideological Study," *ZAW* 101 (1989): 118–24.

63. E.g., Koch, *The Prophets*, 1.98–105; A. S. van der Woude, "Three Classical Prophets," in *Israel's Prophetic Tradition: Essays in Honour of Peter R. Ackroyd*, ed. Richard Coggins et al. (Cambridge: Cambridge University Press, 1982), 52.

64. See Hans Walter Wolff, *Micah the Prophet* (Philadelphia: Fortress Press, 1981), and for a different reading, C. S. Shaw, *The Speeches of Micah: A Rhetorical-Historical Analysis* (Sheffield: JSOT Press, 1993).

65. Bo Reicke, "Liturgical Traditions in Micah 7," *HTR* 60 (1967): 358–60.

66. The expression "holy temple" appears in Pss. 5:7; 11:4; 65:4; 79:1; 138:2; Jonah 2:4, 7.

67. For this interpretation, see J. H. Eaton, "The Origin and Meaning of Habakkuk iii," *ZAW* 76 (1964): 144–171.

68. For theophany in Micah and Isaiah, see Gary Stansell, *Micah and Isaiah: A Form and Tradition Historical Comparison*, SBLDS 85 (Atlanta: Scholars Press, 1988), 9–38.

69. Cf. J. J. M. Roberts, "The Davidic Origin of the Zion Tradition," *JBL* 92 (1973) 329–44; "Zion in the Theology of the Davidic-Solomonic Empire" in *Studies in the Period of David and Solomon and Other Essays*, ed. Tomoo Ishida (Winona Lake, Ind.: Eisenbrauns, 1982), 93–108; A. S. Kapelrud, "Eschatology in the Book of Micah," *VT* 11 (1961): 392–405.

70. For a recent detailed development of the argument, see Shaw, *Speeches of Micah*, 97–225.

71. F. C. Burkitt, "Micah 6 and 7: A Northern Prophecy," *JBL* 45 (1926): 159–61; J. G. Strydom, "Micah of Samaria: Amos's and Hosea's Forgotten Partner," *OTE* 6 (1993): 19–32; J. T. Willis, "A Reapplied Prophetic Hope Oracle," VTSup 26 (1974): 64–76; A. S. van der Woude, "Deutero-Micha: Ein Prophet aus Nord-Israel?" *Nederlands Theologisch Tijdschrift* 25 (1971): 365–78.

72. H. B. Huffmon, "The Covenant Lawsuit in the Prophets," *JBL* 78 (1959): 285–95; Julien Harvey, "Le 'Rîb-Pattern,' Réquisitoire prophètique sur la rupture de l'alliance," *Biblica* 43 (1963): 172–96.

73. Reicke, "Liturgical Traditions in Micah 7," 349–68. Compare this analysis with the parts that regularly appear in the psalms of lament: Complaint, vv. 1–6; expression of

confidence, vv. 7–8; confession of sin, v. 9; renewed confidence, vv. 10–14; oracle, v. 15; confidence, vv. 16–17; praise, vv. 18–20.

74. Micah 7:12 may contain a reference to return from exile, but that is not certain, and if so, it might refer either to the exile of Israel or of Judah.

75. Micah 6:6–8 also addresses any individual: "He has showed you, O human (*'adam*), what is good."

76. Similar uses of "righteous" and "just" as terms for deliverance for the unworthy appear in Pss. 40:10–12; 71:2, 9; 143:1–2, 11; Dan. 9:16, 18.

77. For an excellent, well-balanced introduction to the book, see John Barton, *Isaiah 1–39*, OTG (Sheffield: Sheffield Academic Press, 1995).

78. J. N. Oswalt, *The Book of Isaiah, Chapters 1–39* NICOT (Grand Rapids: Wm. B. Eerdmans Publishing Co., 1986), 23–28.

79. Otto Kaiser, *Isaiah 1–12, A Commentary*, 2nd ed., OTL (Philadelphia: Westminster Press, 1983), vii, 114–98.

80. E.g., R. E. Clements, *Isaiah 1–39*, NCBC (Grand Rapids: Wm. B. Eerdmans Publishing Co., 1980).

81. E.g., Lindblom, *Prophecy in Ancient Israel*, 369.

82. The current efforts to account for the 66 chapters as a meaningful unit are of considerable interest in their own right, but would seem to complicate the approach taken in this book. See Childs, *Introduction to the Old Testament as Scripture*, 311–38. Recent theories attempting to explain the combination of these works into a single scroll also represent promising new approaches to the book. See Christopher R. Seitz, *Zion's Final Destiny: The Development of the Book of Isaiah: A Reassessment of Isaiah 36–39* (Minneapolis: Fortress Press, 1991); H. G. M. Williamson, *The Book Called Isaiah: Deutero-Isaiah's Role in Composition and Redaction* (Oxford: Oxford University Press, 1994).

83. For summaries of other, more complex redaction theories, see A. G. Auld, "Poetry, Prophecy, Hermeneutic: Recent Studies in Isaiah," *SJT* 33 (1980): 567–81; Barton, *Isaiah 1–39*; J. J. Schmitt, *Isaiah and His Interpreters* (Mahwah, N.J.: Paulist Press, 1986).

84. For these discussions, see Brevard S. Childs, *Isaiah and the Assyrian Crisis*, SBT[2] 3 (London: SCM Press, 1967); R. E. Clements, *Isaiah and the Deliverance of Jerusalem: A Study of the Interpretation of Prophecy in the Old Testament*, JSOTSup 13 (Sheffield: JSOT Press, 1980). For a very different reading, claiming chs. 1—33, 36—39 are in chronological order and all written by Isaiah, see John H. Hayes and Stuart A. Irvine, *Isaiah: The Eighth-century Prophet: His Times and His Preaching* (Nashville: Abingdon Press, 1987). Koch (*The Prophets*, 1:105–56) also reads these chapters as for the most part in chronological order, although he does not attribute everything to Isaiah.

85. Among recent commentators, Clements, Kaiser, and Oswalt take ch. 6 as the account of Isaiah's call; Watts, and Hayes and Irvine as a change of Isaiah's commission.

86. For detailed studies of the chapter, see P. Beguerie, "La vocation d'Isaïe," in *Études sur les Profètes d'Israel*, ed. P. Beguerie, J. LeClercq and J. Steinmann, Lectio Divine 14 (Paris: Cerf, 1954), 11–51; I. Engnell, *The Call of Isaiah: An Exegetical and Comparative Study*, Uppsala Universitets Årskrift, 4 (Uppsala: Lundequistska Bokhandeln, 1949); E. Jenni, "Jesajas Berufung in der neueren Forschung," *ThZ* 15 (1959): 321–39; R. Knierim, "The Vocation of Isaiah," *VT* 18 (1968): 47–68; J. Magonet, "The Structure of Isaiah 6," in *Proceedings of the 9th World Congress of Jewish Studies* (Jerusalem: World Union of Jewish Studies, 1986), Division A: The Period of the Bible, 91–97. For background, see Norman Habel, "The Form and Significance of the

Call Narratives," *ZAW* 77 (1965): 297–323; B. O. Long, "Prophetic Call Traditions and Reports of Visions," *ZAW* 84 (1972): 494–500.

87. For the holiness of God as "otherness," see the chapter on "The Numinous" in my *Theology in Exodus*, 25–53.

88. For Exod. 24:9–11, see Ernest Nicholson, *Exodus and Sinai in History and Tradition* (Richmond: John Knox Press, 1973), 67–84.

89. V. Herntrich, *Jesaja 1–12* ATD 17 (Göttingen: Vandenhoeck & Ruprecht, 1957), 97–101; Otto Kaiser, *Isaiah 1–12, A Commentary*, OTL (Philadelphia: Westminster Press, 1972), 78–79; Watts, *Isaiah 1–33*, 67; Koch, *The Prophets*,1.108–109.

90. The appearance of forgiveness probably explains the difference between this passage, in which Isaiah responds positively to the call, and the accounts of the calls of Moses (Exod. 3), Gideon (Judges 6), and Jeremiah (Jeremiah 1), in which the will of God prevails over the resistance of the one called.

91. This leads many interpreters to say these lines must be a result of Isaiah's later reflection on the failure of his work, rather than what God told him his work must be at the beginning. That may be so, but Isaiah does not tell us that.

92. "The holy seed is its stump" has been taken as a promise of new life in the future, but "stump" is almost certainly a mistranslation, in spite of the agreement on it by modern translators. None of the ancient translators or interpreters read it that way, and that meaning first appeared as a guess only in the eighteenth century. The word *matstseveth* denotes a pillar (2 Sam. 18:18) and was probably made of stone. Its association here with oak and terebinth, and with a verb meaning to cast out indicates that this is a reference to the occasional reforms that involved the removal of such cult objects from sanctuaries (e.g., 2 Kings 10:26–27; 23:6, 12). The grammar of the verse is very difficult, but it may mean something like this: "And even if in it is a tenth, again it shall be for destruction, like a terebinth or an oak, when a sacred pillar is cast out with them." [Cf. NEB; Watts, *Isaiah 1–33*, 68] Since "holy seed," in its only other occurrence in the OT (Ezra 9:2) refers to Israel, the final words, "Its sacred pillar is a holy seed," is no promise. For a similar reading, see G. K. Beale, "Isaiah VI 9–13: A Retributive Taunt against Idolatry," *VT* 41 (1991): 257–78.

93. J. T. Willis, "The Genre of Isaiah 5:1–7," *JBL* 96 (1977): 337–62; Kirsten Nielsen, *There Is Hope for a Tree: The Tree as a Metaphor in Isaiah*, JSOTSup 65 (Sheffield: JSOT Press, 1989), 87–123.

94. No combination of English words adequately reproduces the effect of the sounds in Hebrew, but here is a weak effort at echoing the wordplay: "He hoped you'd be fair, but behold, despair! He hoped you'd do right, but behold, fright!"

95. Cf. R. Fey, *Amos und Jesaja. Abhängigkeit und Eigenständigkeit des Jesaja*, WMANT 12 (Neukirchen-Vluyn: Neukirchener Verlag, 1963).

96. Georg Fohrer, "Jesaja 1 als Zusammenfassung der Verkundigung Jesajas," *ZAW* 74 (1962): 251–68.

97. For the use of this exclamation in Isaiah, see J. Vermeylen, *Du prophète Isaïe à l'apolyptique. Isaïe I–XXXV, miroir d'un demi-millénaire d'expérience religieuse en Israël*, Ebib (Paris: J. Gabalda, 1978), II.603–52.

98. See 2 Kings 18–19; Isaiah 36–37; and Sennacherib's own description of his campaign, *ANET*, 287–88.

99. Clements, in his *Isaiah and the Deliverance of Jerusalem* 72–89, has challenged the early date of the Zion tradition, but the evidence for it seems very strong. His chief concern is to show that Isaiah did not teach the invulnerability of Jerusalem, but others have pointed out that although the book of Isaiah speaks of God's deliverance of the city, it does not claim the place will forever be invulnerable; e.g., Th. C. Vriezen,

"Essentials of the Theology of Isaiah," in *Israel's Prophetic Heritage: Essays in Honor of James Muilenburg*, ed. Bernhard W. Anderson and Walter Harrelson (New York: Harper & Row, 1962), 138–41.

100. Roberts, "Zion in the Theology of the Davidic-Solomonic Empire," in Ishida and Sekine, *Studies in the Period of David and Solomon and Other Essays* 93–108.

101. As noted in the discussion of Micah 4:1–4, we cannot be sure of the authorship of this passage, but I believe it is not exilic or later, as many claim. Most of the promises concerning Zion in the prophetic books are later than 587, for they refer to return from exile and restoration of a ruined city. Nothing like that is presupposed in Isa. 2:2–4 and a few other Zion prophecies in Isaiah, suggesting that they originated before the fall of Jerusalem.

102. B. D. Napier, "Isaiah and the Isaian," *VT* 15 (1966): 246–51; Oswalt, *Isaiah 1–39*, 38–39. J. J. M. Roberts reads this passage as additional evidence for Isaiah's interest in the Northern Kingdom: "Isaiah 2 and the Prophetic Message to the North," *JQR* 75 (1985): 290–308.

103. Barton, *Isaiah 1–39*, 49.

104. For bibliography and discussion, see Hans Wildberger, *Isaiah 1–12: A Commentary* (Minneapolis: Fortress Press, 1991), 279–329.

105. I have discussed the use of Emmanuel in Jewish and Christian literature in my *Theology in Exodus, ch. 3*, "I Will Be with You," 54–75.

106. Discussed by Childs, *Isaiah and the Assyrian Crisis*, and Clements, *Isaiah and the Deliverance of Jerusalem*.

107. Peter Machinist, "Assyria and Its Image in the First Isaiah," *JAOS* 103 (1983): 719–37.

108. H. L. Ginsberg, "Reflexes of Sargon in Isaiah after 715 B.C.E.," *JAOS* 88 (1968): 47–53; Clements, *Isaiah 1–39*, 139–40.

109. I discussed the poem and its mythological background in some detail in a monograph, *When Man Becomes God: Humanism and* Hybris *in the Old Testament* PTMS 6 (Pittsburgh: Pickwick Press, 1975), 45–67.

110. The same theme will reappear, also associated with the use of mythological material, in Ezekiel 28, 31, and Daniel 4.

111. G. R. Hamborg, "Reasons for Judgment in the Oracles Against the Nations of the Prophet Isaiah," *VT* 31 (1981): 145–59.

112. Clements, *Isaiah 1–39*, 103–9.

113. For a brief survey of the development of the messianic hope out of these royal oracles, see my *Eschatology in the Old Testament* (Philadelphia: Fortress Press, 1986), 32–42, or *Bridge Between the Testaments: A Reappraisal of Judaism from the Exile to the Birth of Christianity*, 3rd ed., PTMS 14 (Allison Park, Pa: Pickwick Publications, 1986), 387–95. For longer studies, see J. Becker, *Messianic Expectation in the Old Testament* (Philadelphia: Fortress Press, 1980); John J. Collins, *The Scepter and the Star: The Messiahs of the Dead Sea Scrolls and Other Ancient Literature* (New York: Doubleday, 1995); J. Neusner, W. S. Green and J. Z. Smith, eds., *Judaisms and Their Messiahs at the Turn of the Christian Era* (Cambridge: Cambridge University Press, 1987). For the transformation of nature in Jewish eschatology, see my *Eschatology*, 97–120.

114. The question "why" was raised by P. R. Ackroyd, "Isaiah I–XII: Presentation of a Prophet," VTSup 29 (1978): 16–48. Of greater interest theologically than the theories of a school of "Isaianic prophets" that continued for centuries, or of extensive scribal additions, is the fact that the Zion theology in the chs. 1—39 reappears with great prominence in chs. 40—66.

115. For a detailed study supporting a different conclusion, that ch. 35 was written for the purpose of making the connection between Isaiah 1—34 and 40—66, see Odil Hannes Steck, *Bereitete Heimkehr: Jesaja 35 als redaktionelle Brücke zwischen dem Ersten und dem Zweiten Jesaja*, SBS 121 (Stuttgart: Verlag Katholisches Bibelwerk, 1985).

116. For discussion of these matters see, in brief, Clements, *Isaiah 1-39*, 196–200, and at length, D. G. Johnson, *From Chaos to Restoration: An Integrative Reading of Isaiah 24-27*, JSOTSup 61 (Sheffield: Sheffield Academic Press, 1988).

117. Johnson, *Chaos to Restoration*, 80–81. For the traditional reading, see Robert Martin-Achard, *From Death to Life: A Study of the Doctrine of the Resurrection in the Old Testament* (Edinburgh: Oliver & Boyd, 1960), 130–38.

118. A. Feuillet, "Un Sommet Religieux de l'Ancien Testament. L'Oracle d'Isaïe XIX (v. 16–25) sur la Conversion de l'Egypt," *RSR* 39.2–4 (1951): 65–87; J. F. A. Sawyer, "'Blessed Be My People Egypt' (Isaiah 19.25). The Context and Meaning of a Remarkable Passage," in *A Word in Season: Essays in Honour of Wm. McKane*, ed. J. D. Martin and P. R. Davies, JSOT Sup 42 (Sheffield: JSOT Press, 1986), 57–72; W. Vogels, "L'Egypte mon peuple—L'Universalism d'Is 19:16–25," *Biblica* 57 (1976): 494–514; Iain Wilson, "In That Day. From Text to Sermon on Isaiah 19:23–25," *Int* 22 (1967): 66–86.

Chapter 3: The Late Seventh and Early Sixth Centuries: The Neo-Babylonian Threat and the Death of Judah

1. J. McKay, *Religion in Judah under the Assyrians*, SBT[2] 26 (London: SCM Press, 1973); Morton Cogan, *Imperialism and Religion: Assyria, Judah and Israel in the Eighth and Seventh Centuries B.C.E.*, SBLMS 19 (Missoula, Mont.: Scholars Press, 1974).

2. Among a group of recent, helpful commentaries, see Adele Berlin, *Zephaniah: A New Translation with Introduction and Commentary*, AB 25A (New York: Doubleday, 1994); J. J. M. Roberts, *Nahum, Habakkuk, and Zephaniah, A Commentary* OTL (Louisville, Ky.: Westminster/John Knox Press, 1991).

3. Opinions differ on whether Josiah actually did enlarge his kingdom. Cf. Bustany Oded, "Judah and the Exile," in *Israelite and Judaean History*, ed. John H. Hayes and J. Maxwell Miller (Philadelphia: Westminster Press, 1977), 460–65; Ahlström, *History of Ancient Palestine*, 763–68. Evidence is lacking to confirm the theories of Christensen and Sweeney, that Zephaniah was written to support Josiah's programs. Duane L. Christensen, "Zephaniah 2:4–15: A Theological Basis for Josiah's Program of Political Expansion," *CBQ* 46 (1984): 669–82; Marvin A. Sweeney, "A Form-Critical Reassessment of the Book of Zephaniah," *CBQ* 53 (1991): 388–408.

4. Cf. Roberts: "Zephaniah's theology, while it addresses internal Judean problems, seems far more rooted in Judah's earlier prophetic tradition than in a close observation of external political developments." *Nahum, Habakkuk, and Zephaniah*, 155.

5. For discussion of this word, see Berlin, *Zephaniah*, 75–77.

6. The choice of Cush for a brief comment (Zeph. 2:12) is not so easily explained. For a full discussion, see Berlin, *Zephaniah*, 111–14.

7. Zechariah 9:9, (rsv) in which the victorious king is said to be "humble and riding on an ass," is also postexilic, and a special use of the term *'ani*.

8. Hunter: "Gather yourselves as stubble, and remain as stubble, O nation, which has no longing [for Yahweh]," *Seek the Lord!*, 259–71; Berlin: "Gather together, gather like straw, O unwanted nation," *Zephaniah*, 95–102.

9. For a vigorous defense of Nahum, see Elizabeth Achtemeier, *Nahum-Malachi*, Interpretation (Atlanta: John Knox Press, 1986), 5–30. Others with helpful evaluations of the book: Richard J. Coggins, *Israel among the Nations: A Commentary on the Books of Nahum and Obadiah*, ITC (Grand Rapids: Wm. B. Eerdmans Publishing Co., 1985), 5–63; Roberts, *Nahum, Habakkuk, and Zephaniah, 34–73.*

10. In Nahum 2 and 3, God is mentioned only in 2:2, 13 and 3:5.

11. Rex Mason, *Micah, Nahum, Obadiah*, OTG (Sheffield: JSOT Press, 1991), 58.

12. Earlier efforts to find the rest of the alphabet in the succeeding verses required drastic textual emendation, and have been rejected by all recent interpreters. The pattern that has been discovered is very irregular, compared with the acrostics in Psalms and Lamentations. Two nonalphabetical lines intervene between the *aleph* and *beth* lines, and the line that should begin with *daleth* begins with *aleph*. The existence of any acrostic pattern has been challenged by Michael H. Floyd, "The Chimerical Acrostic of Nahum 1:2–10," *JBL* 113 (1994): 421–37.

13. According to geologist Ben Cox.

14. For efforts to be more specific at locating theophany in the cult, see Artur Weiser, "Die Darstellung der Theophanie in den Psalmen und im Festcult," in *Festschrift, Alfred Bertholet zum 80. Geburtstag*, ed. W. Baumgartner (Tübingen: J. C. B. Mohr, 1950), 513–31; Helmer Ringgren, "Einige Schilderungen des göttlichen Zorns," in *Tradition und Situation: Studien zur Alttestamentlichen Prophetie. Artur Weiser zum 70. Geburtstag*, ed. E. Würthwein and O. Kaiser (Göttingen: Vandenhoeck & Ruprecht, 1963), 107–13; H.-P. Müller, "Die kultische Darstellung der Theophanie," *VT* 14 (1964): 183–91.

15. J. H. Eaton, "The Origin and Meaning of Habakkuk iii," *ZAW* 76 (1964): 144–71.

16. This is the *tremendum* aspect of the encounter with God, as described by Rudolf Otto in his *The Idea of the Holy: An Inquiry into the Non-rational Factor in the Idea of the Divine and Its Relation to the Rational* (1917; reprint, New York: Oxford University Press, 1958). I have elaborated on this with reference to the Old Testament material in my *Theology in Exodus*, 25–53.

17. The song of Deborah begins with praise to God expressed in this same way, but these opening verses (Judg. 5:3–5) are poorly connected with the rest of the song, which says nothing of God's intervention to save Israel.

18. On these two words, see the discussions of Nahum 1:2 in the commentaries by Achtemeier, Coggins, and Roberts cited earlier.

19. For readings of the theology of Habakkuk, see Elizabeth Achtemeier, *Nahum–Malachi*, 31–60; Donald E. Gowan, *The Triumph of Faith in Habakkuk* (Atlanta: John Knox Press, 1976); Maria Eszenyei Szeles, *Wrath and Mercy: Habakkuk and Zephaniah*, ITC (Grand Rapids: Wm. B. Eerdmans Publishing Co., 1987).

20. My early article ("Habakkuk and Wisdom," *Perspective* 9 [1968]: 157–166) has often been cited in discussions of wisdom influence on the writings of the Old Testament, but the main point of the article has always been overlooked. I did not claim, as H. W. Wolff did about Amos ("Amos' geistige Heimat," *WMANT* 18 [Neukirchen-Vluyn: Neukirchener Verlag, 1964], and J. Fichtner about Isaiah ("Jesaja unter den Weisen," *TLZ* 64 [1949]: 75–80), that the appearance of wisdom vocabulary and themes in their books identified the stratum of society from which they came. My conclusion was, "If no *special* relationship with the wisdom movement is postulated for the prophet Habakkuk, this fact in itself has some implications for the study of wisdom itself. When we begin to find wisdom influences everywhere in the Old Testament, surely this teaches us that wisdom was not a closed fraternity whose members spoke only with one another and with their pupils, but that it represented a certain outlook on life, conveyed in a special language, which was well-known to the average Israelite" (p. 164).

21. For a survey, see Donn F. Morgan, *Wisdom in the Old Testament Traditions* (Atlanta: John Knox Press, 1981).

22. For an effort to use these relationships to shed light on the conclusion of the book of Job, see Donald E. Gowan, "God's Answer to Job: How Is It an Answer?" *HBT* 8 (1986): 85–102.

23. Roberts, *Nahum, Habakkuk, and Zephaniah*, 141–42.

24. For a theory that the psalm was much earlier than Habakkuk, with discussion as to how it came to be added to the book, see Theodore Hiebert, *God of My Victory: The Ancient Hymn in Habakkuk 3*, HSM 38 (Atlanta: Scholars Press, 1986), 129–49.

25. Quoted from Sigmund Mowinckel's *Jesajadisiplene* by Aage Bentzen, *Introduction to the Old Testament*, 5th ed. (Copenhagen: G. E. C. Gad Publisher, 1959), 2:151–52. Bentzen notes in addition that Marti's commentary left only seven verses of Habakkuk as "genuine," which led Duhm to comment that Marti treated the book just as cruelly as Yahweh, according to 3:13, will treat the house of the ungodly.

26. P. Jöcken surveyed the work of more than 300 scholars in his *Das Buch Habakuk* (Cologne and Bonn: Peter Hanstein, 1977). For a briefer survey, see Rex Mason, *Zephaniah, Habakkuk, Joel*, OTG (Sheffield: JSOT Press, 1994), 60–96.

27. Readings of Hab. 2:1–5 based on emendation continue to be produced, but they vary so widely that I leave them all to one side here. Compare the following recent translations: "Behold, he whose personality within him is not upright will fly away, but the righteous man will live because of his faithfulness. Furthermore, wealth is treacherous, and the proud man will not be successful"; J. A. Emerton, "The Textual and Linguistic Problems of Habakkuk II. 4–5," *JTS* 28 (1977): 1–18. "As for the sluggard, his soul does not go straight on in it; but the righteous by its [i.e., the vision's] reliability shall live"; J. Gerald Janzen, "Habakkuk 2:2–4 in the Light of Recent Philological Advances," *HTR* 73 (1980): 53–78. "If indeed Ophel [will be laid waste] unless its people are upright in it—now the righteous (nation) will live (in divine prosperity in the land) by means of its trustworthiness"; James M. Scott, "A New Approach to Habakkuk II 4–5A," *VT* 35 (1985): 330–40. "Behold, swollen, not smooth, will be his gullet within him, but the righteous because of its fidelity will live. Indeed, (and even more!) since as the mire he deals treacherously, the arrogant man. He surely does not stop!"; Robert D. Haak, *Habakkuk* VTSup 44 (Leiden: E. J. Brill, 1992), 25. "Once someone's greed has grown so great, it has led him astray; but a just person, in his faithfulness, will live. And because wine [*or* wealth] is treacherous, a man grows arrogant, and he will not succeed"; Michael H. Floyd, "Prophecy and Writing in Habakkuk 2,1–5," *ZAW* 105 (1993): 462–81.

28. There are no theological uses of *hayah* in Jeremiah, but it becomes a very important word for Ezekiel, as will be noted shortly.

29. *Tsaddik* also has no significant uses in Jeremiah, but is important for Ezekiel.

30. Faithfulness (*'ĕmunah*) is one of the qualities of the righteous king in Isa. 11:5, but some of his attributes have a supernatural character. Forms of the root *'aman* appear in Isa. 1:21, 26; 7:9; Hos. 11:12 [MT 12:1].

31. Walther Zimmerli, "'Leben' und 'Tod' im Buche des Propheten Ezechiel" in his *Gottes Offenbarung: Gesammelte Aufsätze zum Alten Testament*, TBü 19 (Munich: Chr. Kaiser Verlag, 1963), 178–91; Gerhard von Rad, "'Righteousness' and 'Life' in the Cultic Language of the Psalms," in his *The Problem of the Hexateuch and Other Essays* (New York: McGraw-Hill Book Co., 1966), 243–66.

32. Compare the approach of A. S. van der Woude, "Der Gerechte wird durch seine Treue leben. Erwägungen zu Habakuk 2:4f," in *Studia Biblica et Semitica Theodoro Christiano Vriezen*, ed. W. C. van Unnik and A. S. van der Woude (Wageningen: H. Veenman & Zonen, 1966), 367–75.

33. Proposed in my *Triumph of Faith in Habakkuk*, 51–63. Accepted by Szeles, *Wrath and Mercy*, 35–36, and Anthony Ceresko, "Habakkuk," in *The New Jerome Bible Commentary* (Englewood Cliffs, N.J.: Prentice-Hall, 1990), 263.

34. For more details on theophany, see the discussion of Nahum 1.

35. Jer. 46:2; Donald J. Wiseman, *Chronicles of Chaldean Kings (626–556) in the British Museum* (London: British Museum, 1956), 67.

36. Lists of rations provided to Nebuchadnezzar's captives in Babylon mention Jehoiachin (*Ia-u-kin*, or *Ia-ku-u-ki-nu*), men from Judah (*Ia-a-hu-da-a-a*), and sons of the king of Judah, *ANET,* 308.

37. There is still uncertainty over whether Jerusalem fell in 587 or 586 B.C.E. The issue depends on whether the calendar began in the spring or the fall at that time. Unfortunately, the Babylonia Chronicle published by Wiseman, which corroborates the date of 597 for the first capture of Jerusalem, is fragmentary and continues only through 594.

38. Ahlström, *History of Ancient Palestine*, 804–7.

39. For a collection of representative articles on these subjects, see Leo G. Perdue and Brian W. Kovacs, eds., *A Prophet to the Nations: Essays in Jeremiah Studies* (Winona Lake, Ind.: Eisenbrauns, 1984), 33–127.

40. For helpful surveys of the continuing discussions, see J. L. Crenshaw, "A Living Tradition. The Book of Jeremiah in Current Research," *Int* 37 (1983): 117–29; Leo G. Perdue, "Jeremiah in Modern Research: Approaches and Issues," in Perdue and Kovacs, *A Prophet to the Nations*, 1–32.

41. MT: Egypt, Philistia, Moab, Ammon, Edom, Damascus, Kedar, Elam, Babylon. LXX: Elam, Egypt, Babylon, Philistia, Edom, Ammon, Kedar, Damascus, Moab.

42. For a clear and concise discussion, see Peter C. Craigie, Page H. Kelley, and Joel F. Drinkard, Jr., *Jeremiah 1–25*, WBC (Dallas: Word Books, 1991), xli–xlv.

43. Sigmund Mowinckel, *Zur Komposition des Buches Jeremia* (Kristiania: Jacob Dybwad, 1914).

44. E.g., William L. Holladay, "A Fresh Look at 'Source B' and 'Source C' in Jeremiah," *VT* 25 (1975): 408; following Günter Wanke, *Untersuchungen zur sogennannten Baruchschrift*, BZAW 122, (1971), and Helga Weippert, *Die Prosareden des Jeremiabuches*, BZAW 132 (1973).

45. E.g., John Bright, *Jeremiah*, AB (Garden City, N.Y.: Doubleday & Co., 1965), lxxii.

46. E. W. Nicholson, *Preaching to the Exiles: A Study of the Prose Tradition in the Book of Jeremiah* (Oxford: Blackwell, 1970).

47. Holladay answers in the affirmative, "A Fresh Look," 410.

48. Bright, *Jeremiah*, lxxi.

49. E.g., Bright, *Jeremiah*, lxxxvi–cxviii; W. L. Holladay, "The Years of Jeremiah's Preaching," *Int* 37 (1983): 146–59.

50. Especially in the works of Robert P. Carroll, *From Chaos to Covenant: Prophecy in the Book of Jeremiah* (New York: Crossroad, 1981), and *Jeremiah, A Commentary*.

51. "Jeremiah's proclamation consisted not just of his words, but was represented by his whole life. The prophet not only consistently warned of the coming divine judgment upon the nation, but he participated himself in the judgment of his people. . . . A complete understanding of his ministry demanded elements of both speech and action." Childs, *Introduction to the Old Testament as Scripture*, 349–50.

52. Peter R. Ackroyd, *Exile and Restoration: A Study of Hebrew Thought of the Sixth Century B.C.* (Philadelphia: Westminster Press, 1968), 51.

53. Ronald E. Clements, *Jeremiah*, Interpretation (Atlanta: John Knox Press, 1989), vii.

54. Ward, *Thus Says the Lord*, 122.

55. The most helpful commentaries for the theology of Jeremiah are those of Clements, *Jeremiah*, and of Walter Brueggemann, *To Pluck Up, To Tear Down: Jeremiah 1–25*, ITC (Grand Rapids: Wm. B. Eerdmans Publishing Co., 1988), and *To Build, To Plant: Jeremiah 26–52*, ITC (Grand Rapids: Wm. B. Eerdmans Publishing Co., 1991). On the absence of theology in the recent major commentaries, see Walter Brueggemann, "Jeremiah: Intense Criticism/Thin Interpretation," *Int* 42 (1988): 268–80.

56. So there seems to be little point in looking for material that might have come from the time of Josiah, or reflect the temporary successes of his reforms (2 Kings 22—23), as many have done.

57. Cf. Jer. 4:5–8, 29–31; 6:1–12, 22–26; 9:17–22; 12:10–13; 14:18; 15:7–9.

58. In Jeremiah's call, "send" (Jer. 1:7; Isa. 6:8); "you shall speak whatever I comand you" (Jer. 1:7; Amos 3:8). The visions in Jer. 1:11–16 take the same form as those in Amos 7:1–9; 8:1–2. Jeremiah cites the exodus and wilderness experience in 2:6–7 as Amos did in 2:9–10, and like Amos finds that disasters did not lead the people to repentance (Amos 4:6–11; Jer. 2:30; 5:3). His vision of the dissolution of the world into chaos in 4:23–28 reminds us of Isa. 2:10–22. Isaiah's commission to "stop their ears, and shut their eyes" (Isa. 6:10) had come true according to Jer. 6:10.

59. Thomas W. Overholt, *The Threat of Falsehood*, SBT 16 (London: SCM Press, 1970).

60. Cf. von Rad, *Old Testament Theology*, 2:265

61. Hos. 2:8, 13, 16, 17; 7:16; 9:10; 11:2; 13:1. Jer. 2:8, 23; 7:9; 9:14; 11:13, 17; 12:16; 19:5; 23:13, 27; 32:29, 35. Elsewhere in the prophetic books, only Zeph. 1:4.

62. Heschel, *The Prophets*, 109.

63. Note the wording of the First Commandment: "You shall have no other gods before [or besides] me" (Exod. 20:3).

64. Thomas M. Raitt's book contains a valuable study of the subject, but his reconstruction of development in Jeremiah's message, from early warnings of judgment combined with hope or calls to repentance, followed by use of the failure to repent as a ground for punishment, does not seem well supported by the evidence: *A Theology of Exile: Judgment/Deliverance in Jeremiah and Ezekiel* (Philadelphia: Fortress Press, 1977), 36.

65. Psalm 51:5 is an expression of a deep, personal sense of sinfulness, not a statement of doctrine.

66. Argued recently by Holladay, "A Fresh Look," 408–10; Raitt, *Theology of Exile*, 37; J. Unterman, *From Repentance to Redemption: Jeremiah's Thought in Transition*, JSOT-Sup 54 (Sheffield: JSOT Press, 1987), 176.

67. For a full discussion of the word in Jeremiah, see William L. Holladay, *The Root SHUB in the Old Testament, with Particular Reference to its Usages in Covenantal Contexts* (Leiden: E. J. Brill, 1958), 128–39.

68. For a full discussion, see William L. Holladay, *Jeremiah 1*, Hermeneia (Philadelphia: Fortress Press, 1986), 62–81.

69. von Rad, *Old Testament Theology*, 2:274.

70. Examples of the extensive discussion of these texts: nothing to be ascribed to Jeremiah: E. Gerstenberger, "Jeremiah's Complaints: Observations on Jer. 15:10–21," *JBL* 82 (1963): 393–408; personal outpourings from the prophet: John Bright, "Jeremiah's Complaints: Liturgy or Expressions of Personal Distress?" in *Proclamation and Presence: Festschrift for G. Henton Davies*, ed. J. I. Durham and J. R. Porter (Richmond: John Knox Press, 1970), 189–214.

71. von Rad, *Old Testament Theology*, 2:265.

72. Studies of the symbolic acts of the prophets: S. Amsler, *Les Actes des Prophètes* Essais Bibliques 9 (Geneva: Labor et Fides, 1985); Georg Fohrer, *Die symbolischen Handlungen der Propheten*, 2nd ed., ATANT 54 (Zürich: Zwingli Verlag, 1968); P. Matheny, "Interpretation of Hebrew Prophetic Symbolic Act," *Encounter* 29 (1968): 256–67.

73. H. Kremers, "Leidenschaft mit Gott im AT. Eine Untersuchung der 'biographischen' Berichte im Jeremiabuch," *EvTh* 13 (1953): 122–40. See the critique in Nicholson, *Preaching to the Exiles*, 104–5.

74. Nicholson concludes that the B and C material probably had the same origin, *Preaching to the Exiles*, 34–37.

75. Jeremiah 36 is of considerable interest for efforts to reconstruct the composition of the prophetic books, since it refers to three stages, oral, written, and a written version with supplements, but this need not be discussed in a work on the theology of the finished product.

76. Although see Brueggemann, *Jeremiah 1–25*, 119 (on Jer. 12:14–17); *Jeremiah 26–52*, 226–27, 246–47 (on Jer. 46:25–26 and 48:46–47).

77. The originality of the designation is questioned by Werner E. Lemke, "Nebuchadnezzar, My Servant," *CBQ* 28 (1968): 45–50; defended by Thomas W. Overholt, "King Nebuchadnezzar in the Jeremiah Tradition," *CBQ* 30 (1968): 39–48.

78. Brueggemann, *Jeremiah 26–52*, 213. If, in the MT, chs. 46—51 function as condemnation of Babylon for the havoc it has wreaked on the entire Fertile Crescent, that would account for the inclusion of Elam, which had nothing to do with Judean history.

79. For contrasting points of view, compare Nicholson, *Preaching to the Exiles*, who locates this material in the Babylonian exile, with Raitt, a *Theology of Exile*, who attributes much of it to Jeremiah himself.

80. Said explicitly in Isa. 40:2, but not made explicit in Jeremiah 24. Other interpreters are satisfied with a purely political explanation: These are the words of Babylonian exiles, justifying themselves. That may be so, but there is no reason to deny that a Judean prophet who had taken unpopular positions before might do so again.

81. Walther Zimmerli, "Knowledge of God according to the Book of Ezekiel," in his *I Am Yahweh* (Atlanta: John Knox Press, 1982), 88.

82. Emphasized by Raitt, *Theology of Exile*, 112–19, 144–45.

83. H. W. Hertzberg, "Jeremia und das Nordreich Israel," *TLZ* 77 (1952): 595–602.

84. This is the only OT passage that speaks of a "new covenant." For studies, see Raitt, *Theology of Exile*, 200–206; P. Buis, "La nouvelle alliance," *VT* 18 (1968): 1–15; H. D. Potter, "The New Covenant in Jeremiah xxxi 31–34," *VT* 33 (1983): 347–57; Jože Krašovec, "Vergebung und neuer Bund nach Jer. 31,31–34," *ZAW* 105 (1993): 428–44.

85. On forgiveness in the OT, see Thomas M. Raitt, "Why Does God Forgive?" *HBT* 13 (1991): 38–58.

86. For a full discussion of Obadiah, see John D. W. Watts, *Obadiah: A Critical Exegetical Commentary* (Grand Rapids: Wm. B. Eerdmans Publishing Co., 1969).

87. See J. R. Bartlett, "The Brotherhood of Edom," *JSOT* 4 (1977): 2–27.

88. For surveys of the sketchy evidence from archaeology, see John Lindsay, "The Babylonian Kings and Edom, 605–550 B.C.," *PEQ* 108 (1976): 23–39; J. R. Bartlett, "From Edomites to Nabataeans: A Study in Continuity," *PEQ* 111 (1979): 53–66.

89. Note, however, the favorable picture of Edom in Deut. 2:1–8; 23:7–8.

90. Cf. NIV: "You should not look down on your brother"; Watts: "But you should never look on the day of your brother," *Obadiah*, 40.

91. John Bartlett has questioned the general opinion that the Edomites were directly involved in the fall of Jerusalem, saying that texts such as these reflect long-standing hatred of Edom based on earlier conflicts. J. R. Bartlett, "Edom and the Fall of Jerusalem, 587 B.C.," *PEQ* 114 (1982): 13–24.

92. Cf. Coggins, *Israel among the Nations: A Commentary on the Books of Nahum and Obadiah* 72–74; Mason, *Micah, Nahum, Obadiah*, 89–90.

93. 2 Kings 24:14: 10,000 princes, mighty men, craftsmen, and smiths; 2 Kings 24:16: 7,000 men of valor and 1,000 craftsmen and smiths; Jer. 52:28: 3,023 in 597; Jer. 52:29: 832 in 587; Jer. 52:30: 745 in 582.

94. Lindsay, "Babylonian Kings and Edom," 32–33.

95. Ahlström, *History of Ancient Palestine*, 805, 833.

96. Yohanan Aharoni, "Three Hebrew Ostraca from Arad," *BASOR* 197 (1970): 16–42; Itzhaq Beit-Arieh, "New Light on the Edomites," *BARev* 14.2 (1988): 28–41. Beth-zur is about fifteen miles south of Jerusalem, about five miles north of Hebron. The southernmost town represented in the rebuilding of the walls of Jerusalem, in Nehemiah 3, is Beth-zur (v. 16), and a line of small fortresses was built east to west across the country just south of this town during the Persian period, perhaps to discourage Edomite penetration further north. Ahlström, *History of Ancient Palestine*, 831.

97. The text of Obadiah 20 is very difficult, and it can scarcely be translated literally. Compare the efforts of NRSV, REB, and NIV. The place Sepharad has not yet been located with any certainty.

98. Obadiah may have been located where it is in the prophetic canon because it seemed an appropriate expansion of the promise near the end of Amos, "in order that they may possess the remnant of Edom" (Amos 9:12).

99. Donald E. Gowan, *Ezekiel*, KPG (Atlanta: John Knox Press, 1985). Cf. von Rad, "He was the first prophet consciously to enter this new sphere of activity, which may be described as a 'cure of souls' . . . This pastoral office meant much more for Ezekiel than simply an extension of his prophetic calling, or a special nuance given to it. It was his duty to live for other people, to seek them out, and place himself and his prophetic word at their disposal, and this task affected his own life in deadly earnest" *Old Testament Theology*, 2:231, 232.

100. There are promises added to the messages of judgment in several places: Ezek. 11:14–21; 16:53–63; 17:22–32; 20:32–44; and an offer of repentance and forgiveness in ch. 18.

101. For the history of modern interpretation of Ezekiel, see Henry McKeating, *Ezekiel*, OTG (Sheffield: JSOT Press, 1993), 30–61. For the theology of the book, see Walther Eichrodt, *Ezekiel, A Commentary*, OTL (Philadelphia: Westminster Press, 1970); Walther Zimmerli, *Ezekiel 1: A Commentary on the Book of the Prophet Ezekiel Chapters 1–24*, Hermeneia (Philadelphia: Fortress Press, 1979), and *Ezekiel 2: A Commentary on the Book of the Prophet Ezekiel Chapters 25–48*, Hermeneia (Philadelphia: Fortress Press, 1983); also Zimmerli's collected articles in *I Am Yahweh*.

102. In spite of some recent efforts to dissect the book into several redactional layers, most contemporary commentators agree that its message is remarkably consistent, even though parts of it may be the work of redactors. This is the point of view of Zimmerli's work, cited above, and it will be reflected in my approach. Moshe Greenberg's questions about criteria need to be taken seriously: "What Are Valid Criteria for Determining Inauthentic Matter in Ezekiel?" in *Ezekiel and His Book: Textual and Literary Criticism and their Interrelation*, ed. J. Lust (Louvain: Leuven University Press, 1986), 123–35. The results of Greenberg's "holistic" approach appear in his commentary, *Ezekiel, 1–20*, AB (Garden City, N.Y.: Doubleday & Co., 1983); *Ezekiel 21–37*, AB (New York: Doubleday, 1997).

103. McKeating, *Ezekiel*, 11.

104. Walter Brueggemann, "Weariness, Exile and Chaos (A Motif in Royal Theology)," *CBQ* 34 (1972): 33.

105. In conversation, Ken Bailey, who spent most of his career in the Middle East, expressed his astonishment that Ezekiel could have stayed alive, saying what he did. Bailey had learned about exile from visiting Palestinian refugee camps, finding that what kept those exiles going from day to day was the same kind of fervor Ezekiel fought against. They kept reassuring one another that they were going back, any day now. They would accept no other home but their original homes, and for someone to claim they ought to make a new life elsewhere was treason.

106. The story has always been offensive, but for different reasons at different times. Now, some take it literally (contrary to Ezekiel's intention) as an account of spousal abuse. Not many years ago, it was the explicit sexual language that was shocking. For Ezekiel's congregation it was something else: Jerusalem's fate is sealed, and is deserved.

107. There are two poems in Ezekiel 19. The first speaks of a lioness with two cubs. She must be Josiah's wife Hamutal, since two of her sons, Jehoahaz and Zedekiah, acceded to the kingship. The second depicts the mother as a vine, one of whose branches is destroyed. This probably refers to Hamutal and Zedekiah. There have been other efforts to interpret the imagery in this chapter.

108. Cf. also Ezek. 15; 24:1–14. The promise of a new king in 17:22–24 was very probably added after the death of Zedekiah.

109. I take the difficult Ezek. 20:25 to mean that God made his laws, by which they once could live, invalid. Verse 26 then cites two laws originally intended for life, gifts and the firstborn (referring explicitly to the form of the law in Exod. 13:12, which specifies that the firstborn of humans are to be redeemed). But once God had withdrawn his grace from them, they could be misunderstood and horribly distorted, as in child sacrifice, v. 31. Gowan, *Ezekiel*, 87–89.

110. For recent discussion, Ellen F. Davis, *Swallowing the Scroll: Textuality and the Dynamics of Discourse in Ezekiel's Prophecy*, JSOTSup 78 (Sheffield: Almond Press, 1989), 67–71. From 4:8 we get the impression he was to be immovable for the entire time, but there is little detail provided, and perhaps it was acted out for only a part of each day.

111. Baruch J. Schwartz, "The Bearing of Sin in the Priestly Literature," in *Pomegranates and Golden Balls: Festschrift for Jacob Milgrom*, ed. D. P. Wright et al. (Winona Lake, Ind.: Eisenbrauns, 1995), 3–21, esp. 8–10.

112. Zimmerli, *Ezekiel 1*, 164–65, who does actually speak of "substitutionary sin-bearing." He modifies this by saying later that, by lying bound, Ezekiel became a revealer of guilt, an accuser. Cf. Greenberg, *Ezekiel, 1–20*, 125–27.

113. Othmar Keel, *Jahwe-Visionen und Siegelkunst. Eine neue Deutung der Majestätsschilderungen in Jes. 6, Ez. 1 und 10 und Sach. 4*, SBS 84/85 (Stuttgart: Verlag Katholischer Bibelwerk, 1977).

114. This may be the point of the somewhat cryptic sentence, "I have been a sanctuary to them for a little while in the countries where they have gone" (Ezek. 11:16). Cf. Zimmerli, *Ezekiel 1*, 262.

115. For a study of the use of "name" with reference to God throughout scripture, see my *Theology in Exodus*, ch. 4, 76–97.

116. "For precisely in the Jew's relation with the non-Jew could God's holy name be either most sanctified or most profaned." C. G. Montefiore and H. Loewe, *A Rabbinic Anthology* (Cleveland: World Publishing Co., 1963), xxxiv. "He who steals from a non-

Jew is bound to make restitution to the non-Jew; it is worse to steal from a non-Jew than to steal from an Israelite because of the profanation of the name." Talmud *b.Kiddushin* x, 15.

117. E.g., "If Israel sin not, the whole world is blessed" (*Tanhuma*, Behukkotai, 55a), and in an extravangant way: "When ye are My witnesses, I am God, and when ye are not My witnesses, I am not God," as commentary on "Therefore ye are My witnesses, saith the Lord, and I am God" (Isa. 43:12), in *The Midrash on Psalms*, trans. William G. Braude (New Haven, Conn.: Yale University Press, 1959), 2.303.

118. Zimmerli, "I Am Yahweh," "Knowledge of God according to the Book of Ezekiel," and "The Word of Divine Self-Manifestation (Proof-Saying): A Prophetic Genre," all in his *I Am Yahweh.*

119. Zimmerli, *I Am Yahweh*, 91.

120. Ibid., *I Am Yahweh*, 81–87.

121. For studies of these passages, see Lawrence Boadt, *Ezekiel's Oracles against Egypt: A Literary and Philosophical Study of Ezekiel 29–32* (Rome: Biblical Institute Press, 1980); H. J. van Dijk, *Ezekiel's Prophecy on Tyre (Ez. 26:1–28:19)* (Rome: Pontifical Biblical Institute, 1968). I studied both the mythological parallels and the theme of *hybris* in *When Man Becomes God.*

122. Old Testament writers ordinarily showed little interest in life after death. It is thus important that pictures of Sheol, the realm of the dead appear with some prominence only in connection with foreign kings, here (Ezek. 26:19–21; 31:14–18; 32:17–32) and in Isa. 14:4–21.

123. Walter Vogels, "Restauration de l'Egypte et universalism in Ez 29,13–16," *Biblica* 53/4 (1972): 473–494.

124. von Rad, "'Righteousness' and 'Life' in the Cultic Language of the Psalms," in his *Problem of the Hexateuch and Other Essays*, 243–66; Walther Zimmerli, "'Leben' und 'Tod' im Buche des Propheten Ezechiel," *TLZ* 13 (1957): 494–508; repr. in his *Gottes Offenbarung*, TBü 19 (Munich: Kaiser Verlag, 1963), 178–91.

125. Earlier readers saw this chapter as evidence that Ezekiel was a major party in the introduction of "individualism" into Judaism, but it is understood now that he was simply citing law as it had always been enforced. For a recent study, see Paul Joyce, *Divine Initiative and Human Response in Ezekiel*, JSOTSup 51 (Sheffield: Sheffield Academic Press, 1989). Ezekiel's argument with reference to divine justice seems unrealistic, since in fact we do suffer for the sins of our ancestors and benefit from their righteousness. This must be understood as an ad hominem argument, overstating the case in order to move to the point that a different future is possible by taking personal responsibility and repenting.

126. For a useful article on the subject, see Raitt, "Why Does God Forgive?" 38–58.

127. For the thematic unity of the latter part of the book, see Lawrence Boadt, "The Function of the Salvation Oracles in Ezekiel 33–37," *HAR* 12 (1990): 1–21.

128. Compare the two-stage process—first a body, then breath—with the creation of the human in Genesis 2.

129. Klaus Baltzer, *The Covenant Formulary in Old Testament, Jewish and Early Christian Writings* (Philadelphia: Fortress Press, 1971).

130. The threefold structure of my book *Eschatology in the Old Testament* came from working with the contents of Ezekiel 36. The ideal future will be like the present except that evil has been eradicated; so the prophets speak of transformations of society, of humanity, and even of nature.

131. Ph. de Robert, *Le berger d'Israel. Essai sur le thème pastoral dans l'Ancien Testament*, Cahiers Théologiques 57 (Neuchatel, 1968); B. Willmes, *Die sogennante Hirtenalle-*

gorie Ez 34: Studien zum Bild des Hirten im Alten Testament, BBET 19 (Frankfurt: Peter Lang, 1984).

132. NRSV reads "forget their shame" in Ezek. 39:26, following an emendation of the verb to *nashah*. Ezekiel never uses that verb, however, so *naśú* here is to be taken as a variant spelling of the verb *naśa'*, "bear," which Ezekiel uses with *kĕlimah* in nine other places. See Zimmerli, *Ezekiel 2*, 295.

133. Davis, *Swallowing the Scroll*, 115.

134. For a defense of its originality, see Moshe Greenberg, "The Design and Themes of Ezekiel's Program of Restoration," *Int* 38 (1984): 181–208; repr. in *Interpreting the Prophets*, ed. J. L. Mays and P. J. Achtemeier (Philadelphia: Fortress Press, 1987), 215–36.

135. For a survey, see Phyllis Trible, "Jonah," *NIB* 7 (1996): 480–90.

136. For one form of that reading, see R. E. Clements, "The Purpose of the Book of Jonah," VTSup 28 (1975): 16–28.

137. E.g., H. H. Rowley, *The Missionary Message of the Old Testament* (London: Carey Press, 1945).

138. For various readings throughout history, see Elias Bickerman, *Four Strange Books of the Bible: Jonah, Daniel, Koheleth, Esther* (New York: Schocken Books, 1967), 14–32; R. B. Salters, *Jonah and Lamentations*, OTG (Sheffield: JSOT Press, 1994), 51–61.

139. For detailed studies of literary technique, see Jonathan Magonet, *Form and Meaning: Studies in Literary Techniques in the Book of Jonah*, BBET 2 (Bern: Herbert Lang, and Frankfurt: Peter Lang, 1976; reprint, Sheffield: Almond Press, 1983); Phyllis Trible, *Rhetorical Criticism: Context, Method, and the Book of Jonah*, Guides to Biblical Scholarship (Minneapolis: Fortress Press, 1994).

140. Hans Walter Wolff, *Obadiah and Jonah* (Minneapolis: Augsburg Press, 1977); Jack M. Sasson, *Jonah: A New Translation with Introduction, Commentary, and Interpretation*, AB 24B (New York: Doubleday, 1990); James Limburg, *Jonah, A Commentary*, OTL (Louisville, Ky.: Westminster/John Knox Press, 1993).

141. Cf. Adele Berlin, "A Rejoinder to John A. Miles, Jr. with Some Observations on the Nature of Prophecy," *JQR* 66 (1975/76): 230–35.

142. Most scholars doubt that the psalm was an original part of the book. For arguments that it was, see Magonet, *Form and Meaning*, ch. 2; F. W. Golka, *The Song of Songs and Jonah*, ITC (Grand Rapids: Wm. B. Eerdmans Publishing Co., 1988), 90–94; Limburg, *Jonah*, 31–33.

143. "The most important implication of the story is that the freedom of God is not constrained even by the prophetic word." Blenkinsopp, *History of Prophecy in Israel*, 243.

144. For discussion of those struggles, see Salters, *Jonah and Lamentations*, 34–37.

145. For this reading, see Bickerman, *Four Strange Books*, 34; Berlin, "A Rejoinder," 231.

146. "Whereas some prophets shrank from preaching doom because they saw little or no hope, Jonah shrinks from proclaiming doom because he knows there is hope," Wolff, *Obadiah and Jonah*, 267.

147. Fretheim suggests the book raises the question of justice in that Nineveh is spared while Israel and Judah have been destroyed, but the readers would know that Nineveh had in fact met its demise in real life. Terence E. Fretheim, "Jonah and Theodicy," *ZAW* 90 (1978): 227–37.

148. "The issue turns on the fulfilment of the prophet's word. Jonah resisted because he did not want to be a false prophet. In his response God defends his right as Creator to let his mercy to his creation override the prophetic word." Childs, *Introduction to the Old Testament as Scripture*, 423. "God's pity is open-ended, both in space and in time. Thus

the borders which man erects in defining who may or may not come under God's compassion, themselves disappear into the timelessness of God. . . . If nevertheless we may extract a theme which seems to have become clarified through our analysis, it is precisely the freedom of God to be beyond any definition by which man would limit Him. God is not contained in Jonah's categories." Magonet, *Form and Meaning*, 111–12.

149. "Are not five sparrows sold for two pennies? Yet not one of them is forgotten in God's sight" (Luke 12:6).

150. Bickerman, *Four Strange Books*, 47–48.

Chapter 4: The Mid-Sixth Century and Later: Restoration to the Promised Land

1. Paul-Alain Beaulieu, "King Nabonidus and the Neo-Babylonian Empire," in *Civilizations of the Ancient Near East*, ed. Jack M. Sasson (New York: Charles Scribner's Sons, 1995), 2:969–79.

2. Suggested by J. M. Wilkie, "Nabonidus and the Later Jewish Exiles," *JTS* 2 (1951): 36–44. This may suggest a likely date for other anti-Babylonian passages, such as Isaiah 13; 21; Jeremiah 50—51.

3. Peter Berger, *A Rumor of Angels: Modern Society and the Rediscovery of the Supernatural*, expanded with a new introduction by the author (New York: Doubleday, 1990), 6, and all of ch. 1.

4. H. W. F. Saggs, *The Greatness That Was Babylon* (New York: New American Library, 1968), 256–59.

5. *ANET*, 60–72.

6. Donald J. Wiseman, *Nebuchadrezzar and Babylon* (Oxford: Oxford University Press, 1985), 64–73.

7. H. and H. A. Frankfort, et al., *Intellectual Adventure of Ancient Man*, 168–83, 202–7.

8. Berger, *Rumor of Angels*, 7.

9. Ibid., 21–23.

10. Ibid., 19–21. In a lecture delivered at Pittsburgh Theological Seminary in 1967, Berger used the term "cognitive retrenchment": "Some Sociological Comments on Theological Education," *Perspective* 9 (1968): 127–38.

11. Berger, *Rumor of Angels*, 23–24.

12. "Deutero-Isaiah had two roles: that of Yahweh's messenger conveying to the exiles what Yahweh had to say to them, and that of persuader, endeavouring to convince them of the authenticity of that message." R. N. Whybray, *The Second Isaiah* OTG (Sheffield: JSOT Press, 1983), 43.

13. H. E. von Waldow, "The Message of Deutero-Isaiah," *Int* 22 (1968): 270. A. S. Kapelrud, in "The Main Concern of Second Isaiah," says it is to convince. *VT* 32 (1982): 50–58.

14. For a thorough study of the style and theology of Deutero-Isaiah, see James Muilenburg, *IB*, 5:381–652.

15. Christopher R. North, *The Second Isaiah: Introduction, Translation and Commentary to Chapters XL–LV* (Oxford: Clarendon Press, 1964), 182. The first-person "servant songs" in Isa. 49:1–6 and 50:4–9 may also be self-references.

16. Bebb Wheeler Stone ("Second Isaiah: Prophet to Patriarchy," *JSOT* 56 [1992]: 85–99) makes a case for identifying the prophet as a woman, and there are no obvious reasons why that could not be so. Because of the clumsiness of using "he/she" throughout, the

traditional pronoun "he" will be used here without claiming that tells us anything certain about the prophet.

17. For a recent argument that the location was Jerusalem, H. M. Barstad, *A Way in the Wilderness: The 'Second Exodus' in the Message of Second Isaiah*, Journal of Semitic Studies Monographs 12 (Manchester: University of Manchester, 1989).

18. For our purposes, many of the continuing debates over the book of Isaiah, and Second Isaiah in particular, must be left in the margins; e.g., the question whether chs. 35 and perhaps also 34 come from the author of chs. 40—55; the relationship of chs. 56—66 to Second Isaiah (of which more will be said in a later chapter); questions about structure—larger or smaller basic units; and much of the debate over the "Songs of the Suffering Servant." For good introductions, see Whybray, *The Second Isaiah*, and his commentary, *Isaiah 40–66*, NCB (Grand Rapids: Wm. B. Eerdmans Publishing Co., 1981); North, *The Second Isaiah*; Claus Westermann, *Isaiah 40—66, A Commentary* OTL (Philadelphia: Westminster Press, 1969).

19. Cf. Stuhlmueller's summary, which differs somewhat from this: Carroll Stuhlmueller, "Deutero-Isaiah: Major Transitions in the Prophet's Theology and in Contemporary Scholarship," *CBQ* 42 (1980): 8–9.

20. In Isa. 41:25 he comes from the north, the direction from which the army would have approached Babylon, but also from the "rising of the sun." In 46:11 he is a "bird of prey from the east, the man for my purpose from a far country."

21. "Comfort" (the root *nḥm*) is a favorite word, appearing in Isa. 40:1; 49:13; 51:3, 12, 19; and 52:9.

22. This one time, with the first person plural, the prophet includes himself among the sinners.

23. Isa. 43:22–25; 48:1, 4, 8; 50:1; cf. 47:6. See von Waldow, "Message of Deutero-Isaiah," 270, 280.

24. There is general agreement that here the servant is Israel. For the imagery of blindness, see Philip Stern, "The 'Blind Servant' Imagery of Deutero-Isaiah and Its Implications," *Biblica* 75 (1994): 224–32.

25. Carroll Stuhlmueller, *Creative Redemption in Deutero-Isaiah*, AnBib 43 (Rome: Biblical Institute Press, 1970), 99–131. For the terms "Redeemer" and "Holy One of Israel," see Muilenburg, *IB*, 5:400–401.

26. Dieter Baltzer, *Ezechiel und Deuterojesaja: Berührungen in der Heilserwartung der beiden grossen Exilspropheten*, BZAW 121 (Berlin: Walter de Gruyter, 1971), 98; Koch, *The Prophets*, 2:124.

27. Second Isaiah's ability to resist believing what the majority did must have been analogous to that of the president of the Flat Earth Society in our time, who could say, when told of astronauts orbiting the earth, that when someone could show him some worthwhile evidence that the world was round, he would be willing to consider it.

28. "Thus the whole of the Ancient East is turned upside down for the sole reason that this little people may be conquered or restored to its own land." "The history of the nations is dominated by the fate of the Jewish people." J. D. Senarclens, *Le Mystère de l'histoire* (Geneva, 1949), 163, 182; quoted by Robert Martin-Achard, *A Light to the Nations: A Study of the Old Testament Conception of Israel's Mission to the World* (Edinburgh: Oliver & Boyd, 1962), 13, n. 5.

29. The logical conclusion is then drawn, that Yahweh must have created both good and evil: "I form light and create darkness, I make weal (*shalom*) and create woe (*ra'*, often translated "evil" elsewhere); I the LORD do all these things" (Isa. 45:7). Most Old Testament authors stop short of carrying their monotheism to that extent. For discussion of the problem, see Fredrik Lindstrom, *God and the Origin of Evil: A Contextual*

Analysis of Alleged Monistic Evidence of the Old Testament, CBOTS 21 (Lund: CWK Gleerup, 1983).

30. One translation of Deut. 6:4 also makes the same affirmation: "The Lord is our God, the Lord alone," but there are other possible readings of that verse.

31. Baltzer, *Ezechiel und Deuterojesaja*, 1–72; Westermann, *Isaiah 40–66*, 21–27; Bernhard W. Anderson, "Exodus Typology in Second Isaiah," in Anderson and Harrelson, *Israel's Prophetic Heritage*, 177–95.

32. Instead of "do not remember the former things," Isa. 46:9 insists, "remember the former things," but since it is addressed to "transgressors," it probably refers to other acts of God in the past.

33. For the theme of widowhood, cf. Lam. 1:1–2.

34. For the origins of the oracles against the nations in holy war, see my commentary on Amos 1–2 in *NIB*, 7:354–55.

35. Adolphe Lods, *The Prophets and the Rise of Judaism* (New York: E.P. Dutton & Co., 1937), 248.

36. P. A. H. de Boer, *Second Isaiah's Message*, OTS 11 (Leiden: E. J. Brill, 1956), 101.

37. Martin-Achard, *A Light to the Nations*, 8–31; A. Gelston, "Universalism in Second Isaiah," *JTS* 43 (1992): 377–98. For Martin-Achard's summary, see the conclusion of this section.

38. E.g., North, *The Second Isaiah*, 134.

39. Cf. Psalm 87. The NRSV's use of "adopt" in Isa. 44:5 supports the idea of proselytes more strongly than the Hebrew does.

40. Cf. Gelston's definition, "Universalism in Second Isaiah," 396–97.

41. Martin-Achard, *A Light to the Nations*, 31.

42. E.g., T. N. D. Mettinger, *A Farewell to the Servant Songs: A Critical Examination of an Exegetical Axiom*, Scripta Minora Regiae Societatis Humaniorum Litterarium Lundensis 1982–83: 3 (Lund: Gleerup, 1983).

43. Cf. Stuhlmueller's chart of themes, "Deutero-Isaiah: Major Transitions," 6–7.

44. Christopher R. North, *The Suffering Servant in Deutero-Isaiah: An Historical and Critical Study*, 2nd ed. (Oxford: Oxford University Press, 1956).

45. "Their exegesis must not be controlled by the question, 'Who is this servant of God?' Instead, we must do them justice by recognizing that precisely this is what they neither tell nor intend to tell us. The questions which should control exegesis are: 'What do the texts make known about what transpires, or is to transpire, between God, the servant, and those to whom his task pertains?'" Westermann, *Isaiah 40–66*, 93.

46. Curt Lindhagen, *The Servant Motif in the Old Testament: A Preliminary Study to the "Ebed-Yahweh Problem" in Deutero-Isaiah* (Uppsala: Lundequistaska Bokhandeln, 1950), 56, 155–66.

47. Von Rad, *Old Testament Theology*, 2:251.

48. The collective interpretation has either Israel suffering because of the sins of the nations or a faithful group within Israel suffering for their fellow Jews.

49. Von Rad, *Old Testament Theology*, 2:258–59.

50. Von Waldow, "Message of Deutero-Isaiah," 286–87. Ward calls the servant a symbolic figure, not a historic person. *Thus Says the Lord*, 98. Hans-Jürgen Hermisson speaks of an idealized group of prophets. "Israel und der Gottesknecht bei Deuterojesaja," *ZTK* 79 (1982): 1–24.

51. Paul D. Hanson, *Isaiah 40–66*, Interpretation (Louisville, Ky.: John Knox Press, 1995), 158.

52. Whybray's retelling shows that each word can be understood differently, but his reconstruction of the song as the thanksgiving of the community at the release from prison of their prophet does not do justice to the passage as a whole. R. N. Whybray, *Thanksgiving for a Liberated Prophet: An Interpretation of Isaiah Chapter 53*, JSOT-Sup 4 (Sheffield: JSOT Press, 1978).

53. Whybray, *Second Isaiah*, 80.

54. For a recent survey of the period, with an interpretation of the effects of Darius' activities on Judah, see Jon L. Berquist, *Judaism in Persia's Shadow: A Social and Historical Approach* (Minneapolis: Fortress Press, 1995), 45–65.

55. For known details of the history: Ahlström, *History of Palestine*, 812–906; Georg Widengren, "The Persian Period," in Hayes and Miller (eds.), *Israelite and Judaean History*, 489–538. For the books of Ezra and Nehemiah, see the commentaries by Joseph Blenkinsopp, *Ezra-Nehemiah* OTL (Philadelphia: Westminster Press, 1988); H. G. M. Williamson, *Ezra, Nehemiah* WBC (Waco, Tex.: Word Books, 1985). For the religion of the period, see Rainer Albertz, *A History of Israelite Religion in the Old Testament Period*, vol. 2: *From the Exile to the Maccabees*, OTL (Louisville, Ky.: Westminster/John Knox Press, 1994), 437–533; Berquist, *Judaism in Persia's Shadow*.

56. The scarcity of evidence, both literary and physical, has led to a proliferation of hypotheses, with imagination and bias filling in where evidence is lacking. Examples of bias: The identification by Christian scholars of everything after Second Isaiah as a deterioration of the religion of Israel, as in Julius Wellhausen, *Prolegomena to the History of Ancient Israel* (New York: 1878; reprint, Meridian Books, 1957), 497, 509; Martin Noth, "The Laws in the Pentateuch," in his *The Laws in the Pentateuch and Other Studies* (Edinburgh: Oliver & Boyd, 1966), 80. For a negative view of postexilic prophecy, Franz Hesse, "Haggai," in *Verbannung und Heimkehr: Beiträge zur Geschichte und Theologie Israels im 6. und 5. Jahrhundert v. Chr. Wilhelm Rudolph zum 70. Geburtstage*, ed. A. Kuschke (Tübingen: J.C.B. Mohr, 1961), 109–34. Ackroyd's *Exile and Restoration* was an important move toward correcting these impressions. Examples of imaginative reconstructions: Two opposing parties, theocratic and eschatological, have been identified by Otto Plöger, *Theocracy and Eschatology* (Oxford: Basil Blackwell Publisher, 1968), and Paul D. Hanson, *The Dawn of Apocalyptic*, rev. ed. (Philadelphia: Fortress Press, 1979). Both works have been widely criticized. More extravagant is Philip R. Davies's claim that postexilic Judean society was so productive that the entire Old Testament was written during that period, *In Search of "Ancient Israel,"* JSOTSup 148 (Sheffield: Sheffield Academic Press, 1992), 94–133. For a cautious critique, see Rolf Rendtorff, "The Paradigm Is Changing: Hopes—and Fears," *Biblical Interpretation* 1 (1993): 34–53. For a challenge based on sociological analysis of the area in the Persian period, see Gary N. Knoppers, "The Vanishing Solomon: The Disappearance of the United Monarchy from Recent Histories of Ancient Israel," *JBL* 116 (1997): 19–44, and the literature cited there.

57. Only Hab. 1:1 and Zech. 1:1 include the title "prophet." This may indicate that they held an office, of "cult prophet," but this has been challenged. Respect for prophets seems to have increased greatly in the postexilic period, as a result of the confirmation of the messages of the earlier prophets, with the fall of Jerusalem.

58. Carol L. Meyers and Eric M. Meyers, *Haggai, Zechariah 1–8*, AB 25B (Garden City, N.Y.: Doubleday & Co., 1987), xlvi.

59. Robert P. Carroll, "Second Isaiah and the Failure of Prophecy," *ST* 32 (1978): 121–31.

60. Hans Walter Wolff, *Haggai: A Commentary* (Minneapolis: Augsburg Publishing House, 1988), 41; Peter Ross Bedford, "Discerning the Time: Haggai, Zechariah and the 'Delay' in the Rebuilding of the Jerusalem Temple," in *The Pitcher Is Broken: Memorial Essays for Gösta Ahlström*, ed. S. W. Holloway and L. K. Handy, JSOTSup 190 (Sheffield: Sheffield Academic Press, 1995), 71–94.

61. Paul Hanson's *Dawn of Apocalyptic* is an exception.

62. Elizabeth Achtemeier, *Nahum-Malachi*, 97.

63. Walther Eichrodt, *Theology of the Old Testament*, OTL (Philadelphia: Westminster Press, 1961) 1:467–68.

64. "Haggai and Zechariah must be given enormous credit for using their prophetic ministries to foster the transition of a people from national autonomy to an existence which transcended political definition and which centered upon a view of God and his moral demands." Meyers and Meyers, *Haggai, Zechariah 1–8*, xlii–xliii.

65. Carroll Stuhlmueller, C.P., *Haggai and Zechariah: Rebuilding with Hope*, ITC (Grand Rapids: Wm. B. Eerdmans Publishing Co., 1988), 16.

66. "For five hundred years the temple was to be the backbone of Israel; and for Jesus of Nazareth it was still 'that which is my Father's' (Luke 2.49). The high priest who was in office there really united the whole of the nation in himself, and possessed the highest authority. For this Haggai and Zechariah laid the theoretical foundations." Koch, *The Prophets*, 2:160.

67. A remarkable example of that appeared in a speech delivered in 1979 by Jacobo Timerman, an Argentinian journalist who had been imprisoned and tortured on suspicion of disloyalty: "After one of those long nights of torture, when they had carried me back to my cell, for the first time I had the feeling that I had to involve myself in some sort of positive action, something that would express the act that I was still alive or at the least that I continued to exist. . . . I began to bang on the steel door of my cell so that the guard would come. . . . I told the guard that I wanted to know where the east was so that I could say my prayers facing Jerusalem. I felt that it was my first act of strength, my first positive action to fight for survival. . . . Why did I do this? I do not know. From whence came the question? I do not know. Since my father died, when I was twelve years old, the Jewish religion had disappeared from my home. I ceased to go to the synagogue. I always maintained, proudly, my Jewish identity but I was not an observant Jew. The guard did not tell me, for security reasons, where the east was. Even if he had told me, I didn't know any prayers. Why, in the most difficult moment of my life, why, in the moment of my greatest desperation, the whole world of ideas and culture and knowledge and information that had constituted my life as a man and as a journalist, why was all this not enough to inform me that I was alive, that I wanted to continue to live? . . . I found in some remote place of my being, of my mind, of my consciousness, an act of identity which was linked to the Jewish faith."

68. For archaic cultures, see Mircea Eliade, *The Sacred and the Profane: The Nature of Religion* (New York: Harper & Brothers, 1959), 36–47.

69. Wolff, *Haggai*, 106.

70. Carol L. Meyers and Eric M. Meyers, *Zechariah 9–14*, AB 25C (New York: Doubleday, 1993), 20–27; David L. Petersen, *Zechariah 9–14 and Malachi, A Commentary*, OTL (Louisville, Ky.: Westminster John Knox Press, 1995), 5; Paul L. Redditt, "Nehemiah's First Mission and the Date of Zechariah 9–14," *CBQ* 56 (1994): 664–78.

71. For a survey of this work, see R. J. Coggins, *Haggai, Zechariah, Malachi*, OTG (Sheffield: JSOT Press, 1987), 25–31.

72. For discussion, see Meyers and Meyers, *Zechariah 9–14*, and Petersen, *Zechariah 9–14 and Malachi*, on the relevant passages.

73. A good survey of the message of Zechariah 1—8 appears in the conclusion to Albert Petitjean's commentary, *Les Oracles du Proto-Zacharie: Un programme de restauration pour la communauté juive après l'exil*, Ebib (Paris: J. Gabalda, 1969), 441–44.

74. This makes it possible for us to deal with the "point" of each vision without needing to discuss the choice of images, which are dealt with fully in the commentaries.

75. Compare the outline of my book, *Eschatology in the Old Testament*.

76. Meyers and Meyers, *Zechariah 9–14*, 20–27.

77. Rex A. Mason, "The Relation of Zech. 9—14 to Proto-Zechariah," *ZAW* 88 (1976): 227–39.

78. Stuhlmueller, *Haggai and Zechariah*, 113.

79. Paul L. Redditt, "Israel's Shepherds: Hope and Pessimism in Zechariah 9–14," *CBQ* 51 (1989): 631–42, see 636.

80. Since the house of David appears with some prominence later in these chapters, it is interesting to consider Douglas Jones's suggestion that this strangely unwarlike king is a reflection of the story of David's return to Jerusalem in mournful triumph after Absalom's revolt had been quelled (2 Sam. 15:30–16:2). *Haggai, Zechariah and Malachi*, Torch Bible Commentaries (London: SCM Press, 1962), 130–33.

81. Carol L. Meyers and Eric M. Meyers, "The Future Fortunes of the House of David: The Evidence of Second Zechariah," in *Fortunate the Eyes That See: Essays in Honor of David Noel Freedman in Celebration of His Seventieth Birthday*, ed. A. B. Beck et al. (Grand Rapids: Wm. B. Eerdmans Publishing Co., 1995), 207–22. The reference to elaborate mourning for "one they have pierced" [MT "me whom they have pierced"!] remains a mystery.

82. For a convenient discussion of the issues, Grace I. Emmerson, *Isaiah 56–66*, OTG (Sheffield: JSOT Press, 1992).

83. Westermann, *Isaiah 40–66*, 300–302.

84. Hanson, *Dawn of Apocalyptic*, 32–208 on Isaiah 56—66.

85. Brooks Schramm, *The Opponents of Third Isaiah: Reconstructing the Cultic History of the Restoration*, JSOTSup 193 (Sheffield: Sheffield Academic Press, 1995).

86. I use the third person singular masculine pronoun for convenience in referring to Isaiah 56—66, acknowledging that we do not know whether either the masculine or the singular is correct.

87. "It can be said, at least theoretically, that 'Israel' ceased to be 'a national-ethnic entity' and became 'a confessional community.'" Schramm, *Opponents of Third Isaiah*, 182. Cf. von Rad, *Old Testament Theology*, 2:280.

88. Emmerson, *Isaiah 56–66*, 100–104.

89. Schramm, *Opponents of Third Isaiah*, 126–127, 156, 167–169, 177.

90. A. Rofé, "Isaiah 66.1–4: Judean Sects in the Persian Period as Viewed by Trito-Isaiah," in *Biblical and Related Studies Presented to Samuel Iwry*, ed. A. Kort and S. Morschauser (Winona Lake, Ind.: Eisenbrauns, 1985), 205–17.

91. Isaiah 60—62 are surrounded by two divine warrior texts (59:15b–20 and 63:1–6). Outside these are the two laments (59:1–15a and 63:7–64:12). Chapters 57–58 and 65 both condemn idolatry and reassure the faithful, and 56 and 66 are both concerned with the temple and have an open attitude toward membership in the worshiping community. Cf. Westermann, *Isaiah 40–66*, 297–304; Emmerson, *Isaiah 56–66*, 18–20.

92. Cf. Gowan, *Eschatology in the Old Testament*, 4–20.

93. For a survey of form-critical work on the book, see Petersen, *Zechariah 9–14 and Malachi*, 29–31.

94. For Mal. 2:10–16, considered by some to be a reference to syncretism, see below.

95. For a survey of the debate, see Ralph L. Smith, *Micah–Malachi*, WBC 32 (Waco, Tex.: Word Books, 1984), 321–25. Beth Glazier-McDonald suggests that marriage to a foreign woman was likely to lead to the adoption of aspects of her religion, so both the literal and the metaphorical meaning are relevant. "Intermarriage, Divorce, and the BAT-'EL NEKAR: Insights into Mal 2:10–16" *JBL* 106 (1987): 603–11.

96. There are some problems with A. S. van der Woude's variant interpretation, but it is worth considering. He claims divorce is not the issue, but depriving one's Jewish wife of her rights once the husband has taken a second, foreign wife (cf. Exod. 21:10). "Malachi's Struggle for a Pure Community: Reflections on Malachi 2:10–16," in *Tradition and Re-Interpretation in Jewish and Early Christian Literature. Essays in Honour of Jürgen C. H. Lebram*, SPB 36 (Leiden: E.J. Brill, 1986), 65–71.

97. Deuteronomy claims the right of Levites to serve as priests, a right that was not maintained in the second temple. The most exalted role for the Levites, outside of Malachi, is in Jer. 33:17–26. Cf. also Deut. 33:8–11; Neh. 13:29.

98. God may simply be referred to as "One" in the difficult verse, Mal. 2:15.

99. Elements typical of Deuteronomy: use of the verb "love," the father-son relationship, emphasis on the name of the Lord, the oneness of God, rules for sacrifice and the tithe, special interest in the Levites, and the eschatological messenger of Mal. 3:1 may reflect the promise of the future prophet in Deut. 18:15–18. Deuteronomy's ferocious attacks on syncretism are not echoed in Malachi, supporting the idea that he did not identify this as a serious problem in his time. Steven L. McKenzie and Howard N. Wallace conclude that the covenant with the patriarchs lies behind most of Malachi's uses of the concept. "Covenant Themes in Malachi," *CBQ* 45 (1983): 549–63.

100. E.g., Elizabeth Achtemeier, *Nahum-Malachi*, 177; Beth Glazier-McDonald, *Malachi: The Divine Messenger*, SBLDS 98 (Atlanta: Scholars Press, 1987), 60–61. NIV puts the whole verse in the future tense; NRSV in the present. The first and third clauses in Hebrew are noun clauses, and the second contains two participles, so one would normally read it in the present tense, although participles can be used to refer to the future.

101. For a full discussion of the five readings, see Ralph Smith, *Micah-Malachi*, 313–16.

102. So, Glazier-McDonald, *Malachi: The Divine Messenger*, 217.

103. E.g., Petersen, *Zechariah 9–14 and Malachi*, 220–23. McKenzie and Wallace say that "3:16–21 presumes an inner-Israelite dichotomy which does not exist in the earlier part," and consider the passage to be an addition to the original book, "Covenant Themes in Malachi," 560–63.

104. For such a book, recording those pleasing to God, cf. Exod. 32:32; Ps. 69:28; Dan. 12:1).

105. For discussion, see B. V. Malchow, "The Messenger of the Covenant," *JBL* 103 (1984): 252–55; A. S. van der Woude, "Der Engel des Bundes. Bemerkungen zu Maleachi 3,1c und seinem Kontext," in *Die Botschaft und die Boten: Festschrift für Hans Walter Wolff zum 70. Geburtstag*, ed. J. Jeremias and L. Perlitt (Neukirchen-Vluyn: Neukirchener Verlag, 1981), 289–300.

106. Cf. W. J. Dumbrell, "Malachi and the Ezra-Nehemiah Reforms," *Reformed Theological Review* 35 (1976): 42–52.

107. For a survey of the theories, see Mason, *Zephaniah, Habakkuk, Joel*, 113–116.

108. Ibid., 98.

109. Wolff, *Joel and Amos*, 6–8.

110. James L. Crenshaw, *Joel: A New Translation with Introduction and Commentary*, AB 24C (New York: Doubleday, 1995), 36–37. Compare the lists of parallels cited by

Wolff, *Joel and Amos*, 11; and Ogden, in Graham S. Ogden and Richard R. Deutsch, *Joel and Malachi: A Promise of Hope/A Call to Obedience*, ITC (Grand Rapids: Wm. B. Eerdmans Publishing Co., 1987), 56–57.

111. Wolff, *Joel and Amos*, 9; Ogden and Deutsch, *Joel and Malachi*, 10–12; Graham S. Ogden, "Joel 4 and Prophetic Responses to National Laments," *JSOT* 26 (1983): 97–106.

112. Cf. Crenshaw, *Joel*, 116–17, 128–32.

113. Contrary to Wolff, *Joel and Amos*, 41–42; agreeing with W. S. Prinsloo, *The Theology of the Book of Joel*, BZAW 163 (Berlin: Walter de Gruyter, 1985), 47, and others, to be cited later.

114. See Crenshaw's list, *Joel*, 40.

115. Crenshaw, *Joel*, 41; Ogden, and Deutsch, *Joel and Malachi*, 11.

116. See, especially, the works by Ogden cited above. Also, Ferdinand E. Deist, "Parallels and Reinterpretations in the Book of Joel: A Theology of the Yom Yahweh," in *Text and Context: Old Testament and Semitic Studies for F. C. Fensham*, ed. W. Classen (JSOT Sup 48; Sheffield: JSOT Press, 1988) 63–79. Wolff calls the latter part of the book "literary and composite," *Joel and Amos*, 59. Others speak of it as a liturgical work, or an imitation thereof.

117. Cf. Mason, *Zephaniah, Habakkuk, Joel*, 122.

118. For surveys of the Day of Yahweh theme, as related to Joel, see Crenshaw, *Joel*, 105–6; Wolff, *Joel and Amos*, 33–34.

119. Thomas B. Dozeman, "Inner-Biblical Interpretation of Yahweh's Gracious and Compassionate Character," *JBL* 108 (1989): 207–23.

120. The puzzling reference to "the northerner" in Joel 2:20 is taken by some to mean the locusts of 1:4 and 2:25; but most commentators believe that the prophet is alluding to the enemy from the north of Jer. 1:13–15; 4:6; 6:1, 22 and Ezek. 38:6, 15; 39:2.

Chapter 5: The Continuing Influence of Old Testament Prophecy

1. The Sadducees accepted only the Torah. This was true also of the descendants of the old Northern Israelites, the Samaritans.

2. The LXX text of Jeremiah differed significantly from the Hebrew, as noted earlier, and it also added to Jeremiah the books of Baruch and the Letter of Jeremiah. Lamentations and Daniel were also moved from their places in the Hebrew canon, and added to the prophetic books.

3. Joseph Blenkinsopp offers a detailed reconstruction, but like all others it involves a great deal of speculation: *Prophecy and Canon: A Contribution to the Study of Jewish Origins* (Notre Dame, Ind.: University of Notre Dame Press, 1977).

4. See David E. Aune, *Prophecy in Early Christianity and the Ancient Mediterranean World* (Grand Rapids: Wm. B. Eerdmans Publishing Co., 1983), 103–52; Frederick E. Greenspahn, "Why Prophecy Ceased," *JBL* 108 (1989): 37–49; Barton, *Oracles of God* 105–116.

5. Blenkinsopp finds the key to be rival claims to authority in second temple Jerusalem; *Prophecy and Canon*, 4. Similar theories, with significant differences between them, have been advanced by Plöger, *Theocracy and Eschatology*, and Hanson, *Dawn of Apocalyptic*. Note Barton's critique of these assumptions that there were such rival groups, *Oracles of God* 111–13, 167–70.

6. E.g., "With the appearance of the law came to an end the old freedom, not only in the sphere of worship, now restricted to Jerusalem, but in the sphere of the religious spirit

as well. There was now in existence an authority as objective as could be, and this was the death of prophecy." Wellhausen, *Prolegomena to the History of Ancient Israel*, 402.

7. Ackroyd, *Exile and Restoration*, 1–7.

8. Klaus Koch, *The Rediscovery of Apocalyptic*, SBT² 22 (Naperville, Ill.: Alec R. Allenson, 1970), 36–48.

9. E.P. Sanders, *Paul and Palestinian Judaism* (Philadelphia: Fortress Press, 1977), 33–59.

10. Joseph Blenkinsopp, "Tanakh and the New Testament," in *Biblical Studies: Meeting Ground of Jews and Christians*, ed. L. Boadt et al (New York: Paulist Press, 1980), 96–119; "Old Testament Theology and the Jewish-Christian Connection" *JSOT* 28 (1984): 3–15. See also James Barr, "Le judaïsme postbiblique et la théologie de l'Ancien Testament," *RTP* 18 (1968): 209–17; *Judaism—Its Continuity with the Bible* (Southampton: Camelot Press, 1968).

11. The subtitle of my textbook, *Bridge Between the Testaments: A Reappraisal of Judaism from the Exile to the Birth of Christianity,* PTMS 14 (Allison Park, Pa.; Pickwick Publications, 1986), suggested that I intended to make an effort to present second temple Judaism in a fairer way than had been typical of textbooks written by Christians up to that time. It is heartening that twenty years later the "reappraisal" is now the widely accepted view of Judaism in books on this period.

12. "Theologically speaking, they [Jeremiah and Ezekiel] consigned their audience, and all their contemporaries, to a kingdom of death where they could no longer be reached by the salvation coming from the old saving events." von Rad, *Old Testament Theology*, 2:272. "Because at the Exile the nation died, the Return was interpreted as its revival from the grave after doing full penance for its guilt; and this made it possible from thenceforward to regard the prophetic messages of judgment and new creation as in essentials fulfilled, and to direct the irrepressible energy of men's hopes to removing the remaining obstacles to the world-wide realization of God's dominion." Eichrodt, *Theology of the Old Testament* 1:467.

13. Wellhausen, *Prolegomena*, 27–28.

14. R. H. Pfeiffer, *Religion in the Old Testament: The History of a Spiritual Triumph* (London: A. & C. Black, 1961), 10.

15. Max Weber, *Ancient Judaism* (Glencoe, Ill.: Free Press, 1952), 364. Cf. Lods, *Prophets and the Rise of Judaism*, 1–2; H. Renckens, *The Religion of Israel* (New York: Sheed & Ward, 1966), 223; S. A. Cook, "Le VIᵉ siècle, moment decisif dans l'histoire du judaïsme et dans l'évolution religieuse de l'Orient," *RHPR* 18 (1938): 321–31.

16. Salo Baron, *A Social and Religious History of the Jews* (New York: Columbia University Press, 1952), 1:154.

17. Yehezkel Kaufmann, *The Religion of Israel* (Chicago: University of Chicago Press, 1960), 450–51.

18. James Cameron Todd, *Politics and Religion in Ancient Israel: An Introduction to the Study of the Old Testament* (New York: Macmillan & Co., 1904), 1, 4. James Sanders writes of the "crucifixion-resurrection experience of the sixth and fifth centuries B.C." *Torah and Canon* (Philadelphia: Fortress Press, 1972), xix. A later comment is reminiscent of Todd: "The Bible comes to us out of the ashes of two Temples, the First or Solomonic Temple, destroyed in 586 B.C., and the Second or Herodian Temple, destroyed in A.D. 70," p. 6.

19. Todd, *Politics and Religion*, 306, 308.

20. G. W. Ahlström, *Aspects of Syncretism in Israelite Religion*, Horae Soederblominae 5 (Lund: Gleerup, 1963); Frank E. Eakin Jr., "Yahwism and Baalism before the Exile,"

JBL 84 (1965): 407–14; Gowan, "Prophets, Deuteronomy, and the Syncretistic Cult in Israel," in Rylaarsdam, *Transitions in Biblical Scholarship*, 99–112; Morton Smith, *Palestinian Parties and Politics That Shaped the Old Testament* (New York: Columbia University Press, 1971), ch. 2.

21. Susan Ackerman offers a study of Isaiah 57 and 65, in addition to Jeremiah 7, 44, and Ezekiel 8, in her *Under Every Green Tree: Popular Religion in Sixth-Century Judah*, HSM 46 (Atlanta: Scholars Press, 1992). Morton Smith claimed the syncretistic cult of Yahweh survived the fall of Jerusalem, but even he admitted there was a great decline in syncretism, *Palestinian Parties*, ch. 4, see p. 112.

22. Rosemary Haughton's application of the prophetic interpretation of exile to contemporary Christianity acknowledges this necessity: "That is why we need the second thing that exiles do, and that has to do with the need for differences in order to preserve the hopes of the faith. It is not a matter of being different for the sake of being separate, or different, or trying to be better than other people. It is a matter of finding a way to *create* the homeland in the place of exile." "Prophecy in Exile," *Cross Currents* 39 (1989): 420–30.

23. For the evidence of Jewish resistance to the attractions of Hellenism in the third following centuries B.C.E., see V. Tcherikover, *Hellenistic Civilization and the Jews* (Philadelphia: Jewish Publication Society, 1961); S. K. Eddy, *The King Is Dead: Studies in the Near Eastern Resistance to Hellenism, 334–31 B.C.* (Lincoln: University of Nebraska Press, 1961.)

24. Morton Smith, *Palestinian Parties*, 64. The campaigns are listed in n. 57.

25. A. R. C. Leaney and J. Neusner, "The Roman Era," in Hayes and Miller, *Israelite and Judaean History*, 605–677.

26. For thorough studies: John J. Collins, *The Apocalyptic Imagination* (New York: Crossroad, 1987); Christopher Rowland, *The Open Heaven: A Study of Apocalyptic in Judaism and Early Christianity* (New York: Crossroad, 1982); D. S. Russell, *The Method and Message of Jewish Apocalyptic* (Philadelphia: Westminster Press, 1964). For briefer treatments of the relationship between prophecy and apocalyptic: Michael A. Knibb, "Prophecy and the Emergence of the Jewish Apocalypses," in *Israel's Prophetic Tradition*, ed. Richard Coggins, et al. (Cambridge: Cambridge University Press, 1982), 155–80; Magne Saebo, "Old Testament Apocalyptic in Its Relation to Prophecy and Wisdom: The View of Gerhard von Rad Reconsidered," in *In the Last Days: On Jewish and Christian Apocalyptic and Its Period*, ed. K. Jeppesen et al. (Aarhus: Aarhus University Press, 1994), 78–91; J. C. VanderKam, "The Prophetic-Sapiential Origins of Apocalyptic Thought" in *A Word in Season: Essays in Honour of William McKane*, ed. James D. Martin and Philip R. Davies, JSOTSup 42 (Sheffield: JSOT Press, 1986), 163–76.

27. 2 Baruch 20:1 says time itself will pass more quickly as the end approaches.

28. For studies of these texts, see my essay "The Exile in Jewish Apocalyptic," in *Scripture in History and Theology: Essays in Honor of J. Coert Rylaarsdam*, ed. A. L. Merrill and T. W. Overholt, PTMS 17 (Pittsburgh: Pickwick Press, 1977), 205–23; Michael Knibb, "The Exile in the Literature of the Intertestamental Period," *Heythrop Journal* 17 (1976): 253–72.

29. "The exile is seen as judgement upon the people's life, but more than that it is understood as lying within the purposes of God not simply as judgement but in relation to what he is doing in the life of the world. The response to it must be the response of acceptance, but this involves not merely a repentant attitude, appropriate and necessary though this is, because the disaster is not simply judgment, not simply a condemnation of the past but also a stage within the working out of a larger purpose." Ackroyd, *Exile and Restoration*, 234.

30. Jacob Neusner, *Self-Fulfilling Prophecy: Exile and Return in the History of Judaism* (Boston: Beacon Press, 1987), 34, and see 31–34.

31. The history of the tensions within Judaism between the achievement of faithful existence in the diaspora and the hopes for return to the promised land, an important subject in its own right, cannot be dealt with here, as it involves far more than reference to the prophetic books. For recent discussions, see Neusner, *Self-Fulfilling Prophecy*; A. M. Eisen, *Galut: Modern Jewish Reflection on Homelessness and Homecoming* (Bloomington: Indiana University Press, 1986); Etan Levine, ed., *Diaspora: Exile and the Contemporary Jewish Condition* (New York: Steimatzky/Shapolsky, 1986).

32. Neusner, *Self-Fulfilling Prophecy*, 5–6.

33. Ibid., 41.

34. Amos Funkenstein finds in medieval Judaism four different explanations of the continuing exile: (1) Cathartic—the traditional prophetic way of accounting for it as judgment for sin. (2) Missionary—the dispersion enabled the Jews to spread the knowledge of God among the nations. This also had some basis in the prophetic message. (3) Soteriologic—Israel is the servant suffering for the sins of the nations, based on Isaiah 53 (Rashi). (4) Sacrificial—a whole burnt offering to God, without any specific reference to sin (Maimonides). *Perceptions of Jewish History* (Berkeley: University of California Press, 1993), 202–6. In the twentieth century, none of these explanations has proved adequate in the face of the latest Jewish tragedy, the Holocaust.

35. Chaim Raphael's study of the Midrash now makes 70 the archetypal experience, but the two have merged: "For Jews, one historical event lay for nearly two thousand years in their memory—the loss of Jerusalem. It expressed everything: it accounted for everything." *The Walls of Jerusalem: An Excursion into Jewish History* (New York: Alfred A. Knopf, 1968), xv.

36. Barnabas Lindars, *New Testament Apologetics: The Doctrinal Significance of the Old Testament Quotations* (Philadelphia: Westminster Press, 1961), 272–84.

37. A more literal understanding of contemporary Christianity as life in exile, given the difference between Christian teaching and the predominant culture, is appearing in the works of recent writers, e.g., Stanley Hauerwas and William H. Willimon, *Resident Aliens: Life in the Christian Colony* (Nashville: Abingdon Press, 1989); Karl Rahner, "The Teaching of Vatican II on the Church and the Future Reality of Christian Life," in his *The Christian of the Future* (New York: Herder & Herder, 1967), 77–101; George N. Webber, *Today's Church: A Community of Exiles and Pilgrims* (Nashville: Abingdon Press, 1979).

INDEX OF SCRIPTURE AND OTHER ANCIENT WRITINGS

GENESIS

1:2	27
3:17–18	75
12:7	17
13:15	17
14:18–24	66
15:18	17, 120
17:7–19	17
18:22–33	106, 141
20:7	1
22:18	113
23	17
25:27–28, 32–33	118, 179
32:28	27

EXODUS

3—4	138
3:7–8	16
3:12	150
3:14	40, 42, 130
4:22	30, 48
5:2	33
6:2, 6	130
6:4	17
6:7–8	40, 42
7:12–13	17
6:8	16
10:7	18
12:12, 23	26
12:48–49	173
15:26	42
19—20	55

19	87
19:5–6	17, 30
20:3	42
20:5–6	89
22:21–24	32
22:26–27	31
23:23	181
23:32–33	17
24:9–11	61
32:11–14	27, 106
32:12–14	183
32:13	17
32:34	181
33:19	35, 42
33:20	61
34:6–7	17, 35, 40, 42, 90, 139, 140, 141, 182, 183
34:12	17
34:14–16	42, 44
35:31	184

LEVITICUS

17:7	44
22:20–25	179
25:1–6	21
25:8–17	176
26	20
26:3–10	31
26:34–35, 43	21
26:38	21
26:40–45	17, 21
27:30–33	178

NUMBERS

6:23–27	179
11:29	185
14:13–19	106, 141
15:14–16	173
18:21–32	178
33:55	17

DEUTERONOMY

4—11	18, 105
4	20
4:25–31	19, 21
4:25–26	18
4:26–27	20
4:30–31	17
4:31	21
4:35	34, 152
4:39	152
6:15	19
7:4	19
7:8	179
11:17	19
12:23, 25	32
14:22–29	178
15:12–15	32
15:21	179
17:16	18
18:19–20	19
18:21–22	85, 139, 152
20:19	32
23:1–8	173
28—30	18

28	19, 20
28:36–37, 47–48	19
28:64–68	20
29:18–28	19
30	181
30:1–5	115
30:18	19
31:9–13	179
31:16	44
34:9	185
34:10	1

JOSHUA

1:4	120
23:12–13	18
23:13–16	20
24:20	20

JUDGES

2:1–2	17
2:3	18
6:15	138
6:16	150
8:27	18

1 SAMUEL

10:1	176
11:6	185
16:13	176, 185
18:21	18

2 SAMUEL

1:19, 25	96
8:13–14	118
12:1–7	63
14:1–20	63

1 KINGS

8:27	172
9:6–7	20

12:29	30
14:15–16	20
15:30	38
18	45
20:28	33, 69
22	36
22:19–22	61, 63

2 KINGS

2:9, 15	185
4:32–37	161
9	40
10:28–36	40
10:32–33	24
13:3–7, 22–25	24
14:24–27	24
14:25	5, 24, 138
14:28	24
15:8–22	37
15:20	25, 38
15:23–27	38
15:29	11, 38
16	69
16:5–9	38, 51
17:4	38
17:6	13, 38
17:13	5, 138
17:22–23	11, 29
18—19	5, 71
18:1–6	192
18:7	70
18:9–12	38
18:11	13, 38
18:13–19:36	51
21:1–18	79
21:10–15	5, 8, 79
21:14	20
21:19–26	79
22—23	79, 98, 192
23:10	80
23:26–27	7
23:29	93, 98
23:30–37	98

23:31–34	93
23:34–24:6	93
24:1	93, 98
24:2	20
24:7–17	93
24:10–17	98
24:14	11
24:16	13, 14
24:17–19	98
25:1–21	98
25:21	11, 29
25:27	144

EZRA

1:2–4	145, 162
2:59	14
4:1–3	196
6:3–5	145, 162
6:16–21	196
8:17, 21, 31	14

NEHEMIAH

9:6–37	196
9:8	17
13:10–12	179

ESTHER

3—4	192

PSALMS

2	56, 66
2:7	73
9:10	129
13:1–2	93
15	57, 66
18	34, 87, 96
18:27	83
18:68	55
19:1–2	62
20—21	56, 66

22:1	93
24	57, 66
24:6	35, 94
25:9	83
27:8	35, 94
29	88
34:10	35, 94
44:17–18	183
45—46	56, 66
47	66
48	56, 57, 66
49	97
50:2	87, 88
50:7–15	57
68	96
68:7–10	88
69	57
72	74
72:3, 16	31
73	97
74:9	188
74:10	93
74:12–18	154
76	56, 66
77	55, 88
78:67–72	66
79	57
84, 87	56, 66
88:1, 13	93
89	66
89:46	93
90:10	116
93:95–99	66
97	55, 88, 97
103	141
105:8–11	17
106:39	44
109:21	129
110	56, 66
116:3, 8	97
122, 132	56, 66
137	15
137:4–5	146
137:7	118

138:6	83
149:4	83

PROVERBS

3:34	83
11:2	83
16:19	83

ECCLESIASTES

3:19–22	76

ISAIAH

1—5	61
1:2–3	57, 64, 65
1:4–9	64, 65, 67, 101
1:10–17	57, 64, 66, 67
1:18–20	66
1:21–23	44, 64, 66
1:24–28	96
1:24	89
2:1–4	55, 67
2:6–22	61, 68, 81, 130
3:10	95
3:14, 16	64
3:18–4:1	64
4:2–6	67
5:1–7	63
5:3–7	64
5:7	70
5:8–22	64, 68
5:8	54
5:13	28
5:19	81
5:21	68
5:23	95
5:26–29	72
5:26	93
6	61
6:5	62, 91
6:8	62, 92
6:9–10	63, 65
6:11–12	59, 63
6:11	91

6:13	63
7	110, 111
7:1–17	38, 51, 68, 69
7:9	62
7:18–20	72
8:1–4	69
8:5–8	72
8:14	70
8:18	107
9:2–7	73
9:7	67, 89
9:8–21	69
9:8–10	68, 70
9:15	64
10:1–4	68
10:5–19	68, 72, 80
10:15	82, 130
11:1–9	74, 75
11:1–5	159
11:2	185
11:6–9	176
11:9	67
11:11–16	74
12	57
13—23	73
13	76, 89, 183
13:21–22	75
14:4–21	72, 96, 130
14:7	73
16:1–9	110
16:5	67
16:6	82
17:4–6	69
17:12–14	67
18:7	67
19	110
19:18–24	76
19:24–25	131
20	48, 70, 109
20:1–6	111
20:3	107
20:4	28
24—27	75
24:3–13	75

24:23	67	41:8–10	150	49:22–26	156
25:6–8	67	41:17–20	151	49:26	157
26	110, 111	41:21–29	152	50:4–9	159, 160
26:11	89	42:1–7	158	51:4–5	158
26:19	76	42:1–4	159	51:9–11	154
27:12–13	74, 111	42:1	176	52:9–10	157
28:1–4	69	42:8	62, 158	52:13–53:12	127, 159,
28:7	64	42:18–20, 24	149		160, 199
28:14	64, 71	42:19	181	53:5, 8–12	161
28:22	59, 71	43:1, 4, 25	150	53:6, 11–12	160
29:1–10	56, 64	43:3–4	156	53:10, 12	161
29:1–4, 5–8	59, 71	43:5–7	155, 158	54:1–7	155
29:5–6	55	43:10, 12	157	54:3	157
29:21	95	43:14	145	54:7–8	150
30:1–17	68	43:16–19	154	54:11–12	155
30:1–12	71	43:18–20	147	55:3–5	157
30:15	62, 63, 71	44:3, 5	157	55:12–13	153, 155
30:19–26	67	44:6–8	152	56—66	60
30:27–33	55, 88	44:8	157	56:1	173
31:1–3	68, 71	44:9–20	153	56:3–8	173, 174
31:4–9	71	44:22	150	56:9–57:13	174
31:4	59, 67	44:24–45:7	148	56:9–12	171
32:1	67	44:24	151	57:3–13	170
32:9–11, 17	71, 110	44:26–28	155	57:14–21	174
33:5, 15, 17–24	67	44:26	181	57:15–19	172
34	76	45:3	158	58:3, 6–7	174
34:8	89	45:6	157, 158	59:1–15	171, 175
34:9–15	75	45:13	148, 155	59:9–20	34
35	75, 153	45:14	157	59:15–20	175
36—37	51	45:18	151	60—62	175
36	111	45:21	34	60:4, 9	173
37—45	110	45:20, 22–23, 25	157	60:9, 10, 14, 16	172
37:11–15	111	46:1–4	152	60:10–12, 14	173
37:23–29	68, 72,	47	156	61:1–11	176
	82, 130	47:1–15	145	61:1	92, 185
37:32	89	48:3–5	152	61:3	176
38:1–13, 17–23, 28	111	48:6–7	147	61:4	171
40—55	60	48:11	158	61:5	173
40:1–2	149	48:16	147	63:7–64:12	171, 175
40:3	153	48:20–21	153	63:16	179
40:5	158	49:1–6	159	64:1–12	34
40:7–41:18	110	49:1, 4	160	64:4	172
40:12–17, 21–31	151	49:6–7	157	64:8	179
40:21–23, 27–28	147	49:7–12	153	64:10–11	171
41:2–3	148	49:14–21	155	65:1–12	174

65:1–7, 9, 13–16	175	9:10–11	55
65:17–25	81, 175	9:16	115
66:1–2	172	9:17–22	101, 102
66:2	83	10:20	104
66:3–5	174	10:25	112
66:18–21, 23	173, 174	11:1–13	104
		11:18–23	57, 108

JEREMIAH

		12:1–6	57, 108
		12:7	102
1:4–10	160	12:14–17	113
1:5, 8	109, 112, 160	13:1–11	109
1:6	92, 138	13:10	106
1:7	109	13:17	107
1:8	150	13:23	105, 199
1:10	112	14:11–12	106
2:4–13	57	14:17–18, 19–22	107
2:5	103	15:1–4	106
2:14–15	101	15:10–21	57, 108
2:29	103	15:16–18	108, 160
2:30	105	15:22	116
3:1–4:4	106	16:1–13	109
3:4, 14, 19, 22	104	16:14–15	154
3:15–4:2	170	16:19–21	113
3:15–18	113	17:9–10, 14–18	57, 108
4:2	113	17:9	105, 117, 199
4:16–18	101	17:22	55
4:19–22	103, 107	18:8, 12	106
4:22	104	18:13, 15	103
5:1	105	18:18–23	57, 108
6:6–8	57	19:1–14	109
6:10	105	19:14	104
6:11	107	20:4	115
6:13	104	20:7–18	57, 108
6:18	112	20:7	92
6:26	55, 107	20:8–9	108
6:27–30	107	21:11–22:30	116
7:3–7	106	22:1–5	5
7:5–7	5	22:8, 9	104, 112
7:16	106	22:10–12	93
7:21–23	57	22:11	98
7:25	113	22:18	96
8:5	103	22:24	165
8:8–12	104	23	112
8:18–9:1	102	23:1–8	116
9:5–6	104	23:16–40	104

24	115
24:4–7	106, 136
24:7	151
25:4	113
25:9	112, 113
25:12–26	116
25:15–38	112, 120
25:34–38	55
26:3	106
26:5	113
26:6	112
27—28	36, 109
27—29	104
27:1–3	98
27:7–8	112, 113
27:10, 15	115
28:8–9	85, 140
29:4–7	114, 115
29:10–14	106, 115
30—31	117
30:7	96
31:2–6	116
31:10	112
31:12–14	31
31:19–20	104
31:31–34	117, 185
31:33	192
32:25–44	106
33:5–16	106
33:9	112
33:14–26	116
34:5	96
36:3, 7	106
37:5–11	130
39:6–10	13
40	98
40:1–6	112
41:4–5	114
42	98
42:1–44	112
43:8–11	109
43:10	113
44	114, 192
44:8	112
46:2	93

46:25–26	113	12:6, 11	107	33:23–29	126
48:27	112	12:18–19	126	33:30–33	132
48:29–30	82	12:21–23	123	34:11–13	134
48:46–47	113	12:26–27	124	34:15, 17–22	135
49:1–2	112	14:1	14	34:23–24	136
49:5–6, 34–39	113	14:12–23	128	34:25–31	135
49:9–16	119	16	136	35:10–12	119
50—51	112, 116	16:3–5	124	36	134
50:17	114	16:53–63	134, 136	36:20–21, 23–36	129
50:20	117	16:60	135	36:22–27	151
51:34–37, 49	114	17:3–4, 12	125	36:22–23	158
51:59–64	109	18:2	14, 132	36:24, 28	134, 135
		18:5–9, 24	95	36:25	135

LAMENTATIONS

		18:10–13	129	36:26–27	135, 185
		18:20, 25	132	36:31–32	136
1:3, 12	15	19	125	36:33–38	135
4:21	120	19:1–4	98	37:1–14	9
		20:1–31	125	37:3	161

EZEKIEL

		20:1	14	37:11	15, 134
1	61, 128	20:12–13	174	37:12	198
1:1–3	14	20:33–34	134	37:14	185
1:28	97, 129	20:34–38	48, 135	37:15–22	134, 136, 170
2:1–2	129	20:40–41	135	37:23, 27	135
2:3–4	123	20:43	136	37:25	136
3:7	123	20:49	125	37:26–28	135
3:15	14	23	124	38—39	56, 131
3:16–21	132	24:16–18	127	39:25–28	134, 136
3:21	95	24:24, 27	107	39:29	185
3:24	185	25:1–26:6	130	40—46	137
4	126	25:7, 11, 17	131	43:1–5	158
4:4–8, 16–17	127	25:12	118	44:4–16	173
4:14	92	26:6	131	47:1–48:35	137
5:6	129	27	131		
6:4–6	129	28:1–19, 23	131	**DANIEL**	
6:9	136	28:25	134		
8	114, 192	29:1–5	131	1	192
10:4–19	129	29:6–9	130	3	192
11:5	185	29:6, 9–16	131	6	192
11:14–21	132	29:17–20	130	8:15–26	194
11:15–21	196	30	183	9:2–19	171
11:15	126	31	131	9:2, 24–27	116
11:17–20	134	32:1–16	131	9:4–19	197
11:18–20	135	33	132	10—11	194
11:22–23	129	33:12–13	95	10:9	97

HOSEA

1—7	43
1—3	43, 47
1	40, 109
1:2	42, 44
1:4–5	37, 41, 45
1:6, 9	42
1:7	50
1:10–2:1	40
1:10	38, 41
1:11	41, 53
2	66, 96
2:1	41
2:2–23	48
2:2	44
2:3	39
2:7	49
2:8	44, 45
2:9	49
2:13	44
2:14, 15	42, 44
2:18	43
2:19	45
2:20	42, 45
2:22	41
3:1	42, 44, 47
3:4	48
3:5	42, 45, 47, 48, 49
4	57
4:1–2	45, 46
4:1, 6	45, 185
4:2	42, 44, 45
4:4–9	46, 54, 64
4:9	49
4:10	44
4:13–14	44, 45
4:15	45
5:1, 10	46
5:4	44, 45, 49
5:5	50
5:10, 14	39
5:12–14	50
5:12	40

5:13	42, 46
5:15	49
6:1	42
6:2	94
6:4, 5	46, 50, 57
6:6	45, 64, 185
6:7	43
6:8–9	38, 45
6:11–7:1	49
7:1	42, 45
7:3	46
7:4	44
7:7	46
7:9	45
7:10	49
7:11	46
7:16	49
8:1	43
8:4–6	45
8:4	41, 46
8:8	43
8:9	53
8:10	41, 53
8:11–13	45
8:13	41, 49
9:3	41, 49
9:4–5	45
9:6, 15	39, 41, 53
9:7–8	46
9:17	42
10:1	45
10:4	43
10:5–6, 12	45
11	43, 48
11:1–4	64
11:1	42
11:3	42, 45
11:5	49
11:8	47
11:8–9	49
11:10–11	43, 49
11:12	50
12:1	43, 45
12:2–14	49

12:6	45, 49
12:7	45
12:9, 13	42
12:11	38, 45, 46
12:14	45
13:2	45
13:7–9, 11, 16	39
13:10–11	46
14:4	42, 49
14:7	49, 94
14:9	95

JOEL

1:2–20	182
1:13–14	184
1:15	183
2:1–17	182
2:1–2, 11	183
2:12–17	34, 35, 183, 184
2:15–17	184
2:18–32	182
2:18–19	89, 184
2:21–26	184
2:27	183
2:28–29	184, 185
3:1–21	182, 184
3:14	183
3:17	186
3:18	184
3:21	186

AMOS

1:2	36
1:3–2:3	33, 43, 69
1:3, 11, 13	33
1:5, 6, 9	28
2:1	33
2:4–5	36
2:6–15	31
2:6–8, 9–11	25, 32
2:6	95
2:9–11	57

3:1–2   30, 31, 36, 43
3:3–8   36, 46
3:11   25, 93
3:15   25
4:1–3   31, 53, 64
4:4–5   25, 35
4:6–12   34
4:13   34, 57
5:1–2   26, 64, 96
5:3   63
5:4, 6   35, 94
5:5   25, 28, 29
5:7   31
5:8–9   34, 35, 57
5:10–12   25, 32, 68, 95
5:11   25, 68
5:14   35, 14, 96
5:15   94, 96
5:16–20   35
5:16–17   26, 27, 101
5:18–20   33, 53,
                  64, 183
5:21–24, 26   25, 34,
                   57, 64
5:26   29
6:1–7   28, 31, 53, 64
6:1–3, 13   25
6:1   36, 53
6:4–7   25, 64, 68
6:4   31
6:7   29
6:12   31
6:13–14   24, 25
7:1–3   27
7:2   7, 92
7:4–9   27
7:10–17   27, 29, 111
7:12, 15   36
8:1–3   27
8:2   6
8:3, 10   27
8:4–6   25, 31, 54
8:9–10   27
8:14   25
9:1–4   28

9:1   61
9:5–6   34, 57, 88
9:7   33, 43, 131
9:11–12, 13–15   36

OBADIAH

1—5   117, 119
6—14   117
12—14   119
15—21   118, 120

JONAH

1:9   138
1:17   141
3   139
3:4   138
3:9–10   140
4:2   35, 139, 140
4:6–7   141
4:10–11   139, 141

MICAH

1—3   51
1:3–4   88
1:5–7   51, 52, 54
1:8–16   55
1:8   52
1:9   54
1:10–16   52
1:13   54
1:16   28
2:1–5   51, 53, 55
2:2, 9   54
2:12–13   53
3:1–4, 5–8, 9–12   51, 53
3:1   54
3:2–3   53
3:5–8   64
3:8   176, 185
3:9, 11   54
3:12   51, 52, 53, 56
4—7   51, 52, 55
4:1–4   55, 56

4:6–8   56
4:9–10   56, 58
4:11–13   56, 58
5:2–4   56
5:5–15   58
5:10–15   54
5:14   89
6   57
6:6–16   51, 64
6:10–12   54
7   58
7:1–7   54, 57
7:8–20   57
7:9, 18–20   59

NAHUM

1   86
1:2   89
1:2–11   55
1:2–8   34
1:2–3   90
1:6   89
1:7–8   90
3:1   89
3:8   85
3:19   89

HABAKKUK

1   57
1:2–11   93
1:6   92
1:12   93
1:13   94
2:2–19   96
2:4–5   94
2:20   55
3   34, 55, 89
3:16   96
3:17–19   92, 97

ZEPHANIAH

1:2–18   81, 183
1:8–9   80
1:16   93

1:18	89	9—11	168	22:40	189	
2:1–4	88	9:12–17	170	23—24	198	
2:1–3	83	10:2, 6–12	170	23:30–313	71	
2:3	96	11:4–17	170	28:20	69	
2:5–11	82	12—14	168			
2:13–15	80	12:14	56	**MARK**		
2:15	82	13:1–6	7, 170	12:1–12	63	
3:3–4	80	14:20–21	170			
3:8	89					
3:9–13	82, 84	**MALACHI**		**LUKE**		
3:11–13	96			10:36	63	
3:14–20	84	1—4	168	12:48	30	
		1:2–5	119			
		1:2	178, 179			
HAGGAI		1:3–5	180	**JOHN**		
		1:6–2:9	178	1:18	61	
1:2, 4–8	163	1:6	179			
1:5–6, 9–10	164	1:8	178, 179	**ACTS**		
1:13	164	1:11	180			
2:4	164	1:14	179, 180	2:14–21, 33	185	
2:5–9, 22	163	2:2, 4–7	179	7:52	1	
2:16–19	164	2:10–16	178	8	159	
2:21–23	165	2:10, 14	179	13:15	189	
		2:17	178, 179	28:23	189	
		3:1–5	180, 181			
ZECHARIAH		3:1	177, 179	**ROMANS**		
		3:2–4	178			
1—6	166	3:2–5, 6–7, 17–18	181	1—3	199	
1:1, 7	165	3:8–12	179	6:5	199	
1:2–6	166	3:14	178	7	199	
1:3	181	3:14–18	180	7:19	200	
1:4	7	4:1–3	180, 181	8:19–23	75	
2:9, 11	166	4:1, 4	179	11:3	1	
3:4–10	167					
4:6–10	167					
4:9	166	**MATTHEW**		**GALATIANS**		
4:14	167					
5:1–11	167	1:18–25	69	3:28	185	
6:1–13	167	5:12	1			
6:15	166	5:17	189	**PHILIPPIANS**		
7—8	167	7:12	189			
7:1	165	11:13	189	4:7	97	
7:4–14	166	13:57	1			
7:7, 12	7	19:26	200	**1 THESSALONIANS**		
8:3	168	21:26	1			
8:9	166	21:11	1	2:15	1	
9—14	169					

2 Timothy

2:11	200

Hebrews

11:1	95
11:8–16	198

James

5:10	1

Revelation

16:6	1
21—22	198

Tobit

2	192

Sirach

Prologue	189
48:20, 23	188
49:6, 8, 10	188

Baruch

1:15–3:8	197
3:9–5:9	197

Prayer of Azariah

3—22	197
15	7, 188

1 Maccabees

1:38–40	197
2:7–13	197
3:45	197
4:46	7, 188
9:27	7, 188
14:41	7, 188

2 Maccabees

6:30	97
15:9	189

4 Maccabees

18:10	189

Tobit

1:1–2	14

1 Enoch

85—90	194
91:12–17	194
93	194

2 Baruch

3	197
14:27–35	197
53—74	194
72—74	197

Assumption of Moses

2—10	194
3:5–14	14

2 Esdras

3:28–36	198
13:39–50	14

Mishnah

Sanhedrin

10:3	14

INDEX OF NAMES AND SUBJECTS

A

Achtemeier, Elizabeth, 164, 214 nn.9, 18, 19; 227 n.62, 229 n.100
Ackerman, Susan, 232 n.21
Ackroyd, Peter, 100, 212 n.114, 216 n.52, 226 n.56, 231 n.7, 232 n.29
Aharoni, Yohanan, 219 n.96
Ahlström, Gösta, 205 nn.1, 4; 213 n.3, 216 n.38, 219 nn.95, 96; 226 n.55, 231 n.20
Albertz, Rainer, 226 n.55
Allen, L. C., 209 n.60
Alt, Albrecht, 208 n.50
Amsler, S., 218 n.72
Andersen, Francis I., 205 n.9, 207 n.32
Anderson, Bernhard W., 225 n.31
Auld, A. Graeme, 202 n.15, 210 n.83
Aune, David E., 230 n.4

B

Baal, 44, 45, 48, 49, 104
Bailey, Ken, 220 n.105
Baltzer, Klaus, 221 n.129, 224 n.26, 225 n.31
Barnes, W. E., 53–54, 209 n.62
Baron, Salo, 231 n.16
Barr, James, 231 n.10
Barstad, H. M., 224 n.17
Bartlett, J. R., 218 nn.87, 88; 219 n.91
Barton, John, 1, 68, 201 n.3, 203 nn.28, 30; 206 nn.14, 19; 210 nn.77, 83; 212 n.103, 230 n.5

Baruch, 99, 100
Beale, G. K., 211 n.92
Beaulieu, Paul-Alain, 223 n.1
Becker, J., 212 n.113
Bedford, Peter Ross, 227 n.60
Begg, Christopher, 202 n.22
Beguerie, P., 210 n.86
Beit-Arieh, Itzhaq, 219 n.96
Bentzen, Aage, 215 n.25
Berger, Peter, 145, 146, 223 nn.3, 8, 11
Berlin, Adele, 213 nn.2, 5, 6, 8; 222 n.141
Berquist, Jon L., 226 nn.54, 55
Bickerman, Elias, 222 nn.138, 145; 223 n.150
Bird, Phyllis, 208 nn.41, 45
Blenkinsopp, Joseph, 201 n.1, 222 n.143, 226 n.55, 230 nn.3, 5; 231 n.10
Boadt, Lawrence, 221 nn.121, 127
Bright, John, 216 nn.45, 48, 49; 217 n.70
Brin, Gershon, 54, 209 n.62
Broshi, Magen, 209 n.58
Brueggemann, Walter, 204 nn.57, 58; 207 n.37, 217 n.55, 218 nn.76, 78; 220 n.104
Buis, P., 218 n.84
Burkitt, F. C., 209 n.71
Buss, Martin J., 207 n.30

C

Carroll, Robert P., 202 nn.12, 20; 216 n.50, 226 n.59
Ceresco, Anthony, 216 n.33

Chandler, Edgar H. S., 203 n.32

Childs, Brevard, 6, 202 nn.19, 23; 210 nn.82, 84; 212 n.106, 216 n.51, 222 n.148

Christensen, Duane L., 213 n.3

Clements, Ronald E., 100, 201 nn.1, 7; 202 n.16, 203 n.26, 210 nn.80, 84, 85; 211 n.99, 212 nn.106, 108, 112; 213 n.116, 217 nn.53, 55; 222 n.136

Cogan, Morton, 213 n.1

Coggins, R. J., 209 n.56, 214 nn.9, 18; 219 n.92, 227 n.71

cognitive minority, 145, 146

Collins, John J., 212 n.113, 232 n.26

Cook, S. A., 231 n.15

covenant, 3, 16, 17, 30, 40, 43, 48, 66, 71, 104, 117, 135, 136, 164, 174, 178, 179, 181

Cox, Ben, 214 n.13

Craigie, Peter C., 208 n.40, 216 n.42

creation, Creator, 34

Crenshaw, J. L., 216 n.40, 229 n.110, 230 nn.112, 114, 115, 118

cult, cultic, 2, 35, 55, 57, 87, 91, 95, 171, 186

D

David, Davidic dynasty, 48, 50, 56, 64, 66, 67, 73, 116, 136, 165, 167, 170

Davies, Philip R., 226 n.56

Davis, Ellen F., 136, 220 n.110, 222 n.133

day of the Lord, day of Yahweh, 33, 81, 118, 120, 179, 180, 181, 182, 183, 184, 186

death, 25, 51, 61, 81, 101, 122, 131, 132, 134, 160, 196, 197, 198, 199

de Boer, P. A. H., 225 n.36

Deist, Ferdinand, 230 n.116

Deuteronomistic Historical Work, 5, 24, 28, 29, 160

Diakonoff, I. M., 204 n.43

Dijk, H. J. van, 221 n.121

Dozeman, Thomas B., 230 n.119

Drinkard, Joel F., Jr., 216 n.42

Dumbrell, W. J., 229 n.106

E

Eakin, Frank E., 231 n.20

Eaton, J. H., 87, 209 n.67, 214 n.15

Eddy, S. K., 232 n.23

Eichrodt, Walther, 219 n.101, 227 n.63, 231 n.12

Eisen, A. M., 233 n.31

Eliade, Mircea, 227 n.68

Emerton, J. A., 215 n.27

Emmerson, Grace, 209 n.57, 228 nn.82, 88

Engnell, I., 210 n.86

exile, 10, 28, 29, 41, 42, 43, 52, 56, 58, 63, 84, 98, 99, 100, 106, 111, 115, 116, 121, 122, 145, 146, 148, 157, 161, 164, 166, 167, 170, 171, 172, 190, 191, 193, 195, 196, 197, 198

F

Feuillet, A., 213 n.118

Fey, R., 211 n.95

Fichtner, J., 214 n.20

Floyd, Michael H., 214 n.12, 215 n.27

Fohrer, Georg, 211 n.96, 218 n.72

forgiveness, 59, 62, 117, 128, 132, 135, 136, 148, 150, 151, 172, 177, 181, 185, 196

Frankfort, H. and H. A., 223 n.7

Freedman, David Noel, 204 n.59, 205 n.9, 207 n.32

Fretheim, Terence E., 222 n.147

Funkenstein, Amos, 233 n.34

G

Gadd, C. J., 204 n.47

Galil, Gershom, 207 n.27

Gelston, A., 157, 225 n.40

Gerstenberger, E., 217 n.70

Gibson, J. C. L., 208 n.40

Gilkey, Langdon, 203 n.31

Ginsberg, H. Louis, 205 n.66, 212 n.108

Golka, F. W., 222 n.142

Gowan, Donald E., 202 n.22, 205 nn.65, 5, 8; 206 nn.15, 17, 18, 20; 214 n.19, 215 n.22, 220 n.109, 228 n.92, 232 n.20